POLITICAL WILL

BALBOA.PRESS
A DIVISION OF HAY HOUSE

Peace is to war,
as chess is to checkers.

Both are played on the
same game board.

But peace is a more difficult game.

We bend the arc of history toward peace
and social justice by becoming skillful
advocates; more proficient at creating
political will.

Original illustration by Greg Dearth

PRAISE FOR POLITICAL WILL

"This is a beautiful, engrossing account of the creation of a significant element in the American infrastructure for building peace. Will Spencer provides an insider's analysis of how a citizen's movement was formed that skillfully collaborated with a few members of Congress to establish the United States Institute of Peace. The book blends personal memories and a comprehensive analysis of this remarkable accomplishment. It provides reasons to believe that progress can be made to build a more peaceful United States and world and it also thereby suggests ways that more progress can be made. Will Spencer deserves thanks for helping to do both by writing this book."

Louis Kriesberg, PhD
Professor Emeritus of Sociology, Syracuse University
Founding Director
Program for the Advancement of Research on Conflict Resolution and Collaboration (PARCC)

"Will Spencer has in a quiet voice with remarkable detail woven together three threads: his personal search for meaning in life, finding it in a commitment to embed a culture of peace and conflict resolution in our national life; his relentless and ultimately successful work with dedicated colleagues to generate the political will to make that commitment a reality through the eventually successful campaign to establish what has become the United States Institute of Peace; and finally provides us insight into the rapid maturation in those years of the field of conflict management and resolution. It is a gripping story of tenacity and resilience and a moving account of the human costs of setting one's sights high and living with the human costs of setbacks and loss along the way. Anyone who lived in adjacent vineyards during that period will be moved. It's an inspiration."

Harold H. Saunders, PhD
Former Assistant Secretary of State
Former Director of International Affairs, Kettering Foundation
Founder, Sustaineddialogue.org

"Will Spencer's book is an engaging fusion of an eyewitness account of a major institutional development, a personal memoir, and a conceptual exposition of the United States Institute of Peace as a prominent symbol and potential starting point for new approaches to the conflicts that we inevitably confront in all spheres of public life.

Spencer presents this history in a very personal way, interlaced with an autobiographical account of his learning process, his career choices, and his relationship to other key actors in the ten-year effort that brought this new American institution into being.

In his captivating survey of the ideas underlying the concept of a peace academy or peace institute and the societal processes that shaped it, Spencer makes occasional excursions into the theoretical assumptions that underlie conflict resolution as well as social innovation."

Herbert C. Kelman, PhD
Professor of Ethics Emeritus
Harvard University

"This book is a tribute to all who answered the call to bring this new American institution into existence. It provides guidance for better understanding the strategies and tactics for creating political will in ways that resonate with lasting peace and social justice. The story is both reflective and instructive. Told by the Director of the national campaign to create it and of the Federal Commission that developed it, the story captures the beliefs and values of the major players responsible for USIP."

Ambassador Andrew Young
United States Ambassador to the United Nations

"Powerful and inspiring, Will Spencer's beautiful memoir of his life as a peace advocate and practitioner is a delight to read. At the core of it is the story he tells with captivating detail of the ten-year campaign to build the political will to finally create the U.S. Institute of Peace, only two centuries in the making. Recommended reading for all those interested in peace and indeed anyone passionate to build a better world."

William Ury, PhD
Co-author *Getting to Yes*
Co-founder Program on Negotiation at Harvard Law School.

POLITICAL WILL

Bending the Arc of History

William J. Spencer

Foreword By Ambassador Andrew Young

BALBOA.PRESS

A DIVISION OF HAY HOUSE

Balboa Press books may be ordered through booksellers or by contacting:

Balboa Press
A Division of Hay House
1663 Liberty Drive
Bloomington, IN 47403
www.balboapress.com
844-682-1282

Front Cover photography by Timothy Hursley
Back Cover illustration by Greg Dearth

Print information available on the last page.

ISBN: 978-1-9822-5405-6 (sc)
ISBN: 978-1-9822-5406-3 (e)

Balboa Press rev. date: 10/06/2020

For Dayle
Pathfinder, Partner, Soul Mate

CONTENTS

PART FIVE
Causing Change: Strategies, Challenges, and Concerns

PROLOGUE

The White House,
Friday, October 19, 1984

After catching breakfast about 8:30 AM, the President walked into the Oval Office at 9:35 AM and those who were not already standing stood to greet Mr Reagan. He was about to receive his national security briefing. It would last eleven minutes. The briefing, not one of those intimate one-to-one scenes portrayed in *The West Wing* television series, but more of a kitchen sink of aides including Bob McFarlane, John Poindexter, Jim Baker, Ed Meese, and Michael Deaver, spread out on couches around the oval Presidential seal woven into the carpet—was quick, casual, and comfortable. Mildly impatient, the President's mind was understandably focused on his ninety-minute preparation later in the morning for the second Presidential Debate with Walter Mondale, scheduled in just three days in Kansas City. A little pressed for time, the President wanted to get to the Cabinet Room to prepare. Informality grew into formality, as Oliver North, others from the State Department and, Legislative Affairs, and a Congressman joined the national security team and the Chief of Staff for a quick signing ceremony of the 1984 Act to Combat International Terrorism. The President, graceful as usual, delivered brief remarks and then made his way to the Cabinet Room. About half-past noon the President visited the White House barbershop for a twenty-minute haircut and then returned to the Oval Office at 1:04 PM before retiring to the second floor residence at 1:19 PM, according to his daily diary. The President had lunch in the West Hall at 1:25 P.M. Sometime during the day, the President put his signature on several proclamations and laws, including the Department of Defense Authorization Act of 1985. In that moment, as recorded in paragraph six of eight in a statement by the President released by the White House Press Secretary, the United States Institute of Peace was signed into law, creating the newest American institution.[1]

Malibu, California
Sunday, March 23, 1975

The coastline below the Santa Monica Mountains rose into view, and dropped below the gentle swells in rhythm with my paddling. Ahead, a shimmering, blue-green surface extended to the horizon. It was totally engaging to feel the rolling sea and watch the arc of penetrating sunlight disappear into the deep. I was inches above the water as the sixteen-foot yellow kayak broke through the waves. The hull made a hushed swoosh sound as it passed through the water with each stroke. I loved being out on the ocean in the early morning. It was wondrous to be one with nature and it awakened my soul. The calm sea seemed to be speaking to me.

These moments were often a time for thinking about my life and future. On the water I felt one with my craft. More than a half-mile offshore, the solitude provided the clarity I needed to ponder the decision point I knew was coming. I needed to move on, but to what? The waving blades of floating kelp between the shore and me created a place of sanctuary. I knew as I thrust through the waters off Malibu that a new voyage was ahead, but on a different sea.

It would become a journey of colleagues—partners in working to establish the United States Institute of Peace. Our own life experiences and motivations shaped our shared destination. My task would be to sell concepts to the Congress and the public. I would soon exchange my kayak for a new vessel, a collection of the parts—the skills and mindsets that contributed to the whole of what would become the USIP. Starting with the end in mind, we came together for a discrete voyage to put in place a structure that we hoped would influence the country to become more peace-seeking than war-making; more driven to be peace-building than war-preparing; and more understanding of the dynamics and conditions necessary to create peace. We brought fresh eyes to navigate a new route, building on the experience of others. For me, my yellow kayak symbolized the journey. Ten years later, sometime during his busy day, a sitting President would place his signature on a bill making it law. In a hand stroke, it would almost seem easy. The moment represented a decade of effort, struggle, friendship, learning, and a triumph of political will.

FOREWORD

There was a moment in time for America when its involvement in a costly war in Southeast Asia and the entanglement of the Cold War were coming to a close. Social movements were continuing to define a changing America. The concerns of discrete groups seeking progress in racial equality and social justice, human rights, and environmental sustainability would soon become the institutionalized global struggles of changing societies challenged by redefined national identities, power relationships, economic insecurities, and fear.

Conflict in its many forms and myriad circumstances was on the rise. But big wars were transitioning to many smaller, although still intensely deadly, skirmishes in lands with unfamiliar names and historical ethnic tensions. Antiwar movements were waning and folks were beginning to look for practical and more efficient ways of solving differences. New conflict resolution mechanisms were evolving, along with increasing recognition of the underlying power vacuums and value struggles defined by self-determination. Many parts of American society were looking for ways to overcome an endemic culture of violence.

In this nexus of activism and academia, a small group of people gathered to conceive and carry out a national campaign to create what would become the United States Institute of Peace. This new American institution would be designed to impact and influence our ability to create and sustain peace in our communities and among nations. Building on concepts that had their roots two hundred years earlier, these leaders joined an abiding relay race, of sorts, built on the foresight, advocacy, and commitments of individuals and groups gone before. Overcoming the failed legislative history of one hundred forty prior attempts in the modern period, they were successful in their efforts to create the United States Institute of Peace, or the National Peace Academy, as it was called then. It stands, as a vivid case example of how to create political will in America and offers lessons for overcoming the logjams and clogged politics of Washington, DC, and the divisive state of public policy today.

Between 1976 and 1986 thousands of Americans took up the call to advocate and enshrine a new American commitment to better understand and explore alternatives to the use of force in resolving conflict. It was a natural decision and important obligation for me to have been involved in this cause. The time was finally right to recognize and codify the many experiences and skill sets born of the previous quarter century of lessons learned from labor-management disputes, the civil rights movement and a century of four major wars. Without the efforts of those in the National Peace Academy Campaign, its staff and supporters, a handful of members of Congress and their staffs, and the work of a federal commission, USIP would not exist.

This record of the movement is a snapshot of efforts that helped to define and advance the processes that would become known as alternative dispute resolution. Today, legal systems, governments, businesses, communities, and international partnerships apply these approaches in cost-effective and timesaving ways. This period in our nation's history established a new legitimacy for a field of study seeking new mechanisms, processes, and approaches to advance our understanding of conflicts and our ability to resolve them more effectively, less violently.

This book is a tribute to all who answered the call to bring this new American institution into existence. It is a primer for better understanding the strategies and tactics for creating political will in ways that resonate with lasting peace and social justice. The story is both reflective and instructive. Told by the Director of the national campaign to create it and of the federal commission that developed it, the story captures the beliefs and values of the major players responsible for USIP.

The work of a single peace institution will never be enough, but it can serve to inspire and launch the establishment of a network of federally funded and locally supported peace-related organizations, colleges, and community groups to foster and implement our ongoing commitment of peace and social justice. USIP is itself nearly forty years old, yet its impact and potential is still in its infancy. This is the untold story of how it began.

Ambassador Andrew J. Young
United States Ambassador to the United Nations
(1977–1979)

PART ONE

Setting the Stage

INTRODUCTION

1986 – I started my day sitting in a room with two powerful, well-known parties in conflict.

I had just sat down when the single door to the room opened. The two men entering were wordless, but gesturing simultaneously to one another, arms and palms extended, signaling that the other should enter first. It was an awkward stand off. With additional, and unexpected clumsiness, it got sorted out, and they entered showing considerable reluctance. More silence.

I stood and moved around the small conference table toward the door. It was 8:00 AM straight up, and the late March sun was reaching through the sheer privacy curtains, casting a nondescript image on the barren walls. There were no books; no art; no flowers, only a side table with china and two pots of coffee. For some reason I focused for a moment on the orange tab that indicated one pot was decaf. It was one of the few colors in the room.

Each of us in proper business suits; shook hands and sat in three of the only four chairs in the intimate space. Outside the room, two security men stood stiff and passionless. I had nodded to them earlier as I passed through the corridor. The hallway smelled like fresh paint with a slight adhesive odor due to the new carpet. Still, it all felt fresh, and very business-like.

The prestige and authority of the two men required that I not speak first, beyond a simple greeting. Now, seated, they avoided looking at one another. More awkwardness. The sun fixed on one of their faces, causing one man to slide his chair to get out of the glare. The chair jarred the table, shaking it and we all raised our arms. Nothing was said, but the other man cleared his throat.

I knew that each had let the other down; each man was clearly mad enough to avoid addressing the other. They wore disappointment in their furrowed faces rather than projecting the leadership and captaincy one was accustomed to seeing in these two powerful men. Their shoulders askew, leaning away from the other, they avoided direct eye contact. Instead, they each gradually turned, and with further silence, began to stare at me.

I had been asked to be there because they had each expressed the belief that I could help them resolve a conflict that lingered in the air that morning. At best the division between them would be a major embarrassment to both; and at worst, a very messy legal and financial predicament, inadvertently caused not by ill will, but sadly by miscommunication. Both men admittedly had been too eager to consummate a transaction beneficial to the other. The precarious ledge where they now stood was of their own doing. The three sunrise meetings we were about to hold over the next ten days resolved the conflict and brought new commitments. Our time together clarified the issues, restored the previous trust between them, and provoked each to accept that the other had admitted they were wrong. They rekindled the motivation to continue developing the political will that was so much a part of their lives.

♖ ♗ ♘

I don't consider this book a memoir of my life. But I see my story as a means to share the power of non-violent conflict resolution, and the necessary political will to elevate its usefulness to national recognition and legitimacy. My personal journey has been to cause change, just as the vision for your life may include trying to transform a social dynamic, condition, injustice or policy worthy of your time and passion to change.

What compels a single, twenty-five year old male, living happily on the beach in Malibu – with a fine education; a great job; good fortune, and a BMW – to leave all that to begin an adventure that led to sitting across a small, Formica table from two grieving and very discontented men of the world? The short answer is political will; the long answer follows.

Few things in American life are as inherent as the concept of political will. It has been one of the most consistent, and consequential aspects of our civic DNA since the founding of our Democracy. Political will is simply the art and science of influencing society; it can take many forms, and be applied to unlimited pursuits. Political will celebrates individual or collective action to leverage, or affect the outcome of a decision, usually meant to advance the public welfare. Creating political will is what enables advocacy to work. It is perhaps the most important ingredient in causing social change. In this, there is hope and a challenge.

We change history by becoming skillful advocates and effective at creating political will. Advocacy is about influencing outcomes, including public policy and resource-allocation decisions within political, economic, and social systems and institutions that directly affect people's lives.[2] The two men in the conference room had lived lives of service and been successful advocates for many good causes. It was just in their character. The fact that a serious issue sidetracked them is not part of this story, but it exemplifies that conflict is inevitable and a normal part of our lives.

The story you are about to read is about another such instance, centered on a ten-year journey to create a new American institution intended to influence how our citizens and government perceive and pursue peace. This story is not about resolving a single conflict, as we just saw in the conference room; it is about building a table big enough to seat the world around.

Peace is not merely the absence of war. It is the presence of social justice and the systems necessary to manage conflict without violence or threat of force. It's a group activity. People differ on this perception, as some feel peace can only be achieved by military might. In the work of the National Peace Academy Campaign, NPAC, and the federal commission,[3] our argument was not to limit the military, but to leverage the skills of conflict resolution, collaborative problem solving, negotiation, and mediation.

We sought a different kind of influence, one characterized by understanding and negotiation over military might. Philosopher and historian, David R. Hawkins, MD, wrote that violence is force. Hawkins said, "Force is seductive and manifests itself in false patriotism, prestige and dominance. Often, force is arrogant, whereas power is characterized by humility. Power speaks to trust, reason and optimism. Force speaks to hate, weakness and scorn. Power speaks to truth and can be recognized as self-evident. Power serves others. Force is self-serving."[4]

In our efforts with the National Peace Academy Campaign, we used to say, "Peace is to war, as chess is to checkers." They are both played on the same game board, but peace is a much harder game. While some scholars suggest there are ten theories of why nations go to war,[5] there are far more paths to peace. The question we should be asking ourselves about war is: "What are twelve ways to prevent us from going to war in the first place?"

♜ ♝ ♞

The pursuit of peace should be seen as just as patriotic as the pursuit of war. Historically, societies celebrate the end of wars as recognized moments in time, characterized by defining events, or a "win" that crushes the other side. In reality, wars have lingering effects that fester long after the last devastating blow. When a military operation fails, we seem to understand and expect the next one to be more successful. When international mediation or peace talks fail to deliver a peace agreement, society often sees the outcome as a careless non-achievement when in fact, the game of chess simply takes more time.

This book tells the true story of the significant level of effort needed to bring about the political will necessary to create the United States Institute of Peace, USIP. Social change is often unplanned, and the rate of change can vary. In this historical account an intentional effort was made to accelerate the change. The outcome did not occur by chance. Changes in society usually occur because of the adoption of transformative cultural values; the diffusion and acceptance of new ideas; or demographic friction within or between social groups. Any one or more of these can cause structural change. We intended that the strategic diffusion of new ideas and emphasis on what was not working would combine to eventually impact the structure and functioning of our social system. We believed a new institution, carefully conceived, was capable of legitimizing new values and perceptions of peace.

This is the account of four individuals that made a difference, and chose to undertake the challenge to design a path to create the United States Institute of Peace: a psychiatrist, a professor, a pastor, and a peddler. Three were co-chairs and one, the director of a national campaign. One became Vice Chair of the federal commission, and one the Commission Director. Bryant Wedge advanced the need for better understanding of power and force in national perception and international communications throughout his life. Jim Laue's expertise in the mechanisms of mediation and conflict resolution was defined by his insight about the power of needs and interests over the force of positions. Andy Young's life has been a measure of his study and associations with the thinking of Gandhi and Dr Martin Luther King, Jr. Andy's public service and its impact continue to be shaped by his shared view that nonviolent power is far more effective than the use of force. My life has been about the pursuit of knowledge and best practices, the advocacy to build capacity, and the attainment of solutions to societal challenges. Together, we believed America was and is best positioned to model and pursue peace and social justice if its people could come to see peace as a process different from the use of force.

Over eight years, a national campaign was deployed to influence, and be inspired by, the thousands of people who would become its members. The federal commission on peace—a historic benchmark along the one hundred fifty year history of the concept—would hold twelve hearings across America: providing a formal platform for one hundred twenty invited expert witnesses and more than six hundred public seminar participants from every American region and walk of life. The commission spent more than two hundred thirty hours analyzing seven thousand pages of oral and written testimony and interacting with citizens in fifty major substantive meetings with government, academic, and international organizations. The result was surprisingly successful.[6]

The campaign and commission increased the political support for the USIP by enlisting the sponsorship of two presidents and yielding a twenty-fold increase in Congressional sponsors.[7] This resulted in the critical mass of support that would secure the creation of the United States Institute of Peace.

When the legislative bill authorizing the federal commission was put forward in 1977, there were just twelve co-sponsors in the US House of Representatives. There were three co-sponsors in the US Senate. Five years later in 1982 when legislation to create the United States Academy of Peace was introduced, there were one hundred sixty-three House co-sponsors and over fifty-four Senate co-sponsors.

Sponsors of the final, enacting bill chose the name United States Institute of Peace as a simpler form and to clarify its status apart from the mission of the service academies. The service academies of each branch of the military are designed to train and produce soldiers to think and fight. The USIP mission was envisioned as contributing to the interlocking goals of enhanced national security and the full exercise of peacemaking knowledge and skills. President Reagan signed the bill into law in October 1984.

In 2011, the USIP moved to its permanent headquarters adjacent to the National Mall, twenty-five years after the institute was created—and thirty-two years after its early advocates had envisioned the site a mere two hundred meters from its eventual home. USIP exists as a living symbol for peace in the form of a professional training center for practitioners in conflict prevention, management, and resolution. It is a tribute to those who created the political will to bring it into existence. It serves as an inspiration that can make a difference.

♖ ♗ ♘

The efforts to create political will, also presented unwanted drama and at times unintended negative consequences. Along its legislative journey, the future mission of the USIP was seriously impaired by the removal of specific wording in the enacting legislation, and institute conception that served to validate the important role the USIP could, and should play, in the resolution of conflict in America – within the borders of the country. This omission is an important introductory point. The USIP was never envisioned as an intervention agency of government, but the skills and mindsets it advances are as relative to peace at home, as the peace we seek abroad. This view was clear during the work of both the campaign and the commission.

It is important for the reader of this story to know what a significant mistake this decision may have been. This was not an act done by those who are currently associated with the USIP, nor am I aware of the feelings today on this matter by the staff and leadership of the USIP. It is a reasonable question to ask, however, "Why is it that the USIP does not consider research and study on conflict within the United States as part of its mandate?" I would be remiss in my writing if I did not address this question.

I was in the House-Senate conference hearing room when this mishap occurred. As you will read later, we were caught by surprise when an otherwise supportive, liberal senator from a Northeastern state raised an objection to the language because he incorrectly believed the word "domestic" in the draft legislation referred to married couples, and the Senator felt "it was inappropriate for the US Government to have a legislative role intervening in "domestic conflict." We had not expected the challenge and had not prepared any members of the committee to counter the motion to strike the language. As the various bills moved through Congress, this misunderstanding was never revisited or changed. But for the adopted motion, based on the misperception of "domestic" as a word to describe "national", it is my belief that the USIP would carry in its mandate the charge to research, study and advance our knowledge of internal conflict within the United States.

We envisioned this happening by:

1) Encouraging Land Grant universities to maintain regional data bases of conflict interventions and practitioners in all areas of dispute resolution;
2) Convening practitioners to conduct periodic community briefings and with police, city councils, and public-private roundtables;
3) Sponsoring community leadership councils familiar with alternative conflict resolution processes; and finally,
4) Advocating the principles of economic conversion in communities and Congressional districts where military-related manufacturing form a substantial share of the local economy.

These practitioner-driven programs would compliment the international focus of the USIP; integrate international intellectual capital with community and business experiences; and lastly, network specialty disciplines within the field, populating the USIP expert directory with "national issue" focused scholars and practitioners, as well as those international focused scholars and practitioners already listed.

In my view, if there were a single upgrade or operational advancement for the role and mission of the USIP, it would be this. Conflict resolution has no boundaries; nor should the USIP.

♜ ♝ ♞

My own heroes have always been the facilitators of change. Not necessarily those who would define change, but those who prescribe the process and strategy of how the change would finally come about. Intrigued by these processes, I have been drawn to what it takes to cause change: the cardinal problem of how to create political will.[8]

Learning takes time, practice, and it is hard. So often our optimism is challenged by cyclical setbacks, fears, uncertainty and even wars – whether they are with a COVID virus or bad actor. It will take generations to find the correct course and continue to build the social and institutional infrastructure to succeed. Today with close to forty years of institutional history and experience to its credit, USIP is still growing and evolving as an organization and an influence for change in America.

Economist Kenneth Boulding, whom you will read about later, stated that the intrinsic value of the USIP would emerge only after fifty years or more from its inception. Who knows what influence the USIP will have in coming generations? We know the nature of wars has been dramatically changing; we know the nature of peace is in flux. We are experiencing the trend that peace is no longer just the absence of war; it is the presence of justice. When we stand back, and look from a distant horizon, the changes form an arc.

Those who go before us lay down the foundation toward an ideal that others who follow may also pursue. We built our efforts on a historical path begun by others, but left unfinished. Indeed our own efforts represent just a beginning. We knew our task would eventually end. While we mounted an effective national campaign, even as we carried out the work of the commission, we knew it would be the task of others to put our work in perspective, adapt, develop and revisit.

T.S. Eliot (1888-1965) wrote:

"And to make an end is to make a beginning."[9]

The campaign to create the USIP benefitted from the tools, techniques and strategies of earlier political movements such as the American Labor Movement, Civil Rights Movement, Women's Suffrage Movement, and the 1970's Environmental Movement. All of these movements served to bend the arc of history in meaningful ways. The struggle continues today in each of these significant arenas.

Those that labored before us influenced our work, simulated our endeavor, and cut the rough path that we followed. The United States Institute of Peace, and the work of its mission, will continue to embolden others. Among the recent trailblazers who prompted our pursuits were Senators Jennings Randolph of West Virginia and Vance Harte of Indiana. Their aides, Birdy Kyle and Stephen Cloud deserve credit for sustaining an old idea and creating a foundation of legislation on which to build.

Many Americans have never heard of the organizations that nurtured the concept we developed. History owes a debt of gratitude to CODEP, the Council for a Department of Peace; the Canadian Peace Research Association, and the work of Hanna and Alan Newcombe; COPRED, the Council of Peace Research and Education Development; the work of the American Arbitration Association and its Community Disputes Services Division; SPIDR, the Society of Professionals in Dispute

Resolution; the Board of Church and Society of the United Methodist Church, and Herman Will; and I would be remiss to not acknowledge the work of the Friends Committee on National Legislation, which preceded many of the progressive think tanks and more liberal action-oriented groups we commonly recognize today.

During the work of the campaign and commission, we sought to explore how to create a culture of peace—a cultural shift for America in reframing its meaning and identity with peace. We sought to answer the questions: What might be the essence of a new culture of peace, domestically and internationally? How might we leverage the will to cause such a change?

It is imagery perhaps first observed by Alexis de Tocqueville, the French political thinker and historian who captured the essence of American culture and values in *Democracy in America*.[10] As a sociologist and political theorist, his book is recognized as one of the most influential of the 19th Century. After his extensive travels in the United States, Tocqueville wrote a detailed two-volume treatise on why America developed into the nation it had become. If Tocqueville were alive today, he might well advance a newer version of American exceptionalism – the United States has to fulfill its potential in promoting and living out a new doctrine of peace, internationally and at home. He wrote that the unique spirit of liberty he observed during his visits to America was expressive of the desire for Americans to extend such freedoms everywhere.

America is at its best when it governs from a sense of power, not force. Both Hawkins and Tocqueville would agree that power is the path to peace.[11] The worldviews depicted by the words *force* and *power* collided and defined the landscape of my journey. These opposing views have been in an enduring battle since the nation's founders deliberated on war and peace as it related to our domestic and foreign policy. The balance between them has been perhaps one of our nation's more perplexing debates. The innovative idea that there were alternatives to the use of force thrust this debate into a new perspective in mid-1970. American society began to question traditional authority and how its leaders managed conflict.

Linguist George Lakoff called this leadership dynamic strict versus nurturing.[12] In the end, choosing between these paths defines our moral authority and ultimate effectiveness in the pursuit of peace. Americans began to discover new societal norms and values.

Defined in this way, it is an ongoing challenge. Not only will we require the skills and mindsets to achieve this new world, we must create the political will to succeed in our journey. Every person is a part of peace; each person is asked to discover the strength of his own political will to help create it. Every nation seeks the knowledge that will come from achieving it. This brings us back to the lives of four individuals among many who faced this challenge.

Bryant M. Wedge, MD, *the psychiatrist*, was drawn to advancing our understanding of international relations by applying principles of modern psychiatry, cross-cultural communications, and the insights of political psychology to our task. He first became involved in these issues in the late 1950s. Bryant challenged the foreign policy establishment with his insight, experience, and interdisciplinary thinking. He was a spark. Bryant was fifty-five at the beginning of the campaign. He catalyzed a national campaign by recruiting others and sharing a contagious conviction that a few people could make a big difference. Bryant died in 1987.

The civil rights movement influenced James H. Laue, PhD, *the professor*. He used his experience in the civil rights movement to advance our practical understanding of conflict resolution roles within communities. Jim challenged the establishments of diplomacy and academia to value and utilize the tools of community relations, collaboration, social group dynamics, communications, and third-party processes to elevate their professionalism and effectiveness. Jim not only helped to advance the campaign, he guided the commission as its Vice Chair. Jim was thirty-nine at the beginning of the campaign. He brought academic creditability and boundless networking to the cause, based in no small part to his personal values and enthusiasm. Jim died in 1993.

The Reverend Andrew J. Young, *the pastor*, civil rights leader, and US Ambassador to the United Nations, saw an underlying culture of violence in America that permeated many levels of social interaction and structural injustice. He sought to make the connection between inclusion and social justice, and in so doing challenged the formal power of the foreign policy establishment to accept a wider and more diverse level of participation by the citizenry. Andy's core belief that peace and justice should be the essential objectives of social policy sometimes put him at odds with the American foreign policy establishment that more often viewed peace as an interpretation of US interests abroad, achievable through the use of force. He became a consequential player on the world stage. He brought visibility and esteem to the cause. Andy was forty-four at the beginning of the campaign. He used the power of his life, position, and voice to influence and engage others.

I came to Washington, DC as a recent graduate student, following a brief stent in business. I would become *the peddler*. My role was to coordinate a focused campaign in order to create the political will to advance a legislative process. My job was to persuade others of our vision; explain the practical merits of seeking alternatives to the use of force; manage the energies of those in the campaign effort, and facilitate the work of the commission. Simply put, I became a salesman, pitchman and promoter. I was twenty-six at the beginning of the campaign.

Chapters 1-3 tell how I became a part of this effort, and reveal what we were thinking as we set out on our course. Chapters 4-6 review the strategic moments of the campaign, and how we started and gained momentum. Chapters 7-9 describe the work of the commission and our decision points along the way. Chapters 10-11 chronicle the learning that emerged from our efforts and summarize the six principles that came to inform us when we met resistance. Chapter 12 takes measure of our success and failure, and considers the future rebranding of America as more of a nation of peace and social justice than of violence. The Afterword serves to reflect on answers to the question: Is peace possible?

Sometimes we look back in order to move forward. *Political Will,* this journey you are about to embark upon, is a true story that suggests some of the strategies and tools, to take on the many social and political challenges that will follow the post-Trumpian era. The goal of this book is to inform, enable, and motivate you to follow your individual passion for change. At the conclusion of Chapter 1, I encourage you to pause in your reading by using the prompts and reflect on the meaning of, and your ability to pursue your own passion for change. Then, at your own pace continue to the next chapter.

Rev Dr Martin Luther King, Jr is remembered for using the now famous phrase: "The arc of the moral universe is long, but it bends toward justice." The enduring relevance of his words foretold the sentiments that many came to share in 2020, following the tragic murder of George Floyd. We protest to find justice; Americans are still struggling to find the end of that arc.

Dr King first chose to use this version of this phrase in 1956, following the conclusion of the Montgomery bus boycott, and later in several of his most famous speeches, including his last speech in March 1968 at the National Cathedral.[13]

One of the lessons of his life is that you can bend the arc of history by creating the political will to advance the common good. The passion you choose is yours. The journey chronicled in this book was a personal passage for me; it was a consequential turning point for all of the advocates who shared in the outcome.

At the very end of this book you will find a Summary of Key Chapter Points and Reflections that provides a concise list of the specific Task, Challenge, Gifts and Opportunities I experienced along my path. If you like, use this synopsis to consider your reflections on "bending your own arc of history".

When someone asks the question *"What can I do to make a difference?"* the answer usually resides in that person creating the political will to effect change, in us, in others, or in the policies and behaviors of a community or country. For each of us, we have the choice to act or the choice to observe.

You are perhaps reading this book because you want to make a difference in your life, or learn how others have created institutional change, or influenced society to alter its course. Maybe you are interested in the how the USIP came to be. A unifying characteristic of all descriptions of creating political will is that it revolves around personal choice. The process of creating societal political will is about marketing, but the intended result is based on the volition of the individual. There are scarcely any acts more sacred to Americans than the right to exercise political will as individuals or in the aggregate. Thus, the creation of political will, and the process of doing so, is one of the fulcrum points that encapsulate the essence of American life, innovation and growth.

This book is about a snapshot of history, and the lessons we can learn from it. The history revealed in this story, grew out of both an ideal, and the current events of the times. History and political will, build upon each other. Together, they create an invitation to each of us to view history and the needs of the current situation in fresh analysis. The French novelist, Marcel Proust (1881-1965) wrote:

> "The real voyage of discovery consists
> not in seeing new landscapes,
> but in having new eyes."[14]

With your own "new eyes" you can cause extraordinary things. The passions you feel for social change are not so much about the current terrain as it is, but how it might be. This perspective is among the lessons of history, and of this story. It is also true that individuals sometimes try to move society in a more selfish direction for profit, illicit gain, or political advantage. Fortunately in our democratic system, many of these errant endeavors are usually proven to be subordinate in the long term to the common good.

There are many examples and precedence for creating lasting political will. After the devastation once caused by runaway fires in cities like London and Chicago, societies acted to prevent, rather than merely put out, fires. Necessity drove a process of increased social understanding of the imperative to change and invent better ways of anticipating, mitigating and avoiding the destructive violence of urban fires.

In modern times, fire resistant materials, building codes, and safety awareness came to permeate the culture of our social fabric. Now, professional fire marshals and firefighters have nearly absolute authority to inspect buildings, set occupancy limitations, require sprinkler systems, and regulate exit signage and protocols. It was not always that way. Fire marshals today in American cities have the authority – often over police and town officials – to close down overcrowded indoor public events, or limit citizen access to their homes in active fire zones. This authority is the accountability we give officials to provide for the common good. It insures the liberty of all, and the power of the public right above arbitrary individual action. It is against the law to stand up in a theater and yell, "Fire," if there is none. It is not an issue of free speech, or individual freedom. In our democracy, we grant specific powers to society in balance with the rights granted to individuals. The creation of fire prevention policy was a reflection of the social evolutionary forces that caused hard-fought changes in social policy. Societies learned the hard way—and we changed.

Resistance to social change can be counted on to rise up out of perceived economic self-interest, images locked in the past, ideological positions, or even lack of civic interest. Focused efforts to impact political will serve to inspire change, such as those represented in the fire management example above. The focus of our effort was on specific incremental steps to expand our understanding of peace. It was our hope that citizens would one day challenge their leaders to rebrand America as the recognized world leader in seeking alternatives to the use of force in resolving conflict. That proposition defined the path our efforts would take.

♖ ♗ ♞

Singer, songwriter, and philanthropist Bono wrote in a 2009 *New York Times* Op-Ed piece, "The world wants to believe in America because the world needs to believe in America again." Bono, I believe, was asking Americans to step up to lead the world in jointly addressing global suffering such as extreme poverty, preventable disease and the search for alternatives to violence and war.

America holds a unique position among countries due to our vast natural resources and innovative ideas. Since the 18th Century the world has often looked to American principles and institutions as examples of desirable national values and good statecraft. Americans as well think of themselves as innovators and leaders in the world. Such self-images and the expectations of others call out for American action to engage in the resolution of problems such as these.

The thesis of the book is embodied in the following five elements, or keys that I believe best describe the principles and processes of peace that successfully guided our effort to create USIP:

1) An individual or a small group of people can cause change at the undermost level, and in doing so, be of service to many. The prerequisite is to know what you are doing, and be committed to the effort. Key: ***Create a larger problem definition to achieve a more acceptable solution.***

2) The intent of peace policy goes beyond the conventional parameters of current US foreign policy. Key: ***To succeed, it must include justice and respect for the needs and interests***

of all. The needs and interests of adversaries are as important to sustaining peace as those of allies.

3) Key: ***Peace at home is as important as the peace we seek abroad.*** Peace has to be marketed and sold as a concept, a process and a dynamic. Peace is based on reciprocal relationships that are perceived as authentic in their nature and presentation.

4) To bring about peace at home or abroad, Key: ***it is essential to attack the level of conflict not at the points of highest crisis and violence, but at lower levels of tension*** where norms, expectations and accountability can be set. And finally,

5) The strategies and skills we used can be applied to any cause or movement. They include semantic framing and diffusion strategy that effectively uses the social system itself to remove barriers to acceptance and support. Key: ***Only the system can change the system.***

My challenge to you is to seek opportunities of lifting and inspiring others toward your own passionate ideal. What changes do you want to make now, and into the future? What are the keys to your success?

♖ ♗ ♞

In the early stages of the COVID-19 world, the reality of the important work ahead should be clear to all of us. It is worth repeating that today our American Democracy is caught in an unpleasant and entangled web. Each strand has been woven with remarkable tensile strength by cultural and economic dynamics; each sustaining its own complexity and entanglements. We face enmeshed processes of racism, discrimination, excessive military spending, corporate influence, runaway capitalism, environmental degradation, and the system straining cycles of poverty and injustice. Creating political will is one means to leverage the resistance we need to break these bonds.

The focus of my passionate ideal was peace and understanding the nature of the political will necessary to get there. I arrived at the belief that the pursuit of peace is an evolutionary process, a natural product of human development and learning. Like the biology major I had been in college, I sensed in grad school that American society had not yet matured, or evolved in its public life to perceive peace as we did fire prevention or public health. Organisms, institutions and individuals evolve and develop because we are built that way to survive. With my training in life and behavioral sciences, I regard society as a living organism, fully capable of change. The vital processes that define humans are also defined by the notion of the ecology of cooperation.[15]

Everyone knows that plants require water, sunlight and nutrients to grow. The presence of these conditions influences the ability of the organism to flourish. Humans thrive in much the same way. We benefit from the nurturing institutions around us. We grow, adapt, learn and age.

Distinguished economist and friend Kenneth Boulding wrote in his collection of peace essays, *Stable Peace,*

> "The problem of peace policy is seen not as how to achieve immediate and certain success but as how to introduce a bias into the system that moves it toward stable peace at a more rapid rate."[16]

Dissect the sentence above: the words – *peace policy, bias, stable peace* – could have been the subtitle of this book. Spoiler alert: the storyline of this book is how to create the political will to enable this outcome. Say those words to yourself…*peace policy, bias, stable peace*…please do it now…Now… you can "Drop The Mic."

What I mean by this is not to discourage you from reading the book. Far from it. I invite you to engage the story – my story, so that you will one day write your own. My path happened to lead to advocating for a new institution, and learning the skills to help two powerful individuals continue to do good deeds in the world. Your path is, or will be different.

As this book goes to print in the Fall 2020, our country faces familiar regional strains, and strikingly different views about how best to manage through difficult times. We have faced pandemics and other forms of threat to our national health before. We have overcome the sacrifices necessary to avoid extended suffering, and even extinction.

For many Americans, our national policy of dealing with the COVID-19 pandemic is viewed through political and geographic lenses that date back more than 150 years. General Ulysses S. Grant became our 18th President in 1869. We owe a debt to his moral leadership. For example President Grant addressed the violence and activity of the Ku Klux Klan; created the Department of Justice; set the groundwork for the passage of the 15th Amendment to the Constitution granting African American men the right to vote; advanced African American Civil Rights; reformed Native American public policies; and protected women under Federal law. In addition to these accomplishments, we should recognize President Grant for his view of history.

He wrote the following:

> "If we are to have another contest in the near future of our national experience, I predict that the dividing line will not be Mason and Dixon, but between patriotism, and intelligence on one side, and superstition, ambition and ignorance on the other."[17]

President Grant's insight and prophecy has credibly come back to inform Americans in the first half of 2020 of our past and future. We are perhaps now more divided as a nation than at any other time since the Civil War. We face significant divides over Civil Rights for all, including non-citizens; how to address our American history of slavery and racial discrimination; how to respond to an invisible threat to global health called COVID-19; how to acknowledge and respect gender non-conformity, and how to maintain the separation of church and state called for by the First Amendment. This, of course, is an incomplete list. You surely have your own list.

There is much work to be done, and the methodologies described in this story may be helpful in lending insight to find paths to resolution. How we chose to engage issues such as these represents individual commitment to creating political will. As you read, think about your own journey and what is important to *you*. It is my wish that you will learn as much about yourself in these pages as you learn about my story.

It was our vision forty years ago that the USIP would become an institutional voice to foster new mindsets and skill sets leading to a more peaceful country and world.

Since then, the world has changed significantly; yet many of our nation's finest qualities and greatest deficiencies have not. In this, there is a hope and a challenge. It is my hope that to this end, our work will enliven you to make a beginning.

COPENHILL

Spring 1987 – I emerged from the humid jet way to meet the Secretary-General of the United Nations, but instead was confronted by the shrill voice of Tammy Faye Bakker, who through her tears and running mascara was pleading her innocence to the American people across every television monitor at the Hartsfield International Airport. I struggled to weave between the small crowds standing before each monitor, who seemed to crave the latest news about televangelist Jim Bakker and his $200,000 payoff of church secretary Jessica Hahn. I was already late. The next day was to be a big day for me and I could not afford to stand around, despite the intrigue in the developing story about the total collapse of the PTL network and Heritage USA, the twin duplicitous fundraising vehicles that had propelled the Bakkers first into fabulous wealth and then to their downfall. It was May 27, 1987, and the following day I would facilitate a meeting of eight world leaders who lead international organizations representing the 196 countries of the world. I could not find the Secretary-General amid the waiting limo drivers and scurrying flock in the crowded baggage claim of the airport; I made my own way to the conference hotel.

It had taken more than an airplane flight from Boston for me to reach this point in my career. Indeed, it had been twelve years in the making since I stood in the stacks of the UCLA Research Library to crack open the academic journal on conflict resolution that thrust me on a journey of discovery leading to the creation of a new American institution. Still, despite the battles along the way, I felt nothing but elation and excitement about what I was about to do. A former President of the United States had entrusted me with the task of facilitating this rare gathering of never-before-convened leaders to create a unique list of the intra-national armed conflicts that were clearly off the conscious screens of the world community. The objective of the session was to put in motion hopeful initiatives to keep international conflicts from escalating and to mobilize constituencies of influence that might make a difference in new and innovative ways.

Going into the meeting, we knew there were about thirty-five armed conflicts raging where more than one thousand deaths had occurred. It was about that many every year. My job over the next two days was going to be to draw out the leaders of these sometimes competing organizations to build consensus on a fresh set of ingredients to enable them to succeed in building greater cooperation in targeting the worst and longest running conflicts around the globe. They would be joined by the savvy heads of foundations whose holdings nearly totaled $20 billion in assets, and some of the best dispute resolution minds in the country: men and women who had negotiated the

Panama Canal Treaty, served with President Carter to pull off the Camp David Accords, managed the peacekeeping forces of the United Nations, helped to devise the UN itself, or had authored the bestselling books in the field. What would constitute a good philosophy, plan, and team effort to sustain the existing mechanisms of the world community to better manage international conflict? That was the goal.

What could be a larger strategy – the illusive initiative – to inspire international and domestic political will around the world in creating a new ethos of pursuing peace? Might the group put forward a doctrine or a peace process that might suggest, "everywhere is in everyone's sphere of influence," as one participant would phrase it? Most countries tenaciously embraced the policy that their sovereignty as a nation prevents other nations or international organizations from interfering in the conflicts within their borders, no matter how deadly the disputes. Yet, by far the most number of deadly conflicts and citizen fatalities are within the borders of nations, not between them.

The first of its kind meeting of international leaders charged with managing the conflicts of the world was to set to occur at a place called Copenhill. Originally Copen Hill was a small rise on the outskirts of the railroad crossings that defined Atlanta, founded in 1837. In 1864 Union General William T. Sherman sat atop Copen Hill at his headquarters to oversee the Battle of Atlanta that overwhelmingly defeated the Confederate forces that had gathered to defend the railroads and supply lines of the city. Over thirty-four thousand Union forces had faced off over forty thousand Confederacy troops in a blood bath of more than nine thousand casualties and losses. It was from this hill that Sherman would begin his month-long march to the sea, ending with the capture of the port of Savannah and the destruction of any industry, infrastructure, or civilian property in his way. The carnage Sherman and his troops created was so devastating that modern Atlanta has claimed the mythological reborn phoenix rising from the ashes as its city symbol.

Copenhill was now a neighborhood upon which the present-day Carter Center of Emory University proudly sat, as a nonprofit, nongovernmental organization dedicated to the advancement of human rights, alleviating human suffering, and promoting peaceful solutions to international conflicts. It would be there that the world leaders would gather to assess their past effectiveness and make plans to target the most intransigent of wars. At the hotel most of the participants boarded the bus to travel to the site. The executive transport, a mobile lounge really, was lined with huge tinted gray windows and soft cushy seats.

I had been squeezed in between David Hamburg, President of the Carnegie Corporation and Sir Brian Urquhart, a visiting scholar at the Ford Foundation, but previously the head of UN Peacekeeping forces. David was a medical doctor who had taken over Carnegie just five years earlier. He was passionate about his intent to migrate his organization to "strategic philanthropy," where project support was highly targeted to achieve groundbreaking results. Carnegie had recently set a focus on the danger to world peace posed by the problems of interethnic and regional conflict and they were looking at projects to support that served to diminish the risks of a wider war stemming from civil strife. Brian, who was currently working on his memoir, just recently retired from his duties as Under-Secretary General where he had participated in the shaping and leadership of more peacekeeping and peace-observing forces than any person in history. The next year, the Nobel Peace Prize would be given to UN peacekeeping forces—so in many ways, the prize would be for Sir Brian as well.

Brian's dry wit and lovely, gentle humor had kept David and me in stiches as soon as we had begun the ride to our meeting site. Brian said, "This meeting reminds me of my time as an intelligence officer in England in the run-up to D-Day."[18]

"I was serving in the Airborne Forces to help develop the parachute and glider-borne troop deployment strategies for the invasion. Although I had been forced to jump in my infantry training days, I hated and dreaded jumping. On mornings when we had practice jumps, I would go to great lengths to find other matters to occupy my attention, although the actual descent was usually a wonderful sensation, peaceful, solitary and serene after the hurly-burly and noise of the aircraft. I jumped whenever I could, because I thought I would become less scared of it, but I didn't. Anyway, our activities in the Airborne Forces often attracted increasing numbers of eminent visitors. Mr Churchill liked to come down to the Salisbury Plain for demonstrations of parachuting and gliding, often bringing senior colleagues and distinguished guests. These occasions did not always go smoothly, and on one particularly cold and blustery day, Mr Churchill brought along a newly arrived American Major General, Dwight Eisenhower."

Leaning in to follow his story, David and I both caught the twinkle in Brian's eye as he continued in a deadpan recitation.

"The plan was for all of us to demonstrate our jumping proficiency and show off before the general. Emerging last from our aircraft, I could easily see that the situation was not promising. The line of VIPs, which was supposed to be at a safe distance, seemed rapidly to get nearer as I descended and the wind blew our little group off course. At about 300 feet I could sense the distinction of the lonely line, the prime minister, the air minister, Sir Archibald Sinclair, Lord Cherwell, Chief of the Imperial General Staff, and the American general, as well as my superior officer, General Browning. Shouting a warning and trying to sideslip, I landed with a sickening bump just in front of General Eisenhower. The wind then took my parachute and dragged me at 30 miles an hour straight through the VIP line. Detaching my parachute harness, I came to a halt, stood up, and for want of anything better to do, saluted."

At this point, David and I were laughing and leaning to and fro as the bus maneuvered through the Atlanta suburbs. Other dignitaries in the bus were looking our way, clearly wondering why we were having so much fun on such an otherwise serious ride to an important meeting.

"The British, except for my boss Browning, behaved rather badly, as I recall, muttering 'Disgraceful,' 'Damned poor show,' and so on, and looking very embarrassed. General Eisenhower, on the other hand, was perfectly charming. 'Are you alright, son?' he asked. 'You shouldn't be jumping in this wind anyway.'"

If that had not begun enough laughing among us, Brian went on to say:

"Eisenhower then looked quizzically at the cylindrical cardboard container around my neck. I explained that it contained two carrier pigeons for communicating with headquarters, and I extracted one, attached a message cylinder to its leg, and threw it into the air to launch it on its mission. The pigeon had evidently had enough nonsense for one day and flew to the top of a nearby bush, where it sat cooing and eyeing the company with an evil eye. 'I see we shall have to do something about your communications,' Eisenhower said."

Now our half of the executive bus was laughing, without really knowing why. None of the eminent people down the rows, wanted to be seen as being above a little merriment, so soon everyone began to smile and giggle as if they had been a part of the entire story. David and I had to wipe tears from our eyes.

The story Brian had recounted had emphasized for me in a humorous way that human war itself really is in its imperfections and shortcomings. No matter how extensive the planning or practice, war making is a flawed science, filled with error and misjudgment. Our meetings were to be about improving the science of peace seeking and peacemaking. They, too, were flawed disciplines, but far less injurious than war, and all the more in need of attention. I felt the importance of the day. My unexpected moments of laughter had eased my nervousness and lessoned my anxiety about the day. Just as we pulled into the Carter Center parking lot, Brian once again, this time more quietly said in his soft British accent and country squire demeanor,

> "There is no logical reason why the international community can't stop a dangerous
> and murderous war between two countries that have no armaments industry and
> are both dependent upon a single primary product, namely oil."

He was speaking about the Iran-Iraq War that was just winding down after seven years. It was estimated that the casualties and losses of the conflict had been between 225,000 and 435,000 lives. Iran had experienced an economic loss of $627 billion. Even as we rode in the bus, the war was turning into the deadliest conventional war ever fought between regular armies of developing countries. The seriousness of the extraordinary meeting in which we were about to participate emphasized the importance of the consequences of our actions. There would be the four heads of the major international organizations of the world. The world. This was not going to be a PTA meeting or a Little League Baseball Awards Dinner. As we stepped off the bus, there were the Secretaries-General of the 159-nation United Nations, the 31-nation Organization of American States, the 49-nation Organization of African Unity, and the 48-nation Commonwealth. Each Secretary General that day would become a first-name colleague. I was as nervous as a cat, not only because my hopes were high for the meeting, but because I was going to facilitate the small group to achieve their meeting objectives—kind of a peacemaker among the peacemakers. It was a summit that had never occurred before, and it would remain totally invisible to news coverage. Where often up to seven thousand journalists might cover a superpower summit, none would be present today, except a single reporter, Earl Foell of the *Christian Science Monitor,* a respected and trusted correspondent who covered the UN.

The hallways leading to the Carter Center conference room were a zigzagging maze of beige paint and freshly laid carpet, as the new Presidential Library was still in its infancy. There was a tangible excitement about the meeting as the participants filed off the shuttle bus. There were just twenty-five people in all. President and Mrs Carter were the proud hosts, and Carter Center Fellow for Conflict Resolution, Dayle E. Powell who had designed the meeting. Dayle had been at the Carter Center for three years. Although it was not one of the first events at the Center, it would bring some of the most celebrated leaders in the conflict resolution field together for informal, off-the-record discussions.

The meeting room itself was bright white from the incandescent lights and modern, unadorned walls. The building was so new that no art had been hung. Newsprint was hung instead on the walls and there was no podium, stage, risers, or tables. We sat in a semi-circle, unencumbered by titles, unmovable theater seats, microphones, tape recorders, or an audience. Earl Foell later wrote about the meeting, "What the invisible summit of Atlanta (and some later follow up meetings) sought to discover is whether a system of skilled mediators can be developed which would allow the Secretaries-General to send knowledgeable referees out to calm conflicts before they reach the escalation stage. The analogy often used is that the world needs something like the well-trained, experienced labor-management mediators that exist in many of the industrial democracies."[19]

These two days of meetings engaged the participants in identifying the missing ingredients for success in the use of third-party efforts to bring about a cessation of fighting in many parts of the world. We focused on what were the major obstacles to third-party efforts and, most importantly, where were the current opportunities that existed, what roles would be played by whom, and what were the best possible next steps that could be taken by members of those present to further the objectives of the meeting.

The meeting was a time for this elite gathering of Secretaries-General to get real. Former President Carter had gotten their attention in his invitation because there was a perceived need by all present. I made my way around the room to greet each participant, shaking hands or touching elbows with words of welcome and introduction. I was a member of three "process experts" who had been invited by President Carter to organize a Secretariat of his own called the International Negotiation Network. The trio included William Ury[20], a co-founder of the Harvard Negotiation Project and bestselling co-author of the book, *Getting to Yes*, known around the world as a primer in negotiation, Dayle Powell and myself. Each of the four Secretaries-General had a staff person present and then there were the foundation heads and a handful of resource people who were to be available to the principal participants as advisors or content scholars.

First there was the Commonwealth Secretary-General, Shridath S. Ramphal, who quickly introduced himself as Sonny. He not only had served as the leader of the Commonwealth Secretariat in the United Kingdom, but was the only person to have served on all of the three major international commissions in the decade prior that had gathered the best and brightest of the world to undertake year-long studies on the separate topics of the environment, poverty, and disarmament. Sonny was jovial and immediately engaging. He had previously served as the Foreign Minister of Guyana. Next to him, Secretary- General João Clemente Baena Soares of the Organization of American States had been a Brazilian diplomat before assuming his current role. He was more reserved than Sonny, serious and slightly suspect of the initial informality of what was shaping up to be a more unconventional meeting environment than he was used to attending.

As I moved around the row of chairs, brushing the President, I held out my hand to recognize the UN Secretary-General. What an honor to meet the man who held the office. In that moment I felt a rush of emotions and somehow more connected with all of humanity than ever before. This man, now clasping my hand, was the single most visible symbol of the world's hopes and aspirations for peace. He was Javier Pérez de Cuéllar, a former Peruvian diplomat who had replaced Kurt Waldheim just five years earlier. Pérez de Cuéllar wore Bono-like tinted glasses that were oversized and covered a full third of his face.

I was face-to-face with his office, more than just meeting a man. The Secretary-General too was mildly awkward and had a surprised look about him, much like he was in a daze. He too, seemed to be struck by the easygoing and unceremonious start-up of the meeting. For me, that did not matter. This was the Secretary-General of the United Nations. Not the Pope or a president, not a famous person particularly, or a celebrity whose face brought instant recognition, this man was *THE* guy that most of the world's population put their faith in to bring about understanding and peace. Gosh, I thought. When citizens of the world think of peace, they probably most often visualize the light blue flag of the United Nations. Like the UN or not; close your eyes and that image comes to mind.

I finished my introductory rounds and sat next to a vacant chair that was supposed to be filled by the Secretary-General of the Organization of African Unity. I would meet the OAU SG in the coming weeks. Now the meeting was ready to begin and former President Carter began his welcoming remarks.

I had met with President Carter in July of 1985, after he asked me to serve as one of three mediators in his first foray back into dispute resolution after leaving the White House. Jim Laue had introduced me to Dayle and we came together to plan an intervention with a few more than seventy representatives of the often-harsh conflicting interests in the tobacco debate, most specially in five Southern states.

President Carter had invited Dayle to join his new Carter Center team of nine distinguished Fellows, each in their own area of expertise. When I was first introduced to her I learned that she had served as an Assistant United States Attorney for the Northern District of Alabama and was also law clerk to Chief Judge John R. Brown, of the Fifth US Circuit Court of Appeals in Houston, Texas. Dayle would go on to work with President Carter for almost ten years to develop his approaches to negotiating and mediating international conflicts. In that time Dayle organized negotiations between numerous governments and revolutionary leaders in civil war situations, including Ethiopia and Eritrea; Sudan and the Sudanese People's Liberation Front; and Liberia and the National Patriotic Front of Liberia. She is one of the few Americans to have negotiated directly with the government of North Korea and was instrumental in arranging for peace initiative undertaken by President Carter in that region. Her work in conflict resolution eventually took her to over fifty countries on five continents. Dayle was involved in efforts to end the fighting in fourteen civil wars. Carter was awarded the Nobel Peace Prize for these efforts.

Dayle led the mediation team and had asked Jim to formulate an approach involving three mediators from different disputes resolution disciplines. Tobacco was a health, economic, political, and morale divider among many interest groups and tobacco-related industry concerns. The purpose of the meeting was to see how much agreement disputing parties could make over a four-day time period using three small groups of participants. each group of disputants was led by mediator. It was an academic experiment and it was a real-time venture into measuring the effectiveness of third-party skills to bring disputants together in a very difficult and high-stakes conflict. The model for the event was to observe the techniques of three mediators, each of whom were trained and experienced in one of three different disciplines: civil rights intercession, environmental mediation, and business facilitation—all having shared mind- and skill sets but each with distinct approaches, depending on the personality of the mediator. I had been selected as the business mediator and was extremely proud to be recognized as a practitioner who had demonstrated effectiveness in conducting my craft.

Each of the three mediators had been given a subset of the symposium participants. I had a very lucky draw, as I had in my small group the head of the Centers for Disease Control, a vice president of the Tobacco Institute (which was the lead lobbying industry group for big tobacco in America), the heads of the American Heart Association and American Lung Association, and other prominent leaders from health fields, tobacco grower associations, advertising executives who represented cigarette brands, and a member of Congress from one of the Southern states. Each of the other groups had a similar composition but I was lucky to have quite a few of the decision makers who had influence in the controversy.

To make that long story short, the groups reached enough agreement and integrated their small group outcomes into a consensus of all the participants, to report out several major agreements. Dayle and I were asked by the President and a representative of the Tobacco Institute to continue working with the parties to see if further agreements could be reached. Dayle and I commuted back and forth for ten days from our separate homes in Atlanta and Boston to meet with the disputants and their organizations in Washington, DC. We were able to get the parties to agree on very substantive breakthrough issues, and a month later, the United States Congress passed the Smokeless Tobacco Act of 1986[21], based on our work and the fact that the parties were able to draw together the political will to agree on several important principles that became national legislation. The two major factors that influenced the parties in our exercise to come together in agreement were the uncertainty of multi-state lawsuits pending in various courts, and the knowledge of the anti-tobacco advocates that no lawsuits had ever been won against the tobacco companies. As third parties we were able to highlight these pressures and build a consensus strong enough to support Congressional enactment of new regulations. Our negotiations related to smokeless tobacco—its labeling, pesticide use, and availability to youth. The tobacco industry did not acknowledge that cigarettes caused cancer until ten years later in 1997. In 1998 the industry agreed to pay $206 million to settle a lawsuit brought by the attorneys general in forty-six states. This was a far greater sum than the industry might have had to pay if they had sought an earlier alternative path to resolution, and no doubt thousands of lives might have been saved each year.

President Carter had been impressed and asked me to continuing working with Dayle and the Carter Center to strategize and intervene in several other conflicts, some organizational, some community, and some international. This work and much planning in between had brought my participation in the 1987 meeting with the Secretaries-General and the President.

The President laid out his hopes for the gathering and then turned the agenda over to Dayle, the organizer of the meeting, who outlined the details and proposed outcomes for the day. Dayle described the "mediation gap" that existed among the work and efforts of the international NGOs. When the United Nations and other regional or international peacemaking organizations were developed, they were designed within the context of the then-existing experience with wars. Serious restrictions were placed on the powers of such organizations when the nature of the conflicts of the time was largely transnational. As an example, Article Two, Section Seven of United Nations' Charter prohibits its involvement in the internal affairs of member nations. At the time of our meeting in 1985, Dayle explained there were more than 100 current existing armed conflicts and wars within national boundaries. These conflicts were considered off limits to the peace seeking activity of most international organizations, yet there were millions of people caught up in these internal wars with no where to turn for mediative help. The Peace Research Institute of Oslo, PRIO, estimated that civilian deaths accounted for about three-fourths of all the casualties in in these conflicts.

Dayle went on to present the overview of the thirty-five major wars, where in excess of 1,000 battle-related deaths had occurred. These intranational conflicts incurred great costs, not simply military costs in terms of lives lost, although that would be significant, but costs that included: 1) impeding development, 2) causing excessive childhood morbidity and mortality, 3) creating massive refugee and displaced populations, 4) spreading disease, and 6) causing recurring famine. Each of these conflicts she reviewed also had the potential to spill over into international conflicts and even to escalate region wide.

Next Bill Ury was asked to illustrate a few of these cases, describing why these internal conflicts were so difficult to resolve. At the time, Bill served as an associate director of the Avoiding Nuclear War Project at Harvard University's Kennedy School of Government, where he directed a joint study group on crisis prevention with scholars and policy advisors from the US and the Soviet Union. Bill had received his PhD in social anthropology from Harvard University in 1982. He outlined for the Secretaries-General and others the objectives of trying to find non-military means of reducing these armed conflicts and closing the mediation gap.

Then the President called on me. I explained the agenda and meeting process for the two days and facilitated the participants in listing and discussing their personal expectations and experiences with the topics for the day.

Pretty soon, after the first morning break, the momentum of the meeting picked up. The casualness at the start of the day inspired trust and confidence in the world leaders and they began to highlight and dissect some of the world's most intractable violent conflicts. Some conflicts were in the Horn of Africa and the Sudan; others were in the South Pacific and Central America. Each was a conflict where the sovereign nations of the world refused to intercede in intra-state fighting and civil war due to the protocols of diplomacy, but where the body counts or death rates and destruction of civilians and infrastructure continued without hope of resolution.

Primarily the floor was left to the Secretaries-General to identify the target conflicts. My function as facilitator was to encourage and engage them in the focused brainstorming process without hesitations or fear of judgment by others. Each organization present had hidden away skeletons that represented a lack of intervention efforts for which they might be blamed. After all, the issues that prevented them from interceding were largely structural due to the charters of their international organizations as has been explained. Still, there were lingering perceptions of failure about each of the conflict being identified. These feelings of guilt and awareness of possible failings had to be cast aside. These frustrations themselves were the underlying thesis of the meeting, and the reoccurring problem we were trying to fix.

Now in shirtsleeves, I stood at the front of the room hurriedly writing the names of conflicts with brightly colored markers across a canvas of raging international disputes. I called on each man with the salutation of "Secretary-General?" then wrote down the contribution. Often when recognizing an individual, my voice called out in acknowledgment, "Secretary-General?" and several would respond; they would laugh. They talked over one another with hesitating enthusiasm. The SGs began to get into a rhythm. The pace of this part of the program quickened. It was almost like a purge of their concerns rather than a brainstorming session. Each of the world leaders somehow seem to benefit from finally being able to raise up a failure of international diplomacy and let go of any perceived criminations they may have felt for being on watch while these tragedies occurred. We finished the list and I led them through a cataloging of criteria they might use to prioritize the problems on the three sheets of flipchart paper they had filled. Soon, these world leaders talked and reasoned together on which of the world's raging civil wars most urgently needed a new burst of international attention.

Next, all three SGs were on their feet, coats off and approaching the lists on the wall, assuaging one another's arguments one minute and clarifying a political or ethics difference in another. Each man held marking pens and had set about circling topics and indicating their preferences. President Carter finally stepped in, grabbing the markers out of my hands and marking up the lists himself, highlighting his own sense of what he felt was ripe for intervention. Watching the four men interact in that instant felt like I was viewing enthusiastic young classmates plotting a school trip. The moment was filled with hope, wonderment, and a fleeting ownership that their organizational structures and diplomatic proprieties had prevented them each from experiencing. The other twenty experts in the room sat quietly, taking in the sanguine moment, and reflecting on where the exercise was headed.

As Earl Foell later described, "More than one third of Earth's nations have internal insurrections, potential ethnic splits, or border problems with neighbors. So these nations tend to favor keeping out of other countries' disputes lest others meddle in theirs."[22]

The meeting had achieved its objective. There was indeed a mediation gap in the world and what were needed were the skills, the political will, and the courage to pull together resources to begin to address it. President Carter closed the meeting by urging the process team to move vigorously in distilling the thoughts of the group into bold initiatives for the future. He expressed the hope that, if anything, the Secretaries-General "will tell us that we're going too far for now, rather than we should have gone a little farther." Thus was born the International Negotiation Network, INN. Dayle, Bill and I became the Secretariat, and President Carter it's Chair.

In the decade that was to come, we succeeded in taking the spirit of that meeting to create the political will in a dozen countries to reach cease-fires, mediated settlements, and regional agreements along with the creation of a group of eminent persons as part of the International Negotiation Network, the likes of Archbishop Desmond Tutu, Sonny Ramphal, President Carter, Mikhail Gorbachev, and others. Their standing in the world became a mediative type of flypaper that was used to attract disputants and engage them in third-party-driven processes for peace. Later this innovation in peacemaking and principled process became known as a group called The Elders, sponsored by Sir Richard Branson.

The decade that preceded the meeting with the Secretaries-General had prepared me for this juncture of good fortune and sustained effort: first as a young man intrigued by peace; then as an advocate; and finally as a practitioner of its science. Along this path I discovered lessons that informed the expression and means to inspire political will. As I look back, these exercises were part of my journey to contribute to advancing many of the ideals I believed in, and ultimately to helping to lay the groundwork for the United States Institute of Peace. The passion I had felt for a concept in Malibu; was nurtured to activism in Washington, DC; and had culminated in a notable moment as a practitioner, focused on the means to promote international peace and the resolution of conflicts within and between nations.

That day in 1987, the elevated promontory once called Copen Hill became a fulfilling vista from which to view conflict, one that was heartfelt and personal. The view was not of raging wars, but of the process of peace that lingered on the horizon, a hopeful and aspirant view.

PART TWO

Finding a Way to Make a Difference

CHAPTER 1

Malibu

1975 – As I hauled my kayak out of the surf, thoughts still lingered about where I would go with my life. It was chilly and I kept warm by washing the sand off and loading the boat up through the sunroof of my VW bus. Other paddlers around me were in varying degrees of loading and unloading their crafts and in the distance I could see the surfers beyond the pier. But I was in my own world. There had always been a sort of Zen to the cleanup part of any boat trip. The process slows you down in a good way. There is a certain cleansing, as well as a sense of preparation for the next voyage. I was feeling pensive that today. I was still struggling with the meaning of my life and where it would take me. What choices would I make and would they lead to the fulfillment of my thoughts and dreams? What would those thoughts and dreams become? What would be my calling? Just like the people I would later meet in my evolving story, life was about finding perspective and meaning through others. It's the finding of one's core that presents the challenge and invitation. I was clearly sorting it all out and I knew it.

My uneasiness this day arose from the thoughts that my earlier life experiences had been more activities than a career or a calling. The motivations that inform our actions later in life develop and congeal as we mature to find ourselves. I was changing; at least my perspective was changing. I felt a tug in my core – that sense in your belly that grounds your initiative. Little did I know that in ten years from that moment parts of each of the people I would soon meet would come together as the sum of those parts; the making of a communal core.

My parents were not politically active, but they were patriotic and intuitively active servant leaders in our community. They were givers, not takers, and led by the example of their lives. They were good people: certainly kind, loving, and encouraging of me. My dad had grown up in Minnesota and my mother in Indiana, but they had lived in California for a decade by the time I came along. They were very proud to be Californians. I was too. I had been welcomed into the world as well by a loving sister, Sue, who was two years older. My grandparents lived nearby and often I would go to their house after a day at grammar school, as my parents worked. My grandfather taught me to play chess in his sunroom study and I remember he had small, modest plastic statues of Ike and Mamie Eisenhower on his desk. I thought they were toys, of course, but he had a different view and whenever I snuck them onto the floor to walk them about my model cars, I would be firmly reminded that that was "our President" I was playing with, and he and his wife belonged on the desk, not on the floor. We shared a lot of love and family time in our home. I was fortunate and I knew it. The trade-off was that I was also expected to be good and set an example for others.

We followed current events and my parents provided every opportunity they could afford to expose me to being a good citizen. As a youngster I personally met Richard Nixon, who was then Vice President, in the gardens of the former Huntington Hotel in Pasadena. Ahead of the event I remember being fitted for shiny, new, black leather shoes at a department store in nearby Alhambra. It was no small thing to buy new shoes in those days and in the tradition of our usual family "good judgment," the shoes that were selected were slightly oversized so I would have room to grow. I think my dad thought the polished shoes would be a sign of respect.

I remember the shoes because on the big day when I was to meet the Vice President, the new slippery leather soles did not provide sufficient traction on the uneven, sloping grass lawn where the reception was being held. I stood tall as I approached Mr and Mrs Nixon in the receiving line. But I had to lean back to look up as I prepared to shake his outstretched hand. I slipped and lost my balance. As I began to fall backward, Mr Nixon's hand gripped mine and I recovered. He was nice to me and the Vice President said something about remembering when he had to wear new shoes. My father had said this man was going to be President. It was just after Nixon's famous "kitchen debate" with Soviet Premier Nikita Khrushchev. My dad was impressed and liked him. I never did, but was glad to have met him. I was struck that a national political figure was out in the hot sun shaking hands with kids. Plus, Nixon's presence and influence in national events in the years ahead were to be significant to things that mattered to me. I am sure the encounter made me pay more attention to politics and feel a personal connection with world events. I was nine.

♖ ♗ ♞

At fourteen, I had the opportunity to be part of an innovative program at Los Angeles County General Medical Center–USC Medical School doing melanoma skin cancer research.[23] The premise was to use bright, untrained young people to work side-by-side with highly trained resident pathologists, post-doctoral medical researchers, and lab professionals. The first summer of the program there were two kids; the second summer there were three. The hope was the questions the kids would ask might stimulate or inspire new thinking about the mysteries of cancer and the research protocols to address the deadly diseases. Our task was to watch and do what they did, listen, and ask questions. We were to challenge their assumptions and the acquired medical school discipline in their thinking. It was my first paying job.

As an adult in Malibu ten years later, I began to ask my own questions about why another force, that of war, worked the way it did. What might be done to block its access to the social oxygen that fed its violence? These questions have driven much of my curiosity for much of my life. But, I get ahead of myself.

♖♗♘

My father was a self-described Republican during this period and like so many American families, it was difficult to engage in family discussions about any political ideology beyond that which was espoused by the Grand Old Party. My dad's word was the rule and I generally agreed, in part to get along, but he was also a hero to me and I knew he tried very hard to give us a good life. He did not have the benefit of much education, but I respected how hard he worked for our family. My dad had been an only child and I believe he tried to make up for the absence of his own father in his life by being very present in mine. He tried very hard to be a strict parent, as was the norm for someone of his generation, but he also used humor and his valuable time to invest in me as often as he could. For the first thirteen years of my life, we were fortunate to attend a family church camp in the nearby San Bernardino Mountains. If he were unable to get off work, dad would commute sixty miles up into the mountains to be with my mother and sister and me. Sometimes he would arrive at night on a workday to join us for dinner and campfires, getting up early the next day to drive back into the valley for work. He always attended my sports activities and both he and my mother were my biggest fans. My dad and I played catch in the yard. I helped with mowing the lawns, trimming hedges, washing dishes and windows, and sang in the church choir. Mother helped me with homework and served as a Cub Scout den mother. They had my back. I never wanted to let them down.

As a teenager I remember quite well a turning point that occurred for me when one day my father stated that Spiro Agnew was one of the brightest men he had ever met. I had just turned eighteen. His comment had come at the dinner table, or a built-in dinette really, that dad and I had constructed together in the garage. It provided an intimate space for much of our mealtime family dialogue. We were diagonally across the table from each other, our faces perhaps three feet apart; dinner plates between us but little else except a widening political divide. "The guy is a jerk and a crook," I snapped disrespectfully. My dad turned red and then slammed his flat palm down on the table with such force that all of the plates popped and continued to echo his rage when they landed back down on the table.

"You do not know what you are talking about, son," he asserted. "Agnew is a fine man."

Now I had become accustomed to agreeing with most things my dad said, but this comment not only did not ring true, I could see in that moment that it had the potential to cause a lasting rift with my dad. And I was backed into a corner, literally. I had the inside seat and was trapped. Our family lived in a very small house, and the eat-in area of the kitchen was our dining room, as my sister slept in the real dining room. My dad's comment sent me over the brink in trusting his assessment of people, particularly political figures. My mother and sister had gone silent. I had backed myself further into the tight space and was glad there was a table between us. My dad seemed to sense the challenge I had made to not just his statement, but also his judgment. I could feel his stare penetrating the space around me.

"You do not know what you are talking about," he repeated. I would come to realize later that it wasn't the man my dad was defending; it was his view of what he thought the man stood for. I was expected to learn to respect and cherish my dad's values, or it was clear that my dad would feel he had failed as a parent. Cutting through the intensity around the table, my mother characteristically made an intervention, "I have made a blueberry Oreo dessert with whipped cream. Susan, can you help clear the table?" That announced my escape route and I jumped up to help clear, turning to exit the dinette. My dad could not help himself and said, "After dessert young man, you will go to your room," a phrase that had often ended family debates. I knew better than to respond, and although we later made up as families do, that instant formed the beginning of a crack – or opportunity – in my identity as a young adult.

Never again did I seem to agree with my father's political views or accept his "strict parent"[24] ideology. It was a remarkable moment in my political coming of age. A decade later my own views on the matter were validated when Agnew became the only Vice President in United States history to resign because of criminal charges.

As I made my way through junior high and high school I was increasingly involved in student government and civic engagement. Leadership and service in the community seemed important, and I was rewarded for it with scholarships and parental love. Those rewards came when I was serious and took responsibility, not when I played. So I perhaps took too serious a view of life for a young person. But I was both recognized and incentivized to continue to think deeply about things, as my mother had taught me to do.

Dr Albert Schweitzer died in the fall of my sophomore year in high school. Like many American families, we subscribed to *LIFE Magazine* and the periodical was filled in many issues with images of Schweitzer's life and service in Lambaréné, Gabon (then French Equatorial Africa), where he founded a missionary and medical outpost. Dr Schweitzer became one of my early idols. I did not want to become a fireman or a policeman; I wanted to be like him.

He used his talents as a concert organist to fund his passion. He was not an ordinary medical doctor. Schweitzer was the medical missionary doctor of the generation of my grandfather, also a physician. Although I never met my mother's dad, I grew up with stories of his benevolence and competence as a small-town physician. My grandfather was an idol I never saw; "the doctor of Lambaréné" was real. I felt a connection to both through Schweitzer's story. The model of earning your money doing something you love and carrying out your passion to serve was an early construct of my youthful imagination. Schweitzer exemplified service. He was not just a medical doctor; he was a missionary, New Testament scholar, philosopher, teacher and highly talented organist. He was an independent thinker (and probably would not have thought much of Agnew either). Schweitzer was a humanitarian, an entrepreneur, and a highly principled, thoughtful man. He received the 1952 Nobel Peace Prize for his service and ethical philosophy of *Reverence for Life*. Reading it had left me inspired, as had the tales of his life.

I learned much later that Albert Schweitzer was accused by some of being paternalistic or colonialistic in his attitude towards Africans. I saw him as an honorable man.

Margaret Mead, another famous social scientist of my youth, was also criticized for her good works as an anthropologist. I saw her as a decent woman. Mead had examined social systems and observed localized value sets, vulnerable to outside contact. I considered and learned from her work. As a young person, I might not have seen works by Dr Mead, except two of her books were given to me by a distant uncle in an attempt to interest me in science. I remember the books being worn and dusty. The books were already thirty years old, having been written in 1928 and 1930. As it happened, in 1979 President Carter awarded the Presidential Medal of Freedom to Mead posthumously. Andy Young presented the award to Dr Mead's daughter.

The lesson for me was that innovators are often seen as breaking a few branches and stirring up the waters. They can make others uncomfortable, and may in fact make mistakes, or take unseasoned positions. That lesson would come back to me twenty years ahead. When we tried to advance new thinking and take fresh approaches, sometimes that singular focus was criticized in a context of related, perceived shortcomings. In our efforts to create an institution to focus on peace research and education, some actors faulted our work as being naïve, or that as activists we did not have sufficient standing in the international relations arena to be taken seriously. Still later, in advancing the cause of the INN, we were rebuked by some for challenging convention and hierarchy, while we viewed our work as necessary and filling a void.

Schweitzer wrote: "True philosophy must start from the most immediate and comprehensive fact of consciousness and this may be formulated as follows: 'I am life which wills to live, and I exist in the midst of life which wills to live.'"[25] Schweitzer's observations touched a common theme with similar values I had learned to live as a camper up in the mountains. Every person shares special values with another, and many share those values with a wider world.

I grew to believe as Schweitzer, that living systems would follow basic needs and self-interests in order to survive. However, Schweitzer was particularly instructive to me in his belief that all humans also held a special awareness and sympathy for the will of other beings to live. The inspiration of his message to me was that the ethics of service and of a spiritual philosophy could be one and the same as a kind of evolutionary necessity. This made sense to me.

I remember another story about Schweitzer from my readings at the time. On one particular trip down the river to get supplies, he stopped in to visit a local village. He noticed that many of the villagers, especially males, had broken arms and legs and he was prompted to ask how it happened. He learned that a bad storm that year had demolished many of the huts in the village. The men had worked very hard before the rainy season to replace and repair the roofs. Many villagers had experienced falls and thus the many broken bones. Dr Schweitzer made a note of this, as the story goes, and proceeded down river to obtain the supplies needed for his hospital at Lambaréné.

In negotiating for the needed supplies, he also obtained a number of wooden ladders for the unfortunate village that had suffered so many injuries from the roof repairs. Heading back upriver to his hospital, the good doctor stopped again at the village to deliver the ladders. The village elders were very excited to receive the gifts. They were honored that the doctor had made a return visit and they celebrated his visit with a feast.

The following year the doctor again left his hospital upriver and passed by the small village. He was curious to learn if the ladders had been useful. Upon arriving at the village he noticed that the ladders were nowhere to be seen. He took special care to walk all about the village, but still there were no ladders. So he inquired. "Yes," one village leader said, "the ladders were very helpful and they were much appreciated. Thank you so much." The doctor responded, "You are welcome. But where are the ladders? What happened to them?"

The elder responded, "Oh, we found many uses for them. We used them to hang on the walls of the huts so we could more easily store our food supplies and clothing. They were very helpful in keeping our firewood off the ground and sometimes we even used them for firewood."

Schweitzer said, "But tell me. You did not use them to repair the holes when you climbed up onto the roofs of your huts, or to reach higher into the trees for fruit?" The elder smiled and said, "Oh, no. Why would we do that? Nobody told us you could use the ladders to climb."

The lesson for me, even then, was that cross-cultural communication and shared understandings are incredibly important elements of human behavior.

Schweitzer believed the will-to-life, or respect for the life of others, was the highest principle and the defining purpose of humanity. That principle—of seeing others as equals and valuing the systems we all live in—became an important value for me. Later in my life, and in large part due to working with Andy Young, I came to see that peace was a higher calling than diplomacy, just as nonviolence was a more powerful force than violence.

I received a lot of recognition as a young boy for being responsible. It was a sort of an unspoken bargain I made with my parents. I would be "good" in return for their love. My parents believed in service to the community; they modeled this for me. As I grew older, the challenge became finding the most appropriate path to express my own gifts and inclinations in ways that would be seen as responsible.

During my junior year in high school I had the honor of being selected to attend Boys State, a leadership and citizenship summer program in which over eight hundred boys—one student from each school in the state—were invited by local American Legion chapters to travel to the California State Capitol in Sacramento and deliberate and govern in an intense testosterone-charged setting. We lived under one roof in designated cities where we participated in electoral politics, ran for political office, managed the campaigns of others, and held a variety of local municipal offices. Those elected to the state offices were invited to attend Boys Nation, where a similar experience was staged in electoral politics. At our Boys State, the sitting governor, then Ronald Reagan, was scheduled to address our cadre on the steps of the state capital building. For me, the experience represented a type of draft or summons to a new level of leadership understanding and the political process. Fourteen years later, the Final Report of the federal commission I would direct found its way onto his desk.

♖♗♞

In March of 1968, Robert F. Kennedy was running for President of the United States. His campaign began with him as a front-runner of the Democratic Party. Kennedy appeared at an impromptu campaign event in my small hometown of San Gabriel. His motorcade was proceeding past my high school and stopped for a while at the train track crossing that bordered our high school athletic fields. A number of us were out on the athletic field and noticed the police escort coming up the frontage road. We ran over to see what the excitement was about. Just then a train came along and the motorcade was blocked from crossing over the tracks. We arrived at the candidate's car just as he got out and stood on the roof of the vehicle to deliver a short speech to the fifty or standing around. Someone handed him a megaphone, but he seemed to prefer connecting with the crowd through his own voice. Kennedy had made this type of campaign stop a common practice of his campaign. I was eighteen and very impressed by his words. He inspired me through an authentic, not a divisive, voice. Earlier that same year I had served as high school Student Body President. Leadership was on my mind. The Boys State and Student Body President experiences provided the benefit of practicing on a small scale, but I reflected on how those same skills might serve me later.

At the end of the month, President Johnson stunned the nation by dropping out of the race on March 31, 1968. Vice President Hubert Humphrey then entered the campaign for President, but was too late to stand as a candidate in any of the primaries. Kennedy continued to campaign aggressively all across the country. A war was going on in Southeast Asia; Humphrey was the establishment candidate; Kennedy, with his youthful charisma, was viewed as too challenging. (Coincidentally, nine years later, Senator Humphrey would sign on to a Dear Colleague letter I drafted to confirm his support for the peace academy concept. It would become one of his last missives to his fellow legislators, as he died several weeks after signing the letter.)

A few days later, April 4, 1968, we all learned of the assassination of Dr Martin Luther King, Jr and Kennedy gave another emotional speech, this time in Indianapolis's inner city. He called for reconciliation between the races. Although no protests broke out in Indianapolis, sixty other cities experienced rioting after Dr King's death. My encounter with candidate Kennedy had occurred within a few months of his Indianapolis speech. A month later following his primary victory speech on June 5, Kennedy was shot at the Ambassador Hotel in Los Angeles and died some twenty-six hours later. His death, coming so soon after the killing of Dr King, was deeply disturbing to the country.

Dr King's death and the loss of Kennedy made civil rights come into focus for me. It had been distant; now it was unvarnished by media spin or geographic distance. I felt these traumas. Not only was I in Los Angeles where Kennedy was shot, I had stood near him two months earlier. On Saturday, June 10, I had tickets to take my girlfriend to see the music group the Righteous Brothers perform at the Coconut Grove Room of the Ambassador Hotel. The Embassy Room where Kennedy had been shot was just across the lobby. We debated going, but finally did. It turned out to be a festive night for us, but the blocked off areas of the hotel lobby would remain as an image in my mind.

Once in college I chose a major of premed studies in biology. Even at the undergraduate level, my classes, labs, and concepts got me further on the track of thinking in systems. I took on a second full major in American Studies and graduated with double majors. As part of my undergraduate college experience I did fieldwork in Europe studying the impact of hospital architecture on the decision-making of patients seeking care for certain types of stigmatic diseases. Science was interesting to me, but so was the study of what society did with that knowledge.

My specific project was on the impact of health clinics designed with a new, modern style of architecture versus older, home-like structures that had been converted to clinics. One type of building offered a facade of cement, glass and steel to incoming patents, and the other offered a warmer exterior of wood, porches and grassy lawns. I conducted my overseas study in Lund, Sweden, a university town that was in the process of converting older buildings into a modern hospital clinic. I had completed a similar study in Pasadena, California and intended to make a comparison of cultural difference as well as the impact of the architecture on patient decision-making. At the time, both of the cities I studied had reported high incidences of sexually transmitted diseases, STD, and the willingness of those STD patients to seek treatment was the focus of my research. The Swedish social worker I worked with to conduct the patient interviews and we jointly published our results and passed them onto medical associations in Sweden and the US. I'll let you guess the outcome.

After my study was completed I took the opportunity to travel for two and a half months around Europe. From Sweden, I was able to travel into East Germany and enter East Berlin. The year was 1971. The Berlin Wall would not come down until 1989. From Berlin I traveled into Czechoslovakia, including Prague, which had been invaded by the Russians three years earlier. It was still occupied by Russian soldiers and they briefly detained me, ostensibly due to a traffic violation, but that turned out to be a shakedown for cash. The soldiers knew I had just been required to exchange local currency at the border. I told them I had spent the money on petrol, and was released. The experience of travel broadened my awareness of other cultures and how they were organized, interacted and dealt with conflict.

Out of college, my first job was working with an architecture firm assisting in the design and planning of hospitals. The small company was based in Malibu, California. I began to understand for the first time that public policy took first position to making medicine available and accessible. Good medicine made no difference if there was not a way to get it to the people. Nobody had ever talked to me about supply chains, and here I was seeing the concept play out firsthand, not with a manufacturing process, but with architecture, public policy, and the power of creative planning. Even with solid medicine and caring doctors, the system was not complete or able to fully function without proper physical facilities. Thoughtful hospital design was important to delivering good medicine, and even essential to attracting patients and retaining quality professionals who would want to work in the environment created by good, thoughtful, cost-effective architecture. Perhaps this is what shaped me to see peace as process—a manufacturing supply chain of sorts that had its own variables that contributed and sustain it.

My colleagues and I were tasked with developing a proprietary computer program that facilitated the creation of a master plan for one or more hospitals in days rather than months or years. In some cases this represented a huge cost savings to hospital administrators and executives, particularly those managing large hospital systems such as Veterans' hospitals or those facilities owned by organizations like Kaiser Permanente, religious groups and research universities. Our work represented a breakthrough in hospital architecture and medical planning. The computer-driven program was capable of processing the needed information in a few hours. The master-planning product we created could survey from among one hundred twenty hospital departments and project their combined space needs out into the future. It had been my responsibility to work with space planners and equipment experts to equate space needs with hospital workloads. On the basis of our work, a hospital administrator responsible for seven hospitals, as an example, could forecast the square footage needs and relevant costs and budget requirements for each of their hospitals within weeks rather than many months. Our efforts proved to be a cost-saving tool for our clients. I was recognized for helping to create an attractive product: a service that saved money by reducing planning time; provided a strategic tool for hospital decision-makers, and better positioned them to purchase other services from our firm. I was rewarded for being innovative. My salary was increased, and in those days, making more money than your age was a respectable sum.

I moved from my work in product development to marketing and selling. I started to travel for the business. My first trip was to Chicago to present to the American Hospital Association, then Seattle to meet with administrators in the Catholic Hospital Association, and so forth. I was selling entire systems of hospitals a product that helped executives to better understand their facility needs—and marketing new ideas to change the perceptions of hospital administrators of how to go about their business in different ways. In my time with the firm, I developed my planning, marketing, and selling skills. These competencies would serve me later in my journey, as I became a *peddler* for the concept of peace, something I knew nothing about at the time.

♜ ♝ ♞

Back on the beach at Malibu, I consciously tried to take life less seriously, but like many my age, a lot was on my mind. I was going to amount to something, but I did not yet know what. I had worked myself into a really good business position, but it was never really what I had intended to do. I had a great job. I lived in a beautiful place. I owned two acres overlooking the Pacific and three cars. The challenges and exposure of my first job out of college had been a superb learning experience, and I was motivated, doing well and being rewarded.

Despite my good fortunes and feeling grateful for my life, I found myself uneasy in this world. For example, the musical *Hair* was threatening to me because it pulled me away from the comfort zone of my upbringing into an arena of rebellion I had struggled to avoid. I had just passed through high school and college being highly responsible, and now I was intimidated by the cultural influences around me suggesting a social defiance that was unfamiliar. I tried to balance my internal "tyranny of the shoulds"[26]—my own desires to succeed, please my parents, and exceed the growing expectations of my employer—with a yet unknown calling or meaning to my life. As I prepared to matriculate to manhood I was disoriented. I was unclear about my next step.

Along with the increasing confidence in my business skills and abilities to sell concepts came an uncertainty about who I was versus the person I felt I should be. I was developing my own identity, just as the country seemingly was evolving in its decade of reflecting on a failed war, growing poverty and residual racism. I felt yanked in one direction by a desire for social activism, and the pull of parental imprinting to seek out a traditional career in the other direction. I really wanted both, but did not know how or where to find it.

In Malibu, like elsewhere in the country, the countercultural experience of the 1960s and early 1970s was coming to a close. It felt to me that the social consciousness once inspired by the Kent State shootings was fading; Watergate prosecutions were wrapping up; and Saigon had fallen in April 1975.

America was at the end of a decade where the times they "were a-changing," as Bob Dylan had sung in 1964. Peter, Paul, and Mary had been singing "Puff the Magic Dragon" for ten years and their 1969 release of "Leaving on a Jet Plane," seemed to announce the lift off of a generation into a new American decade. The country was about to shift. The period fulfilled for me the saying of James Allen, "Circumstances do not make the man, they reveal him,"[27] as I was beginning to come into my own.

Streaking, a frivolous expression of fun and freedom burst into featured stories on evening news broadcasts. Clearly a pivot was occurring in the world around me, and I sensed its compelling swing. In retrospect, streaking somehow represented a line in the sand, recognizing the end of the serious side of the counterculture and the war in Southeast Asia. I had strong college memories of sitting on the floor in a crowded dorm room, straining to hear the draft lottery numbers being called out over the muffled sighs of sophomore friends, some soon-to-be soldiers reacting to the hard realities of the draft.

Now just three years later in Malibu, it seemed a decade since those serious moments watching the draft in the dorm room at Occidental. I was in a restaurant at Paradise Cove, Malibu and a group of us at a company TGIF gathering decided to undress and streak. Outside the restaurant, we dropped our clothes and ran between the restaurant windows and the spotlighted ocean, dancing as naked work colleagues across the sand into the darkened shore break. I too was caught up in the triviality. It was fun, and… it left me feeling disengaged and irresponsible. Each of those emotions was an anathema to my self-image.

Along with streaking and the end of the war had come a series of events in 1973–1974 that defined the period and my early professional years. As mentioned, Watergate swung the door closed on the Nixon years and the Vietnam War began to wind down dramatically. All warring parties in the Vietnam War had declared a cease-fire in 1973. Three million Americans had served in the war, with nearly sixty thousand Americans dead, one hundred fifty thousand wounded, and at least one thousand missing in action. It was estimated that 3.8 million Vietnamese died in the conflict.[28] The Vietnam War, conscription, and the draft lottery ended in 1973, just a year after I had started my first post-college job. An Elvis Presley concert in Hawaii was staged and became the first worldwide telecast by an entertainer—watched by more people than had watched the Apollo moon landings. It was a time of release, too, from the psychic inspiration and temporary hold of the counterculture—to a new seriousness of change in different ways. There were new issues and new directions.

America seemed to be turning a corner toward the middle of the decade. New rules, conventions and trends moved center stage in the mid-decade. I knew these turning points represented significant things, but the events themselves seemed to bounce rather than bore into my youthful reality. It would take more clarity on my part to absorb the implications of each aspect of the sea change occurring around me. At this point in my life, I did not yet have, or choose to have skin in the game. The decision on *Roe v. Wade* by the US Supreme Court overturned state bans on abortion. The first American prisoners of war were released from Vietnam. The country was moving on.

The American Indian Movement occupied Wounded Knee on the Pine Ridge Indian Reservation and started a seventy-one-day standoff in South Dakota with federal authorities. Indigenous people, not just in the United States, but also in many other nations, were reasserting their claims on sovereignty and self-determination. The World Trade Center officially opened in New York City with a ribbon cutting ceremony. (It was later of course demolished by a terrorist act in 2001) Secretariat won the Kentucky Derby. The win by Secretariat was significant, as he became the first horse in twenty-five years to win the Triple Crown. Records were broken and it felt like it. Led Zeppelin performed before 56,800 persons at Tampa Stadium, breaking the previous attendance record of 55,600 set by the Beatles at Shea Stadium in 1965. *Skylab*, America's first space station was launched and flew above as Egyptian and Syrian forces attacked Israeli soldiers in the Golan Heights and Sinai Peninsula on the holiday of Yom Kippur. Even long-standing borders were changing on the front page of the newspaper. These seemingly haphazard occurrences slowly began to add up and get my attention. I became more watchful of what was happening and, I suppose, felt more responsible with the realization that I could do more than merely observe the things that were happening. I wondered, what was my stake in all of this?

Gradually I got more political in my understanding of how change occurred and found myself engaging in local political campaigns. Daily news stories were filled with columns about system-wide social and public policy issues such as public health, urban transportation, and other issues that called out for social problem solving. It seemed as though the public policies of the 1950's were asking for a second look. I was intrigued about how all of that might happen. I volunteered in the LA mayoral campaign of Tom Bradley, who was to become the first black mayor of LA. I just made Xerox copies of press events at the campaign headquarters, but it provided further exposure to how campaigns worked. On May 29, 1973, Bradley won and he went on to serve 20 years as mayor. On October 16, Maynard Jackson became the first black mayor of Atlanta, and the first African-American mayor of a major southern city. The times they were a-changing, indeed.

Breakthrough events happened all around. Dr Henry Kissinger began his term as United States Secretary of State, and my father's hero Spiro Agnew was forced to resign as Vice President of the United States. My dad never said a word about it. The American Psychiatric Association removed homosexuality from its Diagnostic and Statistical Manual of Mental Disorders, and Congress passed the Endangered Species Act. Jimmy Carter defeated Gerald Ford. Ronald Reagan was still governor of California, but had begun to campaign for president, unsuccessfully in 1976, but victorious four years later.

This period of change was to some Americans an expression of the best in the American ideals of free speech, equality, and pursuit of happiness. Other people had seen the counterculture as self-indulgent, pointlessly rebellious, unpatriotic, and destructive of America's moral order. In this period, I found myself in the middle.

I never really rebelled, protested only in the safety of my campus, and did not march in the streets. But in my own way, I found the spirited Age of Aquarius. At twenty-five, I was ready, willing, and able for a calling that would in large part become the meaning and identity of my life. It was about service, pride in what I did—and would do—and about playing out my need to be responsible in a new way.

As the sun set in the spring of 1975, I was driving down Pacific Coast Highway listening to Paul Simon belt out "Fifty Ways to Leave Your Lover." I was in route driving the thirty-five miles to UCLA and the vibrancy of the Westwood college environment. It offered up the intellectual stimulation of libraries and the social expectations of meeting girls. Recently my own path of self-awareness had led me to the admission that I was a salesman. That realization was mirrored by the thought: if I was destined to be a salesman, it became important to "sell" something that I could believe in. I needed to find a cause that would help others and would be something that made me feel good about my life and profession. I felt I was destined to do something other than sell hospital design concepts. These thoughts were top of mind to me. Out on the kayak the day before, I had asked myself, "How do I get to where I want to go? How do I discover and become my authentic self? I am not my job. Who am I?"

Most of us ask these kinds of tough questions of ourselves at the critical junctures of our lives. I found myself at such a crossroad. I was at the beginning of some sort of new quest. The Watergate Hearings that began in May of 1973 and continued through August of 1973. During the hearings, I was working in my architectural firm office, but could regularly watch the Hearings on an office television screen. The two of us working on my project had the luxury of sharing a office set apart from the rest of the company and we watched the hearings most days, glued to the television monitor with the latest revelations that unfolded each day. The hearings were of great interest to me, as I was beginning to formulate my own views on politics.

Each day of the hearings brought new revelations to the small TV screen above our work area. Each day new questions were raised about the integrity of government, our leaders and the realities of failings in the stewardship of important American institutions.

I had only been out of college for two years, but I found myself longing for intellectual stimulation. I liked my work colleagues well enough, but they were older and set into their careers. My mind still wanted to engage and I needed to explore ways to get on a different path. The extension classes I enrolled in were subjects that interested me but that I had never had the time to take in my college years due to my double major. I enrolled in a class on astronomy and one on hypnosis. The subjects were fun, engaged me in something other than work, and allowed me to share in classroom interaction. A real upside was that I had the chance to meet new people and engage in new ways of thinking. I would often make the time to study and browse the stacks in the UCLA Research Library before or after class. This was of course before the Internet, so as I walked around I would review periodicals and cross reference books in card catalogues. It was there, over a series of evenings, that I first became attracted to the concept of peace. I was beginning to feel that I had a new calling.

One evening during a period of quiet reading, another student approached and asked if I wanted to take a break and get some coffee. She leaned against my study carrel and said her name was Beth. We visited for a while about small things, and we spoke about the beautiful sunset that day and the things we liked to do.

Then she asked, "So, what are you doing at the library?" With the certain and proud tone of a physician in his residency or a student in her third year in law school, I explained I had encountered two academic journals: *The Bulletin of Peace Proposals* and the *Journal of Conflict Resolution*, and had begun to read about peace research. Boy was I blowing smoke. I had no appreciation for the discipline yet. I mumbled something like; I was fascinated by the arguments of the authors who had written papers seeking to validate what appeared to be an emerging field. I felt a little awkward speaking about something I did not yet know much about. I might have had more confidence if I had been caught reading from a more standard text, such as Psychology or Physics.

I finally came around to a more realistic answer, "I am basically trying to figure out what peace means," I said meekly.

I asked if she was at the library for a class, and she said, "I'm studying to be a geriatric nurse. I had an assignment to study how societies treated their aging, so I came here to do some research." We both laughed as she spoke of why she had chosen nursing, particularly her focus on seniors. She said she found them wise and grateful, and as such, frankly more attractive than kids or other adult populations. Beth was fun. We talked briefly about each of our grandparents and then she twisted in her chair and said, "So, tell me more about this peace thing. I don't really get it, or know if it's possible?"

"I mean, look," she continued,

> "Aren't there people like at the State Department that worry about that stuff and well, isn't war really how we settle things anymore? It all seems so political anyway. We fight about communism, or over oil or some old border that a European king drew a long time ago. I don't really see how you study peace or expect it to happen. Don't we all want it, but secretly believe that it is not possible?"

I opened a bag of M&Ms and offered her some. "I don't know," I said.

> "I guess you're right, but it seems to me a bit like public health, you know. It comes down to knowing about causes and then trying to focus on the prevention of those causes. Many people die of preventable accidents, right? Sometimes the government

or some foundation steps in to try and educate the public. Certain diseases are best treated through prevention. Society has already been shown that early education and engagement regarding preventable illness is easier and more cost effective."

She stuck out her hand for more M&Ms and said, "But why do you think you can stop wars if the arms merchants and African warlords or developing countries can just do what they want? I don't see peace happening any more than people learning to fly. I mean, really?"

"No." I said. "That's *exactly* the point it seems. We *did* learn to fly. Not us, I mean, but we invented the machinery to allow it to happen." Beth laughed. "Society has figured out that fires have to be prevented, not just fought. Doctors have figured out that there is a science to public health information and how it is shared. There is a science to understanding when and where people listen to health information, and how to prevent certain diseases from spreading. In both cases it did not used to be that way. I kind of think there is hope, just like I think your seniors can live more comfortable and satisfying lives, even as they grow older with poor health. You are trying to change that game. Maybe it can be the same with peace."

I stood up to stretch.

"Look, if somehow people can check the mechanisms, or better understand the steps that cause conflict or war, then it makes sense that we can figure it out. People learn how to play new games; you just have to walk them through the new rules. Why can't there be new rules? Who says we have to play the game the same way? Preventive health care is a new thing. Fire prevention is a new thing. They are both working to save lives and the destruction of property. Look at those drapes, or this fabric," I said, pointing to the blue padding on the chair. "I bet they are both made of fire-resistant materials. It did not used to be that way. Society just hasn't figured how to do that yet with war. We haven't learned yet, or thought it was possible to prevent or better manage war."

Getting a little exasperated with myself, and kind of picking up on her doubts, I said,

"In the end, it's where you put your focus. Imagine if we could reduce the possibility of violent conflict by say, fifty percent. We've done that like with certain diseases."

I moved my chair and sat back down. Still uncomfortable with my subject and nervous about what Beth would think of my offbeat interests, I tried to calm down and get control of my awkwardness self-consciousness. I took a deep breath.

She jumped back in, being more casual herself. Beth took it upon herself to change the subject slightly to defuse my intensity. She consolingly offered this,

> "You know I just talked with a herbal healer the other day and he said 'you are what you eat,' and made the point that you can control your health if you watch what you consume. We talked about how seniors can make their lives a lot better by just watching what they eat, if they know how, and what and when."

Then Beth told me a story I had never heard, but have since read many times.[29]

"To make his point he told me that old story about the Cherokee grandfather. Maybe it's like that for you and your peace thing."

"What do you mean?" I asked.

"OK," she said,

> "I heard this fable the other day and stop me if you have heard it before. I found meaning in it. There is an elderly Cherokee man teaching his grandson about life. 'A fight is going on inside me,' he said to the boy. 'It is a terrible fight between two wolves. One is evil—he is filled with anger, envy, sorrow, greed, regret, arrogance, self-pity, lies, false pride, superiority, and ego.' He continued, 'The other is good— he is filled with joy, peace, love, hope, serenity, humility, kindness, benevolence, empathy, generosity, truth, compassion, and faith. The same fight is going on inside you—and inside every other person, too.'

> "The grandson thought about it for a minute and then asked his grandfather, 'Which wolf will win?'

> "The old Cherokee simply replied, 'The one you feed.'"

> "My friend was using the story to make a point about herbs and good food, but I think it applies to what you are saying."

Looking right at me, and picking up her books and papers, she said in a calm, considered voice,

> "What you have to do is help people see they have a choice. Society has a choice, just like the boy in the story. You help people see that things can be better if they learn to have different attitudes, and different expectations of their leaders. We— society I mean—can make it harder to start a fire, contract a disease, or get into a war. It sounds a lot like you are talking about helping people see which wolf they are going to feed, and how that makes a difference."

"I like that," I said. As she spoke, I thought to myself, "How can I make peace research and dispute resolution a serious pursuit, not merely an aspiration?" As I had once trained to understand the healing science of medicine, might there be a future contribution for me to make in this new field? I realized I was looking out the adjacent window, thinking.

My focus came back to Beth. "What you just said was pretty cool." I leaned back in my chair. "So, will we see each other again? I asked. She turned and started to walk away. "Yeah, I expect so. Don't be a stranger if you see me in the library, '*Peace Boy*,' come over and say hi."

♜ ♝ ♞

During those nights at the UCLA Research Library I began to learn more about the related fields of conflict resolution, mediation, peace research and what it might mean to be a practitioner in these pursuits. It was a new world for me. I began to be captivated by the concept of peace, but found no single door through which I could pass to grasp a role for me. I felt disconnected from a field where I was intrigued to find some new sense of meaning and identity. At the same time, I felt it was all outside of who I had been, or how I had seen myself.

A lot of what I read was old stuff—it had been published years earlier. It seemed outdated, but also so insightful that it appeared foundational. I read about Lewis F. Richardson, a pioneer in the mathematical analysis of arms races, authoring *Arms and Insecurity* in 1949 and *Statistics of Deadly Quarrels* in 1950. Quincy Wright, a pioneering political scientist, had authored a major research piece entitled *A Study of War* in 1942. I asked myself what had been the impact of these books written twenty years earlier? Had the implications of these works been integrated into our institutions of foreign and military policy? Surely these works had made an impact.

I read that Harvard scholar Karl Deutsch was also impressed with Wright. He was unknown to me then, but I would later grow to personally admire Professor Deutsch, and I would be fortunate enough to sit in on one of his Harvard lectures later that fall.

Deutsch said of Quincy Wright:

> "War, to be abolished, must be understood. To be understood, it must be studied. No one man worked with more sustained care, compassion, and level-headedness on the study of war, its causes, and its possible prevention than Quincy Wright. He did so for nearly half a century, not only as a defender of man's survival, but also as a scientist. He valued accuracy, facts, and truth more than any more appealing or preferred conclusions; and in his greatest book, *A Study of War,* he gathered, together with his collaborators, a larger body of relevant facts, insights, and far-ranging questions about war than anyone else has done."[30]

I became familiar with mathematician and psychologist Anatol Rapoport's work modeling the psychology of competitive and cooperative behavior. I encountered the writings of Theo. F. Lentz, a pioneer in the promotion of peace research as a discipline. I became aware of the various peace research institutes that had been influenced by Lentz, such as the Center for Research in Conflict Resolution at the University of Michigan (founded in 1957), The Canadian Peace Research Institute (founded in 1961), the Peace Research Group of Des Moines (founded in 1962), and the Peace Research Institute of Oslo (founded in 1964). It became apparent that by mid-1970 the evolving field of peace research, modest as it was, began to accelerate the development of peace education. The growth of a new academic discipline, not unlike the mandate of a new institution, takes on a mushroom shape as its breadth of scope naturally evolves.

I learned that the majority of people who called themselves peace researchers had PhD degrees in the field of psychology, sociology, philosophy, international relations, law, or economics. There also seemed to be a number of researchers from biology, psychiatry, medicine, anthropology, and history. I felt like I was beginning to zero in on a field of life work that interested me. Still, I wanted to learn more.

Entering college I had chosen a premed course of study, and resulting in part from my two-year job as a lab assistant, I thought I would go to medical school. As noted my mother's dad had been a family physician, but I felt more suited to pathology. I was intrigued with why things didn't work. As school went on, I gradually became more drawn to medical issues relating to public health, and then political issues dealing with public health. As I found myself becoming more politically inclined, I thought about going to graduate school. But I still needed to sort out a focus for my studies. Politics, public health and peace, all interests of mine, seemed to be about marketing.

A work friend confided to me that when she decided to go back to school she knew when the time was right. She just had not been certain why. She said, "I've learned that people go to graduate school to either learn something; get credentialed, or make contacts and connections that might further their careers. Sometimes it's was about achieving all three objectives; other times not."

For me, I was happy to be back in an academic environment to be with other people, learning; seeking new ideas. I looked on my night classes in astronomy and hypnosis almost as larks. But as it turned out, my inquiry into these disciplines had implications for my growing understanding of systems theory and marketing. I remember my mind would often race. I tried to make sense of my new interests, but my brain would jump back to my job, new relationships, or my inner narrative of where I was going with my life. All of this was natural I assumed. I knew I was indeed fortunate to even have the luxury of thinking, floundering and testing ideas. I knew there were kids my age just in a survival mode many places in the inner city or other parts of the world. Still, I explored the ideas that interested me. I felt I must do something with my good fortune.

Astronomy, of course, is a natural science focused on celestial objects. But for me, my evening lectures focused on how systems function; how forces collide; how the influences of gravity and mass impact on objects. My mind began to jump from the physics of it all to the political psychology of messaging. Physics was about things bumping into one another. Sales and marketing were about ideas and concepts bumping into one another. This inspired me to think in terms of communication theory and marketing related to conflict resolution and the concept of peace. How do we sell others on our best ideas? How do we influence one another? What analogous forces exist in influencing human behavior that parallels the natural world? I would often leave my classes with my mind racing, so captivated by the pursuit of understanding peace that I began to correlate all of what I was studying and doing into the context of this new field.

Arriving back in Malibu, I would often sit down with my housemate Sam and talk through the questions on my mind. Sam was a physician and a few years older. He always had his own perspective and sometimes these discussions carried over to the breakfast table in the morning. Sam was a pediatrician and loved kids. In some ways he was still a kid himself.

As for my introductory hypnosis class, I began to see the principles of hypnotism in relationship to marketing, perceptions, and alterations of perceptions. Classic hypnosis was about "guiding" another to respond to suggestions for change in actions and perceptions. I began to map my understanding about hypnosis to the management of perceptions. Perceptions that might have to do with how people understood what it took to cause peace. How might the imagination of one individual be opened to accept a vision of peace as a possible reality? I was enthralled by the implications. Unfailingly, my mind raced on the drive home or into a breakfast dialogue with Sam.

Why was there a higher incidence of kids following their parents into service in the military? What were the determinants in our perceptions of patriotism? What were the determinants in our perceptions of peace? Could peace be perceived as patriotic? Could there be a culture of peace? What would a culture of peace look like?

♖ ♗ ♞

Kids grow up playing war, not practicing peace. A childhood friend, Timmy, lived across the street from my grandparents. Often after elementary school was out I stayed with them until my parents got home from work. I played with Timmy nearly every day. He attended a nearby Catholic school, so I never saw him at school. This was before after-school sports kicked in, so we were nearly inseparable for several years. Timmy's older brother was away at West Point attending college.

In Timmy's room was a huge blanket nailed to the wall. It read ARMY on it in big gold letters. The block letters were displayed on a black field of wool. It was impressive in his small bedroom. It stood over us as we played in his room everyday. I only met his brother once, and he was dressed in his elegant uniform. He was cool, fit, erect, and serious. He loved his little brother, and he picked me up too to twirl me around. Timmy's Catholic family prayed for their older son at every meal. Tim and I played army all of the time. We had toy soldiers and plastic tanks.

In those years I was seven or eight years old. Nine years later, after Tim and I had grown apart, he called one day to tell me his brother had been killed in Vietnam. He asked, did I want the blanket? Nobody is his house could bear to see it anymore on the wall. Tim did not feel right getting rid of it.

The concept of patriotism is strongest in times of crisis and united us, as it does every culture. In the US, after September 11, or Hurricane Katrina, millions of American made charitable contributions and reached out to help one another. Patriotism is not about blindly following the beliefs and values of a country, it is about pride, origin, identity and the prosperity of your community. After a mountain flood, "We are Mountain Strong," and after a hurricane we celebrate our resilience and community strength.

♖ ♗ ♞

My evenings at UCLA caused me to reflect on what it would mean to be patriotic within the culture of peace? How could peace seeking be perceived as patriotic as fighting a war or serving in the army? Serving in the Peace Corps was not really comparable. Volunteering with the Red Cross was quite a different thing. I was left with the question: What is the meaning, identity and structure of peace?

Eventually, as I began to travel more and more as part of my work, I could no longer take night classes. As interesting as my evening studies had been, I had to give them up for this more intense work life. I was getting caught up in the day-to-day details of my profession. I thought about my work all of the time. The more successful I became in selling at work, the less time I had to meet and see people my own age. In those days, before the Internet and social media, it was difficult to connect with friends my age. I was spending time on the road with customers and business colleagues. I was twenty-five years old and most of my customers were senior hospital administrators. I began to realize that I had a choice to stay in my current job or seek an advanced degree in planning or architecture, hospital administration, or business administration. None of these pursuits were really of interest to me.

I increasingly focused on what could conceivably become the calling of my life. It was like a puzzle that was beginning to fit together. I realized the concepts I encountered in my UCLA studies needed to be sold. With my increasing success at my company, I confirmed that I was good at selling concepts. I had somehow evolved the skill sets to communicate and convey complex ideas in simple ways that built enthusiasm in others. I enjoyed the reward of watching people see the reason of my pitch and was delighted when clients would purchase the service I was marketing. I believed in the value of what I was selling, but successfully selling ideas related to hospital design and planning was gradually leading me to want to sell something with which I had a more passionate connection.

I came to realize that my motivation to understand and advocate for peace was more intellectual than the hardened, personal experience of my peers who served in the armed forces or in the justice-seeking trenches of the civil rights movement. I had grown to respect those who served in both of these arenas. I knew my calling was not as an activist on the front lines of the anti-war movement or a spiritual calling, informed by any religious tradition. Promoting peace just felt right. It appealed to my rational self and my desire to do good in a meaningful and competent way. It was a bit embarrassing to think if I "sold peace" I would not be ridiculed as a salesman, but that was exactly what I was telling myself.

The science of convincing others of the possibilities of peace is perhaps older than the art of war, but it is often regarded with less veneration. Peace, as a concept, always receives the highest admiration, but the actual teachable techniques to create it and the necessary peace policy to sustain it were less studied and applied. Our understanding of the social levers to achieve peace—and of the necessary social justice to sustain it—remained an evolving art.

As the weeks went by and I could make the time, I dug deeper into my newly discovered field of peace research and concepts of conflict resolution. I learned there were applied tools and ways of thinking about how disputes might be resolved without force, the legal system, or war. I did not understand why society had spent so much money on the military means to conduct war, and so little money on the behavioral ways to prevent or resolve conflicts before they escalated. Why wait for a crisis when conflict could be addressed earlier as in some cases of disease or flooding?

If indeed selling was to be my professional calling, why not sell peace? It was respectable. It was complicated enough to be interesting. There was a need. The field was starting to grow.

In 1963, it was estimated that there were about fifty peace research groups around the world; this number grew to one hundred fifty organizations in 1972 and the numbers were increasing.[31] In the 1960s, the priorities of peace research were primarily focused around disarmament and peacekeeping, world governance and world community. I continued to read and reflect on the works of Ted Lentz, Paul Smoker, William Eckhardt, Gene Sharp, and Jonathan Galtung. I reviewed the literature summaries of Alan and Hanna Newcombe of the Canadian Peace Research Institute. I studied the initiatives of the Institute for World Order and the peace studies curriculum developed by Betty Reardon and others. These papers began to feel like operator manuals for something I wanted to do.

In the 1970s, the nature of conflict shifted to the pursuit of equality, justice, and freedom within nations, as a basic condition for civil and international peace. Many nations were just coming out of their colonial periods and after struggling for independence, competition among indigenous leaders and factions flourished. Internal wars became the sparks in the geo-political underbrush, as cross border wars made more of the headlines. Several new concepts began to permeate the literature.

- Conflict resolution mechanisms and humanism became a new focus of peace research and education, not just the histories of major wars and Cold War policies.
- Researchers began to see structural violence as a basic cause of wars and revolutions.
- Futurists raised new concerns about the growing gap between destructive technologies and constructive technologies in civil society.
- Economists identified and focused research on the growing gap between public expenditures on military research vs. expenditures in peace building and development.
- Scholars, educators, and public policy activists seemed to be saying that the country needed to change the fundamental terms of reference for the entire question of international peace.

I recognized that these researchers were on one end of a worldview of thought, but I thought it was the correct worldview.

I read the works of scholars like Ed Azar at the University of North Carolina at Chapel Hill and J. David Singer at the University of Michigan who through their research on statistical events analysis were building predictability models that might contribute to early warning systems for major conflicts. The social and political needs and interests of warring parties were being picked apart and studied; causes, trends, data tracked. There was a developing science to it; a field and discipline was evolving in both the research and strategy of peace, as well as scholarly steps to document activist practices across a growing set of social interaction.

It was not unlike what my company was trying to do for architectural planning. In my firm my colleagues and I looked at hospital architecture as a system of planned needs over time. Peace, it seemed, needed to be studied and planned as a similar system of preventions for predictable events and processes for necessary interventions based on needs and interests over time. The mechanisms surrounding conflict resolution that were being described in the literature made sense. But the formality and rigidity of the American industry of statecraft seemed to lag behind. From afar it seemed that the dynamics of diplomacy were somehow distant from causing change and more structured to protect stability. Diplomats were seemingly always quoted as having "frank and open discussions" but making little apparent progress to more widely define problems or prevent them from escalating.

From the literature, it was apparent that the beneficiary of peace research was a shifting target, following the changing definition of peace itself. Peace defined as the absence of war in the 1960s shifted in the 1970s to a peace defined in terms of the presence of freedom and justice. The clients of peace research moved from national policy makers to include peace activists, the general public, academic communities, and the United Nations. The old world concept of how nation states conducted war had shifted to how society goes about creating peace.

In the biological sciences, one examines the root causes and effects of a disease. Few elements act in isolation. Things operate in systems. I began to be interested in the concept of peace beyond an isolated, single aspiration of a social system. Peace was a system too. I became increasingly keen in *how* peace was being studied, where it was being studied and the contrasting lenses through which peace was being viewed. The study of peace itself was a system. There were different orbits of exploration.

For some researchers peace could be statistically measured. These scholars were following on with the work of Lewis Richardson who had pioneered the mathematical analysis of various arms races and the statistics of deadly quarrels, as he called them. Quincy Wright and others had made contributions to the peace map I was building by chronicling the historical study of wars and revolutions. Hanna and Alan Newcombe and others were building biographies of the field, to provide some sense of shape, reference and guidance, just as any explorer chronicles the surrounding terrain in order to find this way. Some authors were focusing on the study of attitudes related to peace and war, and others were motivated by the promotion of peace research as a discipline. I began to see the same names in the literature. I fathomed that there was a body of work there. I was interested in its advocacy – the orbit that most fascinated me.

Reviewing the literature in peace research, I tried to see the causes and effects of the apparent forces impacting on the social and political environment. I thought back on what I had been exposed to in melanoma research, the relevance of understanding cycles that could be interrupted to break the development, growth and spread of a disease such as cancer. In that work, the life scientists had been conducting research to break chemical cycles. I asked myself: How could society better advocate and focus behavioral research on breaking the cycles of conflict and war?

It might seem like an outrageous question for a 23 year old to ask, but that was where I was. "How do you get from here to there?" It was a simple question. "How do you break the cycle of violent conflict and war?" The question infatuated me.

Overall it seemed that society tended to view war as a celebrated enterprise—its armies, weapons, slogans, professions were seen as patriotic. War had a history of victories and hardened heroes. Peace, on the other hand, was seen as soft, ethereal, never achievable – and that those who sought it were somehow perceived as less than patriotic. My study overseas in college had been about stigmatized illnesses that could be more easily treated once the stigma was removed or lessened. The question then became: how can one legitimize the pursuit of peace? How can one make peace sciences—and the field of conflict resolution—more viable as a field of study and more acceptable as a profession? How might the barriers be removed to influence society and cause change for the good? How could a person change the context?

In my readings I encountered the writing of Frances Moore Lappé, who published *Diet for a Small Planet* in 1971. I immediately made the leap from the impact of wasteful food production and global food scarcity to similar implications for defense spending. Just as she argued that world hunger was not caused by a lack of food, but by ineffective food policy, I began to see that poor political or military leadership did not cause international conflict, but it was caused by ineffective, or nonexistent peace policy. We did not need more weapons systems to fight the wars; it seemed we needed more public policy to make the peace. I met Lappé later in the fall of 1975. She presented fresh thinking and connected a number of themes across the disciplines I had been studying.

I began to question why society was addressing the problems associated with conflict and war at the least effective point of intervention. We were investing our social resources at the precise point of conflict where it was the most difficult to control. This approach was understandable, if one did not believe in the effectiveness and economic savings of addressing the problems of conflict earlier. If we view conflict as a bell curve, illustrating the escalation of conflict on the upward slope, and then de-escalation on the downward slope, Americans apply most of our social resources at the apex of war, right at the top of the curve where tensions are the highest. It made no sense to me. It seemed as if we were attacking the problem too late. Why use violent force to attempt to resolve problems at the worst possible moment? So if the goal, following this narrative, becomes finding ways to prevent conflict from escalating, how could it be addressed earlier?

It was becoming a calling. For me, scale and context became an important method to break down the topic for better understanding. With a newlywed couple, the importance of sustaining their emotional bank accounts to offset their times of predictable marital conflict seemed obvious. Couples have to work at sustaining the good times so that when they get into trouble, they have a positive foundation to fall back on. Just like individuals, communities, societies, and countries would seem to benefit from such simple yet profoundly influential ideas. Several other ideas began to fall into place for me. For one: conflict resolution as a science was more about understanding the mortar or glue that holds things together than about the study of the blocks themselves. I was interested in the mortar.

Secondly, peacemaking, peace building, peace seeking, or conflict resolution—all as discrete activities—shared social and behavioral technologies that were applicable to all. Society seemed to place a hierarchy on international relations and their complexity, but for me, it began to come together that conflict—and the strategies and tools to address it—was just a matter of scale. I realized that the prevention and solution paths, techniques, escalation dynamics, and opportunities for intervention were more similar than different.

The psychology and dynamics of conflict appeared to be the same, at all levels as well. I began to see the literature in a different light. Some authors were writing about armament dynamics, the history of arms control negotiations, or theories of deterrence. Others wrote of structural solutions such as world governments, strategies of détente, diplomacy, and statecraft. There was literature about operational studies in mediation, conciliation, military and technological studies, legal and philosophical approaches, behavioral studies, and the nature of justice as a necessary part of the DNA of peace. All of these relevant studies and factors of what make up peace studies were applicable to every level of analysis—whether interpersonal, community, or international.

As a backpacker I knew there was value in expecting things to go wrong. Hikers are familiar with rip stop nylon woven with heavy threads mixed with lighter threads to prevent further damage after a tear. Above most American garage workbenches is a roll or two of Duck Tape, a cloth-backed, pressure sensitive tape usually coated with polyethylene. We intuitively know things break. Stuff falls apart; tears, burns, blisters and buckles. With conflict, society has yet to learn what every backpacker and handyman know: life is a process and a fabric that can break or tear. Peace is a living lattice, fragile but resilient. Peace researchers had begun to understand the fragility of peace and the processes to heal when the fabric was torn.

As I tried to map all of these concepts of peace in my mind, I began to see the field of peace sciences and conflict resolution was a big soup of disciplines, not the evolutionary path that I was imagining. Some scholars were stating the problems of peace in ways that would keep the processes of peace from even occurring. Their methods and interests served their discrete fields of study, but not the overall goals of balanced peace and social justice. The missing pieces and gaps in the emerging field seemed to be interdisciplinary and of context and process, more than content.

Somehow in all of this, there was a role for better marketing of peace, for lack of a better term. Peace was a desired state—like whiter teeth or a healthier body—but it was a process as well. Peace, in my mind, was more like the practice of eating healthy foods than pursuing a crash diet. It was less about fighting for justice than living and influencing others to live a just life.

If this was the goal, then what was *the* question? I thought maybe the question was: How can one create a tendency in society to seek early alternatives to the use of force to promote peace and social justice? That would require legitimizing the field of conflict resolution, maximizing the benefits of interdisciplinary study and linking practitioners and practical skills with theoretical scholars and social planners. I had so much to learn. Soon, I found the invitation.

A Moment to Review and Reflect

You may wish to stop reading at this point to consider your own journey in finding meaning and the ability to cause change in your own life. You can do this now or come back later after you finish reading the full story of this book.

One of the purposes of this book is to better understand the extent and development of your own political will to cause change in things that you care about or feel passion toward. To help you facilitate this process, following each chapter of the book is a pause in the story to provide the reader with a moment to reflect. Reflections help you gain new insights that may provide you with choices you may not have considered. The steps below may help you integrate your past experiences and new understanding about those things you may feel the political will to change.

You may find it useful to journal or take notes on the insights that come up for you as you review this chapter, and perhaps the path of your own journey to create political will. Take a closer look at the Task, *the* Challenge, *the* Gift and Opportunity, *and any personal* Reflections *that the preceding chapter may have brought to mind.*

My own personal Summary of Key Chapter Points and Reflections is located at the end of this book.

Chapter 1 Review and Reflection

Task

- Choose one piece of a vision of the "world to be" that appeals to you.
- What condition, situation, or circumstance do you complain most about to others?
- What personal, passionate pursuit of your own do you most describe to others?

Challenge

- Find your source of power to cause change.
- What are the talents, assets or audiences you can tap into to find a power to influence change?
- What subjects or concerns are within your sphere of influence to change? Why?

Gift and Opportunity

- Follow your heart, not your head. What does your heart tell you?
  (Hint: You feel a peaceful feeling in your chest versus a sinking feeling in your stomach.)
- What gifts have you been given in your life that you can build upon to create the opportunity to cause change?
- Who do you know, or can get to know that can create an opportunity for you to make the change you desire?

Reflection

- What feels so wrong to you that you want to change it?
- What has heart and meaning to you?
- What is most important to you?
  (Hint: Things that could be, and are not? Or Concepts that intrigue you? Visions you wish were true?)

CHAPTER 2

Grindstone Island

Summer 1975 – In one of my evening research reading sessions I ran across an advertisement in a journal announcing the Grindstone Island program on Lake Rideau, Ontario, Canada. In the summer of 1975, I decided to take a three-week vacation leave from my job with the medical architectural company and attend the summer camp. It was a luxury. I felt like I was taking a break for myself —and it turned out to be a break in my career.

After arriving at the nearest airport, I took a bus south to Smith Falls, a small town thirty-eight miles southwest of Ottawa, one hundred fifty miles north of Syracuse, NY. There I was transported by pontoon boat to a twelve-acre island in the middle of Lake Rideau. The heavily wooded lake was surrounded by crystal clear water. The pontoon boat was taking me further and further away from what I had known as my world on the California Coast.

Grindstone Island, I would come to learn, was formerly used by Charles Kingsmill, the first Admiral of the Royal Canadian Navy, as his summer residence. Upon the death of the Admiral and his wife Lady Kingsmill, the island went to their daughter, Diana, who in 1963 offered the island to the Canadian Friends Service Committee for their use as a non-profit peace center. The main lodge was built in the early 20th century around an earlier 19th century structure. During the 1960s and 1970s, the island was used as a Quaker conference center. The small cabin I lived in with four other men had thoughtful construction and displayed features like windows with hinged window casements that could be lifted to provide a narrow space below in which to lower the glass window and expose only the screen. All over the island were similar creative design elements in the cabins and out buildings that housed the students and visiting faculty. The summer school itself reflected similar innovation in its curriculum and construct.

Hanna Newcombe, co-founder of Peace Research Abstracts and Peace Research Reviews, ran the summer school with her husband and co-researcher, Alan Newcombe. After meeting Norman Alcock, a physicist who had founded the Canadian Peace Research Institute, Hanna realized that she had found *her* calling: the uses of science to better understand the path to peace. Hanna and Alan were both chemists. Alan died in 1988 and Hanna died in 2011. Without them, I might not have found my way to the path of working to create USIP. Thank you, Hanna and Alan.

On Grindstone Island I was engaged with the ideas and research of visiting faculty and the exchange among students. We met on the open-air porch for eight or more hours per day and because the island was more than a mile out in the middle of Lake Rideau, the conversations, interaction, and community living were intense and uninterrupted for the full three weeks. It was on Grindstone that I became convinced that there was a field of study and discipline of peace. It was not soft; it was logical; it had characteristics of hard research and a little known or applied track record of success in very real situations. This came to me through my exposure to five critical insights that would serve as a platform for the rest of my career.

The First Insight was: we learned from arms race research that ***war preparedness doesn't deter, but rather stimulates, the other side.*** As countries get into some initial stage of competition, the rate of growth of the defense spending of each group is proportional to the actual spending by the competitor.

My Second Insight came in a lecture by Jerry Laulicht, another peace researcher who was also a professor at the University of Pittsburgh. Jerry stood with his back to a calm, glistening Lake Rideau and recited the history of GRIT. Professor Charles Osgood had conceived of the notion of Graduated Reciprocation in Tension-reduction, GRIT. Either side in a conflict can initiate de-escalation without negotiation by making a small, unilateral concession to the other side while communicating the hope that this gesture will be matched with an equal response. If the opponent does so, the first party can then make another concession, creating a peace spiral. Here was a major learning: ***there were distinct processes for actually stimulating and possibly securing peace***. Research had proven results of cause and effect. Social scientists had tested the theory in the lab; statesmen had tested the theory in the field of international conflict.

Other seminars were on theories of aggression, general models of voting patterns of international organizations, gaming theory, and events data analysis which is about using current events data as early warning systems in times of increasing tension between and among countries. There were area studies, such as the Middle East, and the role of the military in civilian society, in peacetime and at war. On a wide wooden porch overlooking Lake Rideau's deep blue waters, peace suddenly had texture; dynamics; content; process; and the concept came alive for me. I listened intensely to visiting speakers and the class commentary of my island colleagues. It wasn't just peace anymore; the mere state of peace became a living system. I saw peace as a weather system; a food chain; there was ecology to peace I had not seen before. I kept trying to pull the string out of the ball of new relationships and tangles I was seeing.

One of the visiting faculty that summer was a young PhD candidate named Lloyd Jeff Dumas, who was just five years my senior. Jeff had received his undergraduate Mathematics degree and both graduate degrees from Columbia University in Engineering and Economics. His mentor, Seymour Melman, was well published in the study of the effects of military/defense spending on the economy and Jeff was continuing in Dr Melman's footsteps. Jeff was really smart and very relatable.

I suppose I really connected with Jeff because of his young age but more over his highly logical and engineering-laced assessment of the state of military/defense spending, the economy, and the robust technologies of war, and the scant existence of alterative peace technologies. Jeff's talks on military conversion were fascinating to me. The notion that there were few "peace technologies" became a critical link in my thinking as I went on to work on the peace academy concept. On Grindstone Island I was presented with the conundrum of why we had so many technologies for war but so few for peace. It was not logical; it was not right and made no sense to me.

Jeff presented me with the ***Third Critical Insight****: the economics of war were in fact the primary driver of violence and destructiveness.* The war system, economy of armaments and myths about the effectiveness of violence, were a separate problem from the processes of conflict and the dynamics of dispute resolution. Interstate conflicts are between established countries; intrastate conflicts are between disputing factions within a nation. The military industrial complex plays a sinister role in both.

Jeff has written: "The fact is, security is not and never has been primarily a matter of weapons and violence. Security is primarily a matter of relationships."[32] In 1969 the federal government spent over $17 billion for scientific research and development. Of this amount, one quarter of was used to improve the means and methods of warfare; one quarter was utilized for space exploration; one-third was earmarked for combating disease, developing energy, and improving agriculture. Of the $17 billion spent, less than 7% was devoted to the study of human behavior.

Out of the total US Federal Budget of $80 billion in 1969, the US government allocated approximately $10 million to the State Department and the Arms Control and Disarmament Agency for the study of the prevention of war.

From 1946–1969, the US government spent over $1 trillion on military goods and services. During that same period it spent approximately $436,000 on peace research and services. By 1969 the Department of Defense employed a full-time staff of over one hundred thousand management specialists, lobbyists, advisors, contractors, procurement specialists, and military spending analysts. The Department of Defense spent $29 million alone in 1969 on public relations – approximately 66 times as much as was spent on Peace Research for the entire 1946–69 periods.[33]

My Fourth Insight came by chance as I picked out a small book from the rickety bookshelf in the main living area of Grindstone Island. The book that caught my eye was *Realities of American Foreign* Policy.[34] It was written by George Kennan, and presented a collection of lectures by the former Ambassador to Russia and later Yugoslavia. He was known for his advocacy of containment toward the Soviets. From reading the book I internalized several other deductions. Ambassador Kennan sealed for me that ***armaments are a symptom, not a cause, of conflict.*** Weapons were "primarily the reflection of international differences and only secondarily the source of them," he wrote.

Jeff Dumas had argued that weapons don't matter; it is about relationships. Kennan argued that weapons are a symptom, not the cause. Much of my own independent study thus far had been focused on disarmament talks and negotiation strategies for reducing the arms race. I had not been focused on the root causes, nor in my view, had most other mainstream thinking. If those seeking peace were focused on the wrong problem, they were probably never going to find the right set of solutions.

The Fifth Realization was an imaginary curve illustrating the rapid escalation of social competition and tension to levels of crisis and violence. The chart showed that ***as a society we were focusing on the wrong aspect point of the escalating conflict dynamics.*** I realized that in misdirecting our attention to negotiating the hardware of warfare, we were seriously missing the all-important behavioral and preventative aspects of conflict management, not unlike society's lack of focus on preventive health in the same years.

Elsewhere in the Kennan book he brought to light that America has a fascination with a kind of utopian endeavor for peace.

> "The evil of this utopian enthusiasm was not only, or even primarily, the wasted time, the misplaced emphasis, the encouragement of false hopes. The evil lay primarily in the fact that these enthusiasms distracted our gaze from the real things that were happening."

He went on to describe the realpolitik of events that were transpiring around the globe. Today, many of our national leaders continue to obsess over the mechanisms of war and focus less on the real causes of unrest and violence.

Kennan thought the pursuit of peace through treaties had preoccupied American statesmanship for long periods of time. Trying to negotiate multilateral agreements and arrangements for disarmament and treaties distracted our leaders. In reality, he stated,

"The United States Government during the period from the turn of the century to the 1930s signed and ratified a total of ninety-seven international agreements dealing with arbitration or conciliation, and negotiated a number of others which, for one reason or another, never took effect. Of the ninety-seven, seven were multinational ones, the remainder bilateral. The time, trouble, and correspondence that went into the negotiation of this great body of contractual material were stupendous." Yet so far as Kennan could ascertain, "only two of these treaties or conventions were ever invoked in any way. Only two disputes were actually arbitrated on the basis of any of these instruments; and there is no reason to suppose that these disputes would not have been arbitrated anyway, on the basis of special agreements, had the general treaties not existed."

He concluded by saying,

"The other ninety-five treaties appear to have remained wholly barren of any practical result. Nor is there any evidence that this ant-like labor had the faintest effect on the development of the terrible wars and upheavals by which the first half of this century was marked."

Kennan pointed out that we as a nation find ourselves distracted at the expense of our feeling for reality by cultivating utopian schemes "flattering to our own image of ourselves." There are real and dangerous enemies in the world. Treaties and armaments do not mitigate or resolve the real issues that drive the conflict. For me there was great insight in his conclusions. Managing a path to peace was more about understanding the underlying interests and needs of parties than negotiating weapons systems or formulating elaborate and unworkable treaties.

Sitting on the expansive former summer porch of Admiral Kingsmill, I wondered about these things:

1) War preparedness doesn't deter, but rather stimulates the other side.
2) There are specific strategies that work to prevent, or deescalate conflict.
3) The economics of war are the primary drivers of major violence and destruction.
4) Armaments are symptoms of conflict not its cause. And finally,
5) As a society we were focusing on the wrong aspect point of the escalating conflict dynamics.

I challenged myself to learn more. It looked to me as if society was stating the problem of peace in a way that it could not be solved.

Far from being an expert in any of these areas of thought or research, I knew it was of great interest and a possible life mission for me. I didn't know the answer to the question: How do we as a society get to where we need to go? But I did now have an opening and a possible way forward. I was becoming my authentic self. I increasingly had the will to find a way to pursue not just the intellectual path to peace, but the way to translate its meaning to others. I came to the conclusion I had to make a break with my well-paying job in Malibu. I pulled Jerry aside and asked how might I best continue my studies and should I apply to graduate school at the University of Pittsburgh's Graduate Program in Public and International Affairs.

In retrospect, I have pondered: How much trial and error do we have to experience to find our best career? How do we know when we are there? At twenty-five, I did not know, but I felt a calling, an intellectual interest, and a growing cadre of faculty and student colleagues who stimulated my interest.

♖ ♗ ♘

The decision to leave my life in Malibu was not an easy one. I was comfortable, learning, and recognized for my work. I had not been trained as an architect or hospital administrator, one of two credentials I might need, as I got older and more entrenched in the work I was doing. I could not see myself pursuing either as a calling, as much as I enjoyed the work and personal lifestyle that my well-paying job provided. My work environment stimulated me, but I wanted more challenge in a field I cared more about. Simply put: I cared more about the meaning and identity of my life that I did about its structure.

After Grindstone Island, I flew to Prescott, Arizona, to meet up with my parents who were visiting friends. Prescott is a lovely mountain community and had been a comfortable family retreat location for us after very close neighbors moved there during my high school years. My mother and dad were staying with these friends. Over dinner my first night there I shared my recent experiences and my desire to return to Malibu, resign, and go to graduate school in Pittsburgh. Our former neighbors listened and looked intrigued. My mother stood up to clear the table. My dad pushed back his chair. My parents clearly did not understand my decision. It was a career pivot and they wanted more explanation. My dad interrupted, "That would be a very silly thing to do. You have a good job. You are in a career. Why mess that up and take the risk on this cloud thinking about peace? You need to go back to Malibu and get back to work. Think about this."

The house was dark with few lights on, as we had been talking since before the sun had set. The mood lighting made my next comments sound even more intense. "I have thought about it. I've had three weeks of thinking about it. No, I've had all the time since I left college to think about it. This is what I want do." I somehow had hoped for a more welcoming reception to a choice that had become obvious to me. I had opened a door that I felt would be warm and sunny and I was now getting nothing but gray clouds. Next there would be lightning bolts; a storm was brewing.

My former neighbors, who had been sitting silently at the table, simultaneously offered in rapid fire, "Good for you. That sounds good. What kind of a degree would you get? When do you have to be at school?"

Mother came back to the table. She said, "I think we have a lot of things to talk about. This sure was a lovely dinner. Anyone want to go for a walk and look at the stars? It seems so clear tonight."

With that my dad exploded. He was vexed. I now know that he was processing what I had said. I was going to leave my well-paying job to go to grad school to study, of all things, peace. In Malibu I was making a higher annual salary than he and he just felt I was about to make a bad career move. I understood his point, but felt that he underestimated my desire, growing intellectual interest, and need for greater social interaction with peers.

I could see my mother's reaction was equally brutal inside for her, but she did not want to talk about it just then. Her reaction was perhaps more understandable, but no less piercing. The evening was getting intense; I silently began to plan to depart the next day by bus for Los Angeles. I had no car. I had to get away. I could not visualize a positive outcome to hanging around for a few more days and then sitting in an unbearably long car ride listening to a family rehash of this evening's concerns.

My mother finally said, *"Who do you think you are, Albert Schweitzer? You are not as bright as Dr Schweitzer and you are throwing your career away."* Her comment, direct and sharp, hurt. That did it. It really hurt. I excused myself and went outside. Her idea to look at the stars suddenly seemed appealing.

As much as her comment hurt, I knew that she did not understand all that the word peace meant or would come to mean to me, as I did not understand it either. I was still struggling to redefine the arc of my own life. I only knew it was a change and a path I had to try. In the end, that choice has guided my life and professional success. I had come to believe that peace is a process, conceived in the mind and felt by the heart, and that would become my life's mantra.

The next morning I talked them into dropping me off at the Prescott bus station. I called my brother-in-law John and asked him to meet me in Pomona, California, at the bus station there. He could drive me back to Malibu the next afternoon. I returned to my job and gave a lot of thought to my resignation letter. When finished, it was fourteen pages long, filled with a bit of unnecessary drama caused by the exchange with my parents. I packed up and I drove to Pittsburgh to begin the fall term. My loving parents later came around to understanding what I was about and grew very close to the colleagues I met along the way. They were as proud of me as they had always been. It just took a little bit of selling, and time, to win them over.

Chapter 2 Review and Reflection

Task

- Search for ways to market a noble idea.

Challenge

- Engage in advocacy.

Gift and Opportunity

- Invite new experiences.

Reflection

- What idea generates hope and questioning in you?
- What is a good fit given your background, skills, and passions?
- Hint: List as many good fits as you can imagine. You can always narrow the choices later.

CHAPTER 3

Pittsburgh

Fall 1975 – Driving across the country to reach Pittsburgh was almost surreal. I felt like I was seeing the nation for the first time, in its purest form. I drove many of the Blue Roads, and tried to bypass the cities. Over and over, I passed the farms, fields, silos, small towns, main streets, schoolhouses, and solitary flags flying in town center parks. I ate in the truck stops and picnicked in roadside pullouts. The highways had the pulse of commerce; it was summer so families were on the move. There were billboards, and more billboards. I drove by small manufacturing plants and car dealerships; strip malls and subdivisions down below the highway overpasses. When I entered the cities, they were like bee hives: vibrant, crowded and churning.

I had never seen America this way. Growing up in Los Angeles, life was one continuous metropolis, filled with an inner city surrounded by fifty-four contiguous, independent towns all running together. The mountains and sea bound LA into an isolated giant of humanity, not the Ritz Cracker-size rural townships I was seeing for the first time along my drive. All of it was America. All of it a visual of the values, life style and commerce we fought wars over. All of it, connected geographies and local cultures rolled up into one "peace proclaiming" nation. But I thought, what does that mean to aspire to peace?

These things I thought as I drove. I was anxious to be back in school again and open to the new experience. I was living with the tension of having left a good job, however, and the strain of having clearly disappointed my parents, perhaps for the first time in my life. Their love and our arguments were on my mind for much of my car journey.

Upon my arrival in Pittsburgh, I was immediately struck by the number of bridges and brick buildings; and the smell and blue-collar feel of the city. I had not known what to expect, but I felt both the age and youth of the city. Pittsburgh is a city of rivers and bridges. It appeared no accident to me that my next months there would be about exploring new rivers of thought and building my own bridges from theory to action. Deindustrialization was just beginning to hit the region. There was still a smell in the air and grit on the buildings that told the story of the history of the many foundries, some of which were still spewing out visible pollution. The area around the City of Pittsburgh had an abundance of coal; a three-river water highway, and its mills had processed coal into steel dating back to 1875. Steel production in the US slowed in the 1970's and the last mills shut down in the early 1980's.

It was a demographic melting pot of cultures and a new world for me of sports teams, blue-collar bars, esteemed academic institutions, museums, and even some stone roadways, which I had never seen. Cobblestone was quaint; I had seen it at Disneyland in Anaheim. This was different. Some of the roadways were made of heavy rectangular stone blocks laid down as if by Romans. Pittsburgh had the hard, solid vibe of a strong place. I was excited to be there. The big sign in the student union of the University of Pittsburgh read "Someplace Special," and it was. The university landmark, the "Tower of Learning" skyscraper loomed over the campus as a sentinel. I began to feel a sense of commitment to my studies and anticipation of what might come from them at the Graduate School of Public and International Affairs.

When at the University of Pittsburgh, three very fine professors heavily influenced me. I remain grateful for their mentorship and influence. The first was Jerry Laulicht, whom I had met at Grindstone Island. It was Jerry who had drawn my attention to continuing my post–Grindstone Island study and apprenticeship at Pitt. He and his wife generously invited me to stay in their home when I first arrived. He seemed to thrive on chaos and was very animated, full of life and socially engaging—a slightly awkward, often disheveled character with a fabulous heart. The second professor was Richard Cottam, a political scientist who was a recognized specialist in Iran and other regional studies. Dick was a humble, smooth, serious man who reminded me of Dick Cavett, or a current-day Mark Ruffalo. He had a slight melancholy to his personality and spoke without notes. The third was Joseph Coffey, a professor of public and international affairs. Dr Coffey wore handsome three-piece suits and hosted informal Friday afternoon receptions in his campus office. He charmed us by serving sherry. He was erudite, very proper, and abnormally formal—even in informal settings—and his reserved nature commanded respect. All of these men became mentors and through my contact with them, I was both inspired and exhilarated to learn about national security affairs, perceptions of political actors, and peace and foreign policy issues.

In the mid-1970s, several major foundations began to fund programs in arms control studies and international affairs. Pitt was a recipient of some of these funds and began to train graduate students, many of whom were mid-career like myself, in area studies, weapons nomenclature, the history of arms control negotiations, and related subjects. Our program was not very large, but it was embedded in a much larger department of International Affairs and the related disciplines of sociology, political science and others. In most of my very small seminar classes, the seven or eight students were—well, shall we say . . . unique? I believed at the time, but never knew for certain, that about two-thirds of my classmates were civilians serving in the military or on mid-career assignment from intelligence agencies. This made for some great discussions, as their backgrounds and disciplined training were reflected in our class debates. My roommate for a time was a student in international relations from Boone, West Virginia. We, along with our professors, seemed to always take the more progressive viewpoint in our class discussions. I dedicated myself to my studies and excelled.

Prior to joining the faculty at Pitt, Jerry Laulicht was a senior researcher at the Canadian Peace Research Institute. Jerry was bespectacled, understated, and carried himself with the gravitas of a newspaper reporter, not an academic. Sometimes his glasses sat on the front of his head. Among the projects he directed were studies on the attitudes of the general public and elite groups on issues of foreign and defense policy. At Pitt, he put together an introductory seminar on peace studies that mimicked the program I had attended on Grindstone Island. Visiting faculty came through weekly and served as resources to the students. They came from many disciplines and universities from across the country. It was a great introduction for me to my areas of interest. I felt like I was in the midst of a smorgasbord of national security main courses. I started to indulge.

During the fall of 1975, I was beginning to define what peace really meant to me. Through my classes and study I began to identify with specific beliefs that had meaning for me. The use of force was to me an optional instrument of decision-making, influenced by cultural identity and perception. To prevent the use of force one could make it culturally unacceptable or clarify the perceptions and images that informed its use. It was pretty simple thinking, but it was my thinking and I had gotten there on my own. I was trying to understand the world of foreign relations and map it on my own experiences with marketing, problem solving, and what I thought of as the psychological dynamics of conflict. I studied and applied values, beliefs, and cognitions to better understand the realities of conflict on the ground. I learned that national perceptions and images were linked to closely held values that in turn influenced decision-making relating to issues of war and peace.

In everything that I studied, I had a sense of looking for the dynamics of the situation and how to change them. The real gifts of my learning were focused on actionable applications. Marketing techniques and the reframing of symbols and national rituals, I argued, could influence images and perceptions. In my final paper I used Lebanon as my area case study and centered my conclusions on a strategy of altering perceptions. I thought and wrote about how those principles might be applied to guide the United States to rely less on the use of force and more on alternatives forms of conflict resolution. I came to believe that if change were to be made in any reasonable time frame, it would require the use of national symbols and rituals in visible ways. This narrative of thinking would later develop into my views of how a national academy of peace might be designed to influence American culture and values using fundamentals of marketing and diffusion of innovations theory.

Laulicht was a recognized researcher and sociologist, focused on public opinion and foreign policy development. His research related to foreign policy issues, specifically attitudes toward nuclear weapons, conventional forces, coexistence policy, the United Nations, and foreign aid. Jerry had found that public opinion can and does affect government policy, but that the public is not a unity, nor are all segments equally influential. Jerry studied how different segments of society influenced opinion, and war and peace.

Again in the fall of 1975, Laulicht brought to class another faculty resource person whose name was Bryant Wedge, MD. Laulicht knew Bryant from their mutual writings and research projects on national perception. Bryant was a practicing psychiatrist based in Washington, DC. The practice was that students could sign up to meet privately with the visiting faculty following their formal presentations. Both Bryant and his lecture topics intrigued me. Bryant had published the very first psychological profile of a head of state—Nikita Khrushchev[35]—and had been appointed to one of the early cadres of the prestigious Eisenhower Fellows from his post as Director of Student Mental Health Programs at Yale. Motivated by his year of travel and writing, he had founded the Institute for the Study of National Behavior. It was a loftily named one-man show that served as Bryant's personal platform for engaging in political and academic intrigue. I made an appointment to meet him.

I arrived at the appointed hour and took a seat in one of those wood and steel classroom desk chairs with the built-in armrest and writing surface common to most classrooms. The colors of fall decorated the trees outside the classroom windows. Bryant entered a few minutes later, a cigarette hanging from his lips, dressed in a rumpled dark business suit and smiling broadly. We sat together, opposite each other. We spoke for hours, well beyond the scheduled time for the appointment.

We exchanged personal stories. Bryant had been born in 1921 in Coldwater, Michigan. He was educated at Kalamazoo College and the University of Michigan Medical School. He trained in psychiatry at Queen's Hospital of Honolulu and the University of Chicago; anthropology at the University of Hawaii; and political sociology and international relations at Yale University and Princeton University. Over the course of his career, he taught at the University of Chicago, Yale, Princeton, George Washington University, the Foreign Service Institute, and the Fletcher School of Law and Diplomacy. I wondered why he had moved around so much. Was it because he was trying to sell something, or trying to find something to sell, more like me?

Bryant founded the Institute for the Study of National Behavior to study the application of social and behavioral science theory and method to problem-solving activity in the field of international and community relations. For most of Bryant's life he sought to advance and integrate the principles of psychiatry and social sciences to our understanding of perceptions, cross-cultural relationships, and conflict resolution.

Earlier on the day of my appointment he had spoken about peace and how to create it using new federal institutions that might one day attract researchers and activists who would influence policy and implementation. In our private session, Bryant shared that a medical doctor had authored an essay in 1799 proposing "A Plan of a Peace Office for the United States." The man was Benjamin Rush, MD, and a signer of the Declaration of Independence. Dr Rush, like Bryant, was a reformer, and an advocate for prison improvements. Bryant spent much of his medical practice as a court-appointed clinician determining the mental state of criminals. Although he had a private psychiatric practice in DC on Wisconsin Avenue, NW, he spent as much time at the mental patient wards at St. Elizabeth Psychiatric Hospital in Southeast DC. Bryant looked like a psychiatrist, so much so that you might easily visualize him testifying in a *Law and Order* episode, taking the stand to answer questions about the defendant. Bryant himself never hesitated to ask normally inappropriate personal questions or awkwardly assert personal observations. Bryant's eyes twinkled. His kindness showed through any abrasiveness. We hit it off.

Bryant was animated and excited as he produced a wrinkled copy of a letter President-elect Eisenhower had received on December 20, 1952 from newspaper publisher Frank E. Gannett who suggested the President create a Department of Peace. Gannett had written, "Peace is too precious to be entirely in the hands of diplomats. It should be all-pervading rather than confined to diplomacy or subordinate to it."

As he stuffed the letter back into his suit pocket, he explained what he thought the letter had meant. The primary purpose of the State Department was the promotion of US national interests in international relations. The primary purpose of most of the legislative proposals over the years was the promotion of peace as a national goal by anticipating and building the long-range conditions necessary for the maintenance of a peaceful world. Bryant pointed out that eleven bills had been introduced in the 91st Congress between January 3, 1969, and April 29, 1969. More than one hundred Congressional sponsors and co-sponsors had offered those bills. Many of these Congressional leaders were still in Congress. Bryant believed there was an opportunity to organize a citizen's effort to move the thrust of their efforts forward.

Bryant asked me to tell him my story. I reviewed the various parts of my past and my current search to find the need to define my life's work as doing something worthwhile, noble, and admirable. I shared with him the work I had done selling architectural design and planning concepts, and that now I was studying to learn more about the fields of peace research and conflict resolution. I expressed frustration that as a society we seemed to be trying to solve problems at the wrong time.

It seemed with regard to preventing war that we treated the solutions as technical advancements, not greater behavioral understanding.

We extended our discussion to the subject of ways to bring about lasting cultural change. We spoke about a variety of disciplines. As we sat together, I was drawn in by our mutual views on systems analysis. I felt we shared many of the same perspectives and sentiments. I think he was struck by my experience as a salesman and my commitment to our shared interests in the practical pursuit of peace.

As our discussions drew to a close, Bryant shared with me the story of new legislation moving through the Congress to create what was then called the George Washington Peace Academy. He briefed me on the progress the bill was making and on his efforts, along with others, to generate interest in and support for the legislation that had been introduced. He invited me to come to Washington to talk further and to attend together the May hearing. Bryant offered to send me some of his academic papers upon his return to DC. I committed to come to DC in the spring. It was October 1975.

♖ ♗ ♞

While in Pittsburgh, I spent most of my day in a library carrel or in small classes. As I had done back in the UCLA library, I used to love taking breaks from my assignments by walking around the library stacks, stopping to peruse whatever current event book interested me. On one occasion, I found myself getting introduced by chance to Everett Rogers, a communications specialist who had authored a book in 1959, titled *Communications of Innovations: A Cross-Cultural Approach.*[36] Professor Rogers had pretty much invented the concept of types of adopters to innovation as illustrated on a bell curve. The book was hugely insightful for me and I became totally intrigued with Rogers's breakdown of adaptor groups into Innovators, Early Adopters, Early Majority, Late Majority, and Laggards. It appealed to me because I saw his work as marketing theory. His thinking and modeling of how social change occurs proved to be key in my work to create a national peace academy and even in my business-consulting career. Years later, I spent a day with him at Stanford University. I greatly admired and learned from the man.

In the fall of 1975 I also traveled from Pittsburgh to Boston to attend an annual meeting of an association called Consortium on Peace, Education, and Development or COPRED. It was also my first opportunity to look around Boston. The COPRED meetings were held over several days at a Quaker retreat site in rainy, cold Concord. I remember my feet being cold as I walked through piles of wet leaves. The fall leaves were at their peak and I found the surroundings of the various universities, historical landmarks, and people exciting and compelling. I had grown up in the West with orange trees, deserts, and mountains. Eastern forests and graveyards, rowed with headstones dating back centuries, were not just charming; they were like being in a Nathaniel Hawthorne novel. It was my first occasion to meet Kenneth and Elise Boulding, who were well-established founders and rock stars of the peace education movement. Both Elise and Kenneth were not only giants of the field; they both carried a special countenance. Ironically, when the Boulding's had to depart for the airport near the close of the meeting, the conference room clock literally stopped. Five years later Elise served as a commissioner on the federal commission, and Kenneth authored several editorials and articles and spoke on behalf of our efforts to engage the country in establishing a national peace academy.

While in graduate school I had the opportunity to sit in on a class at Harvard University taught by Professor Karl Deutsch. It was a lecture on the relatively new topic of peace research and I was stunned by the impact the talk had on my life. Although the Professor's remarks were largely a review of a talk he had given at Middlebury College in Vermont three years earlier, it profoundly raised the assertion, "We must know what we are doing." Throughout his speech Dr Deutsch addressed ways to seek the conditions to make large-scale war less probable, evaluated what makes violent conflict more likely, and in doing so stressed that singular cognitive point. "It isn't enough in medicine to be for health and against disease. We must know what we are doing. The science of medicine – and hence more effective medicine – begins after that point. In the science of peace, it is not enough to be for peace – we must know what we are doing."[37] This mantra stuck with me.

Later that fall I also traveled to Washington, DC, to participate in Pacem Terris IV, an elaborate public seminar put on by the Fund for the Republic and the Santa Barbara–based Center for the Study of Democratic Ideas. The attendee list was made up of the government and academic elite of the American foreign affairs community. I was able to sit in on informal sessions by fifty speakers over the course of a weekend. Much of the discussion centered around the end of the war in Indochina and the false expectation that there would be a peace dividend or shifting of dollars from the war effort to domestic problems in cities and towns across America. In fact, the budgets for military and foreign aid had increased and the problems of domestic inflation had worsened. The word détente was used a lot. It is a French phrase meaning relaxation of tension. The debate in the sessions was focused on the concern that relaxations in one sector—like political détente—could result in redistribution of tension from the technological sector, for example, to the ideological one. As international tensions relaxed, it created a pause for American foreign policy makers to ask. "What is our purpose? What is a clear vision for our country?" Many of the speakers felt that the Vietnam War had been a war created by the decisions of elites and had failed because a broader base of national support was never developed. Right or wrong, the debate raised questions for me about how our American foreign policy establishment influenced the country and vice versa. In much of the discussion and tone of the conference, peace seemed to have no owner. To me, there was a clear need for the country to develop a more concerted bias for peace—some type of institutional advocacy—amid the political and ideological swings of political parties and elites.

The experts at the conference included George Kennan, Richard Barnet, Charles Osgood, Hans Morgenthau, Morton Halperin, James Schlesinger, and US Senators Edward Kennedy, Claiborne Pell, Jacob Javits, and Daniel Moynihan. People like former CIA officials William Colby and Ray Cline, Congressmen Andy Young and Les Aspin, Admirals Elmo Zumwalt and Gene LaRocque. Former Senator Joe Clark, and weapons expert Dr Herb York led the discussions. Not only did the conference hotel have clay tennis courts, which I had never seen, the speakers nearly all seemed like Mount Rushmore figures come alive. I sat in my uncomfortable conference room chair and took it all in. I felt like a little kid at a baseball park lingering down by the sidelines during warm up to get an autograph of a famous Big Leaguer. Just as I had never seen a clay tennis courts, I had never seen a diplomat.

I read about these people in my studies; to see them live in the same forum, interacting and debating was very engaging. Bryant Wedge met me at the conference hotel and we again talked for hours. He brought me some of his published papers and I read them overnight, and we met the next day. Bryant's second foundational belief—with regard to his motivation in pursuing the peace academy concept—was the importance of understanding and benefiting from the study of national perception and its influence on behavior. Bryant wrote several papers about the psychological factors involved in Soviet disarmament negotiations. His thesis was that the United States, more often than not, negotiated with the Soviet Union based upon positional bargaining without fully understanding the basis for Soviet positions and the perceptions that influenced Soviet behavior. Without more fully understanding the Soviet psyche, United States negotiators were at a disadvantage. Bryant's work in the dynamics and power of communication from a psychological perspective was fundamental to transcultural communications. Once again, the *"We must know what we are doing"* Deutsch bells were ringing.

Just before the Christmas holidays I returned to Los Angeles to reconnect with my parents and report on the progress of my search for the illusive peace that I was seeking. I reconciled with my parents as best I could, and talked with them about the new concept of a national center for training and research in conflict resolution. My academic term was over and I felt I had turned a corner. Before leaving Pittsburgh I had completed an application to attend the Fletcher School of Law and Diplomacy at Tuffs. I was hopeful. I was also excited to be returning to Pittsburgh in a few weeks to start more structured classes on area studies.

Back in Pittsburgh I soon had to face one of the realities of being a fulltime graduate student, money. I had saved enough of my Malibu salary to modestly fund my transition to Pittsburgh, but now I was stretched financially pretty thin. The familiar conundrum for students is finding work that pays enough, but does not interfere with class or study time. I was in constant search for odd jobs until I read one day of an asthma study to be conducted with Pitt students who had experienced bronchial asthma as a child. The pay was an insane nine hundred dollars per month for a daily commitment of only thirty-minutes. There was just one catch. I fit the profile of candidates the drug company was looking for, but I was nervous about the daily dose of an unknown, experimental drug that each individual would be administered over the three months of the study. At least there was a fifty percent chance that I would be given the placebo dose and not turn into some sort of wheezing alien. Despite fainting on occasion at our cohort pre-breakfast check-ins I got through the three months with only daily temperature taking; weigh-in; and pill popping. It was my best job in grad school. And yes, as you might ask, I eventually found out that I had been given the harmless placebo, and for three plus months had been inhaling a diluted powdered sugar substance each morning.

I started classes with Professors Richard Cottam and Joseph Coffey. Cottam sounded like he was in the studio set of a television taping. He was always relaxed, conversational and understated. Dick Cottam had earned his PhD from Harvard University. He was awarded a Fulbright Scholarship to carry out a survey for his PhD dissertation in 1951-52. In early 1953 he joined the Central Intelligence Agency and became an operative. In August of 1953, a US-backed coup d'état occurred in Iran overthrowing the government of Mohammad Mosaddeq. Cottam was in country when the coup happened. As a professor, Cottam provided a rare insight into the American intelligence apparatus. He said he strongly opposed the 1953 CIA coup and that it had been a mistake. The Robert Redford and Faye Dunaway action movie about a CIA analyst in Manhattan, *Three Days of the Condor*, came out in 1975. I was beginning to feel like I was in it.

Cottam's classroom discussions were grounded in actual field experience. Not only would I learn my teacher had been a former CIA covert operative, I was able to confirm that more than a few of my fellow students were on educational leave from the National Security Agency or other intelligence organizations. There was something about the way these particular students formulated their questions, each person addressing the query in a similar manner. The questions were often indirect and, although not quite deceptive, certainly odd. It was as if there was a subtle question lurking behind the assumptions embedded in their remark. There were also an assortment of other indicators such as their haircuts, sharp appearance, and lack of socializing with others in the program. I remember sensing at the time that this was my first exposure to intelligence work and how that side of the foreign policy establishment worked.

Professor Cottam had served in Iran under the guise of a political officer at the American Embassy in Tehran from 1956–1958. In these years he developed a close relationship with the National Front, one of the organizations that symbolized Iranians' desires for independence and autonomy. Cottam was not just an expert on Iranian political studies and regional ethic groups, politics, and the motivations of many of the key players, he had experienced the internal American short sighted policy decisions with respect to Mohammad Reza Shah and had played a role in the failed 1958 coup attempt to displace the Shah. He confided to us that his involvement in that unsuccessful covert operation led to his resignation from the agency in 1958.

Cottam believed that the United States' preoccupation with the Cold War and its devastating consequences could be explained through an analysis of the perceptions held by political actors. In the classroom and in his papers and books, he argued that when it came to dealing with developing countries, American political leaders were not only trapped in the Cold War paradigm, but were also afflicted (his words) by an imperial perception intertwined with Western colonial history. His viewpoints, deep expertise, on-the-ground experience, and authenticity as a concerned scholar had a great impact upon me.

Cottam was given the opportunity to interview the exiled Iranian leader Ayatollah Ruhollah Khomeini in Paris at a time when it was becoming clear that Khomeini would lead the Iranian revolution. Much of our classwork was devoted to understanding the misperceptions of the American foreign policy establishment about nationalism. He viewed it not as an ideology, but rather a worldview that greatly influenced behaviors.

In our weekly seminars, he eloquently reviewed the Middle East—country after country, one ethnic group after another, dissecting the behavioral and nationalistic politics of each. I remember that in the study of Lebanon alone, we took into consideration twenty-two different political and ethnic groups. We were tested on the granularity of the motivations of each group. One of our reading assignments was the lengthy essay by Karl Deutsch I had heard him summarize in my fall trip to Cambridge. Now reading the essay in its full form, I saw that Deutsch had written earnestly about the importance of the ethnic dynamics of any regional conflict. Again my eyes locked on to his memorable phrase. It has stayed with me throughout my career, particularly as I came to consider the curriculum for a national peace academy and entered the field of peacemaking as a practitioner.

Dr Coffey was a veteran analyst in national security affairs, having served on both White House staffs and on the Policy Planning Council of the Department of State. I never saw him wearing anything but fine clothes, kind of striking for college professor, I thought. He stood erect and moved his entire body to move his head. My core class with him was on the uses of force in the nuclear age and was a survey course on weapons nomenclature, the history of arms reductions negotiations, and the military and political implications of each.

We had many in-class debates on the effectiveness, or lack of effectiveness, of deterrence policy. In one class, I put my beliefs to the test and surprised my fellow students by arguing a seven-point narrative as to why deterrence, in my view, did not work. My colleagues from the military and intelligence services were in shock as I challenged their thinking about deterrence. They did not buy my argument that the threat of force was not necessarily stabilizing. My simple thesis was if someone was mad enough, no show of force or threat could be great enough to prevent him or her from using force. It was a behavioral connection not a political one. It was not a chess move; it was a checkers move. I used examples from the Middle East and the Cuban Missile Crisis to support my points. I was both surprised and heartened when Professor Coffey quoted some of my arguments in the wrap-up of our debates.

Coffey was highly credible and cultivated in his teaching style. He was fair to both the doves and hawks in our seminars, but I began to realize he believed fully in diplomatic engagement over the use of force. We studied the nature of alliance relationships, communist military strategy and capabilities, nuclear proliferation, and arms control efforts. He refuted the argument and current thinking that American security required "superior" strategic offensive forces or extensive air and missile defenses. The B-1 bomber was in development during these years and we studied the economic implications of its cost of design and production, maintenance, and in-theater effectiveness. It was during these studies that I became convinced that the behavioral side of conflict resolution was far more effective than the technical side of advanced weaponry. The future of peace, to me, was tied to the development of peacemaking and peacekeeping techniques, not to the military-industrial production of increasingly advanced weapons systems.

Each Friday Professor Coffey, again in his three-piece suit, and we students in jeans or chinos, would celebrate the week with a sherry and cheese reception in his oversized, musty campus office. We stood around and acted like I thought diplomats might act, chatting formally about subjects about which we held more private views. On one such occasion, Professor Coffey said to me as we stood by the window bench seat, "I went to West Point and then got my PhD from Georgetown. I don't think you are going to follow a very traditional track, Mr Spencer. What do you think?" I was surprised by his frankness and casual tone. He had always seemed more formal and erudite to me. He addressed everyone in our class as a "Mr" as unfortunately there were no women in the program at that time.

"Well, sir, I don't think arms control is the right path, nor do I think I am cut out to be a diplomat. I want to cause change and those would not seem to be the best options for me." I started to just make up stuff. I really felt I was still incubating and a little unsure of the dots I was connecting.

Professor Coffey just that week returned my term assignment, a seventy-five-page paper[38]. He and I were both well aware of the constructive criticism he had offered of my writing effort. He had given me a letter grade of *A*; in his notes, however, he took care to share a bit of coaching. I began to realize he was just now finding the opportunity to follow up and make a few points for emphasis. I felt he cared about me, as I respected him. His handwritten critique revealed that my paper was too broad. It had been "a mile wide and an inch deep." When I had read his comments earlier in the week, I knew he was correct. I agreed with his notes, but I was even more stimulated by the hard work and intellectual exploration that had gone into the paper. I was on a learning spree and I tried to put too much into my final paper. If I could learn to limit my objectives, I might be more successful with each of my goals.

Still by the window, the fading sun created slanting light as the professor reiterated what he had meant by the postscript below my grade. He encouraged me to focus. Find my niche and execute. He leaned over and grabbed the bottle of sherry and invited himself to refill my glass. He said with a rare unguarded breath, he said, "Too many of us pass through this life seeking to be the best in what we have; too few seek to be the best in what could be." We never spoke of that moment again. His formality and elegance seemed to block any future attempt on my part to pierce his academic veil. I hoped he might again be as real as he was in that moment. I was not so fortunate. Like his books, it was hard to tell where he was coming from until the very end. I admired him for his intellectual honesty, but regretted how he sometimes shielded it with diplomatic charm. I believe that he had not seen that same diplomatic charm in me, but rather a passion for change that he willingly encouraged. I am grateful to him for that.

♖ ♗ ♘

In March I heard back from the Fletcher School of Law and Diplomacy at Tuffs that my application was rejected. I was depressed and angry. How dare they? I thought. I wanted to be in their club. Then I reflected on my discussion with Professor Coffey. Maybe it was all for the good. Perhaps I was destined to be an advocate rather than an academic.

Bryant kept in touch by telephone into the spring and again invited me to visit DC for the Congressional hearings on the George Washington Peace Academy. On the morning of the Congressional hearing I drove the four hours to DC. I proceeded to the center of downtown Washington and parked. I did not know my way around and was worried I might get lost.

I tried to find the right subway to get to Wisconsin Avenue to meet Bryant at his office. I finally hailed a taxi. That May morning, again, Bryant looked like he had slept in his suit. He greeted me holding a cigarette. He gestured dramatically for me to enter the office, as the ashes dribbled onto his suit and tie.

His first-floor psychiatry office had comfortable overstuffed chairs, a couch, and stacks of papers and books along each wall. It was a relaxed place, one that I would visit many times over the next decade, not as a student or patient, but as a colleague. I realized he too was rapidly becoming a mentor. I spoke to him about that and he said he liked that idea. The small, stuffy office would become a quiet retreat where we would scheme and plan, console and inspire. I would come to love, and also feel annoyed by him. Bryant was not easy to love, as he was knowingly abrasive and often inappropriate. I did love him though, as I respected his caring and humanity, combined with intelligence and entrepreneurship. The annoying part was because of the pressures we both felt as we journeyed together; he inventing new routes to take, and me looking for a direct path.

"Coffee?" Bryant asked, as we settled in. "How was the drive down from Pittsburgh?"

"No problems. I am excited to be here." I said.

I asked Bryant if he was ready for his testimony. He smiled and took a long draw in on his cigarette. "I don't think psychoanalysis is going to point the way to the elimination of war, my boy, but I am more optimistic than Freud," he said as he gestured toward the copies of his written testimony stacked on a side table. Cigarette ashes dropped off and floated in that direction. Still smiling he said, "I believe that people are going to agree with us that we must provide a mechanism for steering inputs away from a war system and toward a peace system of relationship."

Leaning back and habitually brushing the ashes from his lapel, he continued, "None of us can move effectively toward the future so long as the war-system dominates. I believe that establishing a peace academy on the federal level is a most significant achievable step—as much for what it symbolizes as for what it will accomplish—and that it will open the way to a range of further actions. You and I can make a difference."

I would come to believe we could.

Bryant continued,

"I am going to tell them that the academy is conceived of as an international as well as a national institution, and its aims go far beyond the pursuit of peace. The rationale for establishing a National

Academy of Peace and Conflict Resolution is quite simply to provide an institution to focus emerging resources and methods—political, ethical, economic, and intellectual—on problems of peace and justice in the contemporary era. No such institution now exists."

He was really pumped. "The United States needs to recapture its leadership as the hope of mankind in its international as well as domestic conduct."

Pausing, and drawing in on his cigarette, he said, "OK, your turn. Why do you care?" Inhaling with a hiss, "You are a young businessman from California. You told me in in Pittsburgh you trained as a biologist; you're smart. For God's sake, you seem to have made things work there in Malibu in that architecture firm." Bryant liked to use flattery to set you up for his next blow. "Why do you care?" he sputtered again, leaning back and again exhaling cigarette smoke. At the risk of overplaying the description of being in Bryant's presence, it was somewhat like experiencing the hissing sound of an ocean mammal surfacing. Bryant waved his flukes and dove again.

Bryant was always direct. Some people found that quality coarse, but I always found him endearing. His style was to go directly to the point, close to the boundary between being abrasive and seeking clarity. It was his way of cutting through the crap and getting to the real issues, as he saw them. Bryant could be simultaneously caring and yet project an uncomfortable edge. He was physically untidy but logically crystal clear. Just as he was confrontational, he was also personable and affirming. If you did not know him, you might guess he was a psychiatrist. He was a complex individual. And I could always count on him to be empowering and encouraging; thoughtful and challenging.

I felt respected by Bryant. I could feel the genuine delight that came through in his comments. I knew he was pleased that I had made the decision to come to DC.

I finally answered his blunt question:

> "You know my work out there taught me I was a good salesman. If you realize you can sell stuff, then what matters is what you sell, right? I like selling concepts. I like to help people understand ideas. Peace is a concept that has many complexities. It's systemic, like biology. But instead of a body, it's about society."

I shifted in my chair and sipped again on my coffee. Continuing, I said,

> "Look, peace interests me and, from what I have already studied and learned, it is in need of selling. It's not a passive science; it's a process science like fluid dynamics.

I believe there are paths to get there; figuring it out intrigues me. It makes sense to me that society should do a better job of creating the environments – the ecosystems really – that nourish it. Peace is not about the hardware that we buy to enforce it. That is clearly treating a symptom not the problem. The key has got to be in the software, the human behavioral and cultural side. That is why I care."

Bryant leaned on his side table and lit another cigarette. I stood and moved to open another office window. The traffic noises outside were beginning to pick up.

Feeling comfortable and safe with Bryant, I said, "I guess I am looking for some meaning and identity in my life that is of my own choosing, something that might cause some real change. Causing peace is something I believe in. Doing this is something that makes intellectual and practical sense to me. I believe it is something anyone can choose to do—and you have given me the added courage to step out and explore what we can do together. Thanks for that."

I lifted my coffee cup in his direction. Bryant raised his cigarette in acknowledgment.

Then he asked what I thought of DC.

My answer was that Washington was an intimidating place. When people ask for whom do you work, they are trying to assess your power. In California they ask what you like to do to figure out your lifestyle preference. In the South the question is do you have family here, to see if you are an outsider. In New York, it's where you live, to assess your wealth. In Cambridge, it's what you think, seemingly to get a read on your intelligence.

Bryant laughed in hearing my assessment. I always got a kick out of Bryant finding such joy in my own take on things.

Bryant and I finished preparations, and he drove us in his faded blue Buick down to the Capitol where I would meet the good Professor, Dr James H. Laue. After parking a distance away, Bryant and I hurried across the Capitol grounds in the early spring Washington humidity, arriving at the Senate hearing room, sweaty and overheated.

Passing uniformed guards and navigating wide and very long hallways, we made it to the hearing room. The high ceiling of the hearing room was impressive enough, but the dark wood paneling and the heavy, courtroom-like magistrate's desk extended wall to wall. Seeing this sight for the first time, I felt small, out of place, and intimidated, as I am sure was the intent.

An enthusiastic man in a gray, three-piece suit crossed the hearing room floor to greet us. Jim Laue was about the sunniest person I had ever met. My sense of intimidation melted to a greater sense of ease. Jim was a Harvard-trained sociologist who was then a vice chancellor at Washington University in St. Louis.

Jim, I would come to learn, was the only white man shown in the *LIFE Magazine's* iconic image of the assassination of Dr Martin Luther King Jr some eight years earlier. In the *LIFE* photo spread of the events at the Loraine Motel in Memphis, Jim can be seen kneeling, placing a towel under the head of Dr King, while the others in the photos – Ralph Abernathy, Andrew Young and Jesse Jackson – excitedly point over the railing to draw attention in the direction of the shooter. Sadly, others gaze down at Dr King's body in disbelief. The pictures captured a terrible moment in American history. Jim was on his knees quietly trying to make a difference.

Jim was a Servant Leader type.[39] He was always jumping into the mix to help out. Bryant had briefed me on Jim, and I was anxious to finally meet him. Approaching Jim, I could see he projected the enthusiasm of a bee, engaging people with a smile, and encouraging Midwestern small talk. Anyone who experienced Jim was quickly drawn in by his disarming, friendly eagerness to please, convince, motivate or flatter. That was Jim in an instant, and that was how I delighted in experiencing Jim Laue for the next seventeen years.

One moment we shook hands, the next, Jim handed me a stack of stapled testimony and asked that I pass it around to some in the hearing room gallery. I had almost completed my assigned task when I dropped a few remaining pages onto the marble floor. I bent over to pick them up and the perspiration from my earlier rush to the building caused my suit pants to adhere to my body, tearing a gaping hole in the seat of my wool pants. Jim came to my side as I arose, red-faced; believing every eye in the Senate audience was upon me. He had seen it all. Jim whispered, "It's O.K., you'll probably not be the last person to tear up something for a good cause." I laughed, and the embarrassing moment passed. My initial indoctrination to Washington, DC, had passed.

Jim would be testifying as well before the Senate that day as a conflict resolution practitioner. He was an expert on systemic conflicts originating from the unfair distribution of power and resources within social systems. After Dr King's death, Jim finished his PhD at Harvard in 1966 and joined the Justice Department as the Director of Program Development and Evaluation at the Community Relations Service. CRS was the part of the Department of Justice that deals with race issues.

In the days and months ahead, Jim would become another mentor, and my closest professional friend. He would eventually introduce me to each of my two future wives; be the Best Man in my first wedding and, with a great sense of loss, I would be one of those to deliver a eulogy in his memory. We always felt very close. He was the kind of friend whose commitment to friendship felt like an old shoe: comfortable, fitting, well matched for all kinds of wear, and right there to slip on when you need an encouraging and familiar embrace. We fit. I still miss him to this day.

I greatly respected Jim. As a conflict analyst, he focused on the structure and roles of conflict. His Harvard dissertation was on Direct Action and Desegregation in the years 1960 to 1962. Out of his experience in the civil rights movement, Jim had come to be a conflict technician. Jim had written:

> "The true resolution of conflict—in contrast to management, winning-losing or mere termination—occurs only through negotiation or some other form of mutual problem-solving. In the last two decades, a growing number of scholar/practitioners had shifted the focus to resolving rather than winning conflicts, with the strategic focus on analysis, problem-solving and negotiation."

Jim was a firm believer that third parties could effectively arm wrestle disputants into agreements by using fair and transparent process. Just as a good lawyer might make any number of arguments to win his or her case, a good mediator had the ability to connect with the interests and needs of the parties in a conflict and present them with alternatives that they would agree to honor.

In this framework all of social life is a negotiated order, and self-interest is best served by engaging in negotiated problem solving with self-interested entities in an uncertain but interdependent world. Where I was interested in the strategies to create peace, Jim was intrigued by the mechanics. He believed that "sustaining and improving the relationship is as important as achieving a satisfactory substantive outcome in conflict."

Jim was well recognized as an expert in the structure and roles of conflicts, the linkage of social justice to conflict, and the ethics of conflict resolution. He was a strong advocate and effective networker. Jim's work was grounded in Christian values and a strong moral code of the servant leader. To Jim, conflict was a natural and inevitable part of all human life. Conflict was understandable, teachable, and necessary to causing justice and change. He believed these things and lived his life as an advocate, encouraging their advancement in the lives of others.

Jim would be the bridge to many who would come to support the concept of a national center for training and research in peace, justice, and conflict resolution. Jim's experiences and work in the civil rights movement would be the cement that drew then Congressman Andrew Young into the political leadership of our efforts. Andy and Jim both believed, as Jim would testify that day,

> "Achieving peace or resolving conflicts is a task at all levels of human social systems, not only the international level. Social conflict is a natural and inevitable part of all social life, and a major ongoing task of all social systems is making constructive use of conflict without either destroying the system or violating the rights of its members."

Together, Jim, Bryant, Andy and I would begin a journey to create what would become USIP. Bryant—*the psychiatrist*—would be the entrepreneur and conceptual strategist, building a movement that spanned the gaps. With experience in international relations and the personal psychology of change, Bryant would shape the vehicle we all drove.

Jim—*the professor*—was the consummate networker: structuring the deal and smoothing the inevitable wrinkles. He provided academic credentialing and legitimizing, and above all, inspired the spiritual underpinning for our heartfelt effort. Jim was a cheerleader for social justice and the civil rights movement.

Soon I would meet Andrew Young—ever *the pastor*. He was the humble civil rights rock star who would bring to our journey the spotlight necessary to attract a famed cadre of other outstanding Americans.

My job would become to hold the campaign together: build the organization, lobby the stakeholders, shape and deliver the narrative, and do the legwork. In short, as a close colleague would say, I became *the peddler* for peace.

The day was June 13, 1976. I had become Political Will.

Chapter 3 Review and Reflection

Task

- Know what you are doing.
- Do you know what you need to know to make the change you desire?
- How might you gain that knowledge?

Challenge

- Evaluate a dream against practical and attainable results.
- How will what you want to change be possible?
- Be clear on what is not possible.

Gift and Opportunity

- Find wisdom in curiosity; self-acceptance of your skills.
- Again, what will you contribute to the whole that is required to cause the change you want?
- What gifts do you need to discover in others?

Reflection

- What barriers must be overcome for you to make a sizable contribution?
- What motivates your search to act?
- What strengths do you have?
- What do you respect in others?

PART THREE

Growing a Campaign

CHAPTER 4

Farragut Square

Summer 1976 – Following the June hearing, I went back to Pittsburgh to think over the offer Bryant had made me to join him in DC. I was just a few classes into my goal of obtaining an advanced degree in international relations and I was torn about what I should do. I went for a walk with my friend Doug in Schenley Park that overlooks the neighborhoods surrounding Carnegie Mellon University and the University of Pittsburgh campuses. We took baseball gloves and a ball. Spring was almost turning to summer in the expansive acreage of the park. The fresh light green of budding tree leaves had matured into the robust foliage of summer. A warm breeze made the day very pleasant. Doug asked, "So, what are you going to do?"

I walked a bit farther before answering and then stopped to take the gloves and ball out of my backpack. "I think this is an opportunity I can't afford to miss. I can always go back to school if things don't work out. I just don't know." Doug backed away a few steps to create room for us to begin throwing the ball.

"What do you want?" Doug said. "I know how excited you are about your classes here. Do you think you can be taken seriously? I mean, that's the center of the universe for international relations. You plan on convincing all of those bureaucrats and politicians they ought to be doing their jobs in a different way?"

I caught and threw the ball a few times before responding to his question. "You know, this psychiatrist Bryant is the only person I know in DC. It's a pretty big risk. On the one hand, I can see that by fall I might be right back here at Pitt. On the other hand, if things go well, I will be right in the middle of causing change—or even moving the country toward a better understanding of peace." Back and forth we tossed.

I missed one of Doug's throws and had to jog off to chase the ball. The ball at first stuck in a clump of grass clippings, but then started to roll down the hill. It picked up speed and I followed.

The chase gave me a minute or two to reflect on my comment about *"moving the country." Really?* I repeated to myself out loud. *Really?* You need to get real and less heady my friend, I whispered to myself. My mind jumped around. Einstein had once said, "Politics are for the moment. An equation is for eternity." His image came to mind. Math was the act of finding a value. I now knew what I valued. Coffey had encouraged me to "seek to be the best in what could be"… that moment of introspection provided me my answer.

I turned back to my friend, "Doug, I think I have to go to DC."

I arrived in Washington, DC, about ten days later, just prior to the Bicentennial Celebration of the American Revolution that had begun to sweep the town. There was a palpable wave of patriotism and nostalgia. Fire hydrants and mailboxes around the area had been painted red, white, and blue. There was bunting everywhere and the new National Air and Space Museum was about to open on the National Mall. The Vietnam War and Watergate seemed far behind, as significant as they both had been. The entire country was poised to celebrate its two hundred years and the next phase of our nation's history.

On my first day in the city I felt like I was no longer the person I had been. It was as if one day I had decided to be someone else—and today was that day. I carried the wisdom of Dr Coffey and my dad: standing in *my own three-piece, gray pinstriped suit*; with my feet hurting in *my freshly polished black shoes*. Both recently acquired. I slowly turned around to take in all that was around me. I stood that moment almost in the exact center of Washington, DC: Farragut Square, on the corner of Connecticut Avenue and 16th Street, NW. The venerable Army and Navy Club stood to my right, as pigeons flew about and careening bicycle messengers cut through the paths of the park where I lingered. I was at long last in the District of Columbia: intimidated, feeling alone—in search of peace.

The hurry and scurry was disorienting as dark figures in business suits and speeding taxis headed by to important places. My head nearly spinning, I took deep breaths to get my bearings and stay grounded. As I gazed around, it appeared that powerful men and women were talking in quiet conversation, and homeless residents of the inner city were pushing a few grocery carts. Up and towering above me was the stoic statue of Admiral David Farragut, who famously said, "Damn the torpedoes, full speed ahead." It seemed a remarkable, and telling moment. The bronze Admiral stood no more than ten feet away, holding his telescope, urging me to do the same.

Seventeen blocks or so from the US Capitol and ten blocks from the White House, I was just eight blocks as the crow flies from what would in ten short years become the building site for the United States Institute of Peace. I tightly gripped the old, familiar leather briefcase from my Malibu days. From that spot I looked up at the rising perspective of glass and steel buildings lining Connecticut Avenue as it disappeared into my new horizon. This day, everything in Washington seemed to be about perspective. I was feeling an odd connection with the others I imagined had walked this same square in pursuit of their own personal cause or grail. In less than eight years the legislation that drove my career and ideals would become the law of the land.

Standing there, I believed that each person could cause change. What people needed were the motivation and the necessary tools. Kenneth Boulding said at a lecture at the University of Texas a year later,

> "The desperate necessities of the nuclear age are forcing us to take peace seriously
> as an object of both personal and national policy. Policy, however, requires a theory
> to sustain it. We cannot, for instance, have an unemployment policy without some
> kind of theory of unemployment."[40]

I felt I had a job to do. I had begun to understand pieces of the theory of peacemaking; now I needed to focus my efforts on leveraging a policy of peace through sustained ways to expand its theories and practice. This would mean stimulating a system to change itself. I knew that life systems, whether scientific or social, were capable of change. The next part of my journey would test that belief.

My greatest lesson would be in learning effective ways to address changing that system. Peace had always been controversial. War was a way to make money; it was a way for military officers to be promoted in the ranks. Peace was both a noble pursuit and a threat that made the establishment uneasy. It usually involves change. Small countries that had been colonized fought for their independence. Large countries that had dominated them, fought for their influence. Peace challenged our national perception of what we hold America to be. Was peace the freedom from civil disturbance or the liberty you fought for?

Following the war of independence our founding leaders wrote extensively about this concern. Americans honor peace as a concept, yet our national behavior manifests a culture of violence. That violence has taken the form of crime, war, domestic violence, school violence, workplace violence, or even the harsh edges of political discourse. We made the use of force and violence an acceptable state of our affairs. Now, in the midst of celebrating two hundred years of nationhood in 1976, different political ideologies and worldviews were questioning the meaning of peace. America was held up to be a great example of freedom, yet many within our sphere of influence were still caught in oppressive entanglements of poverty, discrimination, persecution or limited autonomy.

The concept of peace is applicable in all relationships, domestic, community and international. Peacefulness is the usual manner in which we conduct ourselves. As such, peace can be described as the harmony associated with the way mature personal and business relationships transpire, in loving, kind ways or with upright management, in good times or bad. In community terms, peace can be the orderly resolution of conflict and the means to overcome injustice.

International peace is most often viewed as the pursuit of alternatives to the use of force to manage tension, turmoil, conflict, and war. A culture that accepts violence diminishes the social importance of nonviolence and justice as hallmarks of our nation. To openly address the topic is akin to talking about race, poverty, or obesity in America. We don't like to hear about it. Any discussion tests our will to engage and act to right the wrongs. Most people I had previously known did not talk of peace as anything more than an ideal. Now in the campaign, I was to be surrounded by people who saw it as a process and a mechanism, an achievable goal.

The exercise to create political will – can be seen around us daily. At times it the actions of our elected leaders who seek to win over the people to support their goals. Other times it takes the form of efforts to foment revolution or rebellion. It is the individual act of one person who solely, and without hesitation, takes a stand, undertakes an action, or resolutely acts to nobly influence the thoughts and actions of others. Elements of a successful strategy to cause change can be defined and described. Among the strategies and tactics we utilized were macro-strategies that allowed us to make progress when otherwise we were stuck. I believe that when they are played out over time, the strategies themselves tend to filter out the good from the bad as agreement works its way through a social system. These strategies are described in Chapter 11.

I had come to DC to be a practitioner. Doing peace was more important than advocating for it, or so I thought. Jumping in to help Bryant with this experiment in urban conflict resolution had drawn me away from merely studying peace to actually trying to make a difference on the ground. Bryant and I met to discuss networking to test the interest in the Greater Washington DC Area for the creation of a community conciliation project. I was excited. Bryant was excited too, and we thought we could quickly get on with it. I found an office space with a shared secretary near the corner of K Street and Connecticut Avenue, just off Farragut Square. Bryant paid the rent and provided me a small stipend. I printed stationery and used Bryant's nonprofit organization, set up years before, as our sponsor. We proudly identified the initiative as a program of the Institute for the Study of National Behavior. It was called "Conflict Resolution of Inner-city Stress via Cross-cultural

Recognition Of Self-Interest," CRIS-CROS. It was a silly acronym, I know. But we both believed that through the merits of its design the program might make a positive difference in the city.

Washington DC had experienced riots in 1968 during a four day period of civic unrest. The riots were a direct result of the assassination of Dr King. The inner city communities where riots and looting occurred could still be seen upon my arrival six years later. Many neighborhoods would remain boarded up and in ruin for the next two decades.

The CRIS-CROS program was yet to be tested. The objective was to apply and refine a preemptive program of conflict resolution. The model was designed for urban communities to reduce and control the fragmentation of community structure, prevent crisis and violent conflict without suppressing the potential for social change. It worked by promoting communication across sub community boundaries and systematically utilizing third-party mediators to establish cooperative links based on mutual self-interests. The technical heart of the process—which Bryant had labeled intergroup intercession—was based on creating controlled environments with persons and groups whose interpretations of reality were at radical variance with each other.

Over our years together, I became much attuned to Bryant's intellectual gifts. His passions were people, psychiatry, and conflict resolution. He loved networking and excelled at putting things together. Bryant was constantly dropping cigarette ashes on my desk at our campaign headquarters as he leaned in to make a point, or absentmindedly became just too blunt when first meeting a potential contact or supporter. No doubt, his work as a psychiatrist conditioned him to apply the confronting style he conveyed and poignant realities that he observed. Bryant was anything but a diplomat. He relished sharing the insights of psychiatry and his relevant observations of interpersonal communication to cross-cultural communication and international relations. He carefully studied the nuances of how national perceptions developed and were conveyed within different national cultures—and how they influenced national behavior.

Bryant was first and foremost a medical doctor and psychoanalyst. He cared about healing and spent most of his life trying to pursue the art of healing, not just personal illness, but emotional instability, social tension, and conflict. We shared the desire to consider the larger system, setting, or arena for our applied practice. My memories of Bryant are of his most significant and scholarly writings from the late sixties and early seventies. Part of the excitement of Bryant was engaging him in a conversation on ideas. He affected people with the depth of his thought and exhibited an ability to inspire others. Bryant was a humanist. He put individual dignity at the center of his personal philosophy. He cared greatly about the rights of individuals and the responsibility of society to preserve, protect, and defend those rights.

Bryant believed in creating structures to help both individuals and countries deal with their problems. He once wrote, "When members of different nations establish and institutionalize programs of cooperation – these serve to act as linkages that have the effect of 'tying down Gulliver,' that is, of constraining gigantic forces with many small threads and connections that promote peace."[41] He felt there was a role for government to institutionally address the predictable misperceptions of disputants in international conflict. These were the giants he wanted to tie down.

Bryant was a free spirit. And he was an optimist. He looked for the very best in people and the situation at hand. He was always talking about creating, never focusing, always expanding the view, horizon, or thought. He often reminded me of the Maoist philosophy: a thousand flowers blooming. In my relationship with him, I found I had to develop good gardening skills to keep up with all of the flowers he planted!

In the fall of 1979 Bryant wrote the following in a letter to the editor of our little Campaign Update Newsletter of the National Peace Academy Campaign.

> "Obviously, the Peace Academy Campaign is not a mass movement, at least not yet. It seems incredible that so small a number of active participants have been able to achieve such positive and hopeful outcomes. I am reminded of Isaiah's observation that it is a "very small remnant" that embodies the hopes of mankind."

Delightfully, our working relationship was often punctuated by either of us introducing quotes into our conversations. Bryant was what I would call a conversational teacher. Bryant's Isaiah quote for example brought back to mind this insight from Einstein, who wrote:

> "Times such as ours have always bred defeatism and despair. But there remains, nevertheless, some few among us who believe that man has within him the capacity to meet and overcome even the greatest challenge of this time. If we want to avoid defeat, we must wish to know the truth and have courage, we need not despair."

Virtually all large changes in the course of history were started by a relatively small number of people. Bryant was indeed one of these people. In his own way Bryant was a Don Quixote. He saw the windmill and wanted others to charge it with him. Bryant had convinced me to be there with him for the challenge.

Someone in Pittsburgh had suggested the best way to find a place to live in DC was to go to local merchants, small grocery stores, and corner pharmacies to check what bulletin boards there listed available rooms for rent. On one of my trips to DC, I drove around looking for areas in which I might live. Georgetown, an upscale part of town, had really great tree-lined streets and three to four story townhouses. I parked my car and walked around, finding a corner store that indeed had a room-for-rent listing that sounded appealing. I made my way to a telephone booth and called to express my interest in the room and see if I could set up a visit. The owner was a delightful gentleman named Charles who worked for the Peace Corps. The building on 31st Street NW between O and P Streets was a four-story building with an adjacent vacant, lushly landscaped lot. It was just a couple of blocks from the Metro, had ample street parking, and was about three blocks from the virtual center of the Georgetown area.

Charles lived on the third floor, renting out the top floor as well as the first and second to other people. I would be the third renter. Charles gave me a tour and set up a time for me to meet the other tenants and I passed their inspection, moving in June 1976.

I rented the room in the house in part because the home was truly elegant and would make a good place for receptions and for entertaining guests related to campaign events and the like. I began having mini-receptions at the house on weekends or on weekday evenings. Bryant, Jim or others would mention the opportunity for discussion about the peace academy concept to interested people they encountered, and folks would show up. Groups of fifteen to twenty people might arrive for a few hours of discussion. I would share an overview of the peace academy concept in front of the fireplace or windows. Then ask folks why they were there and what was their interest. The discussions were informal; often quite lively, and a good way for me to meet a wide range of interested professionals in the area.

At one such Sunday gathering a man named Jack Dover introduced himself to the group at the beginning of the afternoon, but remained quiet for a good part of the event. When the discussion concluded, Jack hung back to say a word. He shared with me that he was Special Assistant to Assistant Attorney General Gilbert Pompa, the Director of the Justice Department's Community Relations Service. Gil had asked him to come check me out, after Jim had called on him. At the time, Gil was the highest-ranking Latino in the Carter Administration.

Jim worked for CRS between 1965 and 1969 and Gill and Jim had been friends since 1967.

Jack Dover and his spouse Agnes became close personal friends, and Jack has been an advisor, trusted sounding board and steadfast colleague since that first meeting in Charles' living room.

Bryant and I continually drafted elements of the CRIS-CROS model, and circulated it among community activists, dispute resolution people and possible funding sources. It was largely based on papers Bryant had written resulting from his experiences in analyzing the psychological aspects of conflicts, since his involvement as an Eisenhower Fellow. Much of Bryant's international research had been in the cause and effect of international conflict due to misperceptions in cultural communications. As early as 1963 Bryant was corresponding with scholars like Roger Fischer at the Law School at Harvard University. In 1981, with William Ury, Roger would later publish the classic conflict resolution book, *Getting to Yes*. Bryant was an early and inspiring player in the fields of cross-cultural communications and political psychology.

In 1977, Washington DC again experienced citywide conflict when thirty-five thousand protestors staged large-scale civil disobedience actions in protest over the war in Vietnam. Ten thousand federal troops moved into the city. Twelve hundred protestors were arrested, but most were released. Seventy-nine eventually were convicted. Memories of both of these events were still alive in 1975 when I first spoke with Bryant about conflict prevention techniques. One of the draws of coming to DC was to explore the possible benefits of a citizen mediation program that would be a rigorous, systematic method of facilitating communication, contact, and cooperation across social boundaries by neutral third parties. It would be a form of action research. Due to the recent history of violence and displacement in DC, both Bryant and I felt the city was a good place to test and document the model.

The problem was that the greater Washington community, like other major urban communities, was its rapidly changing physical and demographic characteristics. Administrative structures were not designed for, nor could they fully respond to the changing needs of the citizenry. The outcome was—and continues in many communities to this day – disenfranchised citizens. Ferguson, Missouri is a current example of this type of fragmentation. Community structures and relationships breakdown; frequently community services are competitive; local hostilities develop and street crimes flourish; neighborhoods are abandoned; loss of respect for authority develops quickly; and the integrity of a thriving urban fabric is threatened or completely lost. Bad people do not cause these dynamics. They are systemic situations that foster violence in response to unacceptable conditions. In developing countries these same dynamics and cycles often grow into civil wars or regional conflicts. Unresolved urban conflict can easily transform a community into the kindling of a greater firestorm.

Globally, situations like this had often been the fuel for the spark of intra-national unrest that escalated into urban warfare, regional hostility, and eventually international conflict when fanned by political agendas and border incursions. Studying conflict and its prevention in the urban setting was directly related to better understanding the cause and preventions of international conflict. CRIS-CROS was to be a learning platform and mechanism to impact these types of situations.

Conflict did not stop or begin with national borders, cross-ethnic or political ideologies, or regional natural resources. Conflicts within nations—including America—and between nations shared the same conflict resolution mechanisms and models of escalation and de-escalation.

Kenneth Boulding wrote,

> "The only guarantees of peace are compatible self-images . . .. A problem here . . . is that each party in a relationship tends to create the self-image of the other in a very complex, mutual learning process. To a distressing extent each party in a conflictual relationship is a creation of its enemies. In some degree Napoleon created Bismarck, Bismarck created Clemenceau, Clemenceau created Hitler, Hitler created the Pentagon, and Stalin created the CIA. Perhaps one reason for the biblical injunction to love our enemies is that they make us. One of the critical questions is, what can break this cycle?"[42]

As a clinical psychiatrist, Bryant witnessed values, ideologies, and goals being deeply expressed by people in one cultural context and then misinterpreted by other people in their own ethnocentric belief structures. Cultural values relating to saving face or questions of honor clouded communication between parties. We spent hours in Bryant's home and office discussing real world examples of how early intervention in conflict-prone areas might have prevented otherwise escalating and costly conflicts that were largely based solely on the gap between what was really being communicated and what was really being understood. In situation after situation we discussed how specific cultural interpretations of the same events had led to increased tension. When the parties acted or reacted based on their own ethnocentric interpretations, the situation often quickly escalated.

Our task was going to be to break down cycles of conflict and potential violence in parts of DC using trained mediators. We intended to grow local interest and support around the idea. Along the way, we planned to continue pursuing the follow-up agenda that was emerging from the hearings five weeks before. We started to talk to people; a lot of people.

I was fascinated with the behavioral aspects of our discussions. It was so very different from my studies at Pitt. The behavioral and psychological side of conflict had been missing for me. In Pittsburgh, although I had studied twenty-two ethnic groups and their beliefs in several countries, our class work not focused on the cross-cultural aspects of their communications as contributing to intergroup conflict. Bryant was introducing me not just to the politics of conflict, but also the psychological and cross-cultural aspects as well.

We put together a proposal to explore the feasibility of organizing a program of systemic urban conciliation in the greater Washington, DC, community. It included a feasibility phase, an organizational-consortium building phase, a pilot program phase, and finally proposed a full-scale operation phase where two hundred mediators would be trained and begin third party issue-free dialogue as a preventive process. The concept sought to reduce community tension by improving communication and cooperation on crisis-prone issues as they arose. Rather than wait for a predictable community crisis to erupt, the program would embed trained community third-party conciliation teams from the community, within the communities.

We immediately realized the program concept in its first draft was pretty awkward. Much of the descriptive language in it came out of a clinical, psychiatric model. We clearly had a lot of work to do in order to make the idea more easily understood. The mixture of psychiatric principles, urban conflict resolution, and international relations overtones was pretty hard to grasp. The program was "brain heavy," for lack of a different description. We had a lot of work to do in order to convert theories to something that could be understood, and implemented on the streets.

Moreover, we needed to seek funding, find urban situations to test the validity of the model, and identify methods to evaluate the effectiveness of the process. It was a push strategy, rather than a pull strategy. We had no invitation to enter the socio-political world of the greater Washington, DC, area. We were naively nowhere near being perceived as trusted and credible third parties. This would be a significant barrier. Even if the mechanics worked, the program would not. There was no legitimacy or proclivity to utilize a new social conflict prevention mechanism without first some preconceived notion that it was acceptable. We were quickly learning that even though we had a product that worked, the marketplace was not ready for it without the validation by a higher authority.

I agreed I would write up the concept as a leave-behind and we planned to present it to interested parties around town. Soon, however, everything changed. We began making the rounds to explain our ideas to perceived stakeholders such as the American Arbitration Association, Department of Justice, and others; the peace academy notion kept stirring up more interest than our proposed CRIS-CROS program.

Bryant and I talked about creating a campaign to refocus on the subject of a national peace academy. I wrote Bryant an early draft of what would become our primary NPAC strategy. Even from the very beginnings of the campaign, Bryant and I often experienced a healthy tension between large vision and practical steps for shorter-term gains. Bryant was a bit like a racehorse approaching the starting gate. He wanted to jump ahead, execute the plan before it was formulated, a type of shoot-ready-aim catalytic leader. We would eventually fall short of implementing his vision for CRIS-CROS, but he resurrected it at George Mason University on a different scale. Some considered Bryant's tangential efforts to be a distraction to the campaign, but for Bryant, delays in the legislative process caused him to find ways to push out his big vision and avoid the tedium of focused, practical groundwork to gain passage and appropriations for the commission. Bryant encouraged individuals to pursue as many initiatives as possible. When many of us in the campaign would be focused on a clear strategy and set of tactics, Bryant would come up with a tangential crusade that usually resulted in positive progress, but used campaign resources to chase, contain, reframe, or support. I both loved and was irritated by this side of Bryant. However, the rebel in Bryant was what had drawn me to him in the first place. We would talk through our differences of approach, and then amicably go about pursuing the tactics that suited us individually. In some ways it was humorous; in other ways it was not as effective as it might have been.

♜ ♝ ♞

Jim, in the meantime, was exploring similar themes at his Center for Metropolitan Studies at the University of Missouri–St. Louis, by examining ways to assist cities with the development of conflict resolution processes and mechanisms. Jim and others were active in programs like the Negotiated Investment Strategy, NIS, an experimental approach to intergovernmental relations in Gary, Indiana, St. Paul, Minnesota, and Columbus, Ohio. Each of these efforts sought better means to improve the responsiveness to local needs and to work for better coordination of federal policies and programs. Many of the principles gained from the NIS program would be applied to regional development strategies in conflict areas of the world as a means to offset unrest and violence.

The NIS developed comprehensive investment strategies in a local area to guide negotiations concerning policy decision and program choices. It was assumed that there would be less new monies to go around and those local urban stakeholders competed rather than cooperated to obtain money. Resource providers became an intergovernmental system of bargaining agents, each vying for community stakeholders with often competing interests. NIS became an important model for how public policy could preemptively manage urban disputes. Years later this academic topic became relevant to how regions of many developing nations could benefit from similar principles in collaborative problem solving across a variety of topics. Inner state agencies and activists were encouraged to collaborate rather than compete.

Jim came from a place of seeing conflict as a natural and inevitable part of all human life. He had participated in and studied the biracial lunch counter sit-ins in one hundred fifty southern cities in the fight to desegregate public facilities. He interviewed more than his share of the seven thousand Americans who had been willing to go to jail for participating in the civil rights protests, boycotts, and marches. Jim was a conflict analyst.

He loved diagramming conflicts and understanding the source of conflicts and the directions they might take. He had a knack for and academic interest in selecting goals for intervention and systematically developing strategies and skills for pursuing those goals. Jim was convinced of the importance of focusing on power as the central reality around which social conflict occurs. He saw power imbalances and perceived power imbalances leading to injustice, as the basic underlying cause of social conflict situations. He felt that power was the goal of parties in conflict, either to maintain it, to take it away from the opponent, or to gain more. Jim felt power could be defined as the ability to control or influence decisions about the allocation of resources in a social system. It was on these points that Jim and Andy had agreed when they first met. David Hawkins, more than a half-century later, shared many of these same thoughts.[43]

Jim was proud that our efforts in NPAC had gone further than at any other point in American history. From his vantage point as a sociologist he was witnessing change occur across the country in the language and practice of professional organizations, law firms, and the social policy work of religious organizations. He was excited about what he was beginning to see around the country. People were beginning to act differently around conflict, because of the expectations we were helping to set. Conflict was inevitable, and there were processes to work through it. One could always count on Jim to be quick to sketch diagrams about roles, phases, and the necessary skills to have an effective impact on conflict situations. He was a cheerleader, teacher, and recognized expert, and that combination built confidence in others that the campaign and our efforts to create a national peace academy would be successful.

Jim was a ceaseless networker. In a given week he would be in town, out of town, at a conference, or putting people together to carry on our work. He would call and say, "I've asked so and so to get in touch with you. How are you doing? What do you need? Can you do this or that? Got to run." But under Jim's enthusiasm and affinity for connecting people was a deep regard and understanding of the essence of what we were trying to do.

He wrote a revealing personal postscript in his book *Direct Action and Desegregation, 1960–1962*. In it he says,

> "My adult "career" (more a vocation, to be sure) has carried me from a small minority-less Wisconsin town to activism in a clear-cut moral cause, to analysis and development as a scholar, to work as a third party claiming to help resolve

important social and racial conflicts. My participation in the civil rights movement clearly was the most important formative influence. The moral questions were clear. The people (at least the good guys) were attractive and committed. The combination of risk and incredible leaps in learning was irresistible . . .. So my own odyssey has been one of pushing the edges to advance social justice. The activist background prepared me—as it did a surprisingly large group of my mediator colleagues—to understand power and powerlessness in the pursuit of constructive change through mediation."[44]

Jim came into DC for a strategy session and he and I met with Bryant in a conference room at my K Street office in the summer of 1976. We debriefed the George Washington Peace Academy Act hearings that had been held in May. Together we decided to pursue a strategy of seeking the approval of Congress to establish a federal commission to deliberate on the idea and design of a national peace academy. At the hearings, Senator Claiborne Pell of Rhode Island had suggested that supporters of the idea might do well to "try to get the nose of the camel under the tent" by working to first introduce the idea to Congress via the commission concept. Later, efforts could be continued to seek a larger mandate and implement either a Department of Peace or some other federal institution to pursue our goals.

The camel's nose is a metaphor for a situation where permitting some small, modest action or query can soon grow to a broader situation. The phrase comes from an Arab fable where a begging camel receives permission to insert his nose under the nomad's desert tent. By 1878, the expression was so familiar that part of the story could be left unstated. It meant the humble petition of the camel, which only asks that he may put his nose into the traveler's tent, is so pitiful, so modest, that we must relent and grant its wish. Of course, once the nose was securely in place, the hump, feet, and tail were sure to follow. That fable and Senator Pell's suggestion became the central strategy of our efforts to help Americans see peace in a different way.

Bryant, Jim, and I talked about adding a member of Congress to the leadership of the campaign. Jim valued his past working relationship with Congressman Andrew Young from Georgia. Andy was not only a practitioner; he had come out in support of Jimmy Carter early in the Presidential campaign. Jim had shared with me the closeness he felt to Andy. Later Jim wrote:

> "As Andy Young, one of my mentors and heroes in the movement of the 1960s, sadly in response to my question about what he thought of northern Whites who came down to get involved in the movement: 'It's fine. Once you get shot at in a foxhole down here, you get religion—and you never lose it.'"[45]

"Getting religion" was a phrase often to describe the particular variety of holding the principles of the Civil Rights Movement close to your heart and practice. It also underlined for Andy the importance of the Christian faith in the pursuit of movement objectives. Andy was saying to Jim, you were in the foxholes with me and got shot at. You got religion.

All three men were thoughtful practitioners, each from different disciplines. Whereas many of the citizen groups previously advocating for national legislation to create a Department of Peace, peace academy or peace institute of the leaders of earlier campaigns were individuals working in the peace field. The new NPAC leadership was not from any particular peace group. They came more from the practice of dispute resolution and the shared belief that American international relations would benefit from the core skills and experience of conflict resolution techniques originating out of the internal American history of disputes involving race, environmental concerns, or labor management relations.

Jim was skilled in the more technical aspect of conflict intervention and had contacts in the dispute resolution community. Jim expanded the list of folks he wanted me to meet. At Jim's suggestion, I also dropped by the Capitol Hill office of Representative Young. In those days, one could go and come from the Senate and House offices by only presenting a driver's license and moving through a metal detector. Staff merely showed their badges and foot traffic moved very quickly in and out of any variety of doors. It was possible to walk underground between the Senate and House using a tunnel.

Soon, a young woman from the Congressman's office appeared and came over to greet me. She was Constance Grice, one of several legislative assistants who worked for Andy Young.

Connie was aware of the past relationship between Laue and Andy. She had originally met Andy as a result of working in Volunteers in Service to America, VISTA, in the Mechanicsville area of Atlanta, where Andy was a community organizer. As a VISTA member, Connie had signed up after graduating from Penn to serve full-time for a year at a nonprofit organization or local government agency, working to fight illiteracy, improve health services, and encourage the development of small businesses. VISTA was founded by Congress in 1965 as a national service program designed specifically to fight poverty. It was the domestic version of the Peace Corps, created by Congress a few years earlier in 1960. The program was incorporated into AmeriCorps network of programs in 1993. Connie had fulfilled her contractual obligations to VISTA and had stayed on doing community organizing with Andy and others. When Andy chose to run for political office, Connie became active as a volunteer in his campaign. Following his election to Congress, Andy asked Connie to come to Washington with him to be a legislative aide. Jim suggested I go to the Hill and call on Connie. We might never have met were it not for Jim.

I wouldn't say that in our first meeting we really hit it off, as I was just another lobbyist coming through the door to advocate for another cause. I was surprised, however, that Connie said Andy would be happy to support the legislation and even work to gather co-sponsors for the concept. This development was fantastic.

On a subsequent visit to the Congressional office, I sat with Connie to review possible co-sponsors. She assured me she thought Andy had some in mind and that he would soon be writing what was then called a Dear Colleague letter to request co-sponsorship among other members of the House of Representatives. At some point in one of our meetings, Connie said, "Hey, Andy is here today; would you like to meet him?" I remember that first meeting very well.

Andy was cool. He was soft-spoken and, in his Southern way, gracious in his greeting and demeanor. At the same time, Andy came across to me as a man "in his head," clearly thinking about the next subject, task or event. I asked him how he had time to study all of the legislation that came before him and he replied that it was difficult. He said he often found it necessary to vote on the floor based on how other like-minded colleagues had voted. Sometimes, his closely aligned, like-minded Congressional colleagues voted as he did when they were less familiar with the legislation than Andy. Upon our first meeting we spoke about Jim Laue and about the nature of their relationship back in the movement days. It was obvious there was great respect there.

Having met with several other Congressional Representatives and their staff, it soon became apparent how important the relationship with Andy would become. Andy was born in New Orleans on March 12, 1932, eighteen years my senior. Our birthdays were one day apart and we had both been biology majors in college. I liked Andy immediately that day in his office. Andy eventually did the legislative heavy lifting in the House. He inspired others in the House to support our legislation. He reinvented the legislative momentum in the House that had been born in the 1960s, following the actions in the Senate from the 1950s.

In our first visit, Andy asked me if there were any Blacks on my staff. I said "No," and then added, "Mr Congressman, it's just me, at this point." We laughed, but I remember his seriousness in asking the question. One day in passing three years into the campaign, Andy again asked me that question. I was only able to provide him the same answer, "No," except this time we did not laugh. I said I would take steps to remedy the situation. In the commission hiring process it became important for me to see that we hired a diverse staff and we did. The commission staff was composed of sixty-five percent women professionals and one-third minority professionals.

During the first two years of the campaign, Andy was generous with his time. Connie played a big role in that. When he became Ambassador in 1977, his demeanor did not change. Andy was accessible and helpful. It meant a lot to me personally that he encouraged our efforts, even after joining Carter's cabinet.

Bryant had a common touch; Jim an engaging enthusiasm; and Andy a thoughtful aloofness that was magnetic. It became apparent, as the campaign came together that it would be fueled by distinct contributions from each of us. Bryant had really started the campaign and formed NPAC into a movement. He was an entrepreneur and conceptual strategist. In some ways Bryant had "bought the car" in which we would travel to our goal. He was fifty-five years old at the beginning of the campaign. Jim was the activist and social scientist who "oiled the machine" through his networking, optimism, enthusiasm, and credentials. He had brought Andy into the campaign and Jim later would drive the commission. He smoothed the way for the ride. Jim was thirty-nine at the beginning of the campaign. Andy brought legislative positioning and visibility, integrity and progressive values. He carried the moral authority to add legitimacy to our effort and he reinvented the House ownership of the legislation. He attracted the eminent people as sponsors to the campaign. Andy "provided the wheels" to the campaign. Andy was forty-four at the beginning of the campaign. My task was to hold the campaign together. I built an organization and showed up every day to carry the water. I served as the hub. I connected the pieces and did the leg work that needed doing. I tried as best I could to pull things together, acting like an engine. But more practically I "drove the car" much like a chauffeur, who listens intently to the more experienced riders in the vehicle. Bryant, Jim and Andy were navigators. I tried to keep us on the road, and asked others to climb on for the ride. I was twenty-six years old at the beginning of the campaign.

♖ ♗ ♞

The Vietnam War challenged Americans to think differently about the problem of warfare. The notion of a "good war" had died. The failure of public debate on issues of war and peace prior to the escalation of the war raised mass consciousness toward moving to prevent warfare as an acceptable mode of social behavior. The costs of the Vietnam War, in terms of human and natural resources, and the disproportionate national expenditures on defense as opposed to institutional methods of preventing war, all combined to force Congress to reconsider seeking peace.

In addition to my initial work on CRIS-CROS and NPAC, I began to spend a good deal of my time each day tracking down those who had been active in former efforts to create a peace institute, peace academy, or Department of Peace. The common theme of these previous movements had been to create a framework dedicating the Federal government to expanding its skills, presence, and advocacy for alternatives to force in addressing international and domestic conflict. As it turned out, there were hundreds of identifiable individuals who had played a role or been supporters of citizen and legislative leaders trying to do just that. The trick was to find them. Bryant had identified many of these people and we asked them to be an ad hoc committee for the National Peace Academy Bill. There were thirteen on Bryant's initial list.

In 1969, the Peace Advisory Action Council, PAAC, was organized among twenty-six private associations brought together by Congressman Halpern, (R-NY) and his Congressional aide John Mathews. The Council's functions were stated as sponsoring a searching examination of the implications of the Peace Act Bills and informing the public about the bills and their implications. Some of the individuals on Bryant's early ad hoc lists had been involved in previous efforts to create a Department of Peace or Peace Institute. Senators Hartke and Hatfield and Representatives Halpern and Henry Reuss sent out letters to more than three hundred organizations in 1969. More than seventy-five organizations responded immediately. PAAC was successful in gathering an impressive number of prominent Americans who agreed to be sponsors. Church organizations and publications, newspaper editorial boards, and radio and television personalities were recruited to take a stand on the issue. Drawing support from Johnny Carson, actors like Dick Van Dyke, Bess Myerson, Joanne Woodward, and Barbara Rush plugged the legislation on guest appearances on the *Tonight Show*. The actress Donna Reed served as the Co-Chairwoman of Another Mother for Peace, an advocacy group that campaigned mightily for a Department of Peace. Pamphlets were written and distributed. Groups such as the World Federalists, Concerned Clergy and Laymen, the International League for Peace and Justice, and Women's Strike for Peace sent representatives to Washington to lobby for legislation. The Friends Committee on National legislation and the Board of Church and Society of the United Methodist Church lent support to all of these activities through their national offices and experienced lobbyists. Halpern retired from Congress in 1972, but the momentum continued.

PAAC was formally incorporated as The Council for a Department of Peace (CODEP) in 1971. The leaders of CODEP had worked to promote the Congressional bills that had been introduced in 1969 and other bills. In 1973, CODEP held its first conference of specialists to consider the bills for a Department of Peace and a National Academy of Peace. One hundred and fifty participants attended. Other conferences and newsletters held the supporters together. CODEP's newsletter, *PAX*, was sent out to ten thousand people. Public awareness and lobbying efforts focused on the upcoming Presidential election in 1976 and the American Revolutionary Bicentennial. During this same period a California couple named Dan and Rose Lucy were actively pursuing the peace academy concept. Their Committee for a national Peace Academy was an early affiliate of CODEP. I spoke to the Lucy's in California, CODEP's Mary Liebman in Chicago, and Florence Block in Connecticut about their experiences, later traveling in the spring of 1977 to meet with each of them. We built NPAC's citizen support on the platform of these contacts.

Senators Hartke and Matsunaga introduced legislation for a Department of Peace in 1973, similar in nature to the ones that Senator Jennings Randolph had been introducing since the mid-1940s. Part of the new bill suggested that a joint Congressional committee, known as the Joint Committee on Peace and International Cooperation, be formed with seven members from both houses to make a continuing study of matters relating to the Department of Peace.

The Hartke bill that had been the focus of the May 13, 1976, hearing was a culmination of much of Randolph's work. Hartke's aide Steve Cloud worked diligently to forge the alliances and craft the hearings that produced the first significant public hearing in US history on the subject.

Some of the individuals who testified in the May hearings would become members of the first NPAC Steering Committee. But more importantly, the new leaders of the movement were all proficient and connected activists in the behavioral expertise of causing change: change in civil rights, change in urban policy, change in international perceptions, change in using nonviolence as an alternative to force.

The nexus of these earlier groups was a shared desire for peace. Their competencies were as humanists, religious people, and scholars who had studied alternative outcomes to wars and social conflict, but who were less experienced in the emerging practice of conflict resolution. All were well-intended advocates, but the evolution of the field of dispute resolution had not yet developed a new wave of skilled practitioners that would give the practice of peace-seeking, peacemaking, and peace-building the necessary expertise to make a stronger argument for a national training academy.

At the time of the May 1976 hearings, Senator Vance Hartke was the primary Senate sponsor of the legislation. However, he was engaged in a reelection campaign that he would eventually lose. His staff legislative aide, Steve Cloud, assured us of the Senator's continuing support, but let us know that Senator Hartke would need to be focused on his reelection campaign in the coming months. We had to look for a new principal supporter of the idea.

We began by listing all of the contacts we had in our networks that might be interested or useful. Names were floated from the disciplines of international relations, mediation, and conflict resolution practitioners, academics, members of Congress and other currently serving government officials, religious organizations, businessmen and women, professional associations, possible funding sources, etc. All of us began to work the lists and the communication and contact information began to flow through me.

The initial list developed had thirteen names. I agreed to serve as Campaign Coordinator. As became our practice throughout the campaign, we created a list of resources and then worked to make the most out of whatever we had. Soon the list included forty-three names. We did this over and over again, like taking attendance at grade school. Who were our assets and where could they be plugged in to make a difference? Bryant, Jim and Andy all had thoughts and contacts they wanted me to pursue. It might be dropping by a Congressional staff office; drafting talking points or a newsletter; visiting an government agency; speaking to a small gathering of potential supports; calling on someone from the movement days or a journalist. Andy focused on members; Connie concentrated on Congressional staff; Jim directed his networks toward our efforts; and Bryant kept churning out ideas, finding contributions and recruiting human resources.

Even before the hearings on the George Washington Peace Academy Act, Bryant had created an informal group named the Ad Hoc Committee for a National Peace Academy, a letterhead, and a brochure. This was before I arrived on the scene. Bryant had a career pattern of writing up a list; creating a letterhead; and publishing a brochure describing the activity he was engage in. This served to make whatever cause suddenly seem real and tangible. Forty years later, it may seem trivial, but the early list of individuals who lent their names, modest financial support and reputations to the cause *was* the campaign. Each of those individuals, who were inspired by Bryant, stood with him to ask history to be kind to his ideas.

Early on a pattern was emerging that a few individuals, whose continual participation and contribution helped to steady the course of the campaign and the commission, were the real leaders and strongest advocates for the cause. Other individuals on the list were people such as our printer, accountant, neighbors, former colleagues, or concerned acquaintances who had some connection or somehow touched the campaign. I printed up more brochures and expanded the members of an initial Steering and Advisory Committee. I had an IBM Selectric typewriter that I had purchased when I left Malibu and I began showing up at work every day in my rented office space, working with a part-time secretary, Beverly Orr whom we paid by the hour for clerical services.

Jim, Bryant, and I discussed some of the essential elements necessary to give a national peace academy both grounding and wings. We would revisit these conversations often during the life of the campaign and the work of the commission. Jim emphasized the inseparability of peace from conflict resolution, peace from justice and the related issue of social change toward justice. Jim was adamant that the academy must focus on conflict resolution and the related issues of power imbalances and social justice. Otherwise, for Jim, peace had little operational meaning. It must deal with conflict and change processes at the community, national, and international levels and have a heavy emphasis on the techniques of creating peace. Bryant and Jim were keen on experiential learning, including apprenticeships, in addition to more traditional scholarly approaches to discovering and disseminating knowledge. Andy brought in the wide variety of experiences and veterans from the Civil Rights movement.

We talked about the importance of federal involvement—Bryant bringing his experience with State and intelligence communities—and Jim his experience with the intervention of the Federal government in civil rights issues. The drawbacks of federal involvement were related to how to ensure autonomy and integrity by building a strong, pluralistic base of institutional support. We sorted through alternative structures and organizational models and agreed to use the commission process to identify the best option. Bryant emphasized the importance of focusing on international communication and culture and the signals, messaging, and frameworks that negatively define stereotypes and the images nations have of one another.

Next to the grounding and experienced-based advantage of having three proven practitioners serving as national leaders for our campaign, the decision to seek a commission rather than a full-blown peace academy or Department of Peace was strategic. We followed Senator Pell's advice and focused on the camel's nose initially to make it a proposition that would be acceptable for the Congress and Executive Branch. In the end, this worked.

I got in touch with Pell's Senate aide, Cary Peck, to pursue the strategy. The major players in the Senate would become Senators Hatfield, Randolph, Pell, and Matsunaga. Hartke was defeated in his 1976 Senate campaign by then Indianapolis Mayor Richard Lugar. It was not immediately clear which Senator was going to step up as the lead sponsor for our bills. In the House, it would be Andy. The momentum that Senator Hartke and his aide Steve Cloud created became an important cornerstone. I later asked Steve to serve as a consultant to the commission, to conduct the research on models of alternative institutional frameworks that would be appropriate for a new institution.

Bryant and Jim also were acquainted with Robert Coulson, the President of the American Arbitration Association, AAA. Coulson, in turn, introduced me to the Washington director of AAA's Community Dispute Services, a man named Tom Colosi. I began conversations with Tom, as I did with Bill Lincoln in Boston, the New England head of AAA's Community Dispute Services. During this time, I continued to consult Jack Dover and Gil Pompa at Justice. It is important to note here that my talks with Bob, Tom, Bill, Jack and Gil regarding the development potential for CRIS-CROS, slipped into ways to advance the peace academy idea. Soon these men all became influential supporters of the national peace academy idea.

My usual weekly campaign strategy notes to Bryant, Jim, and Andy, would begin with, "Two things seem most important at this time in the campaign: first, Doing all that we can to ensure that the amendment be passed and the commission established; and second, securing the seed funds to provide a financial base to continue the campaign." Then I would detail the progress in each area. Later, I would produce a more detailed and seasoned campaign plan once we recruited staff and moved into larger offices. However, our organizational dashboard was primarily set by what the legislation was doing, and identifying NPAC supporters in the right places to further that goal. Fundraising took a backseat to the progress of the legislation at any point in time. Gradually my singular staff megaphone became more of a choir and I took on more management duties of the expanding NPAC staff. Soon we were up to seven staff. We stayed close to our Congressional leaders and their staffs. Fundraising accelerated after the commission released our report.

We found that individual NPAC members needed to be instructed as to what they could do to help with the passage of the legislation. Our NPAC office regularly produced a single sheet of instructions that could be mass circulated or sent to appropriate organizations to be included in existing newsletters, seminar program packets, and the like. For example: we might suggest the cost for offset printing would be fifteen dollars for a thousand one-sided copies. This instructional sheet might even include a sample letter that could be duplicated by each individual organization and mailed. People were invited to do whatever they thought they could within their means.

Keeping the legislation moving through Congress was critical to the momentum of the campaign. Often I would tell Bryant, "What is important is not to neglect our short-range needs in favor of longer-range visions and goals. We need to pass the commission legislation. In order to do this, we need visibility and moderate funding. It is imperative that we stay focused on that task and that the energies of the campaign be organized and directed toward reaching these immediate goals."

It seemed like every day of the campaign found tension between just holding our small team together and reaching for the stars. The campaign was challenged by supporters and NPAC members to take on tasks or initiatives that were tangential to our main focus. Part of our success as a campaign was tied to our singular mission. It harkened back to what Dr Coffey had chided me to do – learn to focus.

We began speaking to association groups, churches, business organizations, members of Congress and their staffs, faculty, and students on college campuses, and any groups that we could easily contact. Our message was simple and had four parts:

First, **_education:_** We began every meeting, coffee, speech, or briefing with a historical overview of past efforts to establish an intuitional and intentional bias at the federal level to impact on how Americans manage conflict. With each group or member, we would emphasize a meaningful context, current event, local reference point, or connection to the underpinning of his or her special interest. Perhaps the person or group we were addressing had environmental or business values, spiritual connections or constituent-led interests.

Second, we would ***describe the possible shape and function of a new institution.*** The concept of the national peace academy might include the establishment of a federally chartered corporation that would conduct programs of education and research in the fields of peacemaking and conflict resolution at international, national, and community levels. Such an institution would research the state-of-the-art of the theory and practice of conflict resolution, support existing programs in the field, develop public education materials, and train professionals and private citizens toward the goal of reducing violence and promoting constructive relationships internationally, within the United States and in its communities and institutions. We helped people see just what the institution would look like. Seeing was believing.

The third the topic was always ***legislative advocacy***: We informed our target audience of the status of any legislative action currently in play and the relevance of the position or leadership that their elected representatives were taking. We explored the connections and opportunities for advocacy that our target group had or could be inspired to have. After our initial success in getting traction with the commission idea, we explained what the commission would do. The commission would be charged with conducting an investigation to determine whether to establish a United States Academy of Peace and Conflict Resolution; the size, cost, and location of such an academy; the effects of an academy on existing institutions of higher education; alternatives to the establishment of an academy, such as grants to existing programs, and alternative proposals which would assist the federal government in accomplishing the goal of promoting peace at both the international level and in the communities and institutions of the United States. We would ask for the ideas and thoughts of those we spoke with and, if in a group setting, we would often break down the audience into small groups for reflection and brainstorming.

We would end the third part of our pitch with an invitation to get involved and support the current legislation. Sometimes the legislation in play was in the House or Senate in one of four committees: international relations, foreign affairs, education and labor, or human relations. So the targeted members were changing quite frequently, and this meant different states, Congressional districts and regions of the country were in play. As bills moved through the Senate and House different states became the focus, causing the campaign to direct citizens in those states, or districts to voice their support to each relevant staff in local offices, in addition to members themselves, and their staff located in Washington, DC. It was always best to make contact at the most local level. It was equally important to build relationships with committee staffs, those more professional and senior Congressional staffers, who did the work of the Congressional committees on which the Senators and House members served. Committee staff members provide the continuity for the work of Congress between election cycles. The most successful strategies were focused on getting staff members to talk to other staff members, building on the internal trust that is shared within Congressional offices.

And finally fourth, ***Action:*** Every session we held involved an "ask" for the person or group to become involved in whatever way they might feel comfortable. For example, in a law firm: we might ask for help with pro bono support incorporating campaign entities or studying possible legal frameworks for a new institution. We would also solicit financial contributions and ask that those gathered reach out to their friends and colleagues. In a church or temple setting, we would ask if there was a newsletter or meeting coming up that might feature a blurb about NPAC and the legislation? In some churches, a special Sunday collection was arranged. On quite a few occasions we were asked to provide a sermon or evening program at a church. We asked for people to volunteer and help with mailings and phone bank calls.

In most cities there were a few people who had been advocates in one way or another over the years. They served as hosts and advisors, and provided introductions to local elected officials and organizations in which they were members. We stayed with them when traveling. They also helped at the most basic level to keep the campaign alive financially. Early on, supporters who were already in the campaign drew other people to NPAC because of the strength of the idea; or attracted new supporters through direct mail; arm-twisting by Bryant; referral by Jim, or other forms of introduction, such as by a blurb in the newsletter of a supportive organization. My role was to garner new supportive organizations and to match up supporters with what we needed at the time. Very slowly, our campaign began to get traction, but we faced many stops and starts, always having to check the mail to hopefully deposit a welcomed check for five or twenty-five dollars.

Day-to-day what I personally did was to keep up relationships with the key staff of Congressional sponsors and the members themselves. I sought funds to keep our efforts alive, to focus on whatever legislative bills were in play, and to rally the NPAC membership to influence their Congressional Representatives and Senators. All available time was dedicated to growing our campaign base and advancing the national peace academy concept with conflict resolution practitioners, peace researchers, and citizens in related interest areas. Much of my time was spent networking and targeting the NPAC staff to connect with the NPAC members.

At times I felt like a backhoe operator, working the levers to groom the hillside or fill in a hole. I saw a need and recruited a supporter to take some action, write a letter, or make a call. If you are going to take on a project and seek the political will to inspire it, prepare to roll up your sleeves. You will be doing it all, from collating reports to calling Congressman. Norwegian playwright Henrik Ibsen wrote: "You should never wear your best trousers when you go out to fight for freedom and truth."[46] Our goals were not as heady, but we were in the trenches and struggled to maintain a tight message; overcome resistance and avoid getting our pants dirty.

I cold-called and visited potential leads we might be able to leverage into an action that would advance the legislation. We felt the national peace academy would benefit a lot of sister causes, and believed that the campaign, and a future institution, might act as mortar to further support the "bricks" of the issues of kindred causes. From the start, Bryant was clear that NPAC could best survive and accomplish its goal if it remained a single-issue campaign, committed to close its doors once our objective was achieved. On this Bryant and I agreed. We limited and defended the use of our mailing list. We repelled friendly attempts to ask our supporters to do work on related concerns or agendas. That singular focus made a difference in the end, although throughout much of the campaign It was difficult to turn down individuals and organizations working on important topics.

I wrote testimony for people and encouraged others to draft letters to the editor or write to their Congressperson. I met weekly with Congressional aides and kept their members informed on current talking points about the peace academy concept and its benefits to the country. I tried to tie our messaging to local and national events that would have meaning to each Congressional office. I coached NPAC members in one district about an approach and message that I felt would get that member's attention; and coached a different supporter in a different district on a different narrative based on the local situation. We grew our membership from dozens to many thousands and began to establish greater visibility and legitimacy by creating advisory councils, steering committees, and finally an incredible cadre of prestigious individuals with name and value recognition. Writing and disseminating talking points with common themes and language was essential.

Part of my responsibility was to write issue papers that presented the case for the national peace academy in whatever context it was being presented. Almost every document we produced was educational, advocating, and actionable. We usually emphasized the linkage between the desired state of peace and the means to achieve it. The messaging went something like this: Many ways exist to resolve conflict, but effective conflict resolution that promotes peace is achieved when disputants jointly determine the outcome of their dispute through a negotiated procedure. A third-party intervener may help to facilitate the process. This method of conflict resolution allows constructive change without resorting to violence. It is self-enforcing because it is in the interests of all parties to maintain the agreement.

In one of our early campaign plenary meetings in Alexandria a man named Nachman Gerber appeared. Mr Gerber went by the nickname of Nacky, and he was one of a kind. He was a parking lot owner – lots of parking lots – in Harrisburg, Pennsylvania. He lived outside of Baltimore, Maryland. He had registered his own nonprofit called Peacefully Yours, Inc., and was an example of a generous citizen who acted on his own to do something about peace. Over the years, Nacky provided most of the office furniture, supplies, and in-kind contributions that allowed NPAC to flourish. Without Nacky, the infrastructure of the campaign would have taken too long to build and its usefulness might not have been sustained. I once got a call from Nacky to meet me at our offices on a Sunday morning at 7:00 AM. I arrived a few minutes early and from around the corner came a forty-foot truck filled with desks, chairs, file drawers, office lamps and three men to unload it.

In the next eight years, we pretty much followed the simple outline of my campaign memo, adjusting our priorities when the current legislative initiative was in play and seeking funds as needed to keep our efforts going. It was never our intent to have the campaign be a long-term sustainable venture, but rather to roll over our efforts into a new institution.

After seeing Connie each week to brief her on campaign developments and seek Andy's legislative help, she invited me to drop by a Congressional staff softball game one evening on the National Mall. I was delighted by the invitation and joined the team members at a local bar following the game for pinball and laughs. I really liked the people and felt welcomed by their sense of doing good for the common cause and shared their sense of high commitment for important issues and initiatives. In the coming months this collection of Congressional aides would become the key to our legislative strategy.

Through Connie, this group of friends grew in numbers to include a wide circle of friends who worked for not only Congress, but served as staff in the White House, law firms, HEW, Department of Transportation, journalists, advocacy groups in Veterans Affairs, and other government agencies. One of the delights of living in Washington was the interaction of young people who had come to DC from all parts of the country. Evening baseball games were scheduled on all parts of the open areas adjacent to the National Mall and were played with coed teams, colorful T-shirt uniforms, the requisite beer coolers, and a great deal of fun, mellow companionship. They were surely responsible for many a marriage. Eventually, I was invited to a beach house in Lewes, Delaware, that several of the friends, including Connie, shared.

It was the early summer of 1976 and bicentennial events were beginning to occur in DC and around the country. The national Presidential election was beginning to come together, as Jimmy Carter of Georgia had accumulated enough delegates in the Democratic Party primaries to go into the Convention as the assured candidate. In his first campaign for the White House, President Ford was having to deal with a sluggish economy and was experiencing criticism about his pardon of President Nixon. Carter ran as a Washington outsider and reformer, and eventually won a narrow victory.

On one of my many visits to Bryant's home in Alexandria, VA, he walked me down the street to the former residence of President Ford. Bryant liked to recount the times that both he and then Representative Jerry Ford would wave to one another in their bathrobes as they retrieved their morning newspapers. A few years later, I remembered that moment when I had the opportunity to brief President Ford at a conference I was facilitating at the Carter Center. At a break in the formal large group consultations I met with Presidents Ford and Carter alone to debrief and plan the next part of the program. I took the occasion to inquire of President Ford if he remembered Bryant. President Ford said he didn't remember Bryant, but he still had the bathrobe. Ford had a delightful, down to earth sense of humor in all of my interactions with him.

During the Fall of 1976, I flew to Syracuse, Chicago, and Boston; I took the train to Philadelphia, Connecticut, and New York to call on early NPAC supporters who in some way had been connected to past efforts or were important contacts to confirm and get to know. In Syracuse, for example, sociology Professor Louis Kriesberg was typical of our campaign supporters. Lou participated in writing to members of Congress, sought the endorsement of professional associations, provided written testimony, and attended conferences meant to provide design and planning for the academic and outreach components of the future institution. As a recognized scholar and published expert in the field, Lou, like many others, provided credibility, substantive contributions, and moral support for our effort.

At first in 1976, my travel and that of Bryant or Jim was to visit and speak with individuals – a trip to Columbus or Connecticut because a Congressperson from that district was going to be important to us, or because a former activist currently lived there. One-to-one, in living rooms or in office buildings, we told our story, handed out talking points and asked for support. We were growing our membership, but the reach and effectiveness of the campaign seemed to grow slowly. The NPAC staff grew from one to one and a half to three to six to nine and to a weekly volunteer corps of up to twenty when we might be stuffing mailers or preparing for an event.

After twelve months while Andy was busy recruiting Congressional co-sponsors of a bill, Jim, Bryant, and I were speaking to small groups of people—on campuses, in church basements, at brown-bag lunches, in evening gatherings, and with local organizers, or piggybacked on some other event. Soon, other staff would serve as the speaker or would be paired with a local leader in a community or an organization. Membership names were kept in a little card box. Telephone numbers were kept in a Rolodex on my desk.

The cover of one campaign brochure read:

If you could bring Peace to your neighborhood would you act?
If you could bring Peace to the world would you act?

You can, you know
Join the NATIONAL PEACE ACADEMY CAMPAIGN
A Non-partisan, Public Interest, Non-Profit Organization
An attainable Goal for America
An Attainable Goal for you.

During the life of the National Peace Academy Campaign we published twelve different campaign brochures. I always took care to list on the back cover of any of our brochures the names of the citizen leaders and eminent people who were supporting our efforts to show the broad base of support we were developing.

Florence Block of Connecticut was an early leader in CODEP, Council for a Department of Peace. Prior to the formation of NPAC, she and Mary Liebman of Illinois drew much attention to the concept of a department of peace, which included a national peace academy as part of the design. They built up a following and their support helped to jump-start the work of NPAC. On the CODEP list was Senator Vance Hartke and his aide Steve Cloud, Elise Boulding, Bill Lincoln, Bernard La Fayette, Nacky Gerber and Tom Westropp of Cleveland. Nacky and Tom became two of the campaign's most generous financial donors. More than one half of the names on this initial list contributed written testimony to Congressional Committees, attended academic conferences regarding the future design of the academy, or wrote op-ed pieces or letters to the editor of their local newspapers. Several of the names on the list were, or had been, university presidents and their support was invaluable in establishing legitimacy for the concept.[47]

When NPAC began, Andy, Bryant, and Jim were identified at the top of the list as the Co-Chairpersons. I was responsible for all campaign activity, and had been designated Campaign Coordinator. Upon learning that a man named Bob McCan was a member of the First Baptist Church where the Carters were attending church around the corner from the White House, Bryant added Bob's name as Executive Director. Bob had a PhD credential that lent additional legitimacy to our letterhead. I agreed. Bob moved on after a period of weeks and I became the fully functioning Executive Director. The title change was humbling, but my responsibilities had not changed. As time went on, some names would change and new contacts with perhaps greater influence or different skills and networks nudged former supporters off such lists. Some feathers would be ruffled when somebody was bumped or were perceived as contributing less. Three years into the campaign, a major bump would occur when we created a new level of more eminent citizens, called the NPAC Executive Council.[48]

Financial contributions to the campaign would come to us in small amounts of five or twenty-five dollars. Our tear-out Founder/Member NPAC forms contained Membership option boxes of $15,

$25, $50, and $100 amounts. Some days in 1977 to 1979 the NPAC staff would stand around at mail time encircling our first full-time secretary Joan Mann to witness the opening of the mail. We would gather to celebrate the day's financial take of contributions. Then we would know what programs, travel, printings, or mailings we could plan for the next week. Money was always very tight.

By mid-summer 1976, I worked through a local law firm to incorporate the National Peace Academy Campaign and a second non-profit, the National Peace Education Fund, to serve as legal vehicles for our efforts. The National Peace Education Fund was initially created to receive donations to a future peace academy. I opened bank accounts, printed stationery, and business cards, and began a filing system for tracking the progress of our efforts and members of NPAC.

This is hard to imagine in today's context. Typewriters could only produce small type. Printing of documents or flyers with any kind of design elements was achieved in those days by offset printing. An inked image was transferred to a rubber blanket and then to a printing surface. The act of creating a flyer was expensive and cumbersome. I used to hand transfer large wax letters onto paper to achieve the graphic image we wanted. The print shop could then copy the original and "off set" or transfer the image. The campaign produced a great amount of material. We tried to make it look attractive and to lower our costs; a friendly print shop that could contribute free or reduced cost services was a real asset, playing a critical role in the campaign. Linda Lawton, a printer across the street from our offices, played such a role. Linda became part of the machine that was building political will in our cause. Little things like Linda's generous help came to matter a lot. The various kindnesses extended to our efforts throughout the life of the campaign were uplifting to me and appreciated.

From our small office we just kept pushing out the idea of a peace academy. We would recruit any willing soul to come in and help out at a campaign stuffing party, where we traded hot chocolate or donuts for able hands to help us prepare mailings. Our initial NPAC staff consisted of Bob Paley, Paul Ottens, and Laurie Silver who all served selflessly and without much pay to advance the cause of the campaign.

I used every means possible to invite and host interesting people who might have a useful connection to our effort. For example, you will recall I met Jack Dover at a reception at my home after he was been sent to "check me out," for Gil Pompa. Jack offered to get the word out on what we were trying to accomplish. Jack himself had been active in the Carter Presidential Campaign in Ohio and was also assigned to be part of the transition team after the election. He was recognized for his talents and campaign work and was hired in the new administration. We were the same age and connected on the running and operations of campaigns. Jack was very generous with his networking and matchmaking skills.

Jack began to introduce me to people around Washington. He was responsible for suggesting several key people to serve on my campaign staff. He connected me with Milton C. "Mike" Mapes, whom he had met in the Carter Presidential Campaign. Mike would come to serve as the Campaign Coordinator for NPAC, and later as its Executive Director, when I moved on to become Commission director. Jack also introduced me to Kathy Kozar, a very grounded and competent Ohioan, like Jack, who came to serve as my personal secretary during the most critical time of the campaign.

On Wednesday, September 27, the bill failed to get out of committee in the House. The Senate committee reported it out favorably. This meant that our next legislative battle would be made in the House-Senate conference committee.

On October 4, I met with Herman Will at the Methodist Building across the street from the Supreme Court. Herman was the head of the Board of Church and Society of the United Methodist Church, an influential broker in peace and social justice issues in Washington. I asked for his support and he was very open to endorsing the peace academy concept. His organization would provide stories about the campaign in their national newsletters and mailings and encourage their members and friends to be active. They were also very supportive in lobbying members of Congress in support of our efforts. By the end of the campaign eight years later in the fall of 1984, we had gathered the endorsement and active support of fifty-four religious denominations and professional associations across the country.

In the Methodist Building in DC, I met with the Reverend John Adams, who had been the mediator in the second uprising at Wounded Knee at the Pine Ridge Reservation in South Dakota. John later wrote a book, largely at the urging of Jim Laue, entitled *At the Heart of the Whirlwind*, documenting his experiences in mediation and conciliation in civil unrest.

Through John we reached out to the Native American community. A wonderful story was once told to me by one of the Native Americans present at Wounded Knee. John was a regional Methodist minister and was asked to travel to Pine Ridge when the standoff first started. He arrived, driving a yellow VW Beetle and wearing his clerical collar. There on the bluffs overlooking the protesting Native Americans were hundreds of armed marshals, reservists, and police manning heavy weapons. After a while the situation seemed to be going nowhere and John got agreement to be allowed to drive his Beetle down to the area where the Native Americans were staging their protest. He waived a white flag out the window of his vehicle as he drove toward the armed protestors. At first they captured him and did not believe his story of who he was. Eventually, he convinced the Native American leaders to share with him their demands, as he sought to create the beginning of a negotiation, rather than an armed standoff. One of the demands was that any further talks be conducted in a tepee and that the officials on the bluff had to come to the Native Americans, unarmed, to commence the talks. John carried this demand, and the other requests; back up the hill to the officials standing ready to shoot on the bluff.

The officials agreed to the talks—and set out to find a tepee, among other things, and brief the press and others on the coming talks. Bureau of Land Management men helped John load and balance the canvas and poles of the tepee on the rounded roof of his VW Beetle. Then John headed back down the hill to inform the Native Americans that the officials had agreed to commence the talks. There were many finer details, of course, to actually getting to the process of further negotiations, but among them was the awkward fact that the Native Americans, many of whom were urban activists, were having problem erecting the tepee. The good Reverend Adams had to drive back up the hill, still sporting his white flag, to call for outside resources to help with the proper construction of the negotiation tepee. John loved telling this story himself. That was why peace was more like chess; it always takes more finesse and skill than the brute checkers of war.

Meeting people like Rev. John Adams was inspiring and deepened my commitment and dedication to our effort. It was gratifying and motivating when people with unquestionable integrity and experience on the front lines of conflict resolution believed so much in what we were doing.

I researched and submitted proposals to several foundations to secure funding for both our CRIS-CROS research and in support of the peace academy campaign. This type of fundraising did not prove to be effective. By mid-October I had drafted the second strategy paper for the campaign. At the end of October I took the train to New York City to meet with Robert Pickus of the World Without War Council and others. Andy was in town November 8 and I managed to visit with him about the campaign. Later that week I meet with the Department of Justice training academy.

Andy was again in Washington again on December 2. We met in his Congressional office with Connie and planned the next move in our legislative strategy. On August 26, 1976, Senator Hatfield had offered an amendment to the Higher Education Act, calling for the appointment of a commission to study the peace academy act and alternative proposals.

Senator Hatfield carefully planned the introduction of his amendment. When Hatfield walked to the podium on the floor of the Senate, there were just three Senators on the floor. He asked for unanimous consent that the amendment be accepted. There were no objections from the floor. The amendment passed the Senate.

On September 22, by a House conference vote of six to five, the amendment was struck from the Higher Education Act. The work that we had done since the May hearings on the George Washington Peace Academy Act lost momentum and we needed a new strategy. Visibility for a national peace academy had been increased, but as the legislative session of Congress was coming to a close, we had to start all over again.

November 2, I had planned to attend two election night parties. Bob Gray, a DC lobbyist, hosted one of the parties at his home in Arlington and the other was in town at a DNC event. Beverly Orr was my companion for the evening. As we walked up the entrance to Bob's house, I could hear the party inside just getting started. We knocked, and a woman answered the door saying, "Hi, I am Rosemary Woods. Please come in." Bev and I were in shock and entered to be greeted by Art Buchwald, a journalist and humorist with the *Washington Post*. Rosemary Woods had been Richard Nixon's secretary from his early days in Congress until the end of his political career. In 1974, Ms. Woods had claimed responsibility for inadvertently erasing up to five minutes of the eighteen and a half minute gap of a June 20, 1972, audiotape made during a discussion of Watergate in the Oval Office.

Andy agreed to introduce a new bill at the beginning of the 1977 legislative session. Senators Hatfield, Randolph, and Matsunaga would introduce an identical bill in the Senate.

On the basis of the new relationships I had made on those DC baseball diamonds, and due to Connie's connections and energy, it turned out the first twelve co-sponsors of Andy's bill to authorize the Commission were all members of Congress whose legislative aides played coed softball in the Washington DC summer league. Connie was an organizer of Andy's team, called the "Young Studds" because it was a team made up of the staff of Andy Young's office and the office of Congressman Gerry Studds of Massachusetts.

On the Senate side the trio of Hatfield, Randolph, and Matsunaga emerged as the principal co-sponsors of the next rounds of legislation. Over the next several years, I got to know Senator Hatfield and Senator Randolph and their very fine staffs. Both senators were steadfast in their support of the concept and active in drafting legislation, gathering collegial support and perhaps most importantly, being strategic about making forward progress on the various bills in both houses.

In early December, we finalized the NPAC bylaws. I continued to make the rounds in Washington. I met with academics at local universities and think tanks, numerous legislative assistants, the leadership of sympathetic associations based in Washington, and staff at a variety of government agencies.

In mid-December I had meetings at the Department of State with John Richardson, who was Assistant Secretary of State for Cultural end Educational Affairs. He was very open to the peace academy concept and became both a personal supporter and later provided formal testimony to Congressional committees. He was one of the few State Department people who were openly supportive of the concept.

By the end of the year I had firmly traded graduate school for the politics of DC. I had settled "full speed ahead" into Washington life. We had structured a national campaign and were growing public and Congressional validation for our goal. Connie and I had begun dating. We had spent a lot of time together on campaign issues and were falling in love. She lived on Capital Hill, about twelve blocks behind the Capital dome and I continued to live in Georgetown, across town. The hard work of the campaign was about to begin.

Chapter 4 Review and Reflection

Task

- Create a well-rounded team to get you there.

Challenge

- Sort through the attributes and strengths of the team in hand.

Gift and Opportunity

- Develop meaningful relationships.

Reflection

- How can you meet others that feel the same way?
- What strengths do you have?
- What do you respect in others?

CHAPTER 5

Georgetown

January 1977 – The New Year brought a lot of optimism about achieving the goal of our campaign. Jimmy Carter was President and one of our strongest advocates. UN Ambassador Andrew Young was in his cabinet. In early January 1977, several of us had breakfast with Andy prior to an NPAC Steering Committee meeting. We talked about the legislative agenda for NPAC and which members of Congress would likely be on which committees. Our membership was growing steadily and we had received more and more organizational endorsements. We just needed to restart the legislative consideration of our bill.

The port of Georgetown predates the creation of Washington, DC, by some forty years. The town is situated at the farthest point upstream that boats could navigate the Potomac River. The town was formed and thrived because it served as the start of the Chesapeake and Ohio Canal, originally conceived to extend to the Ohio River and Pittsburgh. In some ways, the canal had brought me to Washington. Georgetown had been my home for the seven months since my relocation from Pittsburgh to DC. The question facing us in the New Year was, could we build the political will to carry the campaign across a continent?

Connie had received tickets to attend one of the Carter Presidential Inaugural Balls to be held on January 20. It was a fancy affair at the National Armory in NE Washington. I had been in DC seven months and found myself renting a tux to accompany Connie, who had purchased a ball gown. The event we attended was the Georgia Ball and was the inaugural venue for many of President Carter's Peanut Brigade, the Georgia Congressional delegation, new White House staff, and others with a Georgia connection. There was a real sense of history and excitement throughout the evening. I began to feel a sense of anticipation and momentum for our campaign as we welcomed the New Year and new administration.

A few days later on January 26, Andy made an important speech at the Shoreham Hotel. It was significant because it was one of Andy's first big appearances after having been named to Carter's Cabinet. In past administrations, there was not an established tradition of recognizing the office of US Ambassador to the United Nations as a cabinet post. Andy's office at the State Department would be on the seventh floor, just around the corner from the office of Cyrus Vance, the newly appointed Secretary of State. In New York, Andy and his family would be living at the Waldorf Astoria Hotel.

Connie and I stood at the back of the hall as Andy prepared to speak. Among Carter's appointments, there was widely shared anticipation about Andy's role, future influence, and contribution to American foreign policy. It was a hot ticket to be in the audience that night at the Shoreham. It was dark where we were standing and Andy was down front, well lit by the stage lights and modestly taking in the admiration of the audience. During the questions and answers someone popped a very tough question that created a dramatic moment in the evening. The audience member called out:

"Do you ever think there will be a Black President of the United States?" The room went silent. Andy thought and focused the entire room with his silence. Then he spoke slowly. "There will never be a Black President of the United States."

The room was stunned with silence and anticipation of what would come next. After quite a pause, either by design or contemplation, Andy finished his thought.

"There will only be a President of all the citizens of these United States."

The audience—including Connie and me standing in the darkened corner—broke into thunderous applause. The next day his assertion was an above the fold headline in many newspapers.

Andy's comment created the kind of moment that could get Andy in to trouble. Those that knew him well recognized that this was not intentional or deliberately provocative. Andy was known to speak his truth, often drawing fire for his honesty. Working together and attending political events, I had the privilege to hear him speak many times. I often observed lesser leaders, or the media, try to bait Andy into an outrageous comment or two. On occasion, Andy was criticized in the press for not being diplomatic enough. The reality for me in watching him was that Andy was very capable of making some people feel very uncomfortable, because he spoke the truth. Quite often, folks of a different political persuasion would denounce Andy, not for the content of what he said, but for saying it!

Connie was invited to Andy's swearing in at the White House. She asked me to go with her. We were then living together and it was an exciting time to be in Washington. My first visit to the White House would be the beginning of Andy's tenure as the UN Ambassador. It was really cool.

We were running when we reached the gate leading to the East Wing of the White House, out of breath and arguing over where we had had to park the car. I thought risking a parking ticket would ensure an on-time arrival for the ceremony. Connie had a different view. It was January 30, 1977. Outside in the cold waiting in line to have our credentials checked, a certain informality was in the air as others in the line spoke quietly of their connection and fondness for Andy.

"Isn't it great?" "Isn't this exciting?" "What is your connection to Andy?" "It means so very much to me that he to be sworn in as the United States Ambassador to the United Nations!" "Can you believe Andy will be a cabinet member in the new administration?" "I am so proud." "My goodness, I can't believe what I am about to see."

Entering the antechamber presented a more humid, slightly anxious, and busy atmosphere. The scene was chaotic. The arriving guests stood in place and went about taking off their heavy outerwear and straightening their apparel. After moving through security, people were frantic to get to their seats.

It was after all, for many of us, our first visit to the White House. I was nervous about just being there. None of us was the honoree that day, but the energy and fidgeting among the small crowd was obvious. We checked our coats and proceeded to the Gold Room for the ceremony, passing Supreme Court Justice Thurgood Marshall, who was waiting in the hall for the President and Andy to enter. I was still a little chilled—the new blue oxford cloth shirt I wanted to wear had been dirty that morning; I had not allowed enough time for the dryer cycle to fully dry its collar and sleeves after washing it. Connie and I had dressed quickly and hurriedly driven the twenty blocks from our house to the White House. My damp shirt caused the chilled January morning air to seemingly crystalize around my body.

My shirt was still damp as Jean Young, Andy's wife, caught Connie's eye and Jean handed off Bo, their toddler. Connie spontaneously offered to babysit Bo through the formality of the ceremony. Jean was visibly relieved and Connie gathered up Bo to contain his youthful energy. The event was brief and tremendous applause and cheering erupted after the President congratulated Andy. By then, I had Bo under my care as all of the audience was invited into a reception line to greet the Carters and the Youngs. We stood and moved slowly toward the bottleneck where Rosalynn, Jean, Andy, and the President were positioned to receive those present. There was great anticipation and joy along the line. Bo grew tired of the wait and started to flail about. He tried to pull away, and I was worried he might begin to disturb others in the reception line. Connie turned and looked at me with a "please do something" look.

Just then, I lifted Bo up on to my shoulders to control his enthusiasm. Suddenly a Marine in full dress uniform was before me. He surprised me when he addressed me in a formal voice saying, "What is the name?"

With Bo on my shoulders struggling to get free of my grasp, I thought: What name? Whose name? Wait, what? I then sheepishly stuttered, "William, ah, Grice." I instinctively used Connie's last name. I somehow thought it would be more likely that the President might recognize her, or Andy or Jean would know what to do. I was clearly in a panic. Drums rolled in my head. I was about to meet the newly elected President of the United States.

Then, with what felt like the fanfare of a cannon going off, the Marine in front of me came to full attention. He stepped aside, gesturing with his white glove, and boomed out, "Mr President, may I present Mr and Mrs William Grice and their son."

I thought again, "Wait, what?"

Bo was still on my shoulders, but now he was climbing up onto my head. I was literally wearing Bo like a hat. He wanted down. I did not want Bo to fall. I struggled to get my hands free in order to shake the hand of the President.

All of the attention, of course, was now on the antics of Bo. He was high up above the crowd and in plain sight of everyone. I flushed in complete embarrassment. Somehow, I felt I was letting the President down. Within sight of his parents, Bo was understandably acting out even more. I was left with no excuse for having the son of the newly sworn in Ambassador on my head.

Everyone nearby burst into laughter, except me. Things seemed to move very quickly. President Carter stepped forward to try to untangle Bo and embrace the toddler. Bo was climbing over the arms of the President to get to his mother. I awkwardly turned to assist with Bo's dismount and share in the attempt of the President to take possession of the boy. I backed up to give the President room to manage Bo's kicking feet and bumped into the saluting Marine. It was a graceless instant for me, but a loving and intimate moment for the President. He now had control of Bo and turned away from Connie and me to engage Jean.

Rosalynn and the President, who of course knew Bo, were being very gracious about the whole thing. I felt weakened and self-conscious. I was tired from having held Bo on my shoulders for so long a period in the receiving line. I could not believe the unimaginable farce that had just happened to me. My blue oxford cloth shirt was now completely darkened by sweat. Little did it matter to anyone else that I had just felt the fool in my first meeting of a President.

Connie recovered the moment by greeting the President and Mrs Carter. Andy and Connie had a brief nod of recognition of the significance of the event—and we moved on for coffee and pastries. So went my first meeting of President Carter. Unbeknownst to me at the time, there would be many more.

At the end of January, Bryant and I traveled to Syracuse, New York to meet with the faculty and students at Syracuse University's Maxwell School's Program for the Advancement of Research on Conflict Resolution and Collaboration, PARCC. It was one of the few graduate programs in the country specifically offering conflict resolution as a curriculum. We had many early NPAC members there. Bryant and I stepped out of the car into a foot of fresh snow. My feet remained cold the entire day as we did a radio show, sat in on meetings, and mingled with faculty and students. I remember it to this day because my feet were so bloody cold. As usual we slept in the homes of NPAC supporters and were kindly shuttled about by these generous people. We would repeat this type of city visit across the country many times during the course of the campaign.

♖ ♗ ♞

In early March of 1977, Bryant and I took the ideas relating to our CRIS-CROS program to the National Institute of Mental Health. It was well received, but there was concern about how such a program could be implemented across such a large urban base. It was the last time we spoke about CRIS-CROS; the work of the campaign instead dominated our time and interest. My hopes of learning to be a practitioner faded as the intensity of the campaign increased.

Connie and I realized that Andy would soon be entering a new world of responsibility and commitments. We realized that if we could leverage Andy's celebrity status and what he stood for we might be able to attract a group of his peers that could carry on the visibility and fortitude of our legislative fight. Andy wrote to fifty Americans—and all responded in the affirmative to join him in serving on an Executive Council for NPAC. This represented a turning point in the campaign, as our efforts began to have credibility, visibility, and reach as a result of Andy's letter. From that point forward, Andy was of course very involved in other matters of state and politics. But his letter was a strategic moment in the life of the campaign. By mid-March, the NPAC efforts were now legitimized and supported by a cavalry of eminent persons who gave us reach, visibility, and advice. I daresay that without this new cadre of fine and distinguished Americans, our efforts may have lapsed.

Those individuals Andy wrote formed a formidable coalition of supporters. The campaign now had a new and improved Executive Council.[49] Many of the same individuals Andy had reached out to had been active a decade earlier, when the eleven Congressional bills had been introduced in the spring of 1969. Some members of the Executive Council were quite famous; all were very accomplished and many were very open to being asked to help us with specific tasks that the campaign would undertake as part of our lobbying efforts. I met with as many as I could immediately after their agreeing to Andy's invitation so that we could solidify their support, give them a face to put with a campaign staff name, and begin to understand how we could best use their goodwill and assistance in our efforts. Many of the meetings were memorable.

As an example, Paul Newman had responded to Andy agreeing to help with our efforts in any way he could. This was great news and I wanted to follow up and see what Mr Newman meant by his offer and how I could coordinate future actions on his part to advance our legislation. Upon learning that he had been appointed to serve as a Special Representative to a UN Conference on Disarmament, I confirmed when he might be in New York and available for a meeting.

I arranged to meet Mr Newman at the United Nations while the disarmament conference was in session. I took the train from Union Station to NYC and stayed overnight with a family of NPAC supporters who lived in the city. Checking in on the first floor of the United Nations is an event. An impressive arc of international flags on the front plaza entrance sets off the deep blue-green windows of the thirty-nine-story building. I received my pass after informing the reception desk that I was there to meet Mr Paul Newman, and proceeded to the floor where I was told he would be meeting me. There a young woman led me to his office door and she knocked. When the door opened, I was looking directly at Mr Newman—intense blue eyes and all. "Hi," he said. "Come on in." He was folksy and quite at ease. He turned and walked around his empty desktop and invited me to sit across from him. The office was small. There was literally nothing in the room on any surface. It was a visiting guest office and it was clear that Mr Newman was just there for a temporary period. I thanked him for agreeing to meet me and asked him how his participation in the disarmament sessions was going. He said they had not started yet, but that he hoped they would be of interest. I started to speak with a respectful; "Mr Newman," and he stopped me. "It's Paul." I was feeling like the entire encounter was a bit surreal. What I do remember most was the intensity of his eyes. We spoke briefly of Andy's invitation and I quickly briefed him on what the National Peace Academy Campaign was, my role, and why I was there. He leaned back, crossed his feet up on the desk, and asked. "How can I help you?"

Paul came across as practical, down-to-earth, and straightforward. Three years later when he founded Newman's Own salad dressings and funded his charity, he was asked his views on philanthropy. He said, "You can only put away so much stuff in your closet." By 2013, Newman's Own had donated all of its post-tax profit and royalties to charity. The amount exceeded $380 million. In media interviews after the creation of Newman's Own, he often responded to the success of his philanthropic venture by saying, "The embarrassing thing is that the salad dressing is out-grossing my films." I found him to be just as funny and engaging as I had experienced him in his films.

I outlined some of the things the campaign was doing, identifying the critical legislators who were currently involved, and shared some of the strategies that we were using. I expressed optimism that with the new administration our cause might receive positive attention. Paul said he would be willing to help in any way he could but one. "What's that?" I said quite naturally. He responded, "Just don't put me in a reception room with a bunch of ladies." We both laughed. We finished up our meeting with more discussion about trying to cause change and my expressing our deepest appreciation for his willingness to lend his name and visibility to the effort.

Paul had been a founding member of the Energy Action Caucus, a group that was trying to counteract the impact of big oil lobbying on the political process with special focus on the environmental consequences of some oil industry practices. He had gone on to the board of the Center for the Study of Democratic Institutions and he seemed to be taking his long interest in halting nuclear proliferation very seriously. In fact he said he had just been in Washington, DC, at the White House for a briefing on the Special Session on Disarmament. He relayed this story. "So, I was walking through a corridor and I literally bumped into President Carter. President Carter asks me, 'What are you doing here?' I said, 'Nothing.' He said, 'Why don't you come on up?' I went into the Oval Office for what I thought was going to be a rare opportunity to discuss arms control with the leader of the free world, only to find out that the President was just like virtually everyone else I met outside of Hollywood. I wanted to talk about SALT II and the President wanted to talk about how you made movies!"

Paul restated how supportive he was and regretted in advance that he might be busy from time to time, but that he would do whatever he could. I asked him what he might like in return. Was there anything we in NPAC could do to help him? I was thinking about possible background papers for his current work at the UN or draft testimony for a future hearing. He playfully said simply, "Oh, you can just get me a six pack of Coors beer!" That brought another big smile and laugh. In those days, Coors had a very limited distribution. It was only available in sixteen states. He had known what he was asking for, and I took it as a personal challenge to get it to him.

I asked how much longer he would be in New York. He said about four more weeks, but that he had an apartment there. He gave me his contact information and we said our goodbyes.

Following our meeting, I wrote him a personal note and saw to it that he indeed received the beer he had jokingly requested. My note read, "On behalf of the National Peace Academy Campaign please enjoy this six pack of Coors with our best wishes." Paul was gracious in allowing the campaign to use his name in our *TIME Magazine* ads.[50]

Another NPAC Executive Council member, Najeeb Halaby, was fascinating too. He had most recently served as the CEO and Chairman of Pan Am Airways. He was born in Dallas, Texas, the son of a Syrian Christian who had immigrated to America in 1891. One evening at one of our NPAC receptions we spent much of the evening together. Najeeb's grandfather had been a provincial magistrate in Ottoman Syria. Mr Halaby his son was an alumnus of Stanford University and Yale Law School; had been a Navy test pilot in WWII, and later served in both the State and Defense Departments. The evening I spent with him the main topic was his daughter, Queen Noor of Jordan, who had just married King Hussein of Jordan in June 1978. We talked Middle East politics and the potential impact a US-based peace institute might have on regional issues around the world. Fortunately I was able to carry my own as I was speaking from the benefit of having had a semester of study on Middle East issues. As an American with deep international connections, Halaby had an interesting perspective on his fellow countrymen and the role of women in the Middle East.

He said what would be most important for a peace institute would be its ability to bring the American people along in understanding peace and how it comes about. "If a peace academy or peace institute is just a building that holds experts, it will fall short of its best opportunity." He said. "America, I have learned, is a country with great talents and insight among its people if they are focused on the true nature of problems and engaged in the solutions. Peace cannot be seen as a distant vision. It must be embraced in every community, state, and region for it to be understood as a viable international objective. Learning to make peace abroad comes from understanding how to make peace at home." It was a reminder of how often our political and military leaders seem to focus on solutions without fully understanding the problem.

On another occasion, I found myself paired with an introvert, like myself, and spent an evening engaged in wonderful conversation with Dr Jonas Salk. His view on why he was credited with the discovery of the polio vaccine and others were not was fascinating. In each conversation with these very accomplished individuals we discussed their views on a national peace academy and why they were supportive of the concept. I am grateful for what each was able to do in support of our efforts.

I played telephone tag with Buckminster Fuller and finally one day, while standing at a telephone booth in the lobby of the Mayflower Hotel, I spoke in detail about the campaign to his wife while Mr Fuller was napping. When I got off the call, I pushed open the flexing doors and exited the telephone booth with a smile on my face. I had just had an in-depth interview with the pillow mate of one of the world's great futurists. I had been glad Mr Fuller was resting, as his wife was fascinating.

Over the course of the campaign, those most helpful and responsive to our requests for direct action were many. Members of the Executive Council wrote testimony, did interviews, wrote magazine and newspaper articles, attended visibility functions, and, perhaps most importantly, personally called members of Congress at the appropriate times. I cannot think of anyone in this group who did not at some point in time help the forward direction of the campaign.

Connie had declined Andy's invitation to accompany him to New York and work at the US Mission to the UN. Instead, she elected to stay in DC and support Andy there, working out of his offices on the seventh floor of the State Department. It was quite a transition for her as she began to monitor international events, follow cable traffic, and sit in on meetings with State Department country desk officers. Cable traffic at the State Department consisted of the flow of messages sent from one embassy to another, or from one country desk to another. If a particular issue or topic were important to Andy, Connie would follow what was going on, and stay current, in order to brief Andy on the status of things. She had left the world of constituent issues and legislation.

I arranged for members of our NPAC Executive Council to visit with Andy at the US Embassy across the street from the United Nations. That corner of New York is an impressive intersection. The beautiful UN building rises on the East River with much grace and symbolism and as you enter the US Mission to the United Nations across the street; you walk under a giant Seal of the United States. The location, occasion, and anticipation of meeting Andy on his home turf was humbling, even for many of our NPAC supporters who were eminent in their own careers and disciplines. There were demonstrations on the street. As we passed through the security arrangements in the lobby, the group got pretty quiet. We were then led into an impressively large conference room in the ultramodern office building. We had been briefed to arrive at an early hour and we were seated around a large square made of mahogany tables around an open floor. We were making small talk, quietly awaiting Andy's arrival. After some time, he arrived with apologies and instantly proceeded to move around the room shaking hands and greeting those gathered. As Andy finished his loop of greetings around the room, he immediately went to the coffee table picking up two steaming coffee pots and a column of Styrofoam cups. To everyone's surprise, he turned back to the conference table and started walking around again, asking folks if they wanted a cup of coffee. He said his day had started early and he had not yet had any. His gesture broke the tension in the room and Andy made everyone comfortable. That was simply the way he was.

Back in the fall of 1976, I had begun talking with an NPAC supporter about hosting a substantive conference to consider the scholarly questions and value-orientation of a future national peace academy. Now it was time to pull the meeting together. This proved to be an important event as it elevated the image of our work and campaign beyond politicking to a more substantive contribution. Professor Gene Bianchi at Emory University organized the academic conference in Atlanta to develop a tangible image of what a future national academy of peace might do. He did a superb job and we worked diligently to attract some of the best people in the field to the meeting. We circulated advance preliminary papers to all participants raising provocative questions. The answers were to be provided in the submitted papers of conflict experts and scholars. Among the participants were: Elise Boulding, Charles Chatfield, Bob Coulson, Jeff Dumas, Ralph Goldman, Jim Laue, Jerry Laulicht, Bill Lincoln, Gene Sharp, David Singer, Norm Walbeck, Bryant Wedge, Dudley Weeks, and Burns Weston. No such detail had ever gone into the planning of the proposed new institution and we believed a conference of scholars and practitioners would not only build support among their colleagues, but also provide a clear sense of vision for legislators in their consideration of the bills moving through Congress. The participating fourteen scholars presented papers that outlined many aspects of how a future institution might operate and impact on topics related to creating peace. All of the viewpoints and momentum developed by the gathering were very helpful to the campaign. These papers might still serve as a resource for USIP.

I made a trip to Boston to engage the academic communities of MIT, Harvard, Boston College and other area colleges. I attended a reception and substantive meeting hosted by the leaders of a group called Interface, a progressive, new age organization offering community mental health services. I took the train to Philly, and then flew to St. Louis, Kansas, and Atlanta, back to NYC, and then to Ohio. In each city I met with campaign supporters to explain the need for timely contact with specific legislators and to raise funds. I pitched our cause to association leaders and engaged the internal support of their organizations. Slowly we grew the campaign.

Andy spoke to the United Nations Association and addressed the need for the national peace academy. Soon thereafter they put out a press release endorsing the campaign and the concept of a national peace academy. As with other such associations, we worked very hard to appeal to their leadership boards and gain the endorsement of the organizations. Once accomplished, we were able to not only list the organization as an endorsing advocate, but also make appeals in their newsletters and access their mailing lists for direct mail solicitations. Eventually we were able to receive the endorsements of over fifty associations and organizations; thirteen religious communities, and about one-fifth of the state legislatures across the country.

We wrote and placed articles wherever we found a positive reception. Some of the most powerful assets in the campaign were editorials and columns authored by named journalists in the *New York Times* and *Washington Post*. We circulated these media reprints and stuffed copies in the NPAC direct mailings and in our briefing packets to legislators and their staff. Kenneth Boulding, Coleman McCarthy, and Father Ted Hesburgh were particularly impactful in their media efforts.

Letters to the Editor in any media market were inexpensive and well-targeted because readers valued the remarks and endorsements of prominent citizens.

Senate hearings were held on June 6, 1977. The legislation continued to make it way through the process. I met in New York with executives at the International Peace Academy and met again with Gil Pompa and several field agents of the Community Relations Service teams from around the country. It became my belief that if there would ever be a Department of Peace in the United States, an existing federal service like CRS might be rolled into the new office of government. The discussions I had during the years of the campaign, and later in the commission with the Directors of CRS, the Peace Corps, and other federal agencies were promising. One of the major arguments that would arise in hearings conducted by the House International Relations Committee, or the Senate Foreign Affairs Committee revolved around whether the Department of State operated as a "Department of Peace"? It was our position that State was the primary advocate for the United States overseas, and therefore functioned not as a mediative influence, but as a champion. Simply stated, the job of State was to advance US interests, not seek the peace.

Bryant was still busy planting his thousand flowers and organized a special in-depth session on Lebanon, as a focal case to draw out the need for the type of expertise that a peace academy would provide. It attracted some high-level participants and was a success in illustrating the importance of cross-cultural communications and perceptions. It was a good example of how the State Department frequently missed the real issue when they entered a conflict zone as they were often blinded by superpower politics, rather than sensitive to the problems on the ground. The result at times was that US foreign policy developed out of fear and overreaction to expressed ideologies and propaganda, and the subsequent military intervention was determined to be unwarranted. Our misreading of local situations has been a contributing factor to what is termed "blowback,"[51] where ill-advised US motivation and action create greater issues. To this day, blow back continues to follow US military interventions and inspire dangerous terrorist actions throughout the world.

When Andy moved up to being honorary chair of the campaign, we needed to replace him with a new co-chair. We worked hard to find a woman for the position and were very lucky to have Lupe Anguiano who agreed to join the campaign in June of 1977 as a co-chair. Lupe was a Catholic sister from Texas who was a national organizer for the United Farm Workers. She had been a founding member of the National Women's Political Caucus and was active in many important movements. Lupe became an important asset in the campaign as we tried to reach out to more women, Latinos and interlink the campaign to social causes beyond the traditional war-peace formulation. Lupe had been a nun from 1949 to 1964 in an order that had a reputation for being advocates of the poor. Her gentle spirit and calm presence encircled a very tough and courageous soul. She helped to bring greater relevance and compassion to our efforts.

♖ ♗ ♞

On March 9, 1977, twelve gunmen, led by Hamaas Abdul Khaalis, took one hundred forty-nine hostages, and seized three buildings in DC. A journalist and a police officer were killed in the event. The conflict ended due to the patience of the DC Police and the FBI and the intervention in the negotiations of three Ambassadors from the Islamic nations of Egypt, Iran, and Pakistan.

After a thirty-nine-hour standoff, all of the hostages were released from the City Hall building, the offices of B'nai B'rith, and the Islamic Center of Washington. The event lasted until March 11 and became known as the Hanafi Siege. Mr Khaalis was a former national secretary of the Nation of Islam before founding a rival Islamic organization known as the Hanafi Movement. Khaalis was born in Indiana and served in the US Army. He changed his name and became prominent in the Islamic associations. The purpose of the hostage situation was to draw attention to differences between his organization and the Nation of Islam. The Hanafi group had suffered the murder of seven of its members in 1973 and Khaalis blamed the Nation of Islam. The conflict was largely philosophical and political within the religious sect. It was was not related to US foreign policy but to internal quarrels and grievances between two rival Islamic groups.

The event brought right into the heart of Washington the significance and relevance of our campaign if people could just see the connection. This type of event was unheard of at the time and significant to Congress as it occurred in its backyard. In the National Peace Academy Campaign we used the Hanafi Siege event as an illustration of what can happen when parties feel aggrieved and third-party skills are used to find peaceful resolution.

♖ ♗ ♞

In Washington, I met with the director of the Peace Corps, also with private and public development agencies and was constantly meeting Congressional staff in their offices. Receptions took place in private homes and in churches, schools and businesses, where we were invited.

In June I traveled again to Boston to meet with a number of academics based in Cambridge, including Nazli Choccri, Howard Raiffa, Roger Fisher, Karl Deutsch, Herb Kelman, Thomas Schelling, and Michael Roemer at Harvard, and Lloyd Etheridge at MIT. These meetings were important, as the support of the leading academics in the field would be influential in countering some of the resistance we were beginning to get from the schools of Foreign Service training and the Foreign Service Institute, whose dean had already testified that they already were doing what a national peace academy might do. These Cambridge scholars knew better.

The July 18, 1977, *TIME Magazine* featured Andy Young on its cover—along with the heading, "Carter's Gadfly." Accompanying the story was A Letter from the Publisher, Ralph Davidson, who introduced the article by writing: "Young proved to be a lively—and inquisitive—subject. His tendency to throw out ideas spontaneously and sometimes underscore convictions with hyperbole may get him into trouble quite a bit." Strobe Talbot, the author of the article, wrote, "But it also makes Young one of the most stimulating public officials I have ever encountered."

This was Andy. Those around him were never surprised by his insights or the honest and spontaneous way he often interacted with them. Many in the establishment, often those with more conservative ideologies, would denounce Andy for his worldview and attack the way he delivered his message by suggesting he spoke out of inexperience or naiveté. For some, Andy was honest and refreshing; for others, his progressive message was leftist, unpatriotic, and inappropriate for an ambassador. Truth was, Andy was always a straight shooter, which is why he was, and is, such a compelling historical figure.

Andy always had the ability to impress people with his humanity and warmth. He was often cool and could be perceived as reserved, but I experienced Andy as engaging and ever playing the servant leader role. Connie once described a contentious meeting Andy was having with a dozen or so leaders of various African nations, Namibia, Zimbabwe, and Angola. There were harsh words and tension with a particular regional statesman. The meeting was not going well and much was at stake. At a particularly heated moment Andy suggested that the group take a break. Andy walked over to the leader with whom he had been arguing and asked the leader to accompany him to the gift shop of the hotel to pick out a gift for Andy to take back to his wife, Jean. During the small talk while they walked to the gift shop, and at some point during the exchange of ideas about whether to purchase African art, clothing, or jewelry, the men made peace. Both had stood in the small gift shop among the clothes racks and pulled on over their suits brightly colored dashikis— the traditional men's garment widely worn in West Africa. The act of the two black men standing together, side-by-side in the embroidered clothing, had set a new tone of respect and common heritage. When the two men returned to the meeting room a bit later, the atmosphere and agenda took a positive turn and agreement was reached on the important points all had come to discuss. No one else knew why, only that Andy had worked some kind of diplomatic magic.

Andy felt that the process of peacemaking, and the body of knowledge and expertise that has been developed, could be applied to address community, national, and international violence with equal effectiveness. Andy believed that a personal commitment to peaceful conflict resolution was an essential prerequisite at each of these levels and contributed to the successful application of similar principles and techniques.

The campaign work went on nonstop. At the end of July I went again to New York. On July 31 Bryant and I addressed the Unitarians outside of Washington. Each day of the campaign was filled with calls to Congressional legislative assistants to track what was happening with the legislation and then I would reach out to the appropriate NPAC members to try and influence further local contact about upcoming legislation, and hearings, Congressional member visits to local districts and States, or through one-off connections with Congressional Members. Whenever Jim Laue was in town, he would stay at our Capitol Hill house. I would meet with Bryant at his Wisconsin Avenue office, in his Alexandria home, or at our NPAC offices. We all seemed to travel constantly.

♜ ♝ ♞

The Congressional legislative process worked like this. We worked diligently to see that our bill was introduced in both the House and Senate at the beginning of each legislative calendar. If the bill did not make it through the full legislative process, it would die that legislative year. Most bills that are introduced in Congress die in this way. Once introduced, a bill would be internally sent to the appropriate committees and then subcommittees that would consider the legislation. Ideally, it is beneficial to introduce a bill in both houses to help ensure that one version, or both, eventually will make its way through the process. The objective was always to have as many sponsors as possible in each house and to have some of the sponsors be on the appropriate committees that would end up considering the bill.

Once our legislation was introduced, it would be sent to the Committee on International Relations in the House of Representatives, as well as the Committee on Education and Labor. In the Senate, the legislation would be sent to the Foreign Relations Committee and Education Committee. The subcommittees of these various bodies would be the actual first decision makers to allow the bill to be sent back to the full committee and then, if favorably passed, on to the full Senate or House. So, usually in each legislative calendar, our bill would have to be passed by four sets of subcommittees (two in each body); four sets of full committees; passed on by the full Senate or House and then, finally, considered in a House-Senate Conference Committee (reconciling the version of the bills from both houses of Congress). After Conference Committee the legislation would go back to each body for final passage, and then to the President for a signature. Then, after being authorized, the bill had to be appropriated, or funded, another legislative gauntlet.

Managing a bill successfully through the Congress was like running through a medieval gauntlet, as the legislation could be knocked out at any point. Another metaphor might be like the old board game Chutes and Ladders, where at any point your player could be sent back down the game board to start over. Milton Bradley introduced the game in the US in 1943, as an adapted game from India first used to teach Hindu children right from wrong. Although marketed as a child's game, it is the same game played in the Congressional legislative process. Of course, after gaining the authorization for the bill, the game started over with a similar process to secure the appropriation funds for the legislation. Most bills, again, never make it thought the gauntlet.

The NPAC staff worked very hard to grow and be in contact with our members, as well as create programs to provide visibility to the campaign. Generally, the average time it took to move a piece of legislation through the Congress in the 1970s and 1980s to a successful conclusion was seven years. We were extremely fortunate to have made the journey in three years, creating the legislation enacting the Commission. It took a bit longer to then secure the appropriations to fund the Commission.

Every step of the legislation—from getting initial co-sponsors in each house, to educating Members of Congress who sat on Committees that would consider the bills, to trying to win over Members who might try to block the passage of the bill—took time and effort. Here is an example of the type of effort we pursued to get our legislation passed. This story is one of the favorite episodes of my NPAC Highlight Reel.

During the summer, we knew that our legislation would come up before specific committees and I made efforts to talk to Congressional aides and members, where possible, about the bill. I would carefully but quickly review talking points that I had written up and would leave behind. Often they would be tailored to the interests of specific members, based on pre-interviews with their staff. As often as possible, I would try to take an NPAC member with me who might be in Washington from the district or state of the member. Along the way this legislative round, I had taken care to meet several times with Congressman Carl Perkins of Kentucky, who served on one of the House Committees that would be considering our bill. I did not have a congenial relationship with him as I did later with Chairman Dante Fascell, but I wanted to stay in front of Perkins if I could. Too much was at stake. A year earlier our amendment had been struck from the House-Senate conference committee and I took precautions to see that the same thing did not happen again.

Carl Perkins entered Congress in 1949, representing a district that included Lexington and was now the Chairman of the important House Committee on Education and Labor. Perkins was a Democrat and many today would consider him a good guy. In 1956 he was one of a few members of Congress from Kentucky, and all southern states in general, not to sign on to the bill that was informally known as the Southern Manifesto. The House bill was signed by 101 congressmen and drafted to counter the landmark Supreme Court Brown v. Board of Education decision in 1954.

To be from the south and vote against this bill took a great amount of character. Voting against it created immense animosity on the part of southern voters and fellow Congressmen.

Congressman Perkins voted in favor of the Civil Rights Act of 1957, 1960, and 1964, as well as the 24th Amendment to the US Constitution[52] and the Voting Rights Act of 1965. Often in these votes, Perkins was the only yes vote from Kentucky.

Remembering that a swift legislative journey can take seven years, a single hiccup can be a big problem. When a bill starts out of the starting gate, it has to stay in its lane based on whatever committee has oversight. The perilous route of a bill moving through Congress is important to emphasize. One of the reasons why the creation of the USIP remains such a big deal is that the concept successfully made its way through the legislative cycle; in a limited timeframe; and with only modest alteration. Most of the bills introduced in Congress do not leave the committee room to which they are assigned after being introduced. They just die. If a bill does move forward, remember the process: it reaches a subcommittee first, then a full committee; maybe a joint-oversight committee; then the floor of the House; then to a House-Senate Conference committee, assuming the bill has made progress in both houses. Our bills were usually launched into four subcommittees to begin their swim up stream. Senator Matsunaga wrote a book in 1978 about the complexity of navigating the legislative process.[53]

I flew to Lexington, Kentucky on August 16 for what would turn out to be one of the more critical meetings of the campaign. Congressman Carl Perkins's support of the bill was critical if we were going to get the bill passed. A veterinarian from Lexington had responded to one of our NPAC legislative alerts, inquiring about constituent connections to key Congress people. In a follow-up telephone conversation with the veterinarian I learned that Congressman Perkins was going to be selling two of his horses in Lexington over the weekend of August 27-28, 1977. The veterinarian would be with the Congressman for most of the weekend, as he was responsible for the health of the Congressman's horses and would be on call for the sale.

I stayed with the vet's family and attended a local high school football game. The vet and I discussed the upcoming visit by the Congressman and took time out to visit to Clairborne Farms, the stable where Secretariat lived. The vet was one of the vets who took care of the special horse. Secretariat stood 16.2 hands tall and was a beautiful, impressive animal. In 1973 the American Thoroughbred racehorse had become the first US Triple Crown winner in twenty-five years, setting race records in the Kentucky Derby, the Preakness Stakes, and the Belmont Stakes, records that still stand today. The veterinary firm was under contract with the well-known three-thousand acre Claiborne Farms stud farm. It was a beautiful place, and in a later meeting with Congressman Perkins in

Washington, I was able to reference having met the horse, subtlety reminding the Congressman of his long-standing and fond relationship with the vet.

The veterinarian later described the meeting with Representative Perkins. He wrote, "I was holding the left rear hock of one of his horses, and the Congressman Leaning over beside me –both of us wearing stable boots—we were literally standing in horse shit."

"Perkins said, 'So Doc, what has been going on with you lately?' I went on to tell him about the peace academy commission legislation and how important I thought it was to the country." The vet said he followed up with the Congressman after the successful sale of the horses and again took care to raise the topic, reminding him of their conversation in the paddock.

That fall when the legislation came up in the Senate-House Conference Committee, I was present in one of the back rows of chairs in the small conference room. I had gotten there early to make certain I had a seat. The room filled up quickly. There were thirteen members present around the table. The air in the room was stale and the members looked bored. I was worried before things even started.

Perkins was chairing. The larger bill was filled with many amendments and subparts that required the members to either vote to include or exclude as differences in the bills brought from each chamber of Congress were reconciled. The fate of a specific section of a larger bill rested with the rapid-fire attention each would receive in the Conference Committee. The Chairman drives this process, and when the bill under consideration is large, the Chair tries to move quickly, with other members only jumping in when a section of the bill is important to them. These deliberations had gone on for most of the morning and sections were being eliminated right and left. The committee took a break.

I was more than a little nervous, as I didn't know where all of the members present stood on our bill. With members of both the Senate and House in the room it was difficult to assess what might happen in the give and take of the discussion. During the break I was able to catch up with the Congressman Perkins in the hallway outside the conference room. I must have come across a bit panicked when I approached Chairman Perkins. "Are you going to get to our bill?" I asked.

He took me by the arm and said; "Walk with me for a moment." Arms locked, he walked me down the hall. "It's going to be OK, son, just have patience." His gesture reminded me of film footage I had seen of Lyndon Johnson when he was in Congress, taking someone by the arm and whispering a word of influence or encouragement. That moment passed and all of the conferees, staff, and lobbyists returned to the conference room.

When it finally came time for our section to come up, Chairman Perkins stated, "Well gentlemen, now we come to this peace academy commission. What is your vote on this legislation?" His head was down and he seemed to intentionally fuss with the papers before him. He was flipping pages back and forth as if he had lost something. I thought: "Oh geez."

A Conference Committee Chair has a great deal of power and influence. By controlling the process of all pieces of legislation in a conference committee, Perkins in this case had direct influence over how his fellow members might vote on what legislation is important to the Chairman if other Congressmen want his support on the legislation that is important to them.

The Chairman said, "Let me have the yeas on retaining the peace academy commission provisions as part of this legislation." There was a yea or two, but then—silence.

The Chairman cleared his throat at a noticeable level. He sat up a bit and repeated his request. He said, "Let me have the yeas on retaining the peace academy commission provisions as part of this legislation." There was silence again. "Oh boy, there goes the ballgame," I thought.

I looked around the room and saw that several members were looking down at their papers and fidgeting. Again, the Chairman cleared his throat. I audibly heard a few more yeas from around the table, but it was clearly not enough to keep our section in the legislative package that would go back for a full vote. I was sweating. Years of work had gone into the effort to get to this point.

The Chairman cleared his throat again. Then he repeated, a little louder and with more eye contact, "OK, let me have the yeas on retaining the peace academy commission provisions as part of this legislation." Silence again.

Then in short order seven "yeas" could be heard from around the table. The Chairman said, "Thank you. OK, so the yeas have it and the provision will be included. Let's move on." Our section was included in the legislation. The vote was recorded as seven to six. He never once asked for the nays and everyone in that room knew that he had wanted the provision included, so he just waited them out. Chairman Perkins got what he wanted. Holy Moly. I sat back in my seat relieved, thinking, *so that's democracy in action.* Sadly, Perkins died in August 1984 before the bill enacting USIP was signed into law.

♖ ♗ ♘

On January 23, 1978, we gathered the leaders of the NPAC Action Committee in Alexandria. I provided an update on the campaign and the co-chairs fielded questions and led strategy discussions.

We got approval on our proposed action plans for February and March. We provided talking points and sent them out to speak with Members of Congress.

On January 24 and 25, 1978, there were hearings on the peace academy before the Subcommittee on International Operations of the Committee on International Relations. Representative Clement Zablocki of Wisconsin was Chairman and Representative Dante Fascell played a very powerful role. Congresswoman Helen Meyner of New Jersey was our main sponsor of the bill, having picked up the lead from Andy when he left Congress one year earlier.

Congresswoman Meyner would lead off the first day's witness list, followed by Tom Westropp, Joe Herzberg, Jim Laue, Bryant Wedge, and Sister Lupe Anguiano. The second day, the witnesses would include the Deputy Director of the Foreign Service Institute, the Dean of the School of International Service at American University, Senator Matsunaga, and Bill Lincoln of the American Arbitration Association. Also appearing would be the Executive Vice President of the International Peace Academy. We had organized the further contributions of forty-five individuals who contributed written testimony, including myself, and a wide range of NPAC supporters. There were three opposing voices—representatives from the Foreign Service Institute and American University and the Dean of the School of Foreign Service at Georgetown University.

Getting a subcommittee to hold hearings on pending legislation lends visibility to a cause and helps to assure that the legislation will move more swiftly through the full committee. Subcommittee hearings are essential to the legislative process due to the decentralization of Congress that made subcommittees more powerful as a result of the Congressional Reform of 1973. In addition, working with Congressional aides of members responsible for the hearing, there is a critical opportunity to suggest (or stack) witnesses who will be delivering the all-important key messages to the committee. An interest group like NPAC has a degree of control over the result of hearings based on personal relationships with Congressional staff. When you lobby members the first threshold is convincing their staff. If you can get through directly to a member, all the better. We distributed information members of Congress sympathetic to our issue. They in turn shared it with other members and their staffs. Some information can be inserted into the Congressional Record—and this can serve to further legitimize the issue. The hearing process is an opportunity to reveal the level of support and source of the bill's proponents. The hearings also provide an occasion for opposition to arise and for public reaction to be judged and estimated. The caliber of witnesses that a group could provide increased or decreased the degree of influence achieved. NPAC worked very hard to provide members of Congress highly influential witnesses whose lives and accomplishments were impressive. The greater the strength of a favorable witness the more horsepower a member would have to drive the cause with other members. Congressman Dante Fascell would become a master for us in pursuing passage of our legislation. As executive Director of NPAC, I was able to represent to the subcommittee members that "Literally thousands of Americans from every walk of life support the concept of a Peace Academy."

At the hearing we began to see two very important opposition themes to the concept of a national peace academy, one dealing with the concern for its need and the other its scope of practice. The level of opposition that would come from the schools of Foreign Service inside the Beltway would become intense. They were threatened, as had been indicated by the Dean of Fletcher School of Law and Diplomacy during the George Washington Peace Academy Act hearing in May of 1976. Clearly they were insecure about any future impact a national peace academy might have on their stature, funding sources, or perceived influence with Washington decision-makers. Anticipating this possible opposition, I had worked with Dr Joe Herzberg to include in his testimony talking points directly designed to offset any negative testimony that might come from the deans. As with most of the witness and citizens who submitted written testimony, we had planned a strategy in advance that laid out the best arguments that might be made by particular witnesses or authors of written testimony. Both Bryant and Jim and other witnesses were prepared to address any negative points that might be addressed by opponents to the idea.

We realized Dr Joe Herzberg would be a highly credible witness. First, he was a medical doctor and psychiatrist. Second, he was a recognized practitioner with professional relationships with many in the State Department. Joe had firsthand knowledge of the Hanafi Siege situation that had occurred one year earlier in the city. Another psychiatrist had managed the official communications with the terrorists and this fact provided credibility to both Bryant and Joe, both of whom knew the inside story. The Hanafi example gave our witnesses the opportunity to address the mechanisms of dispute resolution that were neither taught in the schools of foreign service nor advanced as part of general practice in international relations. In fact, we often noted in our campaign literature and presentations that the Foreign Service Institute of the State Department did not teach negotiation until well into 1979. Most audiences were usually surprised to hear that our diplomats were not trained in negotiation or dispute resolution techniques.

Joe addressed the relationship between international conflict prevention and early warning systems as analogous to preventive medicine and public health. He also addressed the second concerns of some regarding the scope of practice for any future peace academy. Some, Representative Fascell included, and later Senator Javits of New York, were worried about the peace academy becoming a police academy for peace. Senator Javits later single-handedly struck from enacting legislation language that provided for the study of national and domestic conflict. When later pressed on this issue Javits stated that he felt he had confused the meaning of domestic to mean family disputes, and he believed it was not the role of the Federal government to intervene in family disputes.

Throughout consideration of our bills Representative Fascell said that he was worried about the federal government overreaching into local, state, and national issues as a sort of big brother. He shared a concern about unnecessary or inappropriate intervention by the government. The commission struggled with the scope of a future peace institute's role in intervention. In the early days of the campaign, we considered the ethical dilemma of a protest going on outside a future USIP building: Would the staff of USIP get involved? Should they? In what ways: offer services to print up protest materials? Offer strategy advice, or merely ride out the protest and hope that it would go away?

Dr Herzberg tried to preemptively counter the arguments of the diplomatic community regarding their second issue: making policy. Using the analogous legal-institutional model of the National Institutes of Health, he argued the point was moot. As an example, he said, NIH facilitated policy development, not dictated it. NIH was generally regarded not as an intervention agency, but as an advisor, advocate, and reservoir of experts. The success of a future peace institute, not unlike the NIH, would be in its ability to disseminate research, develop practitioner skills, and create an environment for breakthroughs in peace-seeking, peacemaking, and the building of peace building structures in the American society and throughout the world.

Included in Jim Laue's testimony was this poignant exchange with Congressman Fascell.

Dr Laue:

> "Peace does not exist just because tension is low. Peace is a positive concept and it is possible, I think, to cause peace among persons and among groups and among nations in the same way that we talk about the 'causes of war.' Some of those causes of peace are spelled out here. And I call to your attention now."

Mr Fascell:

> "Is that the reason you use the words Peace *and* Conflict Resolution as the title of the Academy?"

Dr Laue:

> "Yes, because we think that if we only talk about peace, and some people read it as a vague and hazy concept and some read it as a threatening concept. We think that any discussion of peace must be linked not only to ways of resolving conflicts that threaten peace, but also to ways of achieving institutional change and social

change that deal with some of the underlying causes of tension. And here we refer to the inadequate distribution of resources, for example, or a sense of injustice on the part of persons who then strike out in individual or social rage to attempt to get their point across. A third major point that I have made in the testimony that I really would like to hold up to you is the focus on peacemaking or doing conflict resolution at the community, neighborhood, and institutional level as well as at the international level . . . So my argument in this section of the testimony is simply that any peace academy would be sorely limiting in its scope and usefulness if it restricts its attention to the international level to the exclusion of community conflict."[54]

Jim went on to describe the value of developing conflict management skills in community and national settings in order to apply them in international settings.

Then Bryant was up and testified that day:

"In twenty years of experience, I have come to learn a great deal about the operations of our international relations in foreign service from the inside in a problem-solving function and my experience convinces me that we can be extremely proud of our professionalism and the dedication and the competence of the foreign policy establishment. We can be certain of their motives in seeking security and the welfare of the Nation. It is an inspiring experience to work with such people on such issues. But it is not enough. Time after time in this process we have encountered circumstances, conflicts, and disputes in which the only or main instruments of solution were force or threat or the application of power in some way or another. Even when the parties were disposed to do otherwise, we had no mechanism, we lacked what this world needs at this point: honest brokers, genuinely impartial third parties. I will emphasize one critical point right now. You cannot be an advocate member of the State Department representing the interests of a country and be impartial in a question in which the State Department is involved."[55]

Bryant continued,

"I want to make a distinction between advocacy roles or mediative roles, as mediative roles require honest brokers or impartiality. This begins to speak to the questions you were raising earlier, Mr Chairman, about whether this can be under the arm of the State Department. I would just remind you of the sad history of the Arms Control and Disarmament Agency, which became co-opted by the foreign policy establishment and has become an arm of strategic negotiations which is far less than was intended when it was first established. You do not hire a referee if you are a sports team, you do not allow one side to hire the referee. There has to be an impartial, neutral person to be the referee. Our job is to try to create the essentially new role, a new social invention, and an honest broker in the world at home and abroad. That is the true impartial, the intermediary . . .. I would say that the purpose of the peace academy is to make available a resource which parties can use as they wish or if they wish. It is not to be a policy agency. By its very nature, it cannot make policy. It can only offer and make available a resource for voluntary use so it does not compete in the policy field."

Bryant got quite directive.

"I want to anticipate some objections. The bureaucracy will not support it. Its arms will officially oppose this—pro forma. The State Department will officially oppose this—pro forma. The Department of Health, Education and Welfare will oppose this—pro forma. The Office of Management and Budget will oppose this—pro forma. You just ask them, I can tell you they will. The State Department will say its job is making peace. Every Secretary of State has been forced in office to say that it is not true, that his job is to press the interests of the United States whether peace or war is involved. I can dig out statements from every Secretary of State without any effort, where it had to be put on the record. They are not impartial, their job is not peace, although its job is sometimes to negotiate a settlement of a social conflict in which the United States is involved. That is fine, but that is not what we have in mind as the impartial role."[56]

Andy Young held the same views as Jim and Bryant. In part, this is why he was placed in a compromising position twenty months later when he chose to play the impartial role of a peacemaker and support a process to avoid escalating an international conflict rather than assume the customary roll of a diplomat and advocate for the stated official US policy, when the peacemaking role clearly better served the national interest. Andy eventually resigned from his position as United States Ambassador to the United Nations over the result of this difference in roles.

Sure enough, later in these same hearings, a representative of the Foreign Service Institute and a graduate school of international service—a feeder to State Department and foreign policy careers— presented testimony along the lines Bryant had predicted. Interestingly, each of the presenters representing what Bryant had called the "foreign policy bureaucracy" chose to read their formal remarks, rather than testify informally, as Bryant and Jim had done. Their actions only further enforced the view that they represented tightly controlled, defensive positions. Carleton Coon, Deputy Director of the Foreign Service Institute of the State Department presented a somewhat condescending view, in my mind, of what Jim and Bryant had addressed the day before. Mr Coon could not quite get his head around the concept that an American could be an impartial third party when it came to issues of international peace where the United States was involved. Under questioning, his responses to Representatives Meyner and Fascell illustrated further defensiveness and distain. Chairman Fascell pushed back on Mr Coon's line of argument. Mr Coon expressed the view that private universities were providing skilled talent for service in the government and we did not need to create a new federal institution to support this training activity. The exchange began to get heated.

Rep. Fascell:

> "I see the difficulty you have with this. At the same time, I appreciate the suggestion that we have a highly skilled corps of people available if people want to use them. I don't see any problem with that. We need negotiators, arbitrators, conciliators and mediators just as we need trained people to go to war. I know you are not opposed to that, you just don't want them in the State Department. I will take that statement back. You do have them in the State Department, you do want them in the State Department and you train them. That is what you say in your statement. What you don't want is a trained group competing with or undermining the diplomats in the State Department."[57]

As the testimony and exchange with the Congressman continued it was apparent that the view of the State Department was that it did not recognize the utility of advancements in conflict resolution mechanisms on the domestic side, nor were they accepting of the relevance of these advancements to those working in international relations. This was exactly the point that we were trying to make in the campaign. Bryant, Joe, and Jim had done a good job of doing it on that day, and those representing the position of the establishment had shown their cards and were found wanting by the members of Congress present.

What the testimony of these hearings indicated was the degree of separation between what we in the NPAC held in our hearts and the defensive position the bureaucracy officially took with regard to examining new ways of doing things. In our view, the United States Government, with its vast resources and influence internationally, could become one of the greatest assets in the world to serve more effectively in the cause to create and sustain peace, so that the international community would be free to focus on pressing issues tied to human survival. America has increasingly possessed this hidden potential to play a new role, sometimes misunderstood or fought by members of established functions within the government or private sector.

In the hearing, Congresswoman Meyner, the lead co-sponsor of our bill in the House, went after the witness:

> "I just want to make one observation and that is it seems very unimaginative of the State Department to not agree to let a commission study the whole situation. It looks as though you are trying to hold your particular jobs or power very closely to your chest. What could possibly be wrong with a commission to just look in the whole thing, to see if we cannot be doing better, to see if a lot of these groups cannot be brought in under one umbrella and let them make recommendations?"

The Congresswoman was directing her comment to Mr Coon, however, Chairman Fascell interjected before Mr Coon could answer. Fascell said,

> "Well, I am going to answer for you. If you put a loaf of bread in the oven, I am afraid you are going to bake it."

His statement was followed by laughter from those present in the hearing room. Fascell knew that our strategy was to achieve a commission mandate and then leverage that into creating a new institution. That is exactly what we did, and with his help and leadership. We got the camel's nose under the tent.

Mr Coon was finally able to respond, albeit in an increasingly defensive tone:

> "I do not want to make this for the record spontaneously as my own personal conviction and also that of all the officers in the Service that I have talked to about this. I don't think we are being parochial in our attitude on this. I don't think we are being territorial. I don't think we are afraid of any competition. This business of the pursuit of peace is central to our own purposes and it is a very big area and we feel there is lots of room in it. We welcome anybody or any entity coming into the field that can make a contribution. Our problem with this specific proposal is that we think it is more likely to provide the leadership that gets in the way eventually than the kind of leadership that stimulates progress."[58]

Rep. Meyner concluded her remarks by stating that she was not certain that the witness understood the scope of what was involved in the proposal to create a national peace academy and how it held a new and different kind of possibility than the State Department was willing to recognize. The next two witnesses that day were Senator Matsunaga and Bill Lincoln. They each made compelling and strong statements, as well as answering clarifying questions from Congresspersons Fascell and Meyner.

Andy was unable to attend the hearings but submitted written testimony from his seventh floor office at the State Department. In part he wrote,

> "The one major difference between these bills was a greater stress in the original legislation on the domestic aspects of these proposals—which I hope will again be included through the committee's final recommendations on the matter. Such an academy could provide an expanded corps of experts available to apply these skills and techniques to the resolution of conflicts throughout our society, without the use of force or violence. This is a need, which is not currently being met. The potential for widespread public education about conflict resolution methods both private and public use is highly encouraging, given the conflict levels we now see domestically and internationally. The United Nations was originally established for many general purposes, one of which is to assist in peacemaking and peacekeeping. It promotes conflict resolution and understanding—but without corresponding institutions at the national level, and without education of the public sector, the type of peace we seek might never be achieved. We need domestic agencies which are dedicated to the promotion of conflict resolution at home, devoid of advocacy and the burden of diplomacy, in order to better understand the role and mechanisms of conflict resolution at the international level."[59]

While we were testifying in Washington, Andy was continuing to make his own lasting impact on United States foreign policy. An analysis of his early contributions representing the United States at the United Nations were said to help:

> "…widen the scope of American foreign relations. He assisted in adding new issues to the agenda, championing racial equality, and fighting hunger and poverty. He focused on previously neglected regions of the world. Andy spoke for the increasingly influential African-American community, as racial minorities and women gained access to the foreign policy establishment…Young facilitated participation in international affairs by a host of institutions beyond the White House and State Department such as Congress, the United Nations, churches and private corporations. Andy broadened the playing field of American foreign relations to allow participation by the diverse and pluralistic society of the United States."[60]

I asked Andy about the resistance we were getting from the State Department, OMB and the various schools of Foreign Service. I noted that the military service academies were generally supportive as were veterans and labor organizations. He began to explain his response to me. Andy had not viewed the white business leaders in Birmingham as bad people; they were just people in a bad situation. It was the way I had come to view bureaucrats in our government. They were limited in what they could say and what they could do, and this influenced their effectiveness in international relations. The formality of protocols, for example, in the American foreign policy establishment often inhibited the role America might otherwise play in problem-solving international issues.

On another occasion when I was alone with Andy in his office, I asked him which among his many roles were most important to him. Was it being an ambassador? Had it been being a Congressman? Perhaps a father, husband, minister, or civil rights advocate? His answer to me was quick and heartfelt. Andy said, "Minister." Andy saw in his own calling the desire to nurture people from any culture or country in ways that promoted peace. He had a personal hierarchy to seek peace over diplomacy, to be an activist world citizen over exhibiting bureaucratic behavior. President Carter saw these same attributes in him and that is one reason the President had selected Andy to serve in his cabinet. Carter also knew that this behavior might well put Andy at odds with the State Department bureaucracy, but that may have been the President's intent.

Andrew De Roche wrote of Andy,

"Young's support for foreign aid reflected his long-held international philosophy that peace and racial justice should be the primary goals. This view came in great part from his Christian faith, which remained central to his life."[61]

Andy invited Hubert Humphrey to be a co-signer on a Dear Colleague letter along with Frances Farenthold and himself. Humphrey and Farenthold agreed. Connie and I wrote up a draft and got the signatures of Farenthold and Andy. Senator Humphrey's was the last we needed. "Sissy" Farenthold as she was called, had been a candidate for governor of Texas and had her name placed in nomination for Vice President of the United States during the 1972 Democratic National Convention. At the time of the letter, Sissy was the President of Wells College in New York and she was the first chair of the National Women's Political Caucus that formed in 1971. The statement emphasized the insignificant cost of the academy when compared to the future benefits. The cost of preparing for war, and going to war is incredible. The cost of benefits to veterans is significant. Humphrey would be a huge influence and I am sure he knew this. The short statement included the line, "This should not be thought of as just a piece of legislation but as a serious obligation." That was powerful stuff to be hearing from a colleague who had great respect among his peers. Sissy's name carried weight, as did Andy's name; but Senator Humphrey's name on the letter was significant, given that our bill would most likely next come up before a Senate committee. The timing of our effort was driven by the fact that Senator Humphrey had rarely been in DC of late due to his illness. It was important to obtain his signature this night.

Washington, DC, seemed to have either those really hot and humid summer days, when I found myself sweating even after a shower, or the really cold days, when to get around comfortably I literally had to wear most of my wardrobe. I remember nearly every summer day that I walked to the Metro; I would begin to sweat under my shirt and tie, and only feel relief once I reached the air-conditioned station. Then walking from the Metro to my office or meeting, the humidity would hit again. In the winter, it was the reverse. Too often I had to wear too many clothes just to stay warm, never getting hot. This was one of those winter evenings when I was too over-dressed to run in a race. But I did.

I literally ran to meet Humphrey on December 14 at a hotel where he was staying for the night. By the time I made it down the various hotel corridors to find the Senator, I had partially disrobed and was carrying an overcoat, jacket, vest, scarf, and the rubber booties that had shielded my feet from the snow. Panting, I knocked on the Senator's door and his longtime aide David Gartner partially cracked the door and greeted me.

I could see the Senator sitting on a couch in the room. David excused himself and took the letter to the Senator for his signature. The letter would later be entered into the Congressional Record and served as Humphrey's last official words to his fellow members of Congress. Senator Humphrey stated in the letter, "I support this legislation and the work that the National Peace Academy Campaign organization is doing . . . . I call upon every American to support this non-partisan cause that will greatly enhance the ability to cope with conflict today and in the future . . .. It's an idea whose time has come."

To create greater legitimacy for the campaign we planned a major Washington event at the Mayflower Hotel on February 6, 1978, about three blocks from our NPAC offices. The Mayflower was known as the second-best address in Washington, DC—the first of course, belonging to the White House at 1600 Pennsylvania Avenue. Presidents, embassies, celebrities, and uncounted politicians have called the Mayflower home. It was first opened in 1925 and is said to contain more gold trim than any other building except the Library of Congress. It was a real financial stretch for NPAC to afford to stage an event there, but it was strategic in claiming our status as a player; with an important cause, worthy of being noted.

We organized fifty big name sponsors – largely out of the Executive Committee – and featured a steel drum band. It actually was a very fun evening. It honored the groundbreaking work done by our primary legislative sponsors, former Congressman Andy Young, Senators Jennings Randolph and Mark Hatfield, and Representative Helen Meyner.

In the weeks prior to the Mayflower event we had conducted an "Art of Peace" competition earlier in the winter by putting a call out to artists in New York City, Baltimore, Philadelphia, and Washington, DC to submit original artwork that captured images of peace or conflict resolution. The winning submittal was an image drawn by local Washington artist, Malik, who referred to himself by one name. The line art drawing illustrated the role of a third party intervening with conflicting parties who were each wearing masks. The initial image of tight fists and stern-looking masks transforms to unmasked faces shaking hands and the third party walking away in the background. We enlarged the art and created posters to sell for fundraising, as well as notecards and other objects carrying the images. We used the images Malik created at the top of campaign mailings and newsletters. At the Mayflower fundraiser we auctioned off the signed posters. The auctioneer was Joan Mondale, wife of the Vice President, and we had learned, an admirer of local artists in the area. It was a grand affair. It had been our strategy to engage Mrs. Mondale to lend further visibility to the campaign and perhaps succeed in messaging to the Vice President the merits of our cause.

We had pulled out all of the stops to pull off the Mayflower party. We were out of cash, our staff was dead tired, we were stalled legislatively—and yet we pulled off a fabulous event.

Sadly, Senator Hubert Humphrey died on January 13 of bladder cancer, just twenty-four days before our event. All of the legislators gathered at the event shared stories about Senator Humphrey in special recognition to him.

Connie had been invited to serve alongside Ambassador Allard Lowenstein as a member of the United States Delegation to the United Nations Human Rights Commission in Geneva. She had departed for Switzerland a few days before our Mayflower event. I was alone in DC.

I remember being among the last to leave after closing down our event, and I walked my secretary Kathy Kozar out to her car. It had begun to snow. In fact, it was a mini blizzard. I got Kathy safely to her car, and then stood in silence gazing down the snow-covered L Street, where we had both parked that afternoon. I was feeling an emotional high that we had carried off the event. We had successfully planned the reception with very few resources and were able to have honored a cabinet member Andrew Young and our primary legislative sponsors. We had the benefit of Senators Matsunaga and Randolph joining us as speakers, along with the others. By all accounts, it was a big success. Yet I was tired and felt very alone.

The coming few months of the campaign would be a turning point. There was much hard work ahead. Our campaign would succeed in maintaining a national headquarters two blocks from the White House, while doubling our membership and beginning to develop a regional coordination system. We would secure the donation of space for full-page advertisements in both *TIME* and Newsweek magazines, without the step of going through the Ad Council. In several weeks we would carry off a major consultation of peace research scholars and practitioners at Emory University in Atlanta. The coming months would find everyone in the campaign presenting professional papers, and delivering speeches, sermons, and living room talks across the country. By November, we would have sponsored the first meeting of the Executive Council at the United States Mission to the United Nations, chaired by Ambassador Young. We were operating a deficit campaign budget but beginning to gain leverage in the media with over twenty-five articles in newspapers from New York to Detroit, Cleveland, and Atlanta. Although we were in the red financially, and owed our staff back salaries, we were moving ahead in very significant ways.

For me personally, I was not sure where my relationship with Connie would go, nor was I at all certain about the future success of our efforts. I just knew we were working very hard and there would be no turning back.

In early March, I flew to Geneva to meet Connie who was just ending her service as a delegate at the UN Conference on Human Rights. The trip gave me the opportunity to put perspective on my life and stand back from the campaign. As I had gotten to know Connie better, I had realized I was in love with her and that we connected around a set of shared values that were important to both of us. Despite the fact that we had grown up on different coasts and were of different backgrounds, we seemed paired for a good match. We both had strong commitments to peace and social justice and each felt we were trying to make a difference with our lives. One evening I proposed to Connie and when we returned from Switzerland we were engaged. We set a date for our wedding.

I expressed to Bill Lincoln my feelings about being such a strong advocate for a cause when I had not experienced being a practitioner. At the University of Pittsburgh, the curriculum had been theoretical and based on case and area studies. One day Bill asked me to join him in attending the eight-week seminar program he was conducting on community dispute resolution. The program was to be in Boston and included introductory curriculum on negotiation, mediation, getting parties to the table, writing up agreements, and many of the behavioral techniques that my studies at Pitt had not covered due to the focus more on theory than behavior. I was, and remain grateful to Bill for the opportunity to begin to make this welcomed leap.

The spring and summer of 1978, leading up to our wedding was a flash of campaign activity. My calendar read like a roadmap, detailing each step of our efforts to get the legislation passed. Over just a two-month period it read: NPAC Steering Committee, Boston meetings and training, meetings with NPAC supporters in DC, Congressional Districts meetings, meetings and endorsements with the American Association for the Advancement of Science, meetings with Bryant and Jim, International Studies Association, Elise Boulding, meetings in New York with World Without War Council leaders, media interviews, Syracuse meetings with faculty, Governor's Conference in DC, Julian Bond, John Adams, Senator Hatfield, John Richardson, Department of Justice, Jack Dover, Herb Kelman at Harvard, Jerry Wiesner at MIT, Representative Helen Meyner, fundraising meetings, Jim Rouse, Bob Coulson and Tom Colosi at AAA, church meetings and speeches, Bob Gray at Hill and Knowlton, meeting with futurists, Tom Westropp in Cleveland, and a UNESCO meeting in New York.

♖ ♗ ♘

On May 4, 1978, the full International Relations Committee, following a contentious markup, approved our bill.

Andy caused controversy when, during a July 1978 interview with French newspaper *Le Matin de Paris*, while discussing the Soviet Union and its treatment of political dissidents, he said, "We still have hundreds of people that I would categorize as political prisoners in our prisons," in reference to jailed civil rights and antiwar protestors. In response, Representative Larry McDonald, (D-GA) sponsored a resolution to impeach Young, but the measure failed 293 to 82. Carter referred to it in a press conference as an "unfortunate statement."

Many of Andy's "unfortunate statements" delighted others. Andy and I were once walking from his office at the Cannon Office Building to the Capitol, back when he was a Congressman. The debate that morning was going to be about the military budget. While in graduate school and again in Washington, there was always a tension between the views of the hawks and the doves when it came to foreign policy. Knowing how he valued Biblical metaphors I asked if the lions and lambs could live together. Andy smiled and replied, "Yes, you just have to keep replacing the lambs."

To this day, whenever I think about neocons, hawks, or conservatives, I reflect on Andy's comment about the need to replace the lambs to get past their obstructionism to peace or their hubris in wanting to be the first to go to war.

As a Congressman, Andy was in a legislative body with many lions and lambs. Often while sitting in the Gallery above the House of Representatives, I would observe the floor dynamics. In the period 1977 to 1979, three conservative Congressmen—Larry McDonald of Georgia, Bob Bauman of Maryland, and John Ashbrook of Ohio—would sit together and laugh or be disruptive of the proceedings of the House. They used parliamentary process to slow the progress of bills that had made it to the floor or to delay the consideration of bills getting to the floor. The dynamics were obvious to all. To some, these legislators were early Tea Party–type heroes, although the Tea Party would not come to exist for another twenty-five years. To others, their antics were troubling, and a good indication of the path politics would take in coming decades when one political party felt disenfranchised and frustrated with the lack of public support for their ideologies. Perhaps deliberative bodies of any democracy have always had such outliers, but for me as a political neophyte, their behavior was quite remarkable.

Larry McDonald was an MD and known for his staunch opposition to communism. He was the second president of the John Birch Society and died onboard Korean Airlines Flight 007 en route to South Korea. The flight was shot down as it entered Soviet airspace on September 1, 1983. The John Birch Society had been on my screen because I grew up not far from their West Coast office in San Marino, California, and often drove by their offices. Their national office was located in Belmont, Massachusetts, where I later lived for two years beginning in 1984. The John Birch Society was founded in 1958 and soon became known as a radical right wing, fringe group of the conservative movement. It was, and still is, an anti-communist and limited government political advocacy group that was a political reference point in my family growing up. On July 13, 1978, Congressman McDonald's motion to impeach Andy Young was defeated.

Bob Bauman was another prominent conservative Congressman and he lost his 1980 reelection bid due to a political scandal involving a male prostitute. He went on to serve as legal counsel for a group dedicated to offshore banking and investment. At the time he was in Congress and while I was observing his conduct, he was known for his knowledge of parliamentary procedure. Bauman was a somewhat antagonistic member toward many of the early Congressional members who supported the legislation to create the Commission.

John Ashbrook was first elected to the US House of Representatives from Ohio in 1961. He was still serving when he died in 1982. He ran in the 1972 Presidential primary against incumbent Richard Nixon because Ashbrook believed that Nixon had turned left on issues such as the budget deficit, affirmative action, the creation of the Environmental Protection Agency, but most of all in Nixon's policy of détente with the Soviet Union and the People's Republic of China. When Nixon became caught up in the Watergate scandal, Ashbrook was the first House Republican to call for Nixon's resignation.

In 1979, Speaker of the House Tip O'Neal surprisingly appointed Congressman Ashbrook to serve as one of two Congressmen on the Federal Commission on Proposals for the National Academy of Peace and Conflict Resolution. The other Congressman was Dan Glickman of Kansas, who would become Secretary of Agriculture under President Clinton. Dan also served as the Chairman and CEO of the Motion Picture Association of America. Glickman had been a co-sponsor of the peace academy bills in various forms as they moved through Congress. During the campaign, I traveled with him to his Kansas Congressional district to speak about the prospects for the national peace academy.

♖ ♗ ♞

In September of 1978, I flew from Washington to meet Kenneth Boulding at the Denver airport to fly together to San Francisco to meet with Roger Heyns, President of the Hewlett Foundation. I had learned in my fundraising research that Roger and Kenneth had been on the faculty together at the University of Michigan in the 1960s. I had crafted a plan to take Kenneth with me to try to persuade Hewlett to fund part of our effort. The Hewlett Foundation at the time was one of the largest and most generous of the corporate foundations funding work in conflict resolution. I felt they might be a sure bet for some funding monies if I handled it right.

Boulding and others had started the Center for Conflict Resolution at the University of Michigan in 1959. It had published *The Journal of Conflict Resolution*, which was one of the periodicals that had persuaded me to begin my journey into the field. Heyns was on the faculty specializing in group dynamics, social conformity, and motivation. He later became vice president for academic affairs at Michigan. In 1965 Dr Heyns had been appointed Chancellor of the University of California at Berkeley, just after the free speech movement had begun at that university.

On the plane out West, Kenneth and I plotted out a strategy that I thought would be a slam-dunk to put NPAC on the track to convince the Hewlett Foundation to invest. Kenneth was an accomplished individual in the field, so much so that if you only just met him or had read about him, you would be impressed and listen to his every word. In this situation, Roger, who was sixty and Kenneth who was sixty-eight at the time, shared professional and generational bonds that spanned their early teaching careers, university affiliations, societal evolution, and a twenty-year friendship. These were very smart men who shared a history and commitment to social change. Kenneth and I rehearsed our plan.

Eighteen months earlier, I had persuaded Kenneth to write a letter to the editor of the *Washington Post*. It ran on June 13, 1977, accompanied by clever artwork by Post cartoonist, Zarko Karabatic, showing two line art doves looking at each other in puzzlement. One dove was holding a piece of barbed wire in its beak and the other dove biting down on an olive branch. I had made sure that Dr Heyns had seen a copy of the clipping prior to our meeting.

The *Washington Post* letter was entitled "A National Peace Academy?" It read:

"The most important legislation is not that which performs a single act, but that which creates an institution that throws its weight into the whole future course of events. Such a proposal is now before the Congress in H.R. 2651 and S. 469, which move toward the establishment of a National Peace Academy. Such an academy would move the whole future in the direction of greater capacity to cope with organized conflict, both domestic and international. Peace is the skillful management of conflict. It has to be learned and organized. In the past generation, considerable progress has been made in the social sciences, in spite of their starvation sciences, in spite of their starvation rations, in the development of a discipline of conflict management. The time is ripe for this discipline to take its place with the other therapeutic disciplines as a recognized and transmittable body of human knowledge, skilled and ongoing research. A National Peace Academy would make an important contribution to this movement. It would have very large potential payoffs for the nation and for the world, for a very small investment. It deserves the support of every thoughtful citizen."[62]

Signed: Kenneth E. Boulding, Professor of Economics, University of Colorado, Boulder

We both dozed off just before landing. Rested and ready for our mission, I was confident of our impending success as I drove our rented car into the Palo Alto parking lot of the Hewlett Foundation.

After warm greetings all around and much obvious mutual affection, the conversation turned to its primary discussion points—not having to do with the peace academy at all, but with a question that had somehow emerged out of our introductory greetings. Roger and Kenneth were locked into a debate over which century and where they would each most liked to have lived. Oh my God. I sat helplessly aside their positions on a sofa, in a chair removed from the action. I had no way to intervene. I could not get Kenneth's attention and their discussion, although fascinating, was eating up the entire meeting time. Both were excitedly reviewing the merits of their chosen decade in mid-seventeenth century Scotland. It was indeed a privilege to be a fly on the wall for the engrossing discourse among such intelligent men, but *Geez,* I thought to myself, *what have I done?*

Finally the clock ticked down. Our meeting was over. My duck was cooked. I am sure Roger had a good time, but must have been left wondering, *what was that about?* The trip had been a waste and we left with no commitment from Heyns, the foundation, or hope of future funding. I was embarrassed. I have thought about that meeting for more than thirty years and still wonder what I might have done differently, save known more about seventeenth century Scotland, and how I could have artfully pivoted the meeting in some way.

I drove Kenneth back to San Francisco where he would be attending other meetings the following day and I took a red-eye back to Washington. Jim Laue, upon later hearing of our disastrous trip, wrote a rather syrupy and chatty letter to Roger following up in the best way he could to try and recover any thread of hope for future funding. We never did receive any money from the Hewlett Foundation, although Roger did send a personal contribution.

On October 9, a full-page advertisement appeared in the national edition of *TIME Magazine*. It would be the first of two ads featuring the NPAC message and listing members of the NPAC Executive Committee. The ads came about as a result of a meeting that one of our fundraising staff, John Holman, had arranged with the chairman of Time Life. We were looking for a corporate contribution but got a nice personal check and a promise to run the ads.

On Oct 14, 1978, five days after the ad ran, and Connie and I were married in a small church in Brewster, Massachusetts on Cape Cod. Andy Young officiated at the service, along with a local minister and Connie's uncle who was a Monsignor priest. Jim Laue was my best man. Bill Lincoln, Bryant Wedge, and others were present. The date was twenty-eight months after I began working on NPAC.

On the day after our wedding, October 15, the commission legislation was finally authorized. Our nose was under the tent at last. We immediately began to kick our work on the appointment of commissioners into high gear.

Chapter 5 Review and Reflection

Task

- Explore your vision of change.
- Define how you get there.

Challenge

- Be clear on your objectives and strategies.

Gift and Opportunity

- Broaden your confidence to be authentic.

Reflection

- What or who affirms your creative spirit to cause change?
- Who are the people who have most inspired you?
- How are you like them?
- How are you different?

CHAPTER 6

Union Station

1979 – Union Station is a major train station and transportation hub in Washington, DC. It is among the busiest train stations in America and is visited by more than thirty million people a year. It opened in 1907 and quickly became the portal to the Capitol. Built on a grand scale and made of white marble it sits just a few blocks from the Capitol. Its convenience to the Capitol makes possible a three-hour ride on Amtrak to New York City or even less time to Philadelphia. As the new year of 1979 started the station became nearly a home for the amount of travel our campaign staff began to undertake. It was a familiar friend. It was a comfort to settle into a train seat for the ride north, free of phones and visitors, and it was reassuring to see its many inspiring architectural elements on a return trip, reminding me of the grandeur of the city where we were increasingly engaged in battle.

We found ourselves caught in the middle of brewing storm clouds. Our hard work was beginning to pay off, but the success of our efforts would draw increased fire in the coming months. The year would be one of more planes, trains, and strains. The State Department, OMB, and others continued to pound members of Congress with letters and testimony that a peace academy commission or a national peace academy was unnecessary, unwarranted, and counterproductive.

We had to organize written pushback from members of Congress to the objecting federal departments who had opposed the most recent bill. For example, we worked with friendly Senate staff to write letters to the Secretaries of HEW, State, OMB, and other departments pushing back on their formal testimony of disapproval. When a powerful member of Congress addresses a cabinet secretary on his stated position, it raises many issues, as these same Senators and members of the House have jurisdiction over other aspects of oversight on the government departments. Heads of federal departments do not want to directly oppose the desires and wishes of members because there may come a time in the future when the secretary of that department might want something from the same members.

The year 1979 was shaping up to be the hardest year of the campaign. NPAC filed its taxes for 1978 and we showed a total income for the year of $59,555. It had been difficult to hold the staff together during these lean times. The fact that our small team of staff stayed together and continued to raise the visibility of the concept was a tribute to their private beliefs in the idea and commitment to its possibilities.

The NPAC staff, again Bob Paley, Paul Ottens, Laurie Silver, Joan Mann, and Mike Mapes, deserve recognition for their fortitude and sacrifice in keeping the campaign moving ahead. Without their efforts I believe the legislation moving through Congress would have died after its introduction, much as the previous 140 bills had perished before they got to the floor of either body.

Over the weekend of February 18 and 19, 1979, a record snowstorm hit the Washington area. Nearly nineteen inches of snow fell within twenty-four hours, shutting down the city. It served as another meteorological metaphor for me. Our campaign had stalled and the city was shut down by snow. I slapped on a pair of cross-country skis and set off to ski the twelve blocks from our rented home to the National Mall. It was a route I usually ran, but with the new snow the city had become a wintery wonderland. The city was caught by surprise by the fast-moving storm. There was no chance of clearing the roads, monuments, or public areas.

Earlier in the month, farmers had planned a protest in Washington to raise the visibility of farm issues. Their strategy had been to drive as many huge tractor-combine harvesters into the city to lend uniqueness and visibility to their protest. The snowstorm had caught the hundreds of machines in its icy wake. The tractors were parked around the National Mall, with a somewhat malevolent presence. The Mayor of Washington and city council were all over the news adopting confrontational postures regarding the tractors and the farmers who had invaded the city. Surprisingly, and unannounced in the midst of the storm, the farmers started up their machines and cleared the streets of Washington, DC, a task that had overwhelmed the city's plowing resources. The unilateral action of the farmers created a lot of goodwill with the citizens of DC and political will with the Congress.

The beginning of the year brought a maturing in the life cycle of the peace academy movement. I wrote a highly detailed action plan to serve as guidance for the remainder of our campaign. It formulated a staff plan in a management-by-objectives format around specific strategies and job descriptions. In the plan we projected an operating budget for the coming years of $630,000. As it turned out, the campaign proved to be successful in its fundraising efforts and our books showed revenues of nearly that amount in the following period.

In March 1979 we tried to jumpstart a slow beginning to the year by staging a recognition reception at the Capitol. One of our supporters, Dasi Grubbs, a local Washington artist, had generously created five busts made out of sculpted terra cotta. Dasi and her husband, Don, had in fact been very loyal supporters of NPAC for three years. Don and I were office suite mates when I first opened the NPAC office on K Street in the summer of 1976 and shared Beverly Orr as our secretary. In those early days, it was as if we were a family.

After Don moved to more permanent offices he often lent our campaign his conference space, copiers, or telephone lines for evening member call banks. Dasi had sculpted busts for Representatives Fascell and Meyner and Senators Hatfield, Matsunaga, and Randolph. As we began the reception, I thanked Dasi and Don for their years of support, and acknowledged Dasi for her artwork. In recognizing the Congressional leaders I greeted them and those gathered in an ornate room in the Dirksen Senate Office Building. I said:

> "The National Peace Academy Campaign is tonight honoring five distinguished members of Congress for their dedication to the ideals of a United States Academy of Peace and Conflict Resolution. By working toward the passage of the Commission on Proposals for the National Academy of Peace and Conflict Resolution, they are helping to bring about a greater federal commitment to research and training in nonviolent means of resolving conflict than this nation has ever seen."[63]

I continued,

> "There are three important reasons why progress is being made now. First, the field of conflict resolution has accelerated in its development. Its recent history provides examples of concrete skills for peacemaking. Peace is now understood to be a dynamic process that can be pursued just as consciously as war or other violent methods. Second, the constituency for a new institution is being organized by the National Peace Academy Campaign, whose sole purpose is to work for the creation of a peace academy. When that goal is achieved, NPAC will cease to exist. Third, strong and respected leadership has emerged in the Congress to push for a peace academy".[64]

I asked each of the members of Congress to come forward and presented them each with the clever, and humorous, ten-inch lifelike busts. Congressman Fascell was first up and I acknowledged "as Chairman of the Subcommittee on International Operations he had held the first hearings ever in the House of Representatives on a peace academy bill. Under his guidance, the committee assembled a strong sampling of viewpoints in the field of conflict resolution, and through his intelligent questioning many of the essential points about the Peace Academy were highlighted for the record."

Senator Hatfield was next and I said, "Senator Hatfield co-sponsored the peace academy commission legislation and helped guide it through the Senate. His commitment to the cause is well known. The essence of a national peace academy was summed up by Senator Hatfield when he offered, 'We must move out into the frontier of new philosophies and techniques of keeping the peace, symbolized not by guns and the bomb, but by the human embrace and the extended hand of friendship and understanding."

When Senator Matsunaga walked up to the podium I acknowledged that, "The Senator's stated fondest dream is to establish a federal commitment to peace research and education to 'launch our nation on a course that may well become the accomplishment for which we will be known in the future and world history, because no other nation dared to do it—the pursuit of peace as art.'"

Representative Meyner, who had just left her service as a Congresswoman from New Jersey, was pleased to be recognized for her recent role as the prime sponsor of the peace academy bill in the House. In handing the art bust to her, I stated, "Her efforts were invaluable in getting the hearings held and in obtaining backing for the concept. On the need for a peace academy, Mrs Meyner has said, "The primary reason why more conflicts have not been resolved by impartial mediation is the lack of trained and experienced mediators. The need for more qualified mediators will increase will the pressures of population growth, increasing competition for scarce resources, and intensified contact and interdependence among peoples and nations.'"

Finally, Senator Randolph came up. I tried to be both respectful and descriptive when I called the Senator "the turtle of the Senate" in referring to the fact that he had persisted in introducing peace institute or peace academy bills more often than any legislator during his service in the Congress since 1945. I hoped I did not hurt his feelings, as I think he appreciated what I was saying. He had a consistent record of doggedly introducing pieces of legislation that eventually became law. Included among those were the right to vote for eighteen-year-olds and the establishment of the National Air and Space Museum, which had just been dedicated in 1976. I said, "The Senator, who has long said the idea of a peace academy has been 'loved to death,' for too long, is determined to see that this effort too will be successful."

These legislators above all others were most responsible for the creation of USIP.

With the legislators standing holding with their commemorative artwork, Dasi Grubbs jumped and up nudged me away from the podium. She kindly asked her husband Don to bring up a sixed bust, one that was in the image of me. I was honored to receive it. I stood there smiling back at my campaign colleagues and the gathering of NPAC supporters.

We aggressively began to advocate for a peace academy model, pushed our NPAC members and legislative sponsors for appropriations, and began identifying the names of individuals for Commission appointments.

♖ ♗ ♞

In the spring of 1979 the resistance to our efforts really began to cause a backlash with some in the foreign policy establishment. We had gained increased support among Congressional and civic leaders, church organizations, conflict resolution professionals, political science and peace research scholars, and an expanding universe of the American citizenry, but one constituency bloc loomed and hovered as a major adversary: the schools of foreign service, the monolithic State Department bureaucracy, and the right wing fringe, whose concern about any dilution of American hegemony seemed an insurmountable obstacle. Peace was seen by some foreign policy establishment professionals as "peace on American terms," and was regarded to be the domain of diplomatic elites. Certainly not every career foreign service officer expressed this view, but many did feel we were treading on their turf. Simply stated: they thought peace belonged to the State Department, clear and simple.

There had been a touch of innocence in my efforts to date. I had been busy trying to win over the gatekeepers and gain organizational endorsements to grow our membership. I believed we had a good idea and that everyone should support it. I believed in the idea that evil men triumph when good men do nothing. We were the good guys and we were doing all that we could. I thought that as long as we worked hard to deliver our message, we would be successful. I was beginning to learn there was more to it than that. I was about to enter a week that would help illuminate the inside politics of how the international non-governmental world was beginning to work, and the importance of the quickly evolving field of community and civic dispute resolution.

In late April 1979 I had a series of meetings that flipped a switch in my head. On Monday at my office, I met with Michael Doyle who was in town from the Center for Collaborative Problem Solving in San Francisco. On Tuesday I met in DC with Peter Schaffer of Development Alternatives, Inc. On Wednesday I traveled to NYC to meet with John Stremlau at the Rockefeller Foundation and then Sandy Jaffe at the Ford Foundation. Thursday I spoke at a community conflict resolution conference at Columbia University, followed by a reception for the peace academy. It was a typical week, but for the first time it made clear to me a new landscape. As I checked in at the Eastern Airlines commuter terminal on Friday to board my plane back to Washington, my mind was abuzz with all that had happened.

Michael Doyle was an architect by training who had started a company with his partner David Straus to advance the use of collaborative problem-solving techniques in making meetings run better and allowing organizations to address change more effectively. Three years later I would join their company, by then renamed Interaction Associates. It was clear to me in talking with Michael that our efforts to shift the way the US government thought about peace was akin to how innovators in the private sector were reinventing how groups and organizations thought about and practiced managing change.

Throughout these meetings in April 1979, a theme began to emerge that suggested a nexus was forming amid different professional discipline, approaches to conflict resolution and collaborative styles of managing organizations. These apparent trends could be seen in the work of nonprofits, corporations, both nationally and internationally. It was clearly just a beginning. Management theories X, Y, and Z were beginning to be contemplated and written about by business consultants. New and different forms of international organizations were sprouting up, tasking activists to reach out to developing communities in innovative ways.

Across town, in the meeting with Peter Schaffer at Development Alternatives, DAI, I was introduced to one new reality new of American foreign policy. It represented a policy shift that would be increasingly popular and carried out by private contractors. Some of these efforts were good, and as it turned out, but others were bad. It was increasingly understood among the foreign policy establishment that part of the way to ensure international peace was to provide international development funds. Three colleagues who I met at the JFK School of Government at Harvard University had founded DAI in 1970. Coming from backgrounds in international development, the men came to believe that economic development could be much more than a philanthropic exercise. They were bright, entrepreneurial, and savvy in the ways of international development. They set about piecing together projects and small contracts to build a business that would eventually earn nearly $400 million in contract funding by 2010. In a company history entitled "The First 40: A History of DAI," they sketched out the changing world of international development. In it they described how the modern idea of foreign aid grew largely out of the American experience after World War II – the Marshall Plan in Europe and other programs designed to bring distressed nations back into the worldwide economy. The motives behind such aid, of course, were complex but could be summarized to three factors: anticommunism, humanitarianism, and a desire to increase international trade and investment.

During the late 1940s and 1950s, US foreign aid was provided mostly in the form of large capital infusions and investments to build dams and highways, and supply heavy machinery manufactured in the United States. The cultures and traditions of impoverished third-world countries, so called in contrast to the "first world" (developed democracies) and the "second world" (communist countries)—were largely ignored by self-confident planners and engineers. By the end of the 1950s, many had begun to question this approach.[65]

More ambitious development approaches came into practice during the Kennedy administration, specifically its New Frontier commitment to spreading freedom and improving the lives of people caught in poverty. Kennedy pushed through the Foreign Assistance Act in 1961 and a new generation of idealists was inspired by approaching development in new ways. The founders of DAI were among these innovators.

In the wholesome spirit of the Peace Corps, founded nine years earlier, DAI entered developing countries to provide technical assistance. However, some companies during this period were tempting avenues for US intelligence agencies to gain influence in targeted nations. Even DAI had been accused in the past as being a front for the CIA.

Peter Shaffer of DAI was interested in what we were doing because it involved advancing new approaches to better managing conflict, a sister skill set to development assistance. The takeaway was that traditional diplomacy, as we had known it was growing into a new enterprise of intelligence activity, regional problem solving, and conflict prevention. That was where the action was going to be.

In New York, my morning meeting at the Rockefeller Foundation was with Dr Stremlau, whose responsibilities included supporting research and training in the fields of international security, arms control, and economic cooperation. I was there to ask him for money to help our campaign. He would later serve as a senior advisor to the Carnegie Commission on Preventing Deadly Conflict and eventually be asked by President Carter to serve as Vice President for Peace Programs at the Carter Center of Emory University. He would replace Dayle Spencer who, of course, had previously held that position when it was designated as the Fellow for Conflict Resolution Programs. John was sympathetic with what we were doing but was not in a position to provide funds to the campaign for our work. He was an advocate of the United States working more effectively through democratic partners in conflict regions.

We spoke about the importance of the nation's search for ways to address conflict without the use of force. We spoke of alternatives to the old ways of doing things and the absolute need to work through others, rather than through elites merely committed to making peace beneficial to the US Government. We understood it was, and is the prerogative of the State Department to carry out American policies to stabilize conflict zones. Stability has always been valued by the State Department, except on those occasions when the US wanted a different leader in power. Indigenous peoples seeking freedom and independence as virtues of self-determination, can run counter to perceived US interests; hence a dilemma.

Sandy Jaffe at the Ford Foundation was my afternoon meeting. Sandy represented a different side of the conflict resolution field. He had been chief of the criminal division in the US Attorney's office in Newark, New Jersey until he became a special assistant to the Attorney General of the US in 1965. In 1967, he was appointed to serve as Executive Director of the Governor's Select Commission on Civil Disorders to evaluate the causes and impact of the civil disorders in Newark and other New Jersey cities. I was meeting with him because he was the Officer in Charge of the Government and Law Program at the Ford Foundation. Ford had just published a report called, 'New Approaches to Conflict Resolution,' in which Sandy had played a part. The report concisely reviewed current practices and promising alternatives in managing national conflicts and disputes relating to racial equality, energy allocation, environmental protection, consumer rights, and equal education opportunity. It addressed alternative models such as arbitration, conciliation, and the importance of systematic reforms where domestic courts and administrative agencies had become entrenched. In short, the report was about "finding better ways of handling disputes outside of the formal system." What was most interesting was that McGeorge Bundy had written the foreword of the report. Bundy was a bright man who had spent most of his professional life in international relations. The connection between national and international dispute resolution was beginning to stick.

Bundy was appointed National Security Advisor to President Kennedy in 1961 after having served as the youngest dean of the Faculty of Arts and Sciences at Harvard at the age of thirty-four. As national Security Advisor for Kennedy, he supported escalating the American involvement in the Vietnam War and the bombing of North Vietnam. Later in his career, he took over as president of the Ford Foundation in 1966.

David Halberstam, in *The Best and the Brightest*, posed the question in part about Bundy, "If he was so smart, how could he get it (Viet Nam) so wrong?"[66] When Bundy died in 1996, he was said to be working on a book about the war whose main message was that Vietnam was a terrible mistake. Mac, as he was called, was bright enough to own up to his mistakes.

Nonetheless, Bundy and the Ford Foundation were seeing the interconnectedness and value of domestic conflict resolution skills and the potential for their possible application in international relations. This linkage was a sign to me that society appeared to be learning from war what it needed to do differently to achieve peace. The oppositional threads of war and peace were fraying as the use of force and traditional diplomatic advocacy were starting to wear thin. The disciplines of peace seeking, peacemaking and transforming the nature of conflict had begun to present local and foreign possibilities. No one I spoke with in the spring of 1979 was overly optimistic, but the sentiment among practitioners was on their minds. The field of peace and the players were changing.

Others associated with the Ford Foundation would later be supportive of our efforts to elevate alternative approaches that integrated dispute resolution techniques and international relations. Sir Brian Urquhart was Senior Scholar at the foundation when I first met him two years later and we sat together on the bus heading to the Carter Center on Copenhill. He had been a member of the British diplomatic staff involved in the setting up of the United Nations in 1945, assisting the Executive Committee of the Preparatory Commission of the United Nations in establishing the administrative framework of the organization that had been created by the UN Charter. He subsequently became an aide to the first Secretary-General of the United Nations and helped handle the administrative and logistical challenges involved in getting the UN established in New York City. When Dag Hammarskjold became the second Secretary-General in 1953, he appointed Urquhart as one of his main advisors, making him responsible for UN peacekeeping and conflict resolution efforts.

During the Suez Crisis of 1956, Brian organized the first UN peacekeeping force, which was designed to separate the Egyptian and Israeli forces then fighting one another in the Sinai Peninsula. To differentiate the peacekeepers from other soldiers, the UN wanted to have the soldiers wear blue berets. Upon learning the berets required six weeks to make, Urquhart proposed the characteristic blue helmets, which could be converted in a day by painting over regular ones. So goes pragmatic peacemaking. Brian Urquhart would later serve as an advisor to the International Negotiation Network at the Carter Center.

It was widely understood in the dispute resolution community that part of the way to ensure urban peace was to provide local development funds. Just like the guys at DAI, Sandy Jaffe understood the linkages we in NPAC were making between the disciplines of dispute resolution and international relations. We spoke about how complex public policy disputes were similar to international conflicts and how the emerging mechanisms to better manage both were in need of greater study and national visibility.

My youth and idealism clouded my understanding of how many parts of DC worked. I was more than a bit secretly embarrassed by my naiveté. Later I realized that I was asking the right questions; pursuing the right goals. Ours was not a battle of ideas based on academic or rational experience as I had thought. It was not a few in the citizenry calling out for change. Our campaign had turned into a classic David and Goliath skirmish between those who understood and valued the emerging field of conflict resolution and some in the foreign policy establishment who were protecting the heretofore-celebrated elites of international relations. The battle was larger than I had ever imagined. I thought back on the Pacem Terris conference I had attended in the fall of 1975. There it all was—and I had missed it. Foreign policy and peacemaking were seen as the domain of the elite. The nature of conflict was changing and the elites had not yet caught up. New forms of peacemaking were strongly informed by the American experience in labor, civil rights, and environmental negotiations. The State Departments' Foreign Service Institute did not teach mediation until the year 1979.

The real duel had not yet begun. Our challenge to those that viewed international relations as their exclusive domain was just beginning to heat up. It felt as if those who controlled the portals to American foreign policy viewed our growing tribe as bohemian upstarts. This relatively small group of international relations gatekeepers publically acknowledged no value in the success of dispute resolution techniques in community sectors and professed not to trust its application in concerns of international affairs. It was not only intimidating, but also fed into my own insecurities and need for legitimization. It was a simple case of elites protecting their power, funding, and prestige. It was a type of intellectual class war. The debates that lay ahead were going to be with the true believers of the foreign policy establishment. They were the foreign policy-holics, largely an inside-the-Beltway set of folks who saw the world through their addiction of viewing the world as it had always been run. There was no room for alternative thinking, at least not yet.

Our campaign efforts to link advances in the domestic dispute resolution sciences with advances in peace research sciences was evidently a nonstarter for these folks. But they seemed to be missing the obvious — excluding national conflict resolution skills from international mindsets would be like excluding national health issues from international health concerns. The world was just too small — and too interrelated to make this argument, even in 1979. In 2014 an Ebola virus crisis illustrated how sensitive and related health issues are in terms of prevention and treatment. In 2020 with the COVID-19 pandemic out of control, foreign policy elites do not argue that health concerns within and across borders can be differentiated into national or international concerns. The world is experiencing the pandemic, and the world is seeking the solutions to appropriate treatment and possible vaccines.

Health concerns extend across national and domestic boundaries, as do air travel policies. The application of conflict resolution mechanisms does as well. Care and professionalism should always be taken to consider culturally sensitivities, but the science of conflict management, like biology, extends across borders.

Many foreign policy professionals seemed to be caught up in old world thinking even as late as 1970. Their premise was that the world was in disorder and needed to be run by rules and expectations that represented the past. The hope for the world could come about by forceful uniters and large armies that used force to bring about peace. Thirty-five years later, Henry Kissinger's book *World Order* still captures this same worldview, including his assessment that we fail in international relations when we see our nation's domestic principles as universally applicable to others in the world community. As I would learn later, the strict father version of foreign policy presented a denial that kids will be kids and should not be nurtured to grow up, but rather must be disciplined instead.

The leaders and organizations I had met with that week were interested in what we in the campaign were doing as we were beginning to split the seams of several colliding disciplines. In a very modest way, our own efforts to bring attention to alternatives to the use of force in managing conflict were coming onto the screens of others. Our campaign was a curiosity, a challenge, and represented a new consciousness. Things were changing and our campaign reflected the change, not necessarily began it. NPAC and its message was not a threat to the foreign policy establishment, but we represented a trend.

To me, the extension of conflict resolution mechanisms and approaches into international relations made sense intuitively. While the old-world order was resisting, the innovators around them were seeking not just to sit at their table, but to introduce new processes and mindsets that were challenging the way the game was played. We saw our work in the campaign as being about identifying individuals who represented these new mindsets; had political positioning to make a difference, and were friendly to our aspirations.

After the passage of the commission authorization, we began to formulate briefing materials for the future commissioners and lists of possible commission candidates that we passed on to the President, Speaker of the House, and President Pro Tempore of the Senate. Our list of names was based on those with: knowledge of the field; familiarity with the legislative history; legislators with longtime representation of strong constituent interests; those who demonstrated concern about the issues; individuals who represented practitioners and researchers, educators, and other professionals; and individuals representing various regions of the country. We worked hard to vet our list with NPAC supporters and those who had led the legislative efforts.

In early June of 1979 I felt worn down by the pace of the campaign and was feeling a bit despondent about how long I could hang in there, leading the campaign and not moving on with my life. I had been married only a few months and had struggled financially along with other campaign staff to just raise enough money to keep the lights turned on and campaign material going out the door. Our legislation was making good progress and I felt confident there was going to be light at the end of the tunnel in terms of establishing the commission. We had been lobbying hard at the White House, Speaker's office, and in the Senate to gain traction on a list of priority candidates to be named commissioners. We believed the commissioners would soon be appointed. Then, the momentum of our campaign efforts would swing dramatically to the effectiveness of the commission.

Eight of the nine names of those ultimately selected were on the NPAC lists we had put forward. We believed that the visibility and work of the commission itself would be a legitimizing event in the acceptance of the peace academy concept, as had been suggested by Senator Pell.

The commission would necessarily become its own orchestra of players, rules, timeframe and impact. I was not planning to be a part of the band. I had to begin to think about moving on to make money and to starting a family.

Charlie E. Smith, one of our NPAC supporters and advisors, invited me to attend a workshop he was delivering to human resource professionals in the DC area. It was to be my first exposure to organizational development, OD, a rapidly emerging profession that had developed from the fields of industrial relations and management sciences. Charlie and his partner and wife Caela Farren, both had PhDs, were enthusiastic about securing my involvement as a possible career option following any departure I might make from the campaign. The meetings went well and Charlie offered for me to begin working with him and supporting his client work. I was intrigued. Organizational Development was a form of conflict resolution as it related to the effectiveness of teams and the human resources of a company.

I met with Bryant and Jim, and obviously talked a lot about my departure from NPAC with Connie. She had a stable position and although she was traveling back and forth from DC to the United Nations in New York, my travel and hers were manageable. I met with Jack Dover, Charlie Smith, Bill Lincoln, and Mike Mapes to discuss my options. Mike would become Executive Director of the campaign if I were to leave. Charlie, Bill and Jack were supportive of whatever decision I had to make. For me, it ultimately was a financial one.

I agreed to do whatever I could to help the campaign, and I also agreed to begin working as an independent consultant with Charlie in his firm to support him on OD work with his clients. I remained on the board of NPAC, but left my management role in the campaign, turning things over to Mike Mapes. During the ensuing months, the board of NPAC changed and we prepared for the work that would be done by the commission.

In the spring of 1979 my buddy Tom Nash was in town and early on a Sunday morning we planned to go for a run. Tom and his wife were close friends from Delaware where we had met them as part of group sharing a beach house. Tom had been one of my groomsmen in our wedding. Our favorite route was down East Capitol to the National Mall and a circle that took in most of the monuments. It was about a seven-mile run for us the way we did it, running twelve blocks behind the Capitol, past its dome around the Tidal Basin to the Jefferson Memorial, out past the Washington Monument, to the Lincoln Memorial. Heading back we usually took in the Vietnam War Memorial, jogged past the various museums and Smithsonian complex, National Gallery of Art, Supreme Court, Library of Congress, back up East Capitol a few blocks, and we would be back for lunch.

Tom was a US history high school teacher and our Washington runs were always punctuated with side conversations about periods of history reflected by the points of interest on the Mall. As we ran it was fun to imagine and make up pretend dialogues that these early American leaders might be having as they called out to one another from their marble and granite homes.

George might say to Abe, "Hey, how come you've got a roof over your head?" and Abe would reply, "Yeah, but you've got the best view." Sometimes we would construct a bit more meaningful dialogue when Thomas, George, and Abe would get into a discussion about slavery or how to preserve the union. We'd laugh and try to out do one another as we ran one of the most visually inspiring runs anyone could ever wish for.

Beyond the fabulous vistas and sense of history, one of the things that made the run so enjoyable was that most of it could be made on the crushed gravel that lined the route. The surface was not only comfortable, but made a satisfying, definitive crunch sound with every step. That particular morning was cool and the skies were clear. It was a great day for a run. After we reached the Lincoln Memorial, we walked up the stairs to view Abe and turned around to enjoy the view of the Capitol about two miles up the Mall. It was a beautiful sight to behold. We next jogged up toward the State Department, where Connie worked, and past the Naval Hospital to the west.

I stopped when we came to the American Pharmaceutical Association, APhA, building located about halfway between the State Department and the Lincoln Memorial, adjacent to the National Academy of Sciences. We started to stretch. I shared with Tom that this spot would make a great location for a future national academy of peace. I had first noticed the building and its location on my trips to drop off or pick up Connie at State. In those days, the APhA site was seemingly never used. It just stood there. It had been dedicated in 1934 and I often wondered to myself why the pharmaceutical industry required a building on the rarified real estate of the national Mall. I just did not get it. With all due respect to the architect and the industry's founding fathers, the building kind of looked like a mausoleum to me. In fairness to the APhA, an addition to the original building was added in 2009. Today, the complex looks less like a tomb because of the modern office building addition.

We retied our shoes and discussed the possibilities.

"Maybe Congress could trade a piece of land someplace else for this location." I said.

In our planning for the peace academy we had foreseen a respectable, ceremonial Washington, DC, presence for the institution, someplace around the Mall. I had surveyed other locations and this spot seemed like the best location, even though it resided in my wildest dreams. Many in the campaign had talked about a campus location probably within a couple hundred miles of the District of Columbia. I had personally explored those options too, taking side trips out into the countryside of Maryland, Virginia, West Virginia, and even Delaware. I had studied how the final location of the UN building in New York had been stolen away from San Francisco. I knew the politics of wealthy individuals and families who had bought up land to tie their family name and generosity to national monuments and parks. Deep down I held a belief that one day a national peace institute might benefit from such benevolence and stand along the National Mall as a symbol of our national commitment to peace. We already had enough war memorials around the Mall. We needed a living building, occupied by peace researchers and policy advocates to further grace the space where currently there was a tomb-like, flat unengaged marble lump.

Tom thought I was being too hard on the APhA folks and their national headquarters. We stretched a bit more and then started our run toward the Capitol up across the grassy knolls around the Vietnam Memorial and once again onto the gravel jogging track of the Mall. What a beautiful run.

♖ ♗ ♘

Later that summer I received an invitation from the Martin Luther King, Jr Center for Nonviolent Social Change to attend their summer institute on nonviolence. I was asked to be a resource person and was flattered but mildly embarrassed to be included in such a forum when I saw myself merely as an advocate, not the practitioner that Dr King, Andy, Jim, or others were, or had been. I just felt a little unworthy. I had not been involved in the Movement. I was prepared to be intimidated in the presence of others I might meet who had been on the front lines of protest, civil disobedience, and had established credentials in the fight for racial equality.

At the meetings, I conducted my sessions and answered the many questions about the national peace academy, peace research, and our legislative progress. Most questions related to the balance of activism and academic study of the institute. I shared my views and those of the academics we had often convened during the life of the campaign. The national peace academy was to be designed as a facilitator of policy, not an implementer. It would not be an intervention agency of the government, but rather provide a bias for new thinking and education, based on research and training as part of its portfolio.

In side discussions with activists attending the King Center program, I found many were grateful for our efforts. Understandably, others were expressly concerned about the role of the government in the area of peace. Their experience with the government's involvement in many situations had not gone well, and they were clearly distrusting of its potential role in a future peace institute. Certainly, there was push back on the idea, and I had a lot of explaining to do to support our campaign assertion that the institute would be a necessary element to help influence the government in changing its conduct. I felt like I was on a hot seat, although there was a shared assumption that we were on the same team. I did not feel defensive, but I knew I had to be clear in my responses. Up to that point in my life, I personally had limited experience in being victimized by the government; however, I appreciated their concerns and tried to learn from them.

One day after the midday sessions broke; Mrs King approached me and asked if I would join her and some other participants for lunch. I was flattered at the invitation. I quickly accepted and a handful of us left the Center building, led by Mrs King as we walked up the street to the birth home of Dr Martin Luther King Jr. When I realized where we were headed, I was quite amazed. I had thought perhaps we would be heading for a fast food place or something, at best maybe a quieter part of the Center for some pre-set lunch. As we filed up onto the porch of the home, I passed the signage commemorating that Dr King had been born in the house on January 15, 1929. We entered the living room and several of the participants from the meetings began to pour juice and water and set up for lunch. Mrs King asked if I would help her in the kitchen. As fast as that, Mrs King began to prepare turnip greens and some other stovetop contributions to our meal. Standing together in the small kitchen, she asked me to fill the pots with water while she cleaned the greens. We just stood and chatted like we were preparing a comfortable Thanksgiving meal, as though it were something we always did.

Mrs King had always seemed a little formal to me, though I suppose it was more because people treated her with such respect. Dr King was always referred to as Dr King and Mrs King was always Mrs King in the circles in which I travelled. Mrs King was always well dressed and appeared rather regal to me.

At this moment, the degree of formality I had previously projected was lost. She was chatty, and engaged in cooking tasks. Occasionally bumping into one another, we worked around the stovetop as if preparing a holiday meal. In the small kitchen, I nearly gasped when upon asking her, "Mrs King, where can I find the butter?" she responded with, "Oh please call me Coretta." That was still very hard for me to do. I knew her as a respected icon of the Civil Rights period, not as an aproned chef preparing a meal together.

While we were crunching up the leaves and stuffing them into the pot, Mrs King said,

> "You know there are vast reservoirs of experienced and talented individuals from the civil rights days who are highly trained in conflict resolution from the movement days. I am so excited about the work you are doing on the peace academy. These people have impressive skills, and talents, although they do not fit a traditional definition of an elite and are therefore unknown and underutilized."[67]

She asked me to hand her another bunch of uncooked greens from the sink. The kitchen was getting a bit steamy as the ingredients boiled. "These people are veterans of the movement and came from every walk of life. The national academy has the potential to bring these people together in the first real unified effort at national peacemaking in American history." I was struck by her vision and practical approach.

"Yes," I said, then added,

"We have hopes that the experience of the civil rights movement will further catalyze not only a focus on nonviolence but also on a linkage of the experience of those community peacemakers with our foreign policy experts. Academics who were part of the movement get this connection. Unfortunately the schools of foreign service people don't seem to appreciate the value of the practitioners who learned their trade on the front lines of the movement. They prefer the tablecloth approach to the raw wood table experience. I don't believe it's as much about elitism as it is about not understanding the true value of dispute resolution that grew out of the hard-boiled realism of the labor, environmental and civil rights movement."

She nodded, and then asked that I go to the living room and invite the other guests to sit at the table. Upon my return to the kitchen, she said,

"I really think that bringing all these people under the umbrella of the national academy will go a long way toward bringing existing organizations into a cooperative unified whole. There is very much for everyone to gain. Whenever Martin spoke with international leaders from around the world, he always remarked to me how much they respected the homegrown American experience with disputes. It will be too bad if our own international diplomats don't see the wisdom in learning more about and practicing what we have done here at home."[68]

It was clear that my very special time with Mrs King had come to an end. I said,

"Coretta, I certainly have enjoyed visiting with you. Thank you for having me to lunch. What a privilege, really." We carried the hot food platters into the other room. As we did she added, "I think too that this approach would help to ensure the integrity, balance, and independence of the academy. The vigor of the movement was generated by the many disciplines and walks of life that contributed to everything we did."[69]

♖ ♗ ♞

In July 1979, Andy Young found out that an upcoming report by the United Nations Division for Palestinian Rights called for the creation of a Palestinian State. Andy wanted to delay the report because the Carter Administration was dealing with too many other issues at the time. He met with the UN representatives of several Arab countries to try to convince them the report should be delayed; they agreed in principle, but insisted that the Palestinian Liberation Organization also had to agree. As a result, on July 20, Young met with Zehdi Terzi, the UN representative of the PLO, at the apartment of the UN Ambassador from Kuwait. On August 10, news of this meeting became public. The meeting was highly controversial, since the United States had already promised Israel that it would not meet directly with the PLO until the PLO recognized Israel's right to exist.

The events that unfolded following the meeting in the home of the Kuwaiti Ambassador underlay several of the problem that peacemakers find when they bump up against the formal portfolio of the State Department, which really acts as an advocate for the United States rather than a advocate for peace and social justice.

The well-intended meeting with Terzi ended Andy's UN ambassadorship. Connie was very upset over the weekend of August 11-12, because of the way Andy was being negatively viewed, rather than in light of his trying to protect Israel. Moreover, Connie was mad because someone had ripped down the official sign over the entrance to his seventh floor office at the State Department. It was assumed that the individual believed that Andy was never the sort of person the United States should have had in the ambassadorship. Connie was livid. As part of Andy's seventh floor staff at State for twenty-eight months, Connie had witnessed and fought the animosity of career diplomats toward Andy because of two things: a perception of Andy as an activist not a credentialed envoy, and racism toward his ethnicity. Andy had often had to fight the bureaucracy of the State Department to serve the country as he felt it should be served. Did I mention Connie was angry? She worked very hard over the weekend to see that a new sign was produced and hung over Andy's office door before he arrived back in Washington.

On Wednesday, August 15, 1979, Andy held a press briefing on the incident at the State Department, attended by many employees. Connie and I stood at the back of the room. James Reston hosted the session. Andy began the press conference by saying,

> "I come before you not at all bloody, and in a way I come because I am unbowed. I find that it is very difficult to do the things that are in the interest of the country and also maintain the standards of protocol and diplomacy that you and many people in the nation make us adhere to. I guess, given the choice, I have felt that perhaps I could best serve my country by asking President Carter if he would accept my resignation as the Permanent Representative to the United Nations and if he would decide just when that resignation should become effective."[70]

He continued,

> "I have tried to interpret to our country some of the mood of the rest of the world. Unfortunately, but by birth, I come from the ranks of those who have known and identified with some level of oppression in the world. And by choice, I continue to identify with what I would say in biblical terms would be the least of these, my brethren. I think because of that and in the attempts to bring about peace and justice in the world in which we live, I get extremely impatient with the slow, plodding way of doing things. I do tend to take things into my own hands, and I willingly take the responsibility for it."[71]

Andy went on to say, as he had told Connie and his staff earlier in the week,

> "The most recent incident, I think, is a case where I found myself caught between two groups of people that were both quite desperate in their own way—I think the Palestinians in some sense desperate for recognition, and the Israelis desperate for security.
>
> In an attempt to respond to the invitations and the pleadings of ambassadors from some of the more moderate Arab countries and in an attempt to forestall a Security Council resolution which I felt would be in nobody's interest, and preparing for my term as the present President of the Security Council of the United Nations, I entered into discussions to attempt to postpone or to arrange a date for a meeting of

the Council that would give us time to reach some decisions that might be helpful. In meeting with Kuwait and Syrian and Lebanese Ambassadors, I was told that they really had no possibility of bringing about a postponement, but that if I would talk to the representative of the PLO, perhaps I might be able to persuade him.

They had successfully persuaded the Arab group to support a very moderate resolution on the question of settlements, thinking that the United States would then vote for it, and we felt it necessary to abstain. So, they had really used up their credibility."[72]

Andy, as he had done many times in the civil rights movement, had tried to meet off-line with leaders to work to find a better path to peace than through confrontation or embarrassment. Some fifteen years earlier in their movement days, he and Jim Laue had met secretly to plan for negotiated arrests the following day, or to inform authorities that a civil disobedience action was planned, in order to avoid the risk of violence or embarrassment that might result in the destruction of property or people.

Andy revealed:

"I said I could not meet with representatives of the PLO, but neither could I refuse an invitation from a member of the Security Council to come to his home to talk Security Council business. And I didn't make any attempts to tell him—in fact, I said deliberately that I can't tell you who you can have in your home, but I will be at your home to discuss with you the postponing of any question of a Palestinian resolution.

"Of course, the PLO representative was there. And I made an effort to gain a postponement for a question, the answers to which we were not, and still are not ready to give. As a result of that I think the insecurities of the Israelis naturally mounted. And because I can understand those insecurities and because throughout all of my days in Congress I was virtually a 100% supporter of the nation of Israel, and still support the nation of Israel, I went to the Israeli Ambassador because I didn't feel as though it was good to beat around the bush or to say things diplomatically. I wanted him to know that I could talk to him as candidly as he had talked with me and that I wanted us to have that kind of frank, open relationship, regardless of the issue at hand.

"I think by doing what I did I helped to preserve our ability to communicate with groups of people who are not able to communicate with each other, but who inevitably must learn to communicate with each other if we are going to have some semblance of peace and prosperity in this world in which we live."[73]

Andy did not want to embarrass Secretary of State Vance or President Carter so he accepted the blame for the incident and resigned. Andy was right in the middle of a delicate leadership role with regard to Namibia and the situation in Rhodesia. By the time of his press conference, Andy had met with both the President and Secretary Vance.

When questioned in the press conference if he felt he was a scapegoat or somehow the victim of some policy or some group, he answered no. He did not see himself as a victim. Andy said to the press and State Department employees that for every time he had spoken out about something during his term as Ambassador to the United Nations, there had been twenty-five to thirty times that he had wanted to speak out and kept silent. He was glad to now lose that level of restraint.

Asked about the incident by *TIME* soon afterward, Young stated, "It is very difficult to do the things that I think are in the interest of the country and maintain the standards of protocol and diplomacy . . .. I really don't feel a bit sorry for anything that I have done."

Andy started a company called Young Ideas after resigning from his ambassadorship. Connie and five or six other political appointees and staff left government service to go with Andy to begin the new venture.

Shortly after Andy's resignation, President Carter asked him to lead a business development mission to twenty African nations. Connie went on the trip to assist the executives who were provided access to the leaders in the countries they visited. Andy provided that access, as he had done to reach out to much of the world as US Ambassador. The trip lasted three weeks and generated several billions of dollars in trade contracts for the American Chief Executive Officers who were packed onto the plane. The trip provided a productive distraction for Andy and Connie after his resignation from the cabinet.

Chapter 6 Review and Reflection

Task

- Discover how to use the power of the system.

Challenge

- Be clear on influencing change versus causing change.

Gift and Opportunity

- See your life in new ways.
- Seek to influence by giving power away.

Reflection

- List five things that you feel are root causes of the situation/problem you wish to change.
- What prevents that change from occurring?
- What societal or ideological forces drive the change you are seeking?

PART FOUR

Carrying out the Commission

CHAPTER 7

2100 M Street

In late December of 1979 I received a call from the office of Senator Matsunaga asking that I come in for an interview with him and Jim Laue. The commission had held its first meeting and the Senator had been elected Chairman and Jim Vice-Chair. The Senator was cordial and complimentary of my efforts to gain the passage of the legislation and asked only one question: Did I believe that I could be neutral in the work of the commission to investigate the need and viability of the peace academy concept?

I was not surprised by his question, but remember digging deep for my answer. I had worked extremely hard for forty-two months to bring our efforts to this moment in time. I felt a sense of loyalty to the thousands of concerned citizens, professional practitioners, members of the research community, and others to carry forward with what we had begun. Could I really give the Senator an honest answer that did not reflect my intense desire and commitment to the benefits that the envisioned institution would bring? Later, I would learn that this very question had been a topic of discussion among the commission members earlier in the week in their first meeting. I was being put on the spot and tested.

The Senator and Jim confided in me that the feelings of the commission as a whole were largely impressed by my familiarity with the issues, and saw my experiences with the campaign as an asset due to the expected fast pace that would be required for the one-year operation of the commission. We needed to hit the ground running and, as Matsunaga himself had been an advocate and co-sponsor of the legislation, our success—and his success as Chair—would be determined by off the block organizational skills, familiarity with the issues, and a high level of commitment to get the job done.

The open question that he had to defend to the other commissioners was: Could I as staff director of the commission be counted on to enter my assignment with an open mind and the self-discipline to genuinely explore all options?

This I truly believed I could do. If anything, I knew—and I believe Matsunaga knew—that I would bend over backwards to explore the concept fully and make the necessary decisions to engage all sides in our work.

I said, "Yes, I will make that commitment, and it would be my honor." The Senator then invited me to be the Director of the Commission on Proposals for the National Academy of Peace and Conflict Resolution. Senator Matsunaga clarified that I would not be a member of his staff, but that the commission would be an independent agency, funded through the Department of Education. I thanked the Senator and Jim for their confidence in me. I told them that as I had already committed three years of my life to advancing the peace academy concept, I was humbled and excited to be part of the work of the commission. I assured the Senator I would do my best to serve him and the other commissioners.

The Senator then asked that I come back *the next day* with a draft budget for his consideration and a draft sketch of what would amount to an operating plan for the commission. As much work as I had put in over the past four years of thinking about a national peace academy, I had never considered the details of an operating budget for a commission.

On December 27, 1979, I was twenty-nine years old and the newly appointed head of a small federal agency with subpoena power. The clock had started and I had stayed up nearly all night at our kitchen table putting down numbers and roughing out a strategy and schedule for the work of the commission. We were off, but not quite running. Public Law 95-561: Education Amendments of 1978, Title XV—Part B that had created the commission and specified that the commission would transmit to the President and Congress a final report not later than one year after the date on which appropriations first became available to carry out the title of the law. The commission itself would cease to exist sixty days after transmitting the final report. Before the inauguration of the next President in twelve months, a final report would be drafted and the work of the commission completed. The clock was already running.

At the second commission meeting in Room 357 of the Russell Senate Office Building, the Senator led the members through the agenda we had prepared and asked me to present my ideas regarding our operations, mechanics, and expectations of the commissioners. The meeting ran two days and covered the following commission start-up topics:

- Staff introductions
- Approval of minutes and proposed agenda from the first commission meeting
- Review of major tasks for the commission
- Order of tasks before the commission
- Decisions on scope and limitations

- Start dates, and proposed schedule of hearings
- Roles of other private and federal agencies
- Arrangements for office space
- Staff salary levels
- List of relevant statutory guidelines
- Organizational charts
- Proposed operations plan
- Timeline of budget limitations and participation by individual commissioners
- List of other commissioner activity; commissioner interests and special requests
- Suggestions regarding the creation of a National Advisory Committee
- Determination of subtopic study groups
- Regional Committee structure
- Criteria for hearing witness testimony
- Subtopic or geographic-orientation for small groups in various cities

The meeting was a grind to prepare for and present.

On the second day I received approval of my draft budget, and discussed the commission decision-making process, voting procedures if commissioners were absent, media strategy for commissioner visibility and we set the agenda for the third meeting of the commission for mid-January, twelve days later.

♖ ♗ ♘

Initially we had the idea of naming a National Advisory Committee to serve as a high-level conduit for testimony to the commission. This was eventually nixed due to staff and commissioner time constraints. There was not enough time or money to do all that we wanted to do. We created at a staff level a number of working groups such as research advisory panels.

After refining the budget in early January I arranged for a General Services Administration, GSA, representative to walk me through the possible office space options that might serve as our Commission offices. I had drawn a small sketch of what space we might require and where in the city might work for our staff. The General Services Administration manages the government office space and transportation assets it owns or leases. GSA was set up in 1949 to help centralize the purchasing power of the government and better manage the things the government needs to run efficiently. Not only would GSA be providing the office space, our desks, conference tables, entry chairs, bookshelves, and files would be rented to us for the term of the commission. That day, we visited five properties that GSA had determined might serve as our commission offices.

The suite of offices I selected was at 2100 M Street, NW, about halfway between DuPont Circle and Washington Circle. The details of what it would take to manage the life of the commission were beginning to come into focus.

Both Washington Circle and DuPont Circle were first drawn on Pierre L'Enfant's 1791 map that laid out grids of streets and, some say, defensive "circles" that were to be placed in strategic locations around the city. Other historians have written that the circles were actually conceived as squares to serve as economic development hubs for the new federal city. Each circle intersected four major roads. Whether the circles were conceived to help slow an invading army or to provide regionally identifiable sections of the city, they still exist as major landmarks and hubs of both residential and business activity.

As the GSA person and I walked into what would become our offices, I noticed that it was filled with discarded diagrams and papers; the space presented in general a pretty messy sight. I was informed that the Three Mile Island Commission had just vacated the space. Three Mile Island near Harrisburg, Pennsylvania, was the site of America's worst accident at a civilian nuclear power plant and occurred on March 28, 1979. Half of the fuel rods melted in one of two nuclear reactors leaking large quantities of radioactivity from the reactor, but most of it was contained. The accident had begun with failures in non-nuclear systems, followed by a relief valve that had accidentally stuck in its open position. I moved a desk to get a better view of the room dimensions—and there on the floor we saw a blueprint, marked up in red ink, clearly indicating a series of valves. Our eyes locked on to the document, and then to each other. Whether the plans were relevant or showed the actual location of the valves was not important. For a moment the two of us suddenly felt like we saw history pass before us. *We were holding history.* Soon, our own commissioners and staff would be taking steps to make our own history.

The twelve-member Presidential Three Mile Island Commission had been established in April 1979 by President Carter to determine the cause of the Three Mile Island accident. It released its final report on October 30, 1979. By their own account, the Three Mile Island Commission, TMI, conducted one hundred fifty depositions and held public hearings, collecting enough "material that will fill about three hundred feet of shelf-space." In their report the TMIC recommended fundamental changes to the Nuclear Regulatory Commission, but the report stated, "We did not claim our proposed recommendations are sufficient to assure the safety of nuclear power." I began to wonder what our Final Report would state and how many feet of shelf-space our documents would require.

A Presidential Commission, like TMI, is created exclusively by the President and reports to his office. Our commission was a federal commission, created by both houses of Congress and the Executive Office. Its nine members represented the House, Senate, and the President and our report would be made to all three sponsoring entities. We had subpoena power but were tasked with no other instructions about how we should conduct our business or the detailed range of our inquiry.

In its Preface, the 179-page TMI Commission report addressed as much about what they did not do, as what they did. In the coming days and months, our staff and commissioners would have to sort out the scope and depth of our own recommendations. Our Final Report to the President and Congress turned out to be 386 pages and would be published in just four hundred days. We literally would be writing history one page at a time for the next twelve months.

♖ ♗ ♞

I began to interview staff at a restaurant on M Street across from what would be the commission offices. With each candidate I spoke about staffing needs and the effort it would take to quickly get the commission up and running, executed, and then shut down—all within one year. Sitting in the bistro-type grill, I looked around at the brick walls, hanging fern plants, and rich darkened booths. I thought how nice it was going to be to finish a workday and pop into the restaurant with staff members to relax and savor what we were doing. That fantasy never happened.

Running the commission was an all-out effort. We went from one day in early January, 1980, with no people, no office, no furniture, no money, no operating plan, and no business cards—to ten days later a bustling, fully furnished, operational 3,500 square foot office, filled with thirty employees learning their new jobs, making phone calls, and beginning to make preliminary witness lists. We hit the ground running very hard.

Most critical in approaching the design of the fast-moving work year of the commission was my consideration of the public hearing schedule and structure. The commission staff would eventually engage in more than fifty significant meetings around the country with NGO leaders at the United Nations, International Peace Academy, military education leaders, conflict resolution experts, academics, and diplomats. But the twelve public seminar programs—as we called them—would be central to our outreach and fulfillment of our Congressional mandate. We had to quickly select the cities we would visit in the public seminar schedule; address specific themes for each hearing location; work out and manage the logistics of travel, venues, witness selection, and public relations to generate attendance; and not least, build our program into the personal schedules of each individual commissioner. To accomplish this, one of my first hires was the Reverend Leslie H. Carter, a former civil rights worker who would become the Director of Program Operations. Les would lead our challenging effort to secure the hearing venues, identify and motivate our local public seminar regional coordinators, and support our team in coordinating and following up on testimony from experts and the public at large. We would eventually receive written testimony from over three thousand citizens and hear extended oral testimony from close to two hundred experts and citizens. Roughly eighteen hundred citizens participated in the public seminar programs over a period of five months. We were hustling.

We selected our public seminar locations based on the interests of the commissioners, legislative relationships, the availability of witnesses, and regional representation. An additional factor in my decision-making was a very thoughtful *Washington Post* article that I had read in March of 1979 by Joel Garreau entitled "The Nine Nations of North America."[74] Mr Garreau drew a new map of the country reflecting the realities of politics, culture, economics, and regional feelings. We were diligent in convening a public hearing in each of the "nine nations" identified by Garreau, and in three other cities. It proved to be a successful and practical strategy. Ultimately, about $150,000 of our commission budget was spent on travel. In conducting the public seminar process the way we did, we eventually garnered the co-sponsorship of more than one-fifth of the Senate and roughly ten percent of the House. These twenty-two Senators and fifty Representatives became the core of support in the Congress that lead to the passage of our legislation.

Each public seminar was conducted over a period of two days. Les worked carefully with our regional coordinators to plan every event, building in time for dialogue, citizen participation, report outs, and commissioner time for informal discussion and engagement with each community. A typical day one consisted of formal testimony followed by questions and answers with the commissioners, then lunch. More formal testimony was followed by question and answer and then public participants were organized into small group, facilitator-led discussions.

Not every commissioner attended every hearing, so we developed an internal method of updating each commissioner on witness bios and testimony summaries, and notes on commission staff meetings with various organizations and agencies. As we settled into the first quarter of the calendar year, I realized that one staff person's time would have to be dedicated to working directly with each of the nine commissioners. Ann Richardson, a very capable and likeable woman, filled this function with great skill as she managed the schedules, expenses, special needs, egos, and briefings of the commissioners.

As the year moved on, we had to hire more administrative personnel to manage our reimbursement process and budgeting constraints imposed by the Office of Education, who served as our official link to bureaucratic Washington. During the course of the year, about forty staff and commissioners came and went through our space, excluding the Chairman's personal Senate staff with whom we coordinated much of our activity. Most of the work of the commission was out of the office.

Not long after the start-up of the commission I was in my office and my secretary brought into me a small package that had arrived a week earlier. She had set it aside as I had been traveling for most of the week. I noticed the package had already been opened, but was repackaged in a haphazard way and I looked up at her as if to say, "What's this?"

She said, "That came for you last week. I opened it but thought you might like to open it yourself." I said, "OK," and preceded to dig into the brown wrapping, bubble wrap, and tissue. I tossed the wrapping paper into my wastebasket and flipped over the object. It was beautiful. Inside was a small bronze replica of my commission business card, mounted on an equally small marble rectangle. Our actual commission business cards were quite impressive. Up in the left corner, each card featured a gold embossed eagle of the United States, holding a bunch of arrows in one talon and a cluster of olive branches in the other. There before me on my desk sat a commemorative version of my own personal business card. The bronze card perfectly recreated my name, title, and our commission address in metal and stone. In a way, it said: "I had done what I had set out to do." It made me so proud; so very proud. Whoever had sent the gift was proud, as well. I looked up with watery eyes to ask my secretary where it had come from.

She looked back at me with a warm smile. The package had contained a remarkable gift, but from whom? I immediately looked for a card. There was none. I looked to her again. She nodded in the direction of my wastebasket and I dug into to retrieve the outer wrapping. Up in the corner of the wrapping was the return address of the sender. It was from my dad.

Five years earlier in Prescott, Arizona, my dad had expressed disbelief and great disappointment in my decision to pursue peace as an academic and professional pursuit. Now his gift was saying to me, "I was wrong. You did it. Congratulations."

During the work of the commission we would hold twelve hearings across America: providing a formal platform for one hundred twenty invited expert witnesses and more than six hundred public seminar participants from every walk of American life and region. The Commissioners spent more than two hundred thirty hours analyzing seven thousand pages of oral and written testimony and interacting with citizens in fifty major substantive meetings with government, academic, and international organizations.

Thirty years after the end of the commission, I had the occasion to interview Judy Bunnell, our youngest staff person, first hire, and last employee of the commission to be on payroll. She had just graduated from Yale University when she joined our staff. She was smart, enthusiastic, and admittedly very new to the politics of organizations and the dynamics of Washington. I asked her what her memories were of the commission some thirty years earlier. She said, "Honestly, I saw the tensions and felt the deadlines among the staff leadership. I remember once when a personnel concern was brought to your attention just after you returned from being on the road for back-to-back hearings. You handled it well, but I specifically recall the look on your face and in your tone that the issue had not been better handled in your absence."

I told Judy that I recalled her frustration one day when we had to make the decision to cancel the Chicago hearing she had been planning. She had had to make a decision that most likely made her feel like she had failed, when Judy had actually recommended exactly the right thing. In the context of the short timeframe the commission had to work with, all staff were called upon to make judgments, shape the composition of witness groups, say no, and share their opinions and decisions quickly, without the aid of email, texting or cell phones, which of course did not exist yet.

In the tight time frames in which we were working there was great pressure to plan quickly, engage, execute, and move on. Our commission staff performed exceptionally well. By the close of the commission, there had been fifty-four human moving parts, all needing direction, coordination, response times, and feedback on their performance so as to perfect our overall effectiveness. This number did not include the various staff members in Congressional offices and government agencies with whom we had to coordinate or inform of our work.

In the Chicago example, our staff and Midwest regional coordinator had not been able to garner enough local support to pull off what we judged a successful event to be. But ultimately the twelve major hearing events we did plan and execute between March and September were very successful, but in our planning we had established a fairly robust set of criteria for regional programs. Each of our planning events were planned to maximize the broadest citizen participation possible; that required a high level of staff effort. Each event required a full media campaign. Mailing lists from the Regional Coordinators we had contracted with had to have been received on time to be effective. Official invitations to participants and witnesses had to be sent out ten to twenty days in advance of the events. Witnesses had to be identified and vetted. Local site arrangements and contracts had to be confirmed before venues could be announced. The Department of Education, our designated host agency responsible for financial management, had an explicit process for contract approvals and often took their time cutting checks and such.

Finally, each of the twelve hearings demanded a short time cycle to print, assemble, and label three hundred pieces of mail and six hundred packets that were to be distributed at the hearing events. The work to simultaneously manage field operations, commissioner schedules, travel logistics, balance witness perspectives, conduct non-hearing related special meetings, etc. kept everyone busy.

Often individual commissioners would express interest in inviting specific groups to hearings, such as veterans, women's organizations, specific peace groups, or policy centers. Tracking down individuals or leaders of groups took time. In our initial hearings, we followed up with every attendee, mailing them a detailed questionnaire to help us improve the perceived value of the participant experience and better target topics to achieve what the commissioners wanted in terms of expert testimony and input. It was a bit like community organizing with a necessarily high level of integrity regarding balance in political, ideological, and regional perspective.

As research had been a large part of our Commission mandate, we organized a meeting of peace research experts, and international relations scholars at our offices. The research needs of the commission fell into two broad categories. The first classification was data collection, synthesis, and summary of the theory and techniques of the peaceful resolution of conflict between nations *and* within communities and nations. In this category we also reviewed existing institutions that assisted in resolving conflict in the areas of foreign and local community relations. We surveyed the national mechanisms that addressed violent conflict. Our staff did research and documentation, and selected witnesses for their experience in these areas. For example, among our expert witnesses were leaders in urban and regional dispute resolution agencies, nonprofit organizations, foundations, and discipline specific mediators and service providers, in addition to diplomats, scholars, and military leaders.

The second category of research was the presentation and analysis of peace academy models, including size, cost, location; relationship to other providers and the government; curriculum and pedagogy, and legal-institutional frameworks. We studied how policy might be set in a peace academy, as well as what steps might be taken to ensure its independence from the federal government. How would the peace academy be accountable, while avoiding being drawn into an intervention role in any given conflict? This was an important criterion for many of the commissioners. We researched the methods by which the peace academy would operate, and the channels, structures and practices it might undertake. How would a peace academy avoid being coopted by competing interests and worldviews of its researchers, sponsors, or branches of government? As part of our research effort, staff visited some fifty existing organizations and made inquiries about their strengths and weaknesses, strategies, scope of practice and measures of success. It was no small undertaking. We had five people on our research team. Each week research products were reviewed by me and progress summaries were provided to the commissioners at appropriate times, depending on their interest or questions. All results were included in our Commissioner Review Notebooks that were generated in the fall of 1980. Our research activities ran parallel to the public hearing schedule, and were quite enterprising all unto themselves. The legislation creating the commission provided a limited description of our research task. Our staff, with help from academics and the leadership of other organizations and agencies, identified the relevant original questions and deployed their resources to find answers. The task of organizing research; identifying expert witnesses; fielding public testimony; integrating testimony and the cosmos of output from more than fifty special meeting and conferences; maintain the interest of commissioners and responding to their individual interest; facilitating the decision process of the commissioners; and writing the Final Report was a considerably larger chore I imagine than drafting the handful of pages that defined the Commission's mandate.

Initially our staff identified thirty-three existing alternative legal-institutional models for consideration. We secured the legislative history of a select group of examples and studied the background and particular provisions of the enacting laws as researched by Steve Cloud, who as previously mentioned had served as an aide to Senator Hartke. We specifically looked at the pros and cons of several intuitional models:

a)   Service academy model
b)   Agency-affiliated model
c)   Agency umbrella model
d)   Endowment corporation model
e)   Increased funding to existing field model
f)   Private sector peace academy model, and
g)   Corporate model

We did a cost-benefit analysis of each, including the structure of three divisions in each model for training, research, and education. It was important in all models that there be an active national clearinghouse for peace information to prepare indexing, abstracting, translating, and other services leading to more effective dissemination of conflict resolution and peace education materials, practitioners' experiences, and peace research findings. One vision of success would be a national center that had regional hub relationships, perhaps with land grant colleges across the country. Each hub would have access to clearinghouse data banks on types of conflicts, strategies used, human resources involved, results, and other information that was deemed useful to professionals in the fields of community, national, and international conflicts.

With regard to the imagery of what the programmatic thrust of a national peace academy might look like, we floated ideas from prior efforts—those we had created as a result of NPAC-sponsored conferences, as well as the suggested scope of activities brought forward by scholars and researchers convened by our own commission research staff. Harvard Professor Herbert Kelman, a longtime friend and more importantly, a highly regarded scholar in the field of international relations, convened one such meeting.

Herb raised a number of very critical, open-ended questions and we circulated them to peace research and conflict resolution scholars around the country. We also sent out a draft academic design model to draw criticism and feedback, based upon what the hearing process was already finding in public and expert testimony.

The meeting produced very thoughtful results and the insights were shared with the members of the commission. For example, the typology of different aspects of conflict was considered, how to ensure that justice would be included, how findings would be integrated and disseminated to parts of the government and public stakeholders, how community conflict resolution and international themes and processes would be integrated, and most importantly, how the core mission of the institution would be protected from compromising its effort due to political or special activity that might serve to squeeze out, budget down, or erode the intended activity of the institution. We observed that there was strong precedent among federal agencies that existing mandates, despite clear intentions from Congress, became watered down or distracted by special demands or degrees of emphasis. The meeting gave examples such as disarmament agencies, ACDA, and AID. Finally, there was a general bias in the group against a big, single location for the academy. There was a strong case made for a central, computer-based information access and emphasis on regional network regarding the success of various practices. Several aspects of the commission's work effort, as well as the conferences sponsored by NPAC, gradually began to stimulate and foment change among agencies, institutions, and Alternative Dispute Resolution applications across the country.

The research meeting we had organized at our offices went so well that it carried on well into the late afternoon. As it happened the air conditioning system in the commercial building in which the commission was housed was automatically turned off at 6:00 PM. Our band of scholars wished to continue talking, but the stagnate air in our conference room became unbearable, so we moved chairs, flip charts, tape recording equipment and lights to the lobby of our building to continue our dialogue.

Gradually the temperature got warmer in the lobby as well. Some of us took measures to cool the lobby down and propped chairs up against the external doors of the building, enabling fresh air to flow into the lobby. After a period, two police cars showed up with lights flashing, and officers entered the lobby space expecting to see robbers fleeing with office equipment or worse. What the officers found was forty researchers and scholars engaged in serious dialogue about a future institution designed to find world peace. We made efforts to invite the police to join in our discussion, but they made us close up shop for the night and we resumed our meetings in the morning. For months after the event, the story was retold around academic communities around the country. It was not wars that were challenging world peace; it was automatic timers on air-conditioning systems.

Following the Research Planning Meeting in April one of the participants, Stephen Sawyer of the Department of Geography at the University of Maryland, wrote to thank the commission staff for being included in the meetings. His note was illustrative of how difficult our work that year was going to become. He wrote:

> "I found the meetings very enlightening, but also frustrating. Most of the frustrations are related to two challenges that deal with managing your immense task within the brief time limits. The first challenge is probably common to most study commissions. How do you maximize the utility of your expert and public meetings? I realize that you have given this considerable thought, but let me make some observations anyway. There is a common tendency to view these meetings as constituent building sessions first and to record relevant input only in an anecdotal manner. This is not only aggravating to the participants, but also suicidal given the magnitude of your task. Our policy planning group could have been much more responsive if we had been provided more specifics. In the first hour of our policy group meeting, we had a very interesting academic discussion, which yielded some information, but in no way near the quantity of precision you need. In the second hour we struggled with issues the staff had probably already resolved after its own lengthy discussions.

> "The second challenge is to adequately evaluate and present the full range of reasonable alternative to a Peace Academy. Given your staff and time constraints, momentum for a Peace Academy proposal to the exclusion of other alternatives is almost inevitable. To ensure that alternatives are assessed, I would suggest an alternative chapter in the commission report. (But I suspect that this alone will be inadequate.) Good luck."[75]

Stephen's letter pointed out the tango of creating political will is often carried out on a slippery dance floor. Our staff study of alternative legal-institutional models was not concluded until late summer. The Research Planning Meeting was in April to help set the agenda for the work the staff needed to do and to tee up the questions which the commissioners would have to decide. Those who would touch the commission process but for a moment had to trust the thoroughness of our work and the integrity of the decision process. The work of the commission began to face challenges of bias based on the perspective of the commissioners and staff, time constraints, and rapid-fire requirements of our process. We were diligent in staying with our plan of a well-designed process. We had few problems until the last months of the commission when we got close to the deadline imposed by our enacting legislation. It all showed that the character and soundness of a process is key to garnering the support of others.

♖ ♗ ♞

The work of the commission was exhilarating, and it was draining on the personal lives of the staff. Everyone worked very hard for the full term of the commission. One day I received a special delivery package from a courier that my spouse Connie had hired to hand deliver an envelope with a handwritten message complaining that I never saw her anymore. I was getting up before dawn, traveling, or getting home exceedingly late; I seemed to never be at home and this was impacting our married life. These stresses played out for me during much of the 18 months of my involvement with the commission's work. It was difficult, and it served as a reminder of just one of the challenges of working to cause far-reaching change.

In formulating the hearings, we tried to invite at least one celebrity-type witness who might help to attract participants to the hearings and public seminar format. In the media run-up to the hearing in each of our twelve cities, the added visibility of a well-known witness served to spike press interest by making the event more newsworthy. In the Atlanta hearings, for example, we would have Coretta Scott King and Andy Young both appear as witnesses. We knew that these individuals had wisdom and experiences to share, and that the media would have an interest in their testimony as well.

At the last minute in preparation for the New York City hearing, we came upon the opportunity to invite former US Attorney General Ramsey Clark to testify. He would be a real headline-grabber for our advance press as he had just returned from Tehran where he had tried to secure the release of the American hostages captured in the seizure of the American Embassy. His trip to the region had been covered worldwide and his speaking with our commission members so soon after his trip would be newsworthy too. He accepted our invitation.

A couple of days before the hearing, which was to be held June 16, and 17, 1980, I found myself very nervous about Mr Clark's appearance. His trip had been controversial. It was a big deal in the papers and on the news. Some were saying he should be prosecuted for violating President Carter's ban on travel to Iran. Others were saying he had been unpatriotic for meeting for forty-five minutes with Iranian President Bani-Sadr to discuss the situation. Media reports had been coming out that Mr Clark had provided unwanted legitimacy to Iran for its continued holding of the fifty-three American hostages who were already in their eighth month of captivity. I was increasingly worried that something might happen to Mr Clark at our hearings. That would be devastating. I did not want anything to happen to him on my watch.

During the life of the commission, I had never really exercised the power of my office as its Director. We had subpoena authority and other powers but had not had the occasion to use them. Now I decided we needed to take steps to protect Mr Clark. I called the Justice Department and requested that the US Marshalls provide security for Mr Clark at our New York hearing.

I was still nervous, but I felt at least I had taken the necessary steps to avoid a potential problem in New York City. Clark continued to take a lot of flak in the press and his presentation in New York would be a public event. I floated the possibility of his appearing in a private session with the commissioners, but in the end we decided to go ahead with the security detail and manage as best we could.

The morning of the hearing, I waited outside the City University of New York building to greet Mr Clark. I was looking down the street for him when he walked up behind me and said hello. We entered the building and with plainclothes security unobtrusively posted about, he provided his testimony and answered questions from the commissioners. After his testimony was finished, I suggested a break so that I could escort him out of the building. I was still nervous that something might happen. We exited through a side door and I walked him to the front of the building where I had first greeted him. Two plain clothed federal marshals trailed us. I assumed there would be a car waiting with his own security. I thanked him and we said goodbye. I asked where his driver was or if he wanted me to wait with him. He said no, he was just going to take the subway back to his office uptown. I was shocked. Here I had been so worried and he was just going to jump on the subway.

Chapter 7 Review and Reflection

Task

- Create a culture of change.

Challenge

- Taking credit for change versus giving credit away.

Gift and Opportunity

- Seeing your life in service to others.

Reflection

- The word "inspire" comes from the term in-spirit; what motivates you in-spirit to be of service to others?
- Where do you find joy in giving credit away?

Andrew J. Young, Ambassador to the
United Nations, *The Preacher*.

James H. Laue, PhD, NPAC Co-Chair,
Commission Vice-Chair, *The Professor*.

William J. Spencer, NPAC Executive Director,
Commission Director, *The Peddler*.

Bryant M. Wedge, MD, NPAC Co-Chair, *The Psychiatrist*.

William Spencer, 1975, Graduate School of Public and
International Affairs, University of Pittsburgh.

William Spencer, 1992, as a Secretariat member of the International Negotiation Network,
presenting to INN Council of world leaders in Atlanta, January 14-17. More than 200
invited guests from 40 countries representing more than 150 organizations or governments
met to focus on the role of non-governmental actors in resolving intra-national conflicts.

(L to R) Commission Director William Spencer, Commission Chair Senator Spark
Matsunaga (HA), and Commission Vice-Chair Jim Laue, St Louis, Missouri
Hearings, US Commission on Proposals for the National Academy of Peace and
Conflict Resolution on April 21, 1980. During the one-year life of the commission,
twelve hearings and more than fifty special meetings were convened. More than
one hundred sixty experts sat with the commission to provide oral testimony.

(L to R) Commission Director William Spencer, Commissioner John Dellenback,
Commission Vice-Chair James Laue, Commission Chair Senator Spark Matsunaga,
Commissioner Elise Boulding, and Commissioner Arthur Barnes, Boston,
Massachusetts Hearings, US Commission on Proposals for the National Academy
of Peace and Conflict Resolution on June 2, 1980. More than 1,800 Americans
participated in the Public Seminar portion of the commission hearing process.

Senator Jennings Randolph (WV) testifying at Hearings of the US Commission on Proposals for the National Academy of Peace and Conflict Resolution, Washington, DC July 22, 1980. Senator Randolph first introduced legislation to create a Department of Peace in 1946, and continued to sponsor similar bills up until the USIP legislation was passed in 1984. Randolph was steadfast for thirty-eight years in his support of the peace academy concept.

(L to R) Rev. Leslie H. Carter, Commission Director of Program Operations, Constance Grice, Special Assistant to Ambassador Andrew Young, and Commissioner John P. Dunfey, Boston, Massachusetts Hearings US Commission on Proposals for the National Academy of Peace and Conflict Resolution, June 2, 1980.

(L to R) Commissioner John R. Dellenback, Senator Mark Hatfield (OR), presenting Commission Director William Spencer a commemorative Yevgeny Vuchetich statue, "Let Us Beat Swords into Plowshares," Washington DC, August 1981. The inscription reads: "To Will Spencer, a pioneer for peace. Best Regards, Mark Hatfield." Dellenback was a former Congressman (1966-1975) and Director of the Peace Corps (1975-1977).

White House Cabinet Room, September 11, 1980, Commission members present Interim Report to President Jimmy Carter. (Left Top Down) Elise Boulding, Arthur Barnes, Jim Laue, President Carter, Senator Matsunaga, Senator Randolph; (Right Top Down) Bill Lincoln, John Dellenback, Jack Dunfey. Following the meeting with Carter, the Commission Interim Report was released to members of the Senate; House of Representatives, government agencies and the public.

Commissioner Elise Boulding. Dr Boulding served as Chair of the Sociology Department, Dartmouth College, and formerly at the Department of Sociology and the Institute of Behavioral Science at the University of Colorado, Boulder.

Milton C. "Mike" Mapes, NPAC Executive Director, testifying to the US Commission on Proposals for the National Academy of Peace and Conflict Resolution, Washington DC, July 23, 1980. Mike's stewardship of the campaign followed the author's three-year service as Executive Director of NPAC after the author was appointed Director of the Commission.

Commission Staff gathering: (L to R) Leslie Carter, Judith Bunnell, Ann Richardson, Ina Risman, Marjorie Dahlin, William Spencer, Senator Matsunaga, Kathy Kozar, Marianna Paige, David Jensen, Mary Downs, Rosemary George. Sixteen additional individuals served on the Commission staff but were not present for this photograph.

(L to R) Mrs Coretta Scott King testifying in Atlanta Hearings: (L to R) Vice-Chair James Laue Commissioner Elise Boulding, Commission, Commission Director William Spencer, and Commissioner William Lincoln. Atlanta Hearings US Commission on Proposals for the National Academy of Peace and Conflict Resolution, June 23, 1980. Mrs King testified "A personal commitment to peaceful conflict resolution on the part of the disputants is the essential pre-requisite at every level."

(L to R) Ambassador Andrew Young testifying in Atlanta Hearings: (L to R) backs to the camera: Commission Vice-Chair James Laue, Commissioner Elise Boulding, Commission Director of Operations Leslie Carter. US Commission on Proposals for the National Academy of Peace and Conflict Resolution, June 23, 1980. Andy testified "The hard part of a negotiation is doing a successful analysis of the various roles being played by the people on the opposite side of the table so you can help build bridges between the two sides."

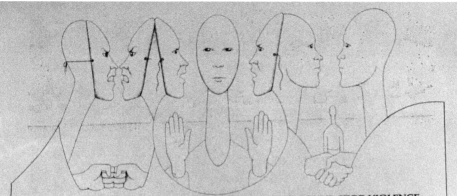

LIKE IT OR NOT,   AND WE NEED EXPERTS,   WHO COULD STOP VIOLENCE
WE LIVE IN A   TRAINED IN A   BEFORE IT HITS US...
VIOLENT WORLD...   NEW SCIENCE...   AND OUR FAMILIES.

Terrorism...riots...community conflicts...labor strife...environmental disputes. All symptoms of a world in turmoil. Creating a situation of constant danger to us all. We live with it. But we feel threatened by it. And fear it. Now, there is a new way of dealing with it.

Conflict resolution skills have been created that can resolve confrontations before they turn violent. Skills and techniques of a science that can be learned. And when they are used, the results are dramatic. Personal security and safety can be protected. And authorities estimate that billions of taxpayer dollars could be saved by reducing violence and avoiding other unnecessary conflicts.

PROVEN TECHNIQUES

During the Hanafi Muslim terrorist seige in Washington, more than 150 lives were saved through the application of these new skills. And they've been proven again and again. At the 1972 Republican and Democratic conventions. In the 1965 Dominican Republic crisis. And in many, more local conflicts, resolved behind the scenes.

A UNITED STATES ACADEMY FOR PEACE AND CONFLICT RESOLUTION

A growing number of citizens and organizations are working to create a federally recognized graduate school dedicated to the science of Conflict Resolution. To research. And to train professional specialists who could intervene in potentially violent and destructive conflicts before explosive, dangerous, even deadly situations go out of control.

This institution, the United States Academy for Peace and Conflict Resolution will not exist without your support. You can help turn back the rising tide of violence and disorder which today threatens our personal safety, our communities, and our nation.

We invite you to join the National Peace Academy Campaign, and to be listed as a Founder-Member. In appreciation of your concern and your gift of $25 or more, we would like to send you a signed, limited edition print of the Peace Academy poster — a fine reproduction of the art seen above. Or, if you would like more information, please write or call us. Today...before it's too late!

NATIONAL PEACE ACADEMY CAMPAIGN
1625 I Street, N.W. Suite 123-4, Washington, D.C. 20006. (202) 466-7670

National Peace Academy Campaign Executive Council

Reverend John P. Adams • Mr. Harry S. Ashmore • Dr. Roland Bainton
Professor James D. Barber • Senator Julian Bond • Professor Elise Boulding • Professor Kenneth Boulding • Mr. Paul Carrington
Mr. Harlan Cleveland • Mr. Robert Coulson • Mr. Norman Cousins • Ms. Frances Farenthold • Dr. Jerome Frank
Mr. Buckminster Fuller • Mr. Robert Gilmore • Mr. Najeeb Halaby • Senator Mark Hatfield • Mr. John Hersey
Father Theodore Hesburgh • Ms. Ruth Hinerfeld • Ms. Mildred Jeffrey • Mr. Vernon E. Jordan • Dr. Herbert Kelman
Mrs. Coretta King • Senator Spark Matsunaga • Ambassador George McGhee • Dr. Karl Menninger
Congresswoman Helen Meyner • Mr. Paul Newman • Ms. Claire Randall • Senator Jennings Randolph • Representative Irma Rangel
Mr. Ogden Reid • Mr. John Richardson, Jr. • Mr. Warren Robbins • Dean Albert M. Sacks • Dr. Jonas Salk, M.D.
Mr. Sargent Shriver • Rabbi Marc H. Tanenbaum • Dr. Jerome Wiesner • Mr. Roger Wilkins
Dr. Herman Will • Dean Colin Williams • Mr. Jerry Wurf • Dr. Herbert York
Ambassador Andrew Young, Honorary Chairman

Full-page advertisement that appeared in *TIME Magazine* as part of the National Peace Academy Campaign 1977. At the bottom of the ad are listed the influential NPAC Executive Council members who brought visibility and legitimacy to the future creation of the USIP. *Newsweek Magazine* also carried full-page public service ads that provided visibility for NPAC.

(L to R) William Spencer, Archbishop Desmond Tutu, President Jimmy
Carter, during Eritrea-Ethiopia peace talks, Nairobi, Kenya 1991. The INN
mediation team including Will and Dayle Spencer was successful in obtaining
agreement for a cease fire among the Eritreans and Ethiopians who had been
at war for almost three decades; the longest running civil war in Africa.

Dayle and William Spencer in Panmunjom, North Korea, while conducting peace
negotiations in Pyongyang 1992. The successful outcome of these negotiations
was the visit of President and Rosalynn Carter to North Korea in June 1994
to meet Kim Il-sung, grandfather of the current leader Kim Jong-un. Carter
was allowed to pass directly through the DMZ as a result of the negotiations,
opening the way for future progress. In October 1994 US President Bill
Clinton signed the *Agreed Framework* with Pyongyang to halt North Korea's
development of nuclear weapons. Peace efforts stopped when US President
George W. Bush in 2001 began to treat North Korea as a rogue state.

(L to R) William Spencer, Dayle Spencer and President Jimmy Carter flying north from Nairobi, Kenya to Khartoum, Sudan and then east to Addis Ababa, Ethiopia while on a mission to further peace talks, famine relief and human rights, November 1989. It is often necessary to meet rebel groups in a country different from the one they were fighting.

President Jimmy Carter and William Spencer prepare for a negotiation, Atlanta 1993. The heads of each national delegation of disputing countries had just left the room.

CHAPTER 8

Ala Moana

1980 – *Ala Moana* in Hawaiian means, "path to the sea" and it seemed fitting that on July 6 and 7, 1980, all but one members of the commission gathered to wrestle with the most critical decisions they would face in their year of deliberations. Senator Matsunaga had selected the Ala Moana Hotel in Waikiki as the venue for the business meeting of the commission, just prior to our next to last public hearing. The ocean itself is sometimes defined as "a great expanse or amount," and that was my view of what decision points the commission members had ahead of them. Nearly three-quarters of our work was completed, yet we had to bring the commission members along. To date the commission had faced outwardly; now the nexus of all of our work would be focused in the minds and hearts of the commissioners.

The first hearing of the commission had been held in Boulder, Colorado, on March 10, 1980. Since that day we had heard from two hundred expert witnesses whose testimony was centered on varying topic areas and we had heard or received written testimony from eighteen hundred individuals. As mentioned, the planned regional hearings, were all carried out – eleven down and one yet to go. Also by this time, commission staff had organized more than forty-eight separate, substantive meetings with academic, military, advocacy, or international organizations. The commission staff identified; contacted; and convened nearly ten special meetings per month, for the six months in the middle of our work. In the ensuing one hundred eighteen days since our first hearing, staff had crunched the overwhelming data of the testimony into manageable themes; notable or memorable witness statements; actionable recommendations and possible decision points, all by July 6. The notes from any meetings we held were dissected, and organized into relevant pieces of information requested by commissioners or thought by staff to be important for the commission decision-making process. All would be ready for presentation to the commissioners on July 22, at the last public hearing to be held in Washington, DC, ahead of the final decision-making meeting of the commission. The task had been monumental. By September 11, we had to have the commissioners prepared to deliver a written Interim Report to President Jimmy Carter, Senate President Pro Tempore, Senator Warren Magnuson, and the Speaker of the House, Congressman Thomas P. "Tip" O'Neill Jr. We were feeling the pressure.

By the conclusion of the Honolulu hearings and public seminar, the commission had heard expert testimony from one hundred thirty men and thirty-two women, including twenty-six African Americans, seven Latinos one Native American, and several Native Hawaiians. Although we heard from individuals of Asian descent, they were not broken out in our numbers. By July 22, we promised the commissioners we would have before them thick, pre-meeting review notebooks that would contain seminar summaries, witness statements, and importantly, a section on models.

In June of 1980 we arranged for a roundtable discussion of "Training and Research for International Conflict Resolution: Ideas for a National Peace Academy" in Boston during the annual meeting of the International Society of Political Psychology. Professor Herb Kelman organized and chaired a panel presentation by specialists including John Burton, Leonard Doob, Roger Fisher, Bryant Wedge, and some invited commission members. I described the history and mission of the commission first and Herb led the panel in ten-to fifteen-minute presentations on the following questions:

- What is the state of existing skills and knowledge in the field of international peacemaking and conflict resolution?
- What are the strengths and weaknesses of the field?
- What needs to be done nationally and internationally to advance training and research in international peacemaking and conflict resolution?
- What are the most appropriate mechanisms for advancing this work?
- What special contributions (if any) could a national peace academy make to this end?
- What special characteristics should the program and structure of such an academy ideally have, if it is to maximize its contributions?
- What are some of the ways in which the commission could help advance training and research in international conflict resolution?

We reserved about forty-five minutes for the commissioners in attendance to interact with the panel and concluded with a half-hour of questions and answers from the audience.

On one of my winter trips to New York for meetings at the United Nations, I noticed outside the entrance to the United Nations a sculpture. It was a striking sculpture named "Let Us Beat Swords into Plowshares" by Russian artist Yevgeny Vuchetich. I remembered seeing it several years earlier and admiring it. Not only was the piece impressive, it was named for a verse found in the Old Testament, Isaiah 2:4, which reads:

> "He shall judge between the nations, and shall decide for many peoples; and they shall beat their swords into plowshares, and their spears into pruning hooks; nation shall not lift up sword against nation, neither shall they learn war no more." (RSV)

I thought a reproduction of the statue might make a fitting and memorable gift for those who had served as commissioners. I felt it would bring some closure to the work of the commission. I put the idea in the back of my mind.

In June 1980, John Dellenback and I attended a seminar, which was given in conjunction with the meeting of the International Society for Political Psychology in Boston. John had been a Republican Congressman from Oregon and was a former Director of the Peace Corps. On the flight back to Washington I was seated in coach and John was in first class. Just as the door was closing, John walked back to retrieve me from my coach seat and insisted I come sit up front with him. I never knew what arrangements he had made with the flight attendants, but it all worked smoothly and we enjoyed a great, intimate discussion during the flight home. Near the end of our talk I mentioned the idea of creating commemorative plaques using the replica of the UN art. John was very excited, and agreed to pay for the awards, but only if I kept his financial sponsorship a secret, and if I did the work to acquire and produce them.

I made inquiries at the UN bookstore and then through a dealer to obtain the artwork as a gift for the nine commissioners, Bryant, Mike Mapes, Senator Hatfield, and myself. The Book of Isaiah also happened to be Bryant's favorite book of the Bible, as it contained a passage he liked about a small remnant. When speaking, he often referred to NPAC supporters as "a small remnant."

The small statue replicas had to be ordered from Russia and I was advised they would take a few months to arrive in Washington.

At the commission business meeting in Honolulu in early July I reported to the commissioners that technically our commission spending authority ceased on September 30. Senator Matsunaga and Congressman Glickman tried to sort through an option to seek further extension of our authorization, not of more funds but of the Congressional approval for the commission to continue working a few more months. I reported that we were working with legislative counsel to have language ready to go and Congressman Glickman suggested it should not be a problem as he said we could use the Congressional provisions for a suspended calendar to achieve our extension.

In early July, after the Honolulu hearings and critical commission meetings, we continued preparation for the final hearing dates that were scheduled to be held in Washington, DC on July 22 and 23. One hearing was held in the Rayburn House Office Building and the other in the Russell Senate Office Building. The hearings at the Capitol were immediately followed by an executive session of the commission to consider the draft Interim Report Time was getting short. We had less than thirty days business days to pull together our Interim Report to transmit to President Carter and Congress. The Interim Report reflected the first seven months of Commission's activity; The commission process had been a foot race interspersed with sprints, politics, and Tocquevillian interaction with 1,800 Americans in eleven States and the five states surrounding Washington, DC.

The commission staff felt they had spoken with one-third of the country. We began to build the pathway to our Final Report that we anticipated would be readied by the following spring, and presented to either President Carter or President Reagan.

On September 11, 1980, Senator Matsunaga sent the letter of transmittal to President Carter, Speaker O'Neill, and the President Pro Tempore Senator Warren Magnuson. I accompanied eight of the nine commissioners to the White House to meet with President Carter.

The commissioners addressed the President and Congress with the following Interim Report:

> "During its first seven months, the Commission met for over 230 hours and collected and analyzed over 7,000 pages of oral and written testimony, research findings and meeting notes.

> "Overwhelmingly, witnesses noted that in recent years teachable, cost-effective, nonviolent methods of resolving conflicts have been developed. These new methods and a rapidly developing body of knowledge are being applied and taught. Negotiation, mediation, conciliation, and arbitration are being used extensively and successfully in domestic labor disputes and in international trade and commercial disputes. Professional experts in conflict resolution are assisting in the peaceful settlement of environmental disputes and terrorist incidents. Private mediators are assisting in delicate international peace negotiations. The United States service academies are beginning to incorporate conflict resolution skill training in their curricula. Research is being done at universities on peaceful conflict resolution.

> "However, the commission found little official organized support for these efforts; existing institutions and mechanisms lack the resources to promote training and research in peacemaking and conflict resolution skills. There is no well-developed

system for responding effectively to conflicts at any level before they erupt into destructive violence.

"Many witnesses voiced their concern that international disputes over natural resources, the environment, international commerce, and the arms race have the potential for escalating into violence if current knowledge of peaceful conflict resolution is not more fully integrated into diplomacy, business, and policy planning. Concerns were expressed that without a significant, coordinated, and ongoing American effort in this area, the possibility of a nuclear war will increase rather than decrease in the years ahead.

"The Commission has concluded that the implementation of a national program of training, research, and public information could potentially save American citizens billions of dollars, directly and indirectly, each year and reduce the level of international violence in both the short and long term. Complete documentation for these findings will be set forth in the Final Report.

"Committing the necessary resources to developing techniques capable of resolving conflicts effectively, nonviolently, and with social justice is the United States' greatest challenge. Broader use of peace and conflict resolution skills is the foundation upon which social justice, social and economic stability, and genuine national security can be built."[76]

There it was. All of our effort typed up into twenty-five pages that would be shared with the President and the Congress. Still to come: the Final Report would later contain close to four hundred pages; the various Commissioner Review Notebooks; eighteen fat binders of verbatim hearing transcripts; and the considerable amount of correspondence and written testimony to the commission.

In June I had written a letter to the General Counsel of the Office of Education to get clarification on our spend rate of commission funds and when our one-year study might legally have to come to a close. The commissioners had held their first meeting on December 12, 1979. Did that mean that we would have to wrap things up by early December 1980? I knew we needed more time to write up our final report and close down everything. We had geared up so quickly, I wanted to get a clear idea of just how long we had before we had to start gearing down. I was told that the commission would have to cease operation one year from when the funds were enacted. According to the General Counsel, that was November 20, 1979, so the commission would have to come to a screaming end by early December, a date that was about six weeks shorter than my original plan.

No private funds could be raised to extend our work, although we had offers from several private citizens. Commissioners Matsunaga and Glickman's efforts to extend the commission's authority as they had hoped failed. It became clear that any commission work after December 1980 would have to be conducted as part of Senator Matsunaga's staff. I hoped this would not have to be the case.

As the fall of 1980 went on, I began to have to let staff go. At the same time, we had draft plans for a fall program intended to inform the public about the commission report and its recommendations. My plan included a cooperative follow-up program with the National Endowment for the Humanities to conduct outreach based on the work of our field operations team earlier in the year. We envisioned special briefings, consultations with the appropriate federal and state agencies and civic organizations, and a series of one-day events in selected cities where commissioners would be invited to participate to expand public discussions of our findings. The budget for the fall program was estimated to be about $75,000. Remaining commission funds and programmatic assistance from the National Endowment would pay the outreach programs of the commission. Most commissioners were excited about the plan. These events would also provide the opportunity to bring some formal closure to the work we had done, including plans to recognize the commissioners. It was my plan to present the commissioners with the commemorative plaques we had created in our final meeting, and end our year on a high. I envisioned the final meeting to be an opportunity to pull the staff back together to be recognized by the commissioners.

All of that came crashing down in early December when Senator Matsunaga asked that I come to his office immediately. I walked into the Senator's office to learn that he wanted to shut down the commission offices and bring whatever staff was necessary into his own Senate offices to finish up the report and administrative steps to end the commission. He requested an accounting of remaining funds and a new budget to carry out his wishes. I left his office and called a staff meeting for the next day, whereupon I explained the Senator's wishes and released most of our remaining staff. It was a very difficult morning. I drafted a budget and met with the Senator again that afternoon to share my proposed plan. I would work on commission affairs half time until February 7 and the consultant who had been selected to edit the final report would continue with his tasks until finished, presumably within six weeks. The government would assume the cost of printing the report. The Senator agreed with the plan, which I felt had been forced on me.

At that moment, the commission no longer existed. Matsunaga wanted to treat all staff as his own. Some of the senior staff had suggested they would volunteer their time to finish up some remaining projects and work out of the Senator's offices. The Senator said no, there was no space and he saw no further need for the work of the commission staff, save the final edits on the report.

After that day, Senator Matsunaga and his staff started referring to the work of the commission as the "Matsunaga Commission," which I found somewhat offensive to the many other members of Congress who had worked so hard to create and support the work of the commission. Some among his own staff seemed a little sheepish when they used the phrase, and staff from other Senate offices kind of just shrugged. I felt bad that I never confronted the Senator about his sudden use of the phrase. As a citizen I felt worse, remembering the critical interventions made by other legislators, such as Hatfield, Randolph, Hartke, Vance, Fascell, Perkins, and Meyner. I chose not to dwell on it, as it simply seemed the way of Washington.

Whether it was separation anxiety, concern of what would come next, or something else. I was hurt. I felt like I had my legs knocked out from under me. The next day I stayed at home and listened to Shubert symphonies lying on a bed in our spare bedroom. I felt I was in a dark tunnel. So much had gone right. We had worked so hard. We had done so much in a short period of time. It felt like the game clock had expired early; the buzzer sounded; and the last run down the court would not count. Rightly or wrongly, it felt like politics had bested our efforts to end the work of the commission in an elegant fashion, putting a bow on the political will we had set out to cultivate.

At the end of 1980, I considered all the seeds we had sowed might as well have fallen on sterile soil. President Reagan had been elected. I was not certain where my career would next take me. Connie was talking about moving to Atlanta, where Andy was going to run for mayor. We had worked very hard to pass the legislation and then had made extraordinary efforts to conduct the business of the commission in such a condensed period. The final report was not yet finished, there had been no closure, the campaign leadership had spun off in different directions, and I was no closer to becoming a practitioner. It was time to regroup. New Year's Day 1981 was filled with soul searching.

On Tuesday, January 13, 1981, Jim Laue was in Washington and we met with Senator Matsunaga to discuss the final report. On January 14, the consultant, Charles D. Smith, we used to edit the final report left a copy on my office desk. The offices were near empty now and I felt a sense of loss for the fine team we had put together, but also that we had not been able to create any sense of final closure for the commissioners themselves. I remembered one of my first days on the job as Commission Director when I began interviewing staff at the restaurant across the street from what would become our commission office. Never had there been time to savor the moments of the commission; now there was no time to savor what we had accomplished. I called the editor to learn if the Senator had seen it and he said, "No." I called the Senator to share a progress report.

January 20 was Inauguration Day, and not by coincidence, the release of the Iran hostages. I stayed home to watch on TV as President Carter left the White House and the Reagan Administration began.

We had planned an NPAC meeting on Friday, January 23, and we somberly went about planning the year, knowing that the final report of the commission would be delayed and that the next cycle of legislation would not benefit from the momentum that we had built.

In late January I flew to Cleveland for meetings with Tom Westropp and other NPAC supporters. Tom had served various volunteer posts in NPAC, including treasurer and had personally paid for a series of newspaper ads that ran in different parts of the county.

In early March I met with Jim in Washington to discuss future legislation and the reorganization of NPAC. On March 9 I met with the editor who was finishing the second draft of the final report of the commission. I was concerned about the timing of our reporting obligation to President Reagan. Who would organize it? Would all of the commissioners be there? Would they be invited? The new administration was working its way through the process of identifying its appointments and sending them over to Congress. The tone and composition of the nominee lists were sliding to the right, as expected. Concerned, may not have been a strong enough word. With my commission hat nearly off, it was time to revisit campaign strategy and consult with Congressional allies. As the spring arrived, seven of the nine commissioners checked in with me and shared optimistic expectations about the next chapter of the work we had started. Their shared interest was how would we get the enacting legislation introduced and passed? Who was going to pick up the relay baton now? How would we establish a new momentum? These were questions we all sat with, just as the cherry trees began to blossom around the Tidal Basin in front of the Jefferson Memorial.

Chapter 8 Review and Reflection

Task

- Develop your message and the ways to deliver it.

Challenge

- Understand your audience.

Gift and Opportunity

- Expand the generosity of your character by developing or enlarging your tolerance for others.

Reflection

- What lessons can you learn from those you do not agree with?
- What wisdom do they offer?

CHAPTER 9

Rayburn

1981 – On the House side of the Capitol there are three House of Representatives office buildings and several office annexes. The main buildings are Cannon, Longworth, and Rayburn and they provide the offices and meeting rooms for House Members and their staffs. The buildings are located immediately adjacent to the Capitol and there are tunnels and surface streets connecting the complex. It appeared that Congressman Dan Glickman would be the primary House sponsor of the next step of our legislative process and Senator Matsunaga would assume that role in the Senate. The campaign began to organize other co-sponsors and rally the NPAC membership to create expectations about the forthcoming bill. Dan was a House co-sponsor previously and during the campaign, he and I had traveled together to his home state of Kansas to meet with several peace church communities that were a sizable component of his constituency.

I remained a bit down and reflective in the late spring of 1981. The work of the commission was done. It had been a fast, high wire act with no breaks. Now it was over. The critical next steps would be back on the floors of Congress. I was without a job. The daily life of commission staff interaction and intense focus was gone. Without proper closure, my colleagues were dispersed to seek other employment and purpose. It was tough, if not traumatic. The end of the commission had come and gone, not as I had planned. Things felt in limbo, untied and open-ended.

Connie was already preparing to head off to Atlanta to be involved in Andy Young's mayoral race. The Young for Atlanta campaign had purchased her an aging, but semi-cute orange Volkswagen station wagon. During the coming months she would be going back and forth to Atlanta with increasing frequency. It was unclear if she would stay on if Andy won, but her first love had always been urban affairs. I was beginning to evaluate my own professional options and was considering several creative tracks, but nothing was solid.

In my down time after such a frantic several years of high pressure, I contemplated what I had done right and what I had done wrong in working to promote and create the Peace Academy.

In the campaign I knew I had been very effective in managing with very few resources. That had been accomplished by winning the trust and contributions of others to keep the movement going. It felt like a breathless campaign much of the time. I had somehow been able to serve as the glue to hold things together. My strength had not been in fundraising but in stirring the pot enough, and in the right direction, to draw others to the table. I had stayed focused on a single issue and refrained from trying to build an organization. As the years after the creation of USIP went on, the nonprofits of NPAC and the National Peace Education Fund developed lives of their own. Those individuals who had been an integral part of the campaign and commission had largely done what we set out to do and we stopped, leaving the field of play to a new team.

I had been fortunate to be a part of successful efforts to create legitimacy for the field of conflict resolution and the concept of a national peace academy. It was a team effort to create political will. We had focused the NPAC organization on the necessary legislative strategy, issue papers, vision statements, research agendas and design elements to facilitate people and efforts to work toward our goal. I worked with Connie and Andy to advance our legitimacy through the formation of the Executive Council. Important credibility across many sectors was established because of the name recognition; integrity and generosity of the many individuals who lent their names and good offices to our cause. The decisions to create downtown offices in premier Washington real estate had served our effort by providing validation of the seriousness of our campaign. It provided a home for volunteer activity and a desirable location for people to gather. The decision to undertake our "Art of Peace" initiative and establish cultural attributes to our political agenda was smart, as was our decision to hold our debut event at the Mayflower Hotel to show that we could be as good as anyone else and deserved a seat at the table among our nonprofit peers. It served to make our efforts believable and its celebration of our midway efforts paid off in boosting the morale of our staff, supporters and legislators. The academic conferences we organized provided not just an exchange of ideas and the shared vision of what the new institution could become, these efforts served to engage scholars whose support and capacity we needed.

Upon reflection, the major mistakes I made in the campaign numbered three. First, I should have delegated more often, and provided training to a cadre of field people rather than just a very few in Washington. My mistake was not making the time to more effectively leverage regional assets. We mobilized many local and national organizations to provide endorsements, and actively engage their members to support NPAC's legislative work. However I failed to strategically assemble a more structured team of volunteers to lead local efforts. In retrospect our day-to-day campaign efforts, as effective as they may have been, were too ad hoc; we were lucky to have accomplished what we did without more horsepower. It was true that the scope of campaign activity was limited by funding and the NPAC principals, myself included, did not want to build a structure designed for organizational longevity. The perceived urgency for action was driven by a legislative cycle that precluded the use of resources that could be focused on organizational development across the country. Still, upon reflection, efforts to develop and leverage more defined leadership might have increased our effectiveness.

Second, in our fundraising efforts I should have utilized more seasoned, more recognized individuals to do the asking. For example, Vernon Jordan was among the members of our Executive Council. His name alone provided visibility and legitimacy to the campaign. However, I have no doubt that if Mr Jordan had paid a visit to the Chairman of Time Life in New York instead of a fundraising consultant and myself, the campaign would have better served. Too often, our young staff tried to do it all, rather than defer to more senior individuals to do the asking. We were highly effective in managing this way with regard to legislation and lobbying, but in the arena of fundraising, we failed. This was the area of the campaign where I most often felt insecure; choosing instead to attend to the immediacy of whatever task was at hand. Fundraising is tough. Our NPAC and NPAF direct mail efforts surged after the commission finished its work, but I regret that I had not been more effective earlier in the campaign in imagining a more productive system of 1:1 fundraising.

Third, as a campaign manager, my personal efforts would have been better leveraged had I created a better span of control within the campaign staff. This was a function primarily of available resources, but existing networks rather than talent searches mostly drove our hiring practices. NPAC drew in individuals who cared about the vision. We were largely a volunteer flock. This is not a slam on the staff of the campaign, but more of a reflection of my own management skills. I felt like there was not going to be enough time to pass some simple tasks on to others, and on other occasions there were no "others" to whom to delegate. Our team accomplished an amazing thing—we were successful beyond all reasonable measure. Everyone who walked through the NPAC doors was able to step up and make a difference in achieving our goal. In my Malibu job, I had managed two staff members and three consultants. I was basically a salesman, without formal management training. Certainly I learned to practice many principles of good management in my three years in Malibu and three years prior to my direction of the commission, but in the campaign, it always seemed a balance between moving the legislation along and developing the staff. As a manager there were many consecutive months when we were unable to meet payroll but we were able to make legislative progress. A more mature manager might have met payroll but failed to move the legislative objective. I suppose it is always a balance. We were young and idealistic and that served our cause, but our staff and families paid a price.

NPAC excelled at helping others to visualize what a national peace academy could look like and how the country might benefit if the model we were advocating came to fruition. We were effective in growing a national membership base and coordinating Congressional support through the mechanisms that existed at the time: mail, personal constituent visits, conferences, telephone calls, and direct interventions by prestigious individuals. I am most gratified that we were successful in enrolling individuals and organizations who believed in an idea; became a part of creating political will; and did so with selflessness and transparency. For these things, I remain very proud.

Perhaps one of the most challenging aspects of the campaign was the near constant change in leadership among our Congressional sponsors. Due to the multiple committees and bodies that had approval authority with our bills, the lobbying target was always changing, as well as the lead legislator with whom we would coordinate our efforts. Whenever the Congressional leadership changed due to an election, review by a different committee, or start of a new Congressional session, we had to adjust. We did that very well. Our posture was always to do what we could to help the legislators and set them up for success. We practiced getting power by giving it away. We saw our task not as one of badgering legislators, but in making them look good to their local constituents and national supporters. We did that very well, but it created a lot of fast pivots, and new trust-building opportunities.

In the work of the commission I made mistakes, but was largely fortunate in my decisions and leadership role. I started out with a singularly poor staff choice due to time and external pressures to make a specific hire. Staffing proved such a critical element of the work that if I had initially gone with my gut, the life of the commission work would have been less stressful. I chalk that up to inexperience, but I have learned that I am not alone in this regard. Years later, I had a client who made similar staffing judgments. The client, now a very close friend, was the Chief Executive Officer of an oil and gas exploration company in South Asia. He had done an incredible job in raising start-up funds over a relatively short period of time. When it came time to staff up his organization, he had a choice to either hire a dream team of highly experienced executives who had never worked together, or hire a band of brothers and sisters, who had spent time together in the trenches as employees in their former professional lives. He chose to staff up with a dream team, which later caused his enterprise to fail within three years due to in-fighting, ego battles, lack of trust, and backstabbing. I learned during the work of the commission that hiring those who were supposed to be the best was not necessarily the prudent course of action. In the campaign, I was able to craft a team of staff dedicated to growing together and supporting the greater good. In the run-up to the staffing of the commission I took the word of others at face value. I paid a heavy price in having to manage my mistake for the duration of the commission's work, as my client and friend later had to do in his organization.

A second mistake I made in the life of the commission was not assigning someone to begin writing the final report from the get-go. Due to the pace of the commission's work, I leaned into hiring staff resources or adjusting responsibilities as we went along. For example, administratively, we were attached to the Department of Education. As such DOE was responsible for cutting checks for our staff and expenses and providing procedures for reimbursements, purchases; basically they were to be our bank. Initially, I imagined no staff position to liaison with the DOE, as I thought this function could be accomplished through my own executive secretary and other multitasking staff members. Boy, was I ever wrong. Eventually, I had to dedicate five staff positions to this function in order to successfully manage all of the administration and to overcome the slower moving parts of our relationship with DOE. I learned that I needed a dedicated staff person to liaison with the commissioners and a lead staff member to interact with the Chairman. I really should have started with the end in mind and dedicated a writer to begin the work on the final report, but somehow that seemed offensive to my promise to the Senator to be open-minded in where our hearings and testimony would take us. In retrospect, I should have managed this issue in a different manner.

Finally, I should have worked smarter to create a better balance in my professional/personal life. I was so focused on the work of the commission that I might have irreparably damaged my marriage. During the 18 months of my service to the commission I made little time to properly nourish and maintain significant personal relationships outside of work. This was a difficult, hard learning. I have given it considerable thought over the years since the passage of the USIP enacting legislation. Certainly as in a political campaign or business start up, we extend ourselves to the limit like we did in NPAC and the commission. We did the work by choice. These endeavors, like an athletic competition, are optional, elective pursuits but can be as punishing as the involuntary aftermath of a disaster, war or survival-driven journey of a refugee. The work was hard, but each of us knowingly had a grander purpose. NPAC Executive Council member Norman Cousins wrote: "The capacity for hope is the most significant fact of life. It provides human beings with a sense of destination and the energy to get started."[77]

As already mentioned, the intensity of the commission's work had an impact on the personal life of all involved. Each staff person and commissioner, including Senator Matsunaga, put in extensive amounts of time and dedication to accomplish our task. The travel schedule alone for commissioners and myself, Les Carter and others consumed more than a third of our budget, to say nothing of the intellectual and emotional energy spent by individuals.

NPAC Executive Council member and futurist Buckminster Fuller is quoted as saying: "You never change things by fighting the existing reality. To change something, build a new model that makes the existing model obsolete."[78] Now he was primarily speaking about architecture, I assume, but it applied to all of our efforts in NPAC and the commission. What we succeeded in doing by all of our work was to simply build a new model – a model of both symbolism and critical mass, to influence how America can choose to manage its future inevitable conflicts in less violent, more just ways. Thank you Bucky.

On the positive side, there were many things we did right during the tenure of the commission. First, we excelled at field operations due to the quality and work ethic of those responsible. We took the time and a measured stance to develop relationships with each commissioner, as we also continued to build relationships with the Congressional leadership who would follow up on the work of the commission. I tried very hard to separate myself from the work of the campaign during the work of the commission. Another early practical step was that we decided to task the research, as distinct from the hearing process. The benefit of this was to separate operational field staff, calendar deadlines and witness testimony from the guidance of expert consultants and staff research managers. This was effective.

♖ ♗ ♘

At the end of March 1981 I took the train to Philadelphia to make a presentation at the International Studies Association meeting. After the ISA meetings, I drove to Princeton to view fifteen hundred acres that an NPAC supporter had offered to donate as a campus for the National Peace Academy. We had received a similar offer for a large tract of land near Apple Valley in California. We had received a similar offer for a large tract of land near Apple Valley in California. The owner, and man who contacted me, had purchased the property years before in anticipation that LAX might need to expand beyond its footprint and force Los Angeles into seeking alternative sites. The need for an alternative airport did not arise and the man was looking for a tax write off as result of donating the sizable parcel to a future institution.

The location of the Princeton property was more appealing because of its position about halfway between New York and DC. It was near a university and had a very rural setting, with five existing old farmhouse structures and the necessary infrastructure such as water, power, roads, and a buffer of surrounding farmland. I spoke with Kenneth Boulding and former members of Rep. Meyner's staff, as the Congresswoman had left office in early 1979. Representative Meyner, who of course had been an important sponsor of the bills, had been married to a former Governor of New Jersey as well as serving as the representative from an adjacent district to the one serving the Princeton area. She was a distant cousin of Adlai Stevenson. I trusted her judgment and thought she might be in a position to provide advice. Kenneth had formerly been a scholar at the Center for Advanced Study at Princeton.

We knew the area; this was an exciting opportunity. In our planning, many of NPAC supporters had wanted a residential campus within several hundred miles of DC and an administrative and symbolic building in a visible location in DC, ideally on the National Mall.

On April 9 I met with John Dellenback and we reviewed the final design of the plaques for the commissioners. We spoke about the next steps for NPAC and the legislative strategy, particularly the support we could count on from Senator Hatfield. On April 13 I followed up with Birdie Kyle and Senator Randolph to review the Senate strategy for the legislation. On April 19 Congressional hearings took place.

During the week of May 17-23 I sat in on a training being conducted in Arlington, Virginia by the Interaction Associates firm from San Francisco that was courting me for a position as a consultant. Michael Doyle – whom I had met a year earlier and his partner David Straus founded their company in 1969 as a management consulting and human resource development firm specializing in the design and implementation of change management and organizational renewal processes. Michael had been drawn to my work as in his view we were trying to cause change at a national level, not unlike the renewal work he and his colleagues were trying to achieve in organizations.

My interest in the company was beginning to grow as I learned more about their approach to collaborative problem-solving, strategic thinking, team development, and organizational effectiveness. These were all core skills to support my interest in mediation, negotiation, and conciliation in organizations and large social systems. In early September I was invited to attend an advanced training in San Francisco. The training was impressive and I came to realize that this was something that might be appropriate for me to do on my journey to becoming a practitioner in the field. I began to talk with Connie about what working with the firm would mean. Initially, this translated to relocating to San Francisco, something I knew Connie was not keen about.

Connie and I had been commuting back and forth between Atlanta and Washington for much of the winter. It was my turn to be in Atlanta. Still unsure of my next career plans, I began to get creative. My job search turned to the Atlanta area. In thinking about my own professional next steps I contacted the Turner Broadcasting System offices regarding an interview at which I had hoped to make a programming pitch to CNN to create a segment on conflict resolution. I envisioned CNN carrying a weekly installment documenting a global conflict and reporting on the progress of its resolution; strategies, personalities, and progress.

CNN, the 24-hour, all-news cable and satellite channel, was launched on June 1, 1980, six months into the work of the Commission. Ted Turner created the innovation and he and its headquarters were in Atlanta. It was a big deal. I had read about Ted and was inspired by his risk-taking style and apparent willingness to take on new things. I thought he might make a great sponsor of a program on conflict resolution and its visibility on his network might help to further legitimize the field.

Mr Turner accepted my proposal for a meeting. I was delighted. On August 20 at 11:00 A.M. I walked into the Atlanta TBS offices and was led into Ted's private office. On the floor were several

24-inch models of 12-meter America's Cup sailboats. They were each beautiful. I was kneeling down on the floor admiring one of the boat models when Ted entered the room behind me.

"Hi there," he said as I stood and said, "Mr Turner." He quickly countered, "Ted."

His wore a loosened tie, and the rolled up sleeves of his white shirt implied, "I'm busy and working." He was vibrating with energy, yet very cool. We shook hands and he walked behind his desk, inviting me to sit across from him, and diagonal to the block of TV monitors silently broadcasting I remember Ted proceeded to place his worn-looking shoes up on his desk and leaned back in his leather chair. As Ted crossed his legs up onto his desk, it reminded me of the exact same move Paul Newman had executed four years earlier at the United Nations. "What brings you here?" he said.

I thanked him for the opportunity to meet and briefly provided an overview of our work in the commission and campaign. The work CNN was now doing and the contribution it was making to the country was impressive. I felt strongly that given my background in conflict resolution there was an opportunity for the network to incorporate into its programming a special segment on conflict resolution. Without skipping a beat, he asked, "What is that and how would it work?"

I had not anticipated such a fast-paced response or the ensuing conversation. I should have expected it. Ted had competed in and won the America's Cup sailboat race in 1977. He struck me as a man who leaned into the wind. I tried to slow the conversation down by saying, "Before we discuss that further, may I just say how beautiful these models are? Congratulations on your sailing victories and on the launch of the new station." I am sure I was a bit intimidated and awkward in the moment. When we began discussing boats, Ted turned graceful and modestly acknowledged his good fortune with both the sailing and the station. Now, I felt a connection and caught my breath enough to proceed.

Reality TV had not yet caught on, although *This Old House* had begun airing in 1979 and *The People's Court* would debut in September. I knew nothing about TV, its production, commercial side, or template for success. I just felt TV might be a good venue for the drama and viewer learning opportunity that would come with a program on conflict resolution. I really did not know where to take the conversation next. Ted apparently did not know either and reached for his telephone, dialing a couple of numbers and said, "Tom, can you please come in here?"

In a flash, Tom Johnson, the President of CNN, rapped on the door and came in. Whether rehearsed or not, Tom listened carefully as Ted reviewed our conversation and Ted, speaking very kindly, suggested to me that Tom would be the better person to speak with about my idea. I felt the handoff, and might have been offended, but these were very successful and busy men. It was fun to meet Ted, and I still had hopes of something developing. I thought my idea made sense.

Tom walked me into his office and again I made my pitch. I had researched that CNN needed programming to fill its 24-hour news cycle. The idea was that CNN consult with me to produce a pilot; then a regular segment, designed to not just report a news story about an event like a specific community protest march, regional conflict or international war, but that CNN differentiate themselves from other networks by featuring the background of the conflict, the approaches to solving the conflict and more. Rather than merely reporting this or that was happening as "news", the CNN story narrative would be hopeful, educational and prescriptive. While most networks focused solely on the drama of the immediate event, CNN could establish their network as leading with background, causation and unorthodox coverage. Rather than a reporter proclaiming, "Wow, there is a big demonstration near the court house," a CNN journalist could report the story without sensationalism or surprise.

As an example, I shared with Tom that the CNN News Anchor might say, "Now we go to our reporter Bruce Dodge at the scene of the long-anticipated demonstration marking the fifth anniversary of the unfortunate shooting of three unarmed boys in a 7-Eleven parking lot. Bruce, what can you tell us about the issues, findings and city's response to the events of five years ago?" The segment would be structured with the tone: "conflict is inevitable and part of life", so what steps can be taken to resolve this one? Tom nodded.

"With CNN now positioned to have reporters in every capitol of the world," I said, "Think Tom about the potential for CNN to be ready to know how to report and analyze breaking stories. While other networks would shout headlines, CNN would be prepared to cover conflict situations with primed experts, authentic and deep analysis and leave the competition behind from the first break in the story."

Each segment would introduce the audience to experts in dispute resolution to define the needs and interests of the parties. File footage would be proactively prepared and used to highlight history of the problem. White boards would be used to explain the possible process steps to resolve it. "Like Ted", I said to Tom, "It would be sleeves-rolled up reporting and analysis."

"Why not?" I asked Tom, who had been sitting still as I had spoken – unlike Ted earlier. "All very interesting, Spencer;" Tom said. "Let me talk with Ted and I will be in touch."

Nothing else came from my meetings with Turner and his people. It was a sign that I would have to be patient in my job hunt.

♖ ♗ ♘

On June 11 there was a NPAC strategy session at the office of Don Grubbs. There were hearings in the house on June 14. The cycle of lobbying, briefings, hearings, and follow up continued.

By now I had found a craftsman who agreed to built the small wooden bases that would hold the replicas of the Yevgeny Vuchetich sculpture. I arranged for the creation of a brass plaque for each individual who was to receive one. Each plaque read:

> In Appreciation for Commitment and Service
>
> [Name]
>
> US Commission on Proposals for the National Academy of Peace and Conflict Resolution
>
> "Let Us Beat Swords Into Plowshares"

In August of 1981 I received a call that the bronze artwork for the plaques had finally arrived at Dulles Airport. As I drove to Dulles to claim them, I was struck by the irony of picking up pieces of art for members of a peace commission at an airport named for the Cold Warrior John Foster Dulles that had been created by a Russian artist.

Surprisingly later that month I received a letter from one of Senator Matsunaga's aides inquiring about the Dulles delivery of the bronze sculptures. The letter contained an attachment letter of notification to me that the sculptures were due to arrive at Dulles. The Senator's office did not know what to think of the letter as it was forwarded to them because our commission office had closed months earlier. Unable to contact me by mail, the cargo office at Dulles had tracked me down by telephone. The aide accused me of using commission resources to obtain the sculptures, without the Senator's permission.

She asked, rather demanded, that I come to the Senator's office the next day to share my story on the situation. When I met with the aide and Senator I explained how the purchase of the art had come about and the purpose for the pieces. I made clear that the purpose of piece was to commemorate the work of the commission and show appreciation to the individual commissioners. I think the

Senator was angry that these commemorative gifts were not from the Senator, as I got the vibe once again that it was "his" commission, and therefore gifts and recognition should come from his office, not me. I apologized to Senator Matsunaga and shared that I had not intended to slight him in any way. I assured him that my loyalty and appreciation for his appointment were unquestioned. With the passage of time, I have come to believe that Senator Matsunaga felt my loyalty to the vision we shared, and the body of work represented by my efforts to achieve it, superseded my allegiance to him. He was probably correct.

Although it had been six months since I had been on a payroll of the commission, the Senator treated me as if gifts of recognition to the commissioners were his prerogative. I informed him that the commemorative plaques, including the bronze images, would be distributed to the commissioners and others soon. I advised him that, in fact, Mr Dellenback and I had already made an appointment with Senator Hatfield to deliver one to him to thank him for his efforts. Senator Matsunaga knew that Hatfield and Dellenback were close, and both were Republicans from Oregon. Dellenback and Matsunaga served in Congress together, overlapping for two terms, before Dellenback was appointed by President Gerald Ford to be the Director of the Peace Corps. Upon learning that Commissioner Dellenback had been involved with the plaques, Senator Matsunaga became quiet. The subject was not discussed between us again.

Later that fall I made appointments to distribute the plaques, thirteen in all, and met personally with as many of the former commissioners as possible. It was my way of trying to bring a sense of closure for the commission members who had done so much work. Regrettably, I was never able to create the opportunity to honor and or thank the commission staff.

Senator Matsunaga was a consequential contributor to the work that was shared, and accomplished by so many others. Certainly he deserves a great deal of credit for both the creation of the commission, and his service as its chairman. I will always be grateful to the Senator for having confidence in me to carry out the work of the commission as its Director.

Senator Matsunaga died on April 15, 1990. There is no doubt that he served his country in outstanding ways both in the military and as a legislator in state and federal government. Every American owes him respect and appreciation for his service to the country. Senator Matsunaga became the lead Senate sponsor of the legislation contained in our Final Report. People who knew the Senator have said he felt his greatest legacy was the United States Institute of Peace.

On August 18, Mike Mapes and I shared a nice lunch at the Mayflower Hotel. We talked about campaign strategy and discussed issues he was having with the staff, donors, and Congress.

On September 28, I finally received my first copy of the printed Final Report. The delay in its printing had somewhat muffled my elation at the final product. I also continued to be quite worried about what President Reagan might do if the appointments to the future peace institute came up in his term. On October 20, 1981, President Reagan received the Final Report of the commission.

Presenting the Final Report to the President were Senator Matsunaga, Senator Jennings Randolph, Senator Mark Hatfield, and former commissioner Jack Dunfey. It was unfortunate that the full commission would not be present to make the presentation, but the meeting with Reagan was set up at the last minute and many of the commissioners could not clear their calendars, including Jim Laue, its Vice Chair. I do not believe that was a slight by Senator Matsunaga; it was more an issue of getting on the President's schedule. I received calls from a few of the commissioners expressing concern that their own schedules had not been considered in the timing of the meeting with President Reagan. It was an unfortunate situation.

I deeply regretted that for the commissioners, as with the commission staff, there was not a fitting sense of closure for all of the hard and demanding work that had taken place. This was among my very few disappointments of the commission.

President Reagan was reported to have commented upon receiving the report that "our worst enemies seem to become our best friends after the war—like Germany and Japan—and that perhaps it was time we learn to do that before the war."

Senator Matsunaga held a press conference at the Capitol. NPAC hosted a reception attended by about two hundred enthusiastic supporters. The current NPAC Chairman, George Hill, noted "This is a great victory for all who support the traditional role of the United States as an international peacemaker. The commission's report is clear and equivocal, and provides the highest level of public endorsement for a concept that is gaining hundreds of followers every day." Mike Mapes added. "Now, with the commission report behind us, we're ready to get on with the larger and more important job—actually creating the US Academy of Peace."

The Final Report was not widely circulated, although it represented the work of the commission and contained many excerpts from the testimony we took throughout the year of its work. The editor did a good job. Members of Congress and some federal departments received copies of the report. It is interesting that Commissioner and Representative Ashbrook felt compelled to request the inclusion of his dissenting views in the Final Report of the commission, although he declined to participate in most of its activity. On pages 206 -209, Congressman Ashbrook attacked the initial "Design Paper" that I had co-authored in March of 1980, and distributed to the commissioners to set the table for their year of investigation. Ashbrook was particularly uncomfortable with the phrase that "when conflict resolution or conflict management is taken to mean pacification, delay, placation, or continuation of the status quo, justice is not served and often more violence is apt to occur." Ashbrook's worldview was that "In the real world, the status quo is often the least violent, least unjust choice available." The Congressman completely missed the point of expert and citizen testimony, findings of peace research, and the personal experiences of many witnesses in the public seminars that structural violence of the status quo is a form of injustice and violence.

Ashbrook was fearful that a future institution might have a "pseudo-cosmopolitan outlook that prevails at places like the United Nations." The Congressman rejected many of the findings of the Commission's work. Ashbrook declined to sign the Final Report. He felt it would be "foolish" for Congress to create a federal peace academy and he stressed in his dissenting remarks that such an institution would become a "haven for our Andrew Youngs and Ramsey Clarks and others who believe that the way to peace with the assorted ayatollahs and other titled bandits of today's world is to grovel."

In the end, I hope Congressman Ashbrook was right, as that is indeed what most of those on the commission and its supporters were trying to achieve, that is to say, *progress toward peace with justice and understanding.* Congressman John Ashbrook died on April 24, 1982. President Ronald Reagan said as part of Ashbrook's remembrance: "…his articulate and passionate calls for a return to old-fashion American values earned him the respect of all that knew him."

In early October I traveled to Terra Haute, Indiana to make a presentation on the Peace Academy, and thanked a number of NPAC supporters. Around the country, members of NPAC and many who had participated in the hearings continued to provide support critical to keeping the focus on new legislation. They wanted to know what was happening and how the story might end. As I traveled for other reasons during this time, I tried to meet with individuals and groups of supporters as often as I could. I was not the only NPAC advisor doing so, and we coordinated our visits; built upon one another's contacts, and shared what was happening in DC.

♖ ♗ ♘

Connie had been in Atlanta for most of the summer working in Andy's mayoral campaign. Near the end of October I flew to Atlanta to join her. Connie had responsibility for several geographic sections of Atlanta. She was included in all of the inner-circle campaign meetings. I was invited along as a spouse. When I was in town I would help out delivering yard signs to people that had requested them or canvasing in neighborhoods as directed by others. I would ring doorbells and hand out buttons and brochures. In the November elections, Andy was elected mayor of Atlanta.

After the election, Connie and I had a lot to talk about and our own future hung in the balance. We took some time off and went to St Simons Island, Georgia to talk through our future plans. Connie was pregnant. I had a job offer in California; Connie had a job offer to stay with Andy in Atlanta.

Our discussion about our future was pretty intense. Connie had been with Andy for nearly a decade, serving first as a community organizer, then legislative assistant and then special assistant when he was appointed Ambassador. She had worked with him at Young Ideas, and traveled to twenty African nations with him before starting to work on his campaign in the Atlanta mayor's race. On the one hand, Connie wanted to stay with Andy and focus on urban policy issues. She liked Atlanta and, of course, was very loyal to Andy. On the other hand, she was tired and was ready for a change. Connie made it clear that if she were to leave Andy, I would have to drag her away, which she admitted might not be a bad thing. As much as she loved Washington, DC, neither of us felt it was a good place to raise a child. She was not wild about my job offer in San Francisco, as she was unsure about being away from her family and friends on the East Coast. Finally, with some persuading, she agreed that we would move to California.

On the road trip back home to DC from St Simons Connie had a miscarriage in Charleston, South Carolina.

In early December Jim and I met to talk about the legislation and campaign going forward. I shared with him that we were going to move to San Francisco. We discussed my desire to become a practitioner in our field, and he was exceedingly encouraging. Over the next decade, Jim moved from his academic position at the University of Missouri- St Louis to Washington, DC, where he was appointed a Professor at George Mason University and served as President and Executive Director of the Conflict Clinic, Inc., a non-profit dispute resolution organization.

Leaning into this same decade, I was about to begin a fresh career as a business consultant and conflict resolution professional. Our efforts to advance the concept of a peace academy or institute were now parallel tracks to our mutual labors pushing out the boundaries of the field as practitioners.

Chapter 9 Review and Reflection

Task

- Learn to manage failure and loss.

Challenge

- Find your resilience.

Gift and Opportunity

- Learn to be fearless, with nonattachment to self-importance, ego, or absolute control.

Reflection

- What do you trust unshakably in yourself?
- How can you help others change themselves?

PART FIVE

Causing Change: Strategies, Challenges, and Concerns

CHAPTER 10

China Basin

1981 - China Basin is a San Francisco industrial and residential area built alongside San Francisco Bay. In July of 1981 I traveled there for a job interview and to observe a public training in facilitation and collaborative problem solving by Interaction Associates[79], IA, to determine if there would be a fit for my joining the firm as a senior consultant.

China Basin originally was a wharf area built into a landfill waterfront just south of the historic San Francisco Embarcadero, which meant "place to embark" in Spanish. As the city of San Francisco grew, a large offshore seawall was built and the surrounding mudflats were filled in, creating what is today's Financial District. Before the construction of the Bay Bridge, the embarcadero plaza in front of the Ferry Building was one of the busiest areas of foot traffic in the world; only Charing Cross Station in London and Grand Central Terminal in New York City were busier. By 1981, this area south of Market in San Francisco had become an incubator of pioneering organizations and initiatives. It was in China Basin that I would embark on a new phase of my journey—to become a dispute resolution practitioner.

I began my work with IA in early 1982 by learning to perfect the teaching of collaborative problem-solving and taking on consulting assignments. There too, I hit the ground running, feeling the self-imposed pressure to get up to speed in teaching and consulting as soon as possible. I was motivated to begin demonstrating the skills that I had advocated for the previous half-decade.

On February 23, 1982, Mike Mapes called to ask if I would consider going onto the board of directors of NPAC. I said yes, as I was very happy to do so and felt grounded enough in my new responsibilities to support the campaign. In mid-March I was back in Washington, DC, leading a two-day seminar on collaborative problem-solving and facilitation skills. I met with Mike and some of the NPAC members on my visit. The following day, March 17, I had been asked to meet with the personnel department of the Central Intelligence Agency in Rosslyn, Virginia, to discuss an internal conflict that had been brewing at the CIA's language school. The agency maintained a discreetly located language school right in the heart of Rosslyn. Several members of the faculty were apparently in conflict due to cultural differences regarding teaching hours, punctuality, and other behaviors that impacted on the sense of community at the facility. I spent a couple of days interviewing faculty members and providing feedback to the school staff and faculty. Back in the Bay Area on Friday, I had marketing meetings and checked in by telephone with some of the leadership of the National Institute of Dispute Resolution.

Then I led a six-day seminar back in San Francisco the week of March 29, with client trips in between. April 14 was an NPAC Annual Meeting, just ahead of peace academy hearings before Representatives Fascell and Zablocki in the House. I did not attend the hearings, but called Nacky Gerber to get a report on how they had gone. Senate hearings were scheduled for April 21, but I was teaching a five-day program in San Francisco and was not available to attend. In the formal testimony that I submitted to the Senate Subcommittee I reviewed the work of the commission; the significance of the future peace institute and emphasized the cost savings that would occur as a result of its formation. Regarding the economics and return on investment of the US academy of peace, I stated:

> "Recently, a study made by one of the largest corporations in America indicated the potential for a 64% return on their investment in the same types of skills and techniques which would be central to the learning at the academy of peace. The study conservatively estimated the potential savings to the company to be close to $50 million per year."

With regard to the significance of the US academy of peace, I stated to the committee members:

> "In the coming decades, Americans will be faced with more change than ever in their history. The boundaries of our tradition, culture, commerce and way of life will be pressed severely by our growing population, decreasing resources and escalating reliance upon technology to solve our problems. The forces of change in our society will be so incredible that in order to manage conflict within society and to preserve our American heritage, we as a nation will have to adapt to change so profound that we will have no way to predict the effects of such change. Those Americans who will be challenged in international diplomacy, business, and social affairs to deal with change must become managers of the process of change as much as managers of the changes themselves.

> "The major problem caused by change is how you proceed to deal with it. The thrust of the US Academy of Peace is to prepare our leaders and future leaders to understand the process of change. We can predict, respond and mange the process of change, but we will never be able to predict the changes themselves. Therefore,

the hope for international peace rests with the efforts to manage the process. The peacemakers of the future will be the managers of process, more than of the causes of the disputes."

♜ ♗ ♞

Connie and I both traveled to DC in late May. We reconnected with Washington friends and work colleagues. June 3 was a peace academy event and on June 4 I met with Professor Ralph Goldman, who was an early peace academy supporter. As a specialist in American and transnational political parties, he was recognized for his advocacy of the use of parties as the institutional alternative to civil and international war. He believed political parties were crucial to overcoming terrorist and anti-democratic movements. Over the years, Ralph and I had spent hours discussing the institutional structure of a future peace academy and how to insulate it from potentially harmful government interference. Ralph was as assertive in his beliefs as he was astute in his political and social observations.

The end of June found me back in DC teaching for a week and I was able to meet with several Congressional staffers as well as reconnect with campaign and commission consultant Charlie E. Smith. Back in San Francisco, I again met with Professor Goldman regarding peace academy testimony and talked with the people at NIDR about their Dispute Resolution Newsletter.

July 6 was Elise Boulding's birthday. It brought back fond memories of our celebrating her birthday two years earlier on a catamaran sailing off Waikiki during a much-needed break in the business meeting of the commission. In the first day of commissioner deliberations, the commissioners were really stuck. Things were not going well, and the tension and spirit in the conference room clashed against the idyllic surroundings. Elise spoke up saying, "Well, this does not appear to be going anywhere. It's my birthday and I need a break." I suggested we go sailing. We agreed to take a break. Commissioner John Dellenback, Elise, Connie, and several others joined in before returning to the meetings later in the evening. Whether it had been strategic or not by Elise, the break in our deliberations proved to be highly beneficial.

August 10 and 12, I met with Commissioner Bill Lincoln who was advocating using singer Burl Ives to promote the peace academy concept. Mr Ives joined us for lunch. Bill continued to advocate for his idea of selling red bricks as a way to fundraise for NPAC. He had made a mock-up sample for me when I was Executive Director of NPAC. It featured a brass plaque with my name and made for a lovely nameplate on my office desk. As clever as the idea was, the cost of postage for a brick was always of concern to me. Bill had proposed that once a national peace academy was physically built, all of the donors would be asked to return their bricks to be crafted into a founder's wall. I loved the concept, but was never really able to get my head around mailing bricks to and fro around the country.

Also during this time period, I held meetings with the leadership of American Society for Training and Development, helping them plan for their national conference in DC in 1983. I met with leaders from EVOLVE, an environmental group, and I was doing consulting work with the ATARI computer game-tech firm, the CORO Foundation, Proctor and Gamble, and teaching a full seminar schedule. The American Bar Association National Conference was in San Francisco and I dropped by the conference hotels to meet with leaders from various ADR groups. On these various business trips and conference gatherings I continued my advocacy of whatever was happening in Washington, DC.

The week of September 6, I met several times with Jim Laue and Peggy Hermann, who were both involved in planning an upcoming meeting of a new association of conflict resolution professionals called the National Consortium on Peace and Conflict Resolution, NCPCR. It was one of a number of emerging professional networks that resulted from the work of the campaign, commission and the development of an expanding field of ADR.

At the first NCPCR meeting, held in St Louis, I arrived late due to some travel delays. Jim was at the podium welcoming the attendees when he saw me walk into the back of the room. He altered his remarks to recognize me. He asked the attendees to turn and greet me as I walked in to sit down. Jim proudly said, "Ladies and gentlemen, please join me in recognizing William Spencer, director of the recent federal peace academy commission and former Executive Director of NPAC." I was overwhelmed when the meeting participants stood to give me a standing ovation. It was the first I had ever received any recognition of my work to create the Peace Academy. There was nothing I could say; no way I could deflect the recognition as I was far from the speaker's lectern. My heart soared. Jim set up that moment for me and I will be eternally grateful, as I am for so many of his gracious gestures toward me.

That moment, I was instantly recharged with a new sense of dedication and delight for the goals I had set for myself seven years earlier. I was on my way to becoming a practitioner. My hardest years and the ordeal of the campaign and commission were over. Despite the adjustment that Connie and I were making with our move to the West Coast, and her loss of some identity and meaning in her life as she parted ways with Andy, we had made a new beginning of our lives together. It felt like a corner had been turned. Connie and I tried again to have a family.

In November we learned that Connie was pregnant again. In late December, we traveled to Averill Park, New York to spend part of the holidays with Connie's family. On December 30, I met in DC with Jim, Bryant, Jack Dover, and NPAC and NPAF people.

While in Washington, I stopped in at the University of Maryland Medical Center in Baltimore to see Mike Mapes who was seriously ill with lymphoma. We spent about an hour talking. Mike was already weak. He had a lot of courage and we spoke together as friends who had shared a great deal.

Mike Mapes was loyal, kind, and very committed. When I first met him I was impressed that he had been a Boy Scout Leader for more than eighteen years. He owned racehorses, which surprised me, and he was the only person I ever knew who kept his morning coffee mug on a little electric stand that heated the cup all day long. He had his quirks, as we all do, but his commitment and advocacy to our cause was instructive to anyone looking for a model of dedication to creating political will. Mike was a graduate of the Naval Academy at Annapolis and of Yale Law School. I admired him as a friend; valued his patience and calm as a manager; appreciated his service to NPAC and the advancement of the cause leading to the creation of USIP. Mike and I had spent the better part of the past six years working together, in close touch; sowing fields and developing a concept.

After our hospital meeting, I called one of my physician friends in DC to confirm the diagnosis and learned that the mortality rate for his specific disease was 70%. It was very sad, and apparently there would be no remission, even with aggressive treatment. We on the board of NPAC began to make arrangements to lessen Mike's responsibilities with the campaign so he could focus on his health and family. I was deeply saddened by Mike's health situation. I found myself seeking the distraction of working harder at my training and consulting activity.

♖♗♘

As my second year as a consultant began, it was important to me to prove that the approaches and techniques my colleagues and I had been advocating were capable of creating measurable results in business and society. It was one of the ways I felt I could further validate the Peace Academy concept and influence the forward process of our efforts. The year 1983 was shaping up to be a year of personal recommitment to the campaign, and continued professional growth and exploration of collaborative problem-solving techniques. There was a self-imposed pressure to grow a business practice that could make a difference in the life of the clients we served and further demonstrate the value of alternative methods of planning and dispute intervention.

I began the planning for a large community intervention in Riverside, CA and started working with EPA in planning one of their upcoming events in Sacramento. My colleagues and I in IA were fortunate to be among the pioneering West Coast firms being recognized for our work in skill building and collaborative consulting. With my background in dispute resolution, I started to take on new assignments.

I had meetings with three representatives of the Aleutian Pribilof Island Association, a Native Alaskan corporation, based in Anchorage. I was asked to help representatives of the tribe with a leadership development program. In Alaska the mineral rights belonging to Native Alaskans became available for sale twenty years after the Alaska Native Claims Settlement Act of 1971. The Act was the largest land claims settlement in United States history, intended to resolve the long-standing issues surrounding aboriginal land claims in Alaska. The Act provided for the transfer of land titles to twelve Native Alaskan regional corporations and over two hundred local villages. A provision was later made for Native Alaskans living outside of the state.

When Atlantic-Richfield Company discovered oil at Prudhoe Bay in 1968, the issue of land ownership became controversial and an urgent settlement was reached. The 1971 Act attempted to enable Natives to stay in their local villages and benefit from the oil revenues flowing to the Native corporations. More than one hundred thousand Native Alaskans were impacted by the act. Roughly forty-four million acres were involved in the exchange for $963 million paid to the villages and tribal corporations. One provision of the act set forth that mineral rights and shares could not be sold by Native Alaskans for twenty years, so that the corporations and local Native leadership could forge the necessary skills to manage the funds and educate others in their communities about ownership rights.

With the year 1991 on the horizon, the twenty-year buffer was about to expire and the tribal council wanted to ensure that its members were willing and able to deal with the transition that was coming. The area managed by the tribal council was about one hundred thousand square miles and extended eleven hundred miles down an archipelago from the southwestern tip of Alaska. I learned that the tribal council served thirteen village communities along the Aleutian Chain. Each Native Alaskan corporation provided for the health care, education, and security of its geographic area. The objective of my assistance to the tribe was in support of strategies to preserve their traditions and help their leaders prepare the population for the coming changes brought on by the final implementation of the Act.

During the next four years I spent many intense experiences in Alaska with elders, youth, senior corporation managers, and village representatives to meet the objectives we had set. My work in Alaska was an amazing experience that afforded me the opportunity to engage in cross-cultural work that would prepare me for what was to come. I learned that native peoples have an incredible sense of the authenticity of people, particularly outsiders, who offer to help. It was both an honor to be accepted among them and to learn from their culture.

January 1983, I was back in Dearborn continuing to work with the Ford Motor Company. Ford at the time had about 320,000 employees worldwide, including sixty thousand employees who were involved in the product development business in Dearborn. My client was the Chief Design Executive and Vice President of North American Design, an important part of the North American Automotive Operations. During the next four years I worked with the 2,500 members of the design staff to create and implement a new vision of where their efforts would take them, and more specifically, the philosophy, mission, and values that served to bind them together as an organization. The environment in which Ford designers were operating was quickly changing, and corporate financial losses were creating tension between the designers of vehicles and the sea of engineering professionals that made up the balance of the research and development park. In the year before I began working with Ford, they had lost two billion dollars. To solve this problem, we worked create better relations between the designers and engineers and led a collaborative problem-solving process to shrink the time of their product development process. In the design community, we addressed the design philosophy; their increased understanding and use of technology, the human resource leadership and effectiveness of the staff, and improved the overall skills of the organization to better manage change. Within the larger product development enterprise, my colleagues and I helped them identify eight hundred problems—sorting them into twelve categories—and led a two year problem-solving process that resulted in cutting their time to market in half and saving, by Ford's own estimate, close to a billion dollars per year. The scope and investment of time in the contract was considerable. It proved to be the largest change management program I have ever been involved with. The project was a lot of work and represented the scale of change effort faced by many major companies at the time.

My extensive trips to Detroit enabled me to make side trips to Washington and stay in personal touch with several commission staff members, NPAC supporters and staff and members of Congress as needed. I was in frequent communication with Tom Westropp, Jack Dunfey, Bill Lincoln, Bryant, and Jim. Bryant nurtured George Mason University to develop a graduate, degree-granting program in conflict management. It became known as Institute for Conflict Analysis and Research, ICAR. Jim and his wife Mariann had made their move from St. Louis to Northern Virginia to assume his teaching position at George Mason University. Andy was busy being mayor of Atlanta.

By March 16, there was a Senate subcommittee meeting on the peace academy legislation and support had increased to include fifty-three Senate co-sponsors. I along with others continued networking and supporting NPAC's efforts to move the legislation along.

In 1983 I was asked to design a program for the United States Conference of Mayors, to be held on the Queen Mary cruise liner in Long Beach. The venerable cruise ship had been converted into a hotel and was to serve as the venue for a series of forums to explore critical urban issues in six in-depth workshops, each constructed to include experts and identify solutions that would benefit public-private partnership in addressing the topics. President Reagan provided a welcoming letter to the participants who were mayors and executives from all across the country. Coleman Young, the mayor of Detroit was the co-convener, along with William Kieschnick, the Chief Executive Officer of the Atlantic Richfield Company. Many other national organizations participated, including The Conference Board, the White House Office of Private Sector Initiatives, the AFL-CIO, American Enterprise Institute, the Aspen Institute, the Business Roundtable, and others. The topics under discussion were Infrastructure/Transportation; Mediating Structures / Human Services; Taxation and Fiscal Policy; Municipal Services; and Jobs, Education, and Training. After designing the meeting format and decision process for the conferees, I was asked to deliver a lunchtime keynote on how to go about reaching agreement on the initiatives the conferees were to take back to their cities and urban partnerships.

By the spring of 1983, NPAC had secured the endorsement of major organizations that carried weight with Members of Congress and their staffs. At this point in the campaign, NPAC had been able to gain the official support of fourteen national associations, twenty significant organizations, fifteen religious denominations, and garnered the support and endorsing resolutions of ten state legislatures. On April 14, a House subcommittee did a final mark-up on the bill.

♖ ♗ ♞

I was traveling to client assignments and was having difficulty making it to the birthing classes that we were taking in preparation for the birth of our son, Matthew. In April, I was in Alaska, Detroit, Phoenix, Washington, DC, and Los Angeles working with clients and sitting in on meetings with the National Institute for Dispute Resolution, NDIR, and NPAC meetings.

May 10–12 I was in Detroit and the following day the Senate bill was marked up. On May 15, I managed to run in the seven-mile Bay to Breakers fun run in San Francisco in a throng of eighty thousand fellow runners. After finishing, I headed to the airport to catch a plane to Washington via Detroit, for a joint NPAC-NPEF meeting that included Jim, Dante Fascell, and Jack Dunfey on May 23. I led training in Atlanta on May 26-27 and then headed back to the Bay Area to begin work at a GE plant in San Jose on June 2-3.

One of General Electric's business units was called Nuclear Energy Business Organization, NEBO, and had the primary responsibility for the design of nuclear plants around the world. The operation was significant and housed five thousand engineers in a research and design complex that included a full-scale mock-up reactor, built mostly underground so as not to concern the neighboring businesses and residential areas. It was not an active plant, meaning it did not produce power or contain uranium, but it was fully functioning in all other ways so the engineers could test new processes and diagnose problems that might appear in their online operational plants. The presenting problem of our consulting work was that very few new nuclear plants had been ordered since the Three Mile Island disaster. The business unit of GE did not want to break up the cadre of brainpower that they had built up over the years, but the parent company GE was concerned about the financial losses of the company, as well as the increasing public displeasure with nuclear power that some stockholders felt was diminishing the overall GE brand. Our job was to help the company figure out what to do by way of economic conversion of their expertise and human resources. Ultimately, the five thousand engineers began to make a successful business out of decommissioning the nuclear plants rather than designing and building them.

On June 6-7, I led a public training at our San Francisco offices and then entertained Bill Lincoln who was in town to talk about the current legislation. I was scheduled to lead an advanced training for trainers during the period of June 12-17, but midway into the program found a substitute because Connie went into labor. Our son Matthew was born on June 16, 1983 at nearby Alta Bates Hospital in Berkeley. He was born in a birthing room that enabled Connie, Matt, and me to spend the night together in one large bed. That night I wrapped Matt up and took him to the rooftop of the hospital in TV series *Roots* fashion—presenting him to the skyline of San Francisco across the bay.

The day before, on June 15, the peace academy bill was voted out of committee. On June 23, I joined in by telephone to participate on an NPAC meeting in DC.

With NPAC, we began to expand the citizen base of support we had enlarged as a result of the work of the commission. We had gained momentum and were more rapidly increasing the scope of political will necessary for us to reach our goals. At the same time, ADR was picking up speed, as well as other applications of conflict resolution across the country. During the campaign and commission we had worked very hard to place newspaper articles and letters to the editors to gain visibility. Now, as more parts of society were beginning to use alternative mechanisms, coverage grew. For example, courts were beginning to utilize night prosecutor's offices to more easily and informally process specific types of conflicts, usually in the evening as alternatives to more traditional day courts. Other examples included a trend toward more neighborhood justice centers being established around the country to process local disputes in non-litigious ways; local school boards were adopting school mediation services; and couples facing divorce now had the option of using divorce mediation in place of expensive and often hurtful court proceedings. Arbitration clauses were becoming more common in business deals and lawyers were going back to school to learn more about the behavioral aspects of mediation to supplement their legal training. Our efforts to promote alternative conflict resolution skills and mindsets were part of a wave of interest and new approaches to managing disputes.

The end of the first week of July I met in Sacramento with some of State House Speaker Willie Brown's staff regarding using better agenda planning and collaborative problem-solving methods in the way the California State Assembly functioned. The discussions eventually did not go very far, as it was apparent that the Speaker was trying to use the tools to further certain political agendas rather than advance more participatory goals. I enjoyed meeting Speaker Brown, as he was quite the character, and being from California I found him very interesting. In early July I also worked with Ford in Dearborn and with NEBO in San Jose.

My schedule of client work, company management, and new parent responsibilities continued through the end of the year. The momentum of the campaign simmered, as we continued our efforts to broaden public support for passing national legislation.

My work at Interaction Associates had been an answer to my craving to become a practitioner, not just an advocate. In those years, IA was small; there were just five of us. I worked diligently along with my colleagues to build a business and expand on the visions of the founders. I took satisfaction from working with the company on marketing issues and learning to lead the training courses offered by the company. I shadowed each of the other consultants. I mimicked and modeled their skills and behaviors. I copied what they did—I even told their same jokes in our public training sessions. They gave me constant feedback and helped me to improve my game. Our firm grew.

Years later whenever clients asked me over meals at corporate retreats how I came to learn my skills, my answer was always that it had been by doing it over and over again in these early years. My early years at IA were the years I matured from being an advocate to being a practitioner. By being exposed to the conflicts in organizations and the dynamics of corporate organizational change, I got better at the practice of problem-solving, negotiation, mediation, and organizational development. As I did more and more training, I became more accomplished at corporate consulting because I understood the politics of organizations and the dynamics of conflict. The opportunity Bill Lincoln had provided in encouraging me to attend the AAA ten-week course in community dispute resolution training in Boston had provided a base from which to begin. The dashing off to weekly Eastern Airlines flights commuting to Boston had proved very worthwhile. I had been afforded the opportunity to learn the behavioral stuff that had been missing in graduate school.

Working with organizations – large and small – provided me the experience and confidence of practice. Each company had its own culture, organizational dynamics, power relationships and usually unique problems to solve. By 1988 my experience base of working to facilitate the resolution of client problems exceeded two hundred and fifty corporations. This work was preparing me to one-day work with larger systems in more intense conflict. As I began a parallel track of working for companies *and* assisting countries and alliances in their dysfunctions, the territory was familiar and non-threatening to me. The skill and mind sets of serving both arenas was not unlike what I imagined the experience of a physician to be who practiced medicine at home and abroad. There were differences of culture, poverty, and limitations of support services, but at the end of the day: medicine was medicine. For me, conflict resolution practices were effectively adaptable to each setting. I felt in my heart that these learnings were similar to the narratives we had pushed out over the prior decade.

I came to fully realize in these years that the peace academy—or USIP—would be more effective and in fact better off if it incorporated a blend of practical skills with the important theoretical ones. At my small company, we required all of our consultants to continue to do training and teach skills seminars precisely to keep their mindsets grounded in practical techniques. We did this specifically to maintain congruence between talking about it and being able to model the desired behaviors necessary for change. As the company grew, some new hires that came from academic backgrounds objected, but we held to our belief that it was important, and I believe it made a difference in our future success. I was able to hone my own skills working with corporate organizations and communities so that when the opportunity arose to execute on international problems and conflicts I had the confidence that I knew what I was doing.

♖♗♞

This was the model many of us had envisioned for a national peace academy. Practice and training on community and national disputes created the opportunity for master skills and mindsets that could be applied to international conflicts. The marketing of these new behavioral technologies—collaborative problem solving, facilitation, mediation, and negotiation—were key to helping societies better manage their problems and conflicts. It was an early formulation of Bryant and Jim, both practitioners in their fields, brought together by the discipline of conflict resolution. The practice of selling these types of mediative services was also an essential skill. One of the toughest phases of conflict resolution is getting the parties to the table. That is to say: developing the political will among the disputants to get together is critical to the follow on steps of greater understanding of the issues and formulation of agreements. As Mahatma Gandhi is reported to have said: "Be the change that you wish to see in the world."[80] We were trying to be the change we wanted American society to embody and prove new ways of being that could serve as models for the American foreign policy establishment.

During this period I served as a facilitator for the City of Riverside, California, to agree on goals for the city and surrounding towns of the region. At the time, the "Inland Empire" of California was composed of the adjacent cities of Ontario, San Bernardino and Riverside. Together the region had a population of about four million people, making it one of the top ten urban regions in the country. The area remains the fourth largest urban area of California; the most populous state in the union. This is to say the project had scope and importance.

The City of Riverside, its major newspaper, and the Junior League sponsored the event. For weeks prior to the three-day meeting, the local newspaper had run full-page spreads listing the proposed goals for the region. Following the work of many small groups whose task was to clarify, massage, and bring the issues back to a large group, I lead a decision process of the entire gathering. In less than a day we whittled the fifteen hundred proposals down to a short list of one hundred twenty that the participants vetted to be worthy for implementation by the city. We did so by utilizing a new technology at the time of hand held voting devices similar to the concept of virtual voting used today.

In the Riverside event, the small devices we used provided an instant result via a daisy chain of wires connected to individual handheld units, running throughout the audience of participants. In today's world, voting devices commonly send results wirelessly to a central instrument. Although our methodology would seem antiquated today, the process worked and was an incredible effort. The Junior League did a fantastic job at organizing the event and the process worked. This type of business-community, public-private partnership work provided me experience in facilitating multiparty, complex negotiations that I would use later in my career.

These types of highly visible, high-stakes events honed my practitioner skills, along with the corporate problem-solving work I was doing with companies across a large spectrum of industries. I was using the world of corporate and community problem-solving as preparation for what was to come. I was convinced more than ever, as we had messaged during the campaign and commission, that there was value in the educational and experiential dimensions of performing dispute resolution at the local level in preparation for international applications.

In the campaign, we had begun with the end in mind. Those who came together to create the Peace Academy were looking beyond the establishment of an organization. We were clear we were fostering a new environment to leverage what was known about peace.

Living in San Francisco and removed from my former day-to-day responsibilities with the campaign and commission, I was able to spend more time reflecting on our what had made our efforts successful. Faced with the new challenges presented by my clients, I thought about what we had accomplished and just how we had done it. Buckminster Fuller once said, "I'm not trying to copy nature. I'm trying to find the principles she's using."[81] As we made our case to the Congress and public, Bryant, Jim, Andy, and I applied principles and strategies that seemed to have worked. We were not copying any particular formula for change. These principles, I believe, emerged out of the combined skills and orientations of our backgrounds as professor, psychiatrist, pastor, and peddler.

♖♗♞

With all of my travels and intense consulting experiences, I found myself using new skills I had learned and inventing others. Important in my reflections were my memories of the times in graduate school when I had first encountered the work of Everett Rogers.

Rogers was a communication scholar and sociologist who introduced the term early adopter in his writings. I knew instantly that his writings held within them the very strategies I might need to sell peace.

Professor Roger's book was first published in 1962 when he was thirty and an assistant professor of sociology at Ohio State University. In the mid-2000s, his follow-on book, *The Diffusion of Innovations,*[82] has been cited as the second-most referenced book in the social sciences. I was lucky to have found it that day in the University of Pittsburgh research library.

What had caught my eye in his book was the proposition that the adopters of any new innovation could be sorted into categories of adoption rates for everything from using new seeds (which is where he first developed the idea) or new processes, mechanical devices or innovations having to do with health, hygiene, family planning, or other aspects of social invention. His thesis was that each adopter's willingness to adopt an innovation was dependent on their awareness, interest, trial, and evaluation. To change a social system required first impacting the Innovators and Early Adopters of the system, who in turn would influence the others—described in Roger's work as the Early Majority, Late Majority, and Laggards.

The learning for me was huge as it suggested that if one were intending to work toward social change, one needn't set out to convince everyone, just a smaller population that Rogers estimated to be about 15% of the target population. In 1979, when I had I encountered "The Nine States of America" article by Joel Garreau I had been likewise captivated. It became an important organizing tool for me in both the campaign and the commission.

These insights became significant in my efforts to create the USIP. We started the campaign with these things in mind. I harkened back to Professor Deutsch's phase, "You have got to know what you are doing." Understanding how to effectively target the 15% of innovators and early adopters and focus on the nine defined regions of the country was a beginning to *knowing what I was doing*.

Not only did I use Rogers's insights in my consulting work, as I had in the campaign and work of the commission, they stayed with me as I continued to think about creating political will and causing social change as I eased into international mediation toward the end of the decade.

In the late 1980s I learned that Everett Rogers was in residence at Stanford as a Visiting Scholar. I called him and arranged to meet him for lunch one day on campus. We spent a half-day together, walking and talking. He was an influential mentor to me, although I never studied under him. Never underestimate the power of writing a book!

Many societies have demonstrated the capacity to resolve conflicts peacefully. Most cross-border conflicts are in fact resolved peacefully. Thousands of issues, conflicts, and problems are resolved daily between nation states and within countries. Yet, in the most destructive of conflicts the use of force, aggression, or violence remains a preferred strategy of disputants.

Is there a way to change the way nations and leaders see conflict and the use of violence? The work Rogers did in diffusion research is of interest to scholars and practitioners because it explains how social change occurs at the micro level. Historically, the diffusion of innovations has occurred, from the spread of steel axes within one community to the use of facsimile machines within another. It was applied to AIDS education in the worldwide effort to inform people about the disease. Since the early 1970s more than four thousand publications about the diffusion of innovation have been written. Although few of these studies have focused on the rapid growth of the dispute resolution field, many of the findings seem relevant to our understanding of how alternative dispute solving techniques can be more readily acceptable and applied in the post-Cold War period.

If alternatives to the use of force exist, why have societies not embraced them? Why have the innovations of alternative conflict resolution approaches, dispute resolution systems, or other nonviolent techniques not been more enthusiastically received? What are the barriers to adoption? What are the strategies to gain more widespread acceptance? Finally, what lessons can we draw from the field of diffusion research to better understand what actions might be necessary to transform the nature of conflict from violence to joint problem-solving?

During the years we were actively campaigning to create the commission and through the eighteen months of the commission's life, into the mid 1980s, the field of ADR was coming into its own. In business, the US court system, public policy development, and environmental issues, ADR began to blossom. Law schools began teaching it; business contracts began including it; and the courts began to use ADR strategically to increase the effectiveness and efficiency of managing their caseloads. It took over thirty years, but arbitration, for example, is now used to resolve approximately 60% of all business-related conflicts. Court-referred ADR programs have grown to carry approximately 30% of the workload of all civil cases in the United States.

Only recently have sovereign states begun to create coalitions to intervene in regional or state-to-state conflicts. This activity was considered totally inappropriate just a few years ago. Formal NGOs like the United Nations still will not intervene in the affairs of sovereign nations. The rate of adoption of arbitration and peace-seeking activities by the mainstream are examples of the delays typically found in the introduction of other new ideas before their widespread adoption.

The rate of adoption of new ideas is a fascinating topic and has direct implications for the future effectiveness of the USIP. For instance, more than fourteen years were required for hybrid seed corn to reach complete adoption in Iowa in the first half of the last century. US public schools required fifty years to adopt the idea of the kindergarten in the 1930s and 1940s and more recently it took about five to six years in the 1960s for schools to accept modern math. The laptop computer was conceived nearly forty years ago but only came into marketplace acceptance in the mid-1990s. Cell telephones and what were then called, Personal Digital Assistants, PDAs, replaced laptops. Kenneth Boulding wrote in the 1970s that, "There is a long, painful, slow, but persistent historical movement from the stable war into the unstable war into unstable peace into stable peace."[83] The main objective of peace policy is to speed up the transition by deliberate decision. Achieving that objective will require political will.

♜ ♝ ♞

For the past forty years ideological barriers have played an important role in limiting the development of alternative dispute solving mechanisms. In many parts of the world conflict has been too intense to rethink how it is managed. During the last half of the past century the major powers provided a significant barrier by creating and perpetuating theaters of conflict in Africa, Latin America, and Asia. For example, since 1960, Africa has experienced no less than eighteen wars, twelve of which are still raging to this day. The loss of life from these wars is estimated to be more than six million people, not to mention substantial material damage to infrastructure and economies in the affected countries. There are more than five million refugees today. The existence of such massive turmoil does not provide a rich soil for adopting innovations in conflict resolution. People caught in a world of subsistence and survivals have little opportunity to innovate.

In the campaign we utilized diffusion of innovations techniques to spread the word and gain acceptance of our cause. Today, USIP and others have the opportunity to target populations to transform not just conflicts, but also the social systems we develop to resolve them. US leadership is essential in this task and can usher in a new epoch in the way we conduct foreign policy. It can form the basic core of a new American Exceptionalism. It is not all about the weapons.

Through our efforts to understand the barriers to adopting new methods of managing internal and cross-border conflicts, and the creative regional strategies to overcome these barriers, the United States might succeed in hastening a wider spread use of alternatives to the use of force in resolving conflicts. New networks of innovators and early adopters are emerging, accompanied by the spread of technology. Together these new opportunities for diffusion of ideas relating to nonviolence may help to offset causes of conflict including arms transfers, the psychological dimensions of conflict, and the lack of leadership by political officials.

Those of us closely involved in the National Peace Academy Campaign were presented with a huge learning curve as we invented, evolved, and borrowed tactics and strategies to make our case across the country—and particularly with the Congress and Executive Branch. The civil rights movement, environmental movement, and research in the fields of communication theory and sociology had influenced and helped our progress in organizing support for the campaign. Activists and scholars in conflict resolution practice, theory, political science, and political psychology helped to feed the content of our arguments, but the process to present our case to Congress and the citizenry at large became a real-time exercise in learning how to cause change at a national level. We were lobbying for what was perceived by some as an ethereal state and by others as a peace ensured by the threat of violence. In our work we tried to focus on the practical side of peace and make it relevant for every audience, in their own context. We tried to illustrate what peace really was, how it could be caused and sustained, and whose role it was to build the systems to create it.

Did this function peacemaking belong to State, DOD, the White House, and how would any federal agency sustain the necessary focus on peace to nurture it among all the other competing interests? In our minds, none of the above agencies had very good answers, but of course, all saw their role as being the primary peacemaker in the country. At times we had to work against prejudices and assumptions that linked any concept of peace with antiwar activists, New Age apostles, or simply to the answer to a prayer. We learned to separate what was myth from what was practical, factual, logical, and based on field research and rigorous academic consideration.

In retrospect, five macro-strategies played a role whenever we got stuck or hit a wall. They were simple concepts, yet they enabled us to break through resistance and directly impact on systems that otherwise appeared to be too well established, or too intimidating to influence.

The word "macro" comes from the Greek and means long, tall, high or large. I use the term macro, because it connotes a large or prominent tool that is utilized in exceptional circumstances. For example, you use a macro tool when you are working with relatively large quantities or on a large scale. A common example of its usage is in the term macroeconomics.

During the work of NPAC and the commission we were not consciously aware of these tools; nor did we invent them. We did employ them. Only later was I able to give them names. Following my work withy the commission, I was exposed to versions of similar tools that my colleagues and I experimented with in working on complex, large-scale corporate change efforts while at Interaction Associates. I am indebted to David Straus, Michael Doyle and Charles E. Smith for synthesizing the construct of these tools. The effectiveness of the macro-strategies became more apparent when I integrated them with the work of Everett Rogers. They are examples of concepts, steps, or macro-strategies that help create political will. Each is expressed here in a short phrase. We developed our version of them over time, out of real-life experience. Other people may know them by other names. They work.

A word of encouragement and caution:

*As you read through the next seven pages or so, you may have difficulty visualizing how each tool works. That is expected and occurs because each tool represents out-of-the box thinking; and that is precisely why they work. Most often when anyone is involved in social the tools are designed to be used when you get stuck in trying to cause change. change or creating political will, the scale and scope of the activity can be quite large. It is easy to get stuck along the way. These tools are actually much simpler than they are portrayed in the context, details and examples that follow. Keep in mind **the tools are designed to be used when you get stuck in trying to cause change.*** Try one or two. You don't have to use them all at the same time.

Summarizing, the five macro-strategies are:

- When in ***doubt***, go out: reframe to a wider field
- ***Open*** the problem space: invent a shared reality
- Target the ***early*** adopters: focus on people with influence; customize the message
- Get their attention: use an uncharacteristic ***strategy***
- Break through the inertia: change the ***structure***; change the perception

Over the course of the activities of the campaign and the commission, we acted to use each of them as macro-strategies and they were equally useful later in my life when I began doing change management work with companies and in international mediation. To facilitate remembering the macro-strategies, I have labeled them with the simple mnemonic DOESS. A mnemonic is a tool that uses a pattern of letters, or numbers to help you recall an idea or phrase.

I refer to this suite of macro-strategies, as the DOESS process to create and nurture political will.

- D—**Doubt** – when in doubt, go out; reframe to a wider field
- O—**Open** the problem space; invent a shared reality
- E—**Early** adopters – focus on the people with influence; customize the message
- S—**Strategy** – be uncharacteristic; get their attention
- S – **Structure** – change the structure; change the perception

Macro-strategy 1.   D—When in *doubt*, go out; reframe to a wider field

We reframed a lot when we met or anticipated resistance. Bryant was particularly good at this because of his work in communications and his relationships with the innovative researchers. I found later that the work of George Lakoff encapsulated some of these same ideas in his books: *Moral Politics*, published in 1996 and in *Don't Think of an Elephant*, in 2004. The trick is in the framing of the topic.

We took steps to consciously link peace and social justice, economic development, and community collaboration, and we:

- Provided a historical context
- Changed the image and narrative to peace and how to achieve it
- Reframed resistance to positive narratives for support based on known facts
- Showed evidence of wide social implications, not just gains for special interest groups
- Linked to spiritual, moral, and social grounding based on values, not specific issues
- Demonstrated the range of appeal of idea by breath and character of organizational support
- Appealed to stakeholders based on teachable behaviors, not present attitudes
- Introduced federal issues if focused on state issues; if focused on federal issues, we introduced state issues
- Accepted and legitimized concerns; translated invitations to solve into challenge to support
- Created positive momentum by featuring tangible examples of progress
- Talked about peace as an everyday reality
- Invented a narrative that challenged people to think beyond what was expected

Macro-strategy 2.   O—*Open* the problem space; invent a shared reality

Opening the problem space enlarges the universe of possible solutions. It provides an opportunity to address new perceptions of the appropriate political will. Open the problem space: invent a shared reality. In the campaign we told stories in ways that they could be told again and again. We defined social problems in ways that increased the size of the vision of solutions, to encompass the new institution we sought. The larger the problem space, the larger the solution space.[84] We created narratives that could be shared across diverse notions of self-interest. We talked about peace as an everyday reality that was teachable and achievable. We sought agreement on the problems before trying to get agreement on the solution.

We talked about peace in explicit ways that got people on the same page. We grounded people on shared benefits. We encouraged public meetings and seminars to share expressions of what a National Peace Academy might be like. We defined peace broadly to be inclusive of multiple self-interests.

When a group or individual tried to make arguments against the concept of a national peace academy, we would often counter their points by expanding the debate from a narrow message to a more widely shared perspective. When people at the State Department and the schools of Foreign Service or diplomacy argued that training for peace was already their job, we took the argument to a larger audience. Peace was increasingly being seen as not just the domain of the elites who acted in large part to protect the status quo. It was becoming an art form that went beyond. By expanding the argument to include other individuals and perspectives from beyond the narrow focus of the debate, as framed by the opposing side, we were able to better make our case. Instead of just using peacemaking as the prerogative of diplomacy, we expanded it to public health, prison life, urban planning, school desegregation, environmental policy, and many other aspects of community affairs. The linkage was rational and expanded people's perception of what the real problems were as well as expanding their willingness to consider a greater range of solutions, such as the creation of a national center to promote and address the expanding knowledge base and practice of conflict resolution.

Macro-strategy 3.   E—***Early*** adopters; focus on the people with the most influence; customize the message

The third macro-strategy: Target the early adopters and customize the message. We focused on individuals and specific groups of innovators and early adopters to legitimize and sell the idea. We used Innovators and early adopters in specific interest areas to advocate and sell the early majority. We made multiple touches with the same individuals and groups. We went to them as opposed to expecting them to come to us. We focused our message on individual leaders tried to inspire them to motivate others. We had a singular product with multiple applications.

Target the early adopters: In DOESS, both conservative and progressive arguments can be presented to the early majorities. Imagine the innovators and early adopters on the left side of the bell curve as being progressives. This 15% of true believers is trying to capture and influence the middle thirds of the early majority and the later majority. In the mind of the progressive, the laggards, on the far right would be the conservatives. The lesson of target the early adopter is to use the system to influence the rest of the system. Don't waste your time on the laggards.

Now imagine the innovators and early adopters on the left side of the bell curve as being conservatives. This 15% of true believers is trying to capture and influence the middle thirds of the early majority and the late majority. In the mind of the conservative, the laggards on the far right would be the progressives. Progressives would tend to view conservatives as hopeless causes in the same way that conservatives would tend to view progressives. However, people can be progressives on some issues and conservative on others.

Experience shows that when trying to work the bell curve in this way, a conservative argument will lose momentum in its journey across the population groups in the curve because the wisdom of the crowds will take over and most often, the populations in the curve will select the nurturing dialectic over the strict dialectic. Staying with the example of resistance in the diplomatic training business, we worked hard to identify individual leaders within a given community to influence others within that community. Where the dean of one school of diplomacy issued a letter dismissing the concept of a national peace academy, we found another more progressive dean to issue an endorsement. We used diffusion strategies to cause the people in a system to influence others in the same system. We organized the early adopters to influence other individuals in the bell curve array of adopter categories in social systems, as described by Rogers.

Sometimes to make sense of how society develops political will, I imagine a village of no more than one hundred citizens. I find that thinking about change in this context and scale is revealing. Think about your own experience with a Parent Teacher Association, community association, or Home Owners' Association. Out of this small population, probably fifteen or so would emerge as leaders, sixty or so might just be along for the ride, fifteen might find cause to challenge any decisions of the group and ten or so might move in and out of the subgroups. If I am trying to get the PTA to change course, I know to invest my time with the more open-minded movers and shakers, who are the innovators and early adopters. When they support a new idea they sell it to the others and I don't have to do all the heavy lifting. Societies and other social entities work in the same way.

Macro-strategy 4. ***Strategy***; be uncharacteristic; get their attention

Lastly, these two macro-strategies, strategy and structure, can help get a campaign, argument, or movement unstuck.

Uncharacteristic strategy is a way to get people to focus on your issue because you draw their attention to it via an unusual vehicle, imagery, situation, place, context, or vantage point. It serves to break patterns of hierarchy and states of perceived priority because it surprises parties into thinking differently. This attention-getting action can help create the opportunity to grow the political will.

Get their attention: Use an uncharacteristic strategy. We used unusual ways to get the attention of significant groups. We developed support through historically grounded, value-based, practical skill-driven relevance. We modeled how to transfer skills to others. The commission took the time to hear public testimony in open microphone question and answer sessions and facilitated seminar breakouts designed around interest areas. We convened visibility events and recognized members of Congress as partners in our efforts. We held substantive academic conferences to be the change we wanted to make. We held Swiss cheese meetings that helped participants assume the existence of the peace academy (the cheese), while focusing them on the topic (the holes) that we thought best served their interests and needs. We created an executive committee of highly regarded individuals for legitimacy and visibility. We gave away credit and recognition. We linked organizational and constituent closely held needs and wants to the future vision of what a national peace academy could achieve.

There were many areas of the campaign and Commission's activities that were not successful, but in large part we were successful by being uncharacteristic in our approaches. For example: with regard to the Congressional legislation itself, we chose to initially ask for a commission, not the entire institution, as had been the trend over the 135 years of prior legislation. Once we got our nose under the tent, we later sought the full legislation. We got people to think about peace in different ways by using individuals from different walks of life and professional esteem to make our case. Andy's successful approaches to diplomacy were uncharacteristic, as were Bryant's approaches to psychiatry as applied to international relations. Jim's understanding of roles and the structures of community conflicts were different and instructive to policy leaders and members of Congress. The NPAC strategy was one of focusing on only one issue—and that was uncharacteristic in a city where issue advocacy was more often tied to a wider agenda of special interests. We lined up Republicans and Democrats as co-sponsors on every bill that was introduced and used both progressive and conservative messages to make our case. We combined a value-based, historically grounded narrative along with a practical, skill-driven relevance.

To get their attention we used uncharacteristic strategies in the following ways:

- The commission took public testimony, held breakout sessions, and hosted question and answer sessions
- Used the Mayflower Hotel event to signal ourselves as a substantial player
- Recognized members of Congress
- Held academic conferences that looked like a USIP
- Held Swiss cheese meetings—making the existence of the peace academy the topic, assumed it would come into existence
- Create executive committee (for legitimacy and visibility)
- Engaged and grew public support through design of seminar program
- Focused on a single issue and were bipartisan
- Gave awards and recognition to legislative leaders
- Provided historical context and sense of place (a building on the National Mall, campus site)
- Linked organizational and constituent local and closely-held needs and wants to vision of a peace academy

Macro-strategy 5.   S – **Structure**; change the structure; change the perception

Changing the structure is a way to change the dynamic of how parties perceive an issue. It might be a physical alteration to seating, how people meet, where they meet or how an issue is discussed—changing the focus from things written, to diagrams, to cartoons, to a movie or even the use of music. Changing the structure helps to provide an opportunity to change perception and be more open to creating political will.

We used "Change the Structure" in these ways:

- Created a new American institution
- Held commission meetings in different locations (not all in DC)
- Changed the image and narrative as peace and how to achieve it
- Gathered public testimony, not just expert opinion at hearings
- Engaged perceived stakeholders in private meetings (fifty) – listen and legitimize concerns
- Convened experts in field and facilitated their visualizing the potential and benefits
- Shared the skills and mindsets of conflict resolution to a wider public
- Involved and empowered more minorities and women in the conflict resolution process
- Linked social justice and conflict resolution
- Address the issue of structural violence by educating and empowering access

To summarize, when trying to create political will it may be useful to apply the DOESS approach when your efforts, planning, selling process, or intervention get bogged down. Remember: the tool is for when you get stuck. It DOESS work. Here's how it worked for us.

Andy Young tried to change the playing board of US foreign policy development by engaging new stakeholders who had never really been involved in the process before. When in doubt, go out: Reframe to a wider field.

Jim Laue changed the perception people held of conflict by reframing it as natural and inevitable and constructive to achieving social justice. Open the problem space: Invent a shared reality.

Bryant Wedge was effective in creating early support for the Peace Academy by reaching out to fellow psychiatrists and physicians (68% direct mail return). Target the early adopters: Customize the message.

We used the legislative process of creating the commission as a vehicle to get the nose of the camel under the tent. Get their attention. Use an uncharacteristic strategy and break through the inertia: change the structure.

Chapter 10 Review and Reflection

Task

- Manage people up and down the leadership ladder.

Challenge

- Manage mentors, allies, and the people who do not agree with you.

Gift and Opportunity

- Become facilitative, not forceful.
- Strive to influence, not intimidate.

Reflection

- Where do people say you lead by example?
- When are you a good follower?
- What of your gifts help others?

CHAPTER 11

Cambridge

1984 – At a partnership meeting of Interaction Associates, we decided to open a new office in Cambridge, Massachusetts, to better serve our clients. David Straus and I would immediately move east with our families. Our wives, Connie and Patty, were very happy at this development as they had both grown up in New England and their extended families and hearts were more in that region than out west.

For someone who likes books, ideas, and thoughtful people, Cambridge is magical. Harvard University and Massachusetts Institute of Technology are among the academic institutions gracing it along the Charles River. Our new IA offices were just off Harvard Square on Mt. Auburn Street also on the Charles River just adjacent to the Kennedy School of Government. Returning to Cambridge to open a new office in 1984 after first visiting the place in 1975 was really quite a joy. As much love as I had for San Francisco, I knew I would be visiting it at least once per calendar quarter and I still had many clients out west. I was excited about again being on the East Coast, closer to New York, Washington, DC, and, as it turned out, Atlanta.

As a business consultant I was beginning to come into my own, and in Cambridge, I found myself back in a rich learning environment with opportunities for practitioners of cooperation to hone their skills. It was a chance to demonstrate what graduates from a Peace Academy might do, or what a peace institute could accomplish separate from the role of the State Department. My business travel facilitated my ability to attend NPAC board meetings. NPAC had grown in its membership and staff due to the success of its direct mail program.

I was now already practicing all of these skills in some very large corporate systems, implementing change management assignments, and dealing with some very large internal organizational conflicts. My work at Ford had involved an employee base of 320,000 people and my specific projects were focused on the sixty thousand people in the product development part of their business. Another client, John Hancock Financial Services, had more than twenty thousand people impacted by their efforts to change the company. GE's NEBO had been five thousand people; and a new client, Andersen Consulting, had a staff of eighty-five thousand consultants operating worldwide. Soon the opportunity to practice what I had learned in these environments to issues and concerns in the international arena would come my way. All of this had been made possible because I first focused on organizations, then communities, large international companies, and countries. It all underscored for me the importance of blending domestic and community conflict with international issues in the programmatic efforts and constitution of USIP.

Connie started a new job as the Executive Director of the Albert Einstein Institution in Cambridge, a nonprofit organization set up by my friend Dr Gene Sharp to advance the use of strategic nonviolent action in various conflicts around the world. In the mid-1980s there was a significant increase in the amount of nonviolent struggle being deliberately practiced throughout the world to deal with the problems of dictatorships, genocide, oppression, and war. Gene and his colleagues organized research and scholarship around these issues to expand the availability and understanding of nonviolent forms of struggle. Connie helped Gene create the administrative infrastructure to promote these concepts. She located an office just off Harvard Square, and organized a staff and engaged in fundraising. After staying home for a while after Matt's birth, she was very happy to be committed once again to a cause and be with intelligent, motivated people each day. It improved our relationship because we each were achieving the things we had set out to do.

In the coming decade, I was able to assist others with collaborative problem-solving in the private and community sectors and make contributions to other processes that created political will in the international arena such as in Burundi and the South Pacific. Just as I had helped Riverside better manage its goal setting for collaborative undertakings, I had worked with the US Conference of Mayors to advance the ways urban areas across the nation successfully create public-private partnerships.

Blending these techniques, skill sets, and mindsets is what we had meant in the campaign as domestic conflict resolution expertise and practice. Senator Javits had misunderstood the language and connection. I repeat here because the integration of skill sets is important.

There is a subtle, but perceptible hierarchy in the social level of where one addresses conflict. It is easy to acquire an enlarged ego when one acts at the international level. It is a bit more complex to work on international, or foreign national conflicts. This is because it is easier to make a mistake with an inappropriate cultural nuance, and therefore more akin to walking a tight rope, because mistakes can be far-reaching. But the foundational skills and behaviors are the same. In my own journey of discovery, I had gotten good at understanding systems, then selling and advocating for new ideas, and coming to understand the importance of needs and interests over positions. I developed the mindset and learned to value the importance of power over force. I learned the skills of negotiation, mediation, and problem solving, then training, and finally the consulting craft. In 1984 these skills and abilities all began to come together as one package.

I had become a practitioner, as well as an advocate for causing peace. Both were ways to make peace happen, or at least to move in that direction. These were the skills and practices of the peacemaker, not of diplomacy. These approaches—which defined what a National Peace Academy would train people to do—were uncommon within the foreign service community. Their job was advocacy for the US Government, not advocacy and action for peace, whether at home or abroad. I came to realize at a very personal level why the schools of foreign and international service had found the idea of a national peace academy or peace institute redundant or unnecessary. They simply did not yet seem to understand the new strategies and tools that had developed out of the American experience with dispute resolution.

Following the successful Tobacco Symposium, President Carter had asked me to think about how he might go forward to accomplish the goals he shared. I put together a draft paper on ways that he and Rosalynn might use the Carter Center to impact on the issues they cared about. I suspected President Carter was asking others the same questions. I followed through when asked to help some of the center fellows with meetings and symposia on topics ranging from American business competitiveness, to Middle East relations, to other conflict resolution–related forums. I planned and facilitated a staff retreat and even performed a bit of dispute resolution between Carter and the President of Emory University, Jim Laney. I was flattered to be asked to mediate the issues between them, and honored that they had trusted me to help them in achieving a positive outcome.

I was pleased that much of the strategic plan for the campaign we had formulated in 1979 had come to fruition. The operating scale of NPAC had matured, allowing sustained influence and funding. During the years between 1979 and the end of 1981, the focus of NPAC supporters was primarily on the work of the commission. Beginning in 1982, the peace academy campaign received more visibility due to the prominence of the commission's work and subsequent legislative proposals.

By September 30, 1984, NPAC had taken in total public support dollars amounting to $549,813.68. About 40% of the revenue was from our membership donations and 55% of the dollars had come in from direct mail program. However, as is often the case with nonprofits, the campaign was about $37,000 in debt, mostly due to direct mail costs. Mike Mapes, my successor as Executive Director of NPAC, had done an outstanding job. Mike died in 1984. The NPAC board and core supporters met on November 2, 1984, to consider the options.

Over the prior eighteen months, the board of directors had been reconfigured and some of the longer-term supporters of its mission had again stepped in and were present and active in the decision-making relating to next steps. The board of directors of NPAC now included former commissioners Jack Dunfey, Jim Laue, Bill Lincoln, myself, and early NPAC supporters Nachy Gerber Tom Westropp and Charlie E. Smith. Other members included Arthur Gregg, Rev. George Hill, John Moore, Elsa Porter, Mary Purcell, Vice-Admiral Ralph Weymouth, Ellis Woodward, Raul Yzaguirre, and David Straus.

We met at the National 4-H Center in Chevy Chase, Maryland, and were joined by Henry Barringer, Harry Hogan, Nancy Ramsey, Gail Ranadive, Libby Rouse, as well as four staff members—Robert J. Conlan, who had replaced Mike Mapes as acting Executive Director, Marilyn Hill, Martha Manning, and Pat Washburn. NPAC had a current staff of seven.

We ratified the appointment of Bob Conlan as NPAC Executive Director to formally replace Mike. We voted to terminate all employees of NPAC effective December 31, 1984, essentially ending the campaign after one hundred one months of effort. We agreed to take steps to pay off the existing debt and support the transition of the campaign into activities driven by the fund.

It was projected that NPAC would require about $146,000 to continue working through the end of 1984 and to fund additional expenses anticipated in 1985. Eight of the gathered board members pledged to raise about $40,000 before the end of the 1984 to allow NPAC to continue. Bob Conlan identified twenty-six individuals who had given a $1,000 or more to the NPAC in the recent period. Six of us divided up the names and committed to make calls to raise whatever funds we could beyond the pledges we had already made. One of the agenda items for the board was the question of from whom and how NPAC would solicit recommendations for the USIP Board of Directors. At the meeting, we laid out the criteria and representation that the Board felt was necessary for the new institution. Leaving the meeting, many of us went to hit the phones to ask for the money that was needed to support the final months of the movement.

During the next phases of legislative consideration of the bills, the name United States Academy of Peace and Conflict Resolution was changed to United States Institute of Peace. Some legislators and the new administration did not like the academy concept and deleted several of the recommendations of the commission, including that provision.

As our lobbying efforts continued, it was widely felt that the strength of the neoconservatives in the Reagan Administration presented a dangerous risk to any institution born during his term as President. Reagan was heading toward the close of his first term and was in an election campaign for his second term, challenged by Democratic Presidential candidate Walter Mondale. Polling indicated that Reagan would win the election, and indeed he did.

Reagan's first term had been characterized by an escalation of the Cold War and a massive buildup of United States Armed Forces. In 1983, the Reagan Administration's introduction of the Strategic Defense Initiative, or Star Wars as it came to be called, and the funding and deployment of the CIA to Afghanistan and Pakistan were of great concern to most who had worked so hard to bring a National Peace Academy into being. In 1984, concerns were raised when it became apparent that the enacting legislation to create USIP would be included in the Department of Defense Authorization Act of 1985. It was recognized that many successful and well-received programs have been attached to defense bills, including the legislation that transformed the highways of America. More of a concern was the reality that President Reagan, a conservative Republican, might use the occasion of creating USIP as a part of his policy agenda.

At the time Reagan took office the largest amount of money going into what they called peace research was through the Defense Advanced Research Projects Agency. DARPA defined their work around eight major thrusts perceived to have potential importance to national defense. It is another example of how our government defined peace at that time. The 1980 DARPA investments in peace were carried out through their programmatic areas of Space Applications; Undersea Vehicles; Undersea Surveillance; Land Combat; Command, Control, and Communication; Nuclear Monitoring Research; Lower Defense Costs Through Technology; and Laying the Groundwork for Further Technological Revolutions.

During the campaign and in the work of the commission we never attacked the military and actually benefitted from the support of many military leaders. The military plays an important role in the execution of foreign policy and in regional assistance for natural disaster and for intervening in criminal behaviors that impact on humanity. Unfortunately, American history reads with a scattering of antiwar movements where military personnel were mistakenly targeted rather than policy makers. President Eisenhower's memoirs were entitled *Waging Peace* and warned of the dangers of the military-industrial complex, not of individual soldiers, pilots, or sailors. Eisenhower believed it was the politics and economics of the military that can set in motion destructive dynamics, not the profession itself.

♖ ♗ ♞

At a gathering of NPAC supporters in Washington, DC, in 1984, tensions increased about the issue of President Reagan being in a position to make the first appointments to the USIP Board of Directors. I spoke with Jim Laue and met with Kenneth Boulding. We were in a bit of a panic.

I placed a telephone call and got through to Congressman Dante Fascell, who by that time had become the Chairman of the House Committee on Foreign Affairs. He asked that I come by the office rather than discuss the matter on the telephone.

I caught up with the Congressman as he was leaving his Congressional office. He briskly said, "Walk with me." Congressman Fascell said he would try to take the enacting legislation out of the defense bill if that was necessary. "What do you think?" he said. I relayed to him the conversations I had held with Jim and Kenneth, particularly emphasizing Boulding's orientation to take the long view. Congressman Fascell said he too felt it was better to go ahead and get the bill passed rather than have to begin all over again. I asked the Congressman for some time, and checked back with other leaders from the campaign. I called Kenneth. He said about the same as the Chairman Fascell, but in a different way. Kenneth told me, "Any new institution will need fifty or more years to find its true feet. The sooner we can get the bill passed, the earlier the seeds of USIP will be planted and the institution will be allowed to grow." Other NPAC supporters were called and it seemed to be the consensus that the institute should be created.

Early in the afternoon, I was still unsure as I caught up to Congressman Fascell in a hallway in the Cannon Congressional Office Building. We discussed the topic again. It was agreed to leave the enacting language in the bill.

On the day the President Reagan signed the USIP into law, many of the same men who would embroil Reagan in the Iran-Contra scandal were at his side.

♜ ♝ ♞

Following the enactment of USIP, Bryant was ecstatic about the passage of the enacting legislation. He continued his psychiatric practice. Jim Laue became a professor at ICAR at George Mason University.

Andy Young was reelected Mayor of Atlanta in 1985 with more than 80% of the vote. He prepared the way for Atlanta to host the Democratic National Convention in 1988. He made a run to be elected Governor of Georgia in 1990 but lost. Next Andy took a job as Chairman of the international operations of Law Engineering, a 1,400-person firm operating in thirty countries.

Upon learning that President Reagan had signed the bill authorizing USIP, I was pleased and hopeful that in time the new American institution would overcome the ideological leaning of any one President.

Elise Boulding sent a sonnet that Kenneth wrote for me. The paper in the thin envelop was crinkled and typed with the exception of what Elise had hand scribbled at the top of the page,

"Dear Will, you will cherish this! Elise." I was greatly honored.

SONNET

On the creation of an Institute of Peace, by the United States Congress, October 1984

There are realms and regions of time. We cross
From one to another, often unaware
That our tomorrow may be a strange new year
In which another system is the boss.
Sometimes, indeed, the past is no great loss;
Time pushes us, without much wear and tear,
Into a future that is much more fair,
In which new gold is made from ancient dross.

Could this be happening now? Could we have reached
An invisible gate, beyond which lies true peace,
Where ancient war, sudden as dawn, will cease,
And granted is—what we have long beseeched?

For when we plant even the tiniest seed
The past's dethroned. The world is changed indeed.[85]

Kenneth Boulding, and he had signed just Kenneth.

Elise was right. I do cherish the moment and his words.

Following the passage of the Defense Authorization Act, it took a while for the new institution to get traction. The first president of USIP was Robert F. Turner, appointed by President Reagan. The first board of directors of USIP was sworn in on February 25, 1986. The organization set up shop off of Lafayette Square across the park from the White House. These first USIP offices were located three-tenths of a mile from where I had first arrived at Farragut Square ten years earlier.

USIP began its life in the Reagan Administration and got off to a fairly slow start, influenced by the policy makers and conservative orientation that characterized his term in office from 1981 to 1989. In 1986, the Reagan Administration was involved in the Iran-Contra Affair, the largest political scandal of the 1980s, where members of the administration illegally used money from covert arms sales to Iran to fund the Contras in Nicaragua; direct funds to the Contras had been specifically outlawed by an act of Congress in the Boland Amendment. The International Court of Justice also ruled that the United States had violated international law and breached treaties in Nicaragua in various ways. Part of the Reagan legacy would become that weapons provided in 1992 to the Mujahidin forces fighting the Soviet Army in Afghanistan would be used against US troops in the 2000s.

By the time of the first USIP board of director's meeting in 1986, concerns still lingered about what would be the agenda for the new institution. Congress mandated that the USIP's work be "nonpartisan, non-ideological, and rooted in the highest standards of scholarly and professional integrity." USIP, however, received early criticism as being a research arm of the government rather than an independent academic institution. Some saw the initial USIP Board of Directors as a partial Who's Who of right-wing academia and government. The struggle to find the appropriate balance of the work of USIP will no doubt continue into the future, as predicted by Kenneth Boulding and rationalized by Congressman Dante Fascell in our emergency meetings during the summer of 1984.

As Reagan's successor, President George H. W. Bush carried on much of the Reagan agenda and USIP struggled to find a balance between the intent of its founders in education, training, applied research, and information services.

As one might expect, the organizations receiving the largest number of grants are groups reflecting the policies of the Reagan and Bush administrations. In its initial years USIP grantees reflected Cold War ideologies. More recently, area studies tend to reflect problems and strategies of low intensity conflict and subjects dealing with the changing political situation in the former USSR and Eastern Europe. The institutions receiving the largest number of grants over the life of the USIP have been the Fletcher School of Law and Diplomacy, the Institute for Foreign Policy Analysis at Tufts University, the School for Advanced International Studies at Johns Hopkins University and the RAND Corporation. Several of these organizations presented testimony against the creation of the national peace academy concept as it moved through Congress in the years 1976 to 1981.

As USIP began its development it had five interrelated program areas: grants to individuals and organizations, fellowships, research and studies, education and training, and library and information services. USIP awards both solicited and unsolicited grants to both foreign nationals and US citizens. Most grants are for one to two years and range from $25,000 to $35,000. Distinguished Fellows, Peace Fellows, and Peace Scholars are selected under the Jennings Randolph Fellowship

Program. Fellows come from around the globe and are invited on the basis of their stature and experience. Peace Scholars are PhD students from American universities.

USIP's research and studies program includes working-group projects which run for a year or more, study groups, which run for four to six months and public workshops presenting a three-hour discussion group on a current topic. The first two generate books or lengthy studies.

For some practitioners and scholars, activists and legislators, USIP has yet to reach its full potential, as conceived by many of its founding supporters. Experts and citizens dramatically shared their visions of what the USIP could become throughout the period of 1976 to 1984. The public record is documented by the various academic gatherings convened by NPAC and the eighteen volumes of public testimony gathered by the commission, commissioner dialogue, and discussion. The resulting Final Report of the commission is a summary of this work. Together they provide a very clear image of the vision and mission envisioned by advocates of a national peace academy and peace institute.

♖ ♗ ♞

Some peace advocates have pondered "Did we win the battle, but lose the war?" when we successfully passed legislation to create a new institution, but fell short of the mission and operation intended by its founders. Periodic and on-going reminders of the original intention of the founders may be a refreshing inspiration to USIP leadership. The next steps to creating a more peaceful world through the good offices of USIP now rest within the institution and the bodies that created it. The nature of war has clearly changed, even in the short span of thirty years since our efforts were begun. Nobody knows this better than scholars at USIP.

USIP has its work cut out for it. Traditional wars, those based on geopolitical or ethic tensions, will continue. The conflicts over critical resources such as oil, water, privacy, and ownership of data are new challenges. Cyber terrorism, social media, drone technology, and other developments suggest unchartered horizons for research and the application of conflict resolution mechanisms. The desire for regional sovereignty, within the United States and around the world, continues to grow as a potential conflict area. There are many new and critical venues in which to extend and create cultures of peace in geographic regions of America and abroad.

In response to armed aggression, political and economic sanctions by the global community are proving more effective and less expensive than escalating troop movements or the threat of violence. The study and application of more technical problem-solving and conflict resolution techniques in preventive diplomacy will continue to be a major area of study. Among these areas of conflict are issues relating to environmental degradation, nuclear disarmament, poverty and economic injustice, universal education, human rights, and others. The future of peacemaking will mature into a patchwork of military, diplomatic, and peacemaker professionalism.

The opportunity to advance my work to an international arena came from former President Jimmy Carter in 1985, and Dayle Powell, the Fellow in charge of conflict resolution programs at the Carter Center, as explained in the Chapter Copenhill. I was able to blend organizational development skills and demonstrate their viability to conflict situations. The experiences of my teachers had been modeled by professors Cottam, Coffey, Bryant, Jim, and Andy, and stayed with me. They had been doing it every day—living their practice. I was just beginning to catch up. I began to more fully understand the importance of building into the USIP the ability to be able to actively apply the new skills, as well as talk about them.

In June 1986, I went to Ireland and Northern Ireland with Dayle and Dr Thomas Rice, one of my business partners, to do exploratory dispute resolution work, using the country's very serious and shared issues of youth unemployment as our access point. Our trip was undertaken at the invitation of a professor at the Strategic Research Institute, University College Dublin. The purpose of the trip was exploratory. We were interested in learning more about Ireland's youth unemployment problem and how it tied to other economic and political issues. We wanted to determine how our own skills might lend themselves to these issues. We also shared a commitment to reach beyond the confines of our cultural experience to learn the limitations of our concepts, frameworks, and attitudes toward other people. Ireland, it seemed, could benefit from some of the resources we saw being applied to advantage in other troubled places.

As with social strife in many areas of the world, the more one learns about Northern Ireland, the more complex the reality becomes. While many relate to the Troubles and violence in Ireland as a religious conflict, it was, and continues to be based on social class, economic disparities, and ethnic identities.

In Belfast, Derry, Dublin, and many smaller cities on the island we met with individuals and groups to better understand the conflict and issues surrounding the Troubles. Our hope was to expand the networks of collaboration to create new partnerships for the long-term improvement of the conditions on the ground. As outsiders we were cautious about the limitations of our own roles, but also aware that the inquiry and advocacy of third parties can sometimes benefit those who are caught up in the escalation of bitter conflict.

Although our trip was brief—only three weeks on the ground and covering 1,858 miles of car travel—we were able to engage representatives from all side of the conflict, including reconciliation groups, academics, social service agencies, political parties, Cabinet secretaries, religious leaders, and citizens ranging from peace advocates to hard men who used violence to achieve their goals.

We tried to share resources and strategies, skills and frameworks that we saw being applied to advantage in other troubled places. While our approach was sometimes criticized for being a practice landing intervention, where experts merely touch down briefly to assess and influence a conflict, our continuing work with some of the parties helped to advance mindsets and skill sets for reconciliation and peace.

♖ ♗ ♞

After one of our Atlanta meetings with the Secretaries-General, the meeting participants shared a dinner together at a midtown Atlanta hotel. We had two more days of meetings among our little secretariat group, advisory council and with President Carter. As our group dinner began to wind down, I excused myself from the group to telephone Connie from the hotel lobby to check in. She had undergone some medical tests that day and I was concerned how things had gone. I was startled, and flabbergasted to learn that based on her blood test results she was referred to an oncologist she was scheduled to meet the next day. She asked if I could come home to Boston.

I hurried back to the lobby dining room and told Dayle that I had to depart immediately by taxi to get to Hartsfield to attempt to catch the last plane to Boston. It would be close. I was not going to check out—only leave immediately with hopes to somehow make the plane.

Now in those years there was no TSA or time-consuming security at airports. Of course there were also no cell phones or email so I asked Dayle to call to make a reservation and I ran to catch a cab. Upon arriving at the airport I managed to quickly get my ticket, but was told I had to hurry, as the plane was ready to back away. The ticket agent said, "You might not make it, but you can try." I ran down the escalators and to the train. Bursting out of the train doors, I ran up the escalator and down the corridor out to the gate. I slowed up, out of breath at my gate. The gate area was empty except for a gate agent standing calmly at the Jet way door. She said, "Mr Spencer?" Surprised but pleased by the recognition, I gave her my ticket and boarded the aircraft to see every eye on the plane directed at me to see who had held up their departure. I did not learn until three years later that President Carter had called the airlines himself and requested that the plane be held.

Meeting the next day with the oncologist we learned that Connie had been diagnosed with small cell non-Hodgkin's lymphoma, a variation of the same disease that had killed Mike Mapes, my successor in the campaign. We were told Connie had a 50% chance of survival if she could qualify for the protocol for a bone marrow transplant. The transplant itself was experimental—only two hundred had been performed in the country at the time of her diagnosis—but fortunately, one of the two hospitals where the transplants were being performed was in Boston.

Over the next two and a half years Connie was in and out of local hospitals and major medical centers to qualify for the protocol leading up to her bone marrow transplant. Six months after her transplant at the Dana Farber Institute, the lymphoma came back. Connie died six months later on January 16, 1990. We had been together thirteen years. Her death and the preceding years of illness were difficult. Andy was kind to fly to Boston to officiate her memorial service for at the Harvard University Chapel. We had been a couple for twelve years. Connie had served beside Andy for seventeen years.

In his remarks, Andy spoke of the Beatitudes, emphasizing the peacemakers. Jim Laue had not been able to attend due to the weather. Bryant had already died. My son Matt, at age 6, and I sat in the front pew of the chapel. I chose not to speak. Matt and I took time off from school and work to process the grief of Connie's passing.

In life, we encounter death. The passing of a loved one is staggering to understand. Their absence is unreal and disquieting in all you do. Connie's death was not a "good death', because she suffered and was aware of her possible fate for nearly thirty months of uncertainty, hope, chemotherapy, recovery and then regression. The myriad ups and downs took a toll on our family, her mother and sisters, friends and co-workers. I suppose the meaning of her death was not that a loved one passed on, although Connie was an essential part of my journey; it was that Connie cared. She engaged and cared. The lasting meaning of her death for me is to be found in her caring about people, all peoples. Caring is the emotional bedrock of political will. That was the lesson she taught me. That was her bequest to me, and the inheritance I hope to pass on to others.

♖ ♗ ♞

Following the initial meetings with the Secretaries-General at the Carter Center, Dayle, Bill Ury, and I pushed out the concept of the International Negotiation Network. After further meetings with eminent persons and NGO leaderships we initiated separate interventions in several countries. Our Carter Center–based INN Secretariat began working with the Secretariat of the UN and other NGOs to advance these trips and seek agreements to provide technical assistance in the form of interpreters, security assistance, and introductions.

On November 5, 1987, Dayle and I again had the opportunity to meet with the Secretary-General Javier Pérez de Cuéllar of the United Nations at his office in the UN headquarters on the East River. My visit to the seventeen-acre site of the UN complex included a pilgrimage once again to the *Swords into Plowshares* statue by Yevgeny Vuchetich. It felt like seeing an old friend. We were briefing the Secretary-General on our planned trip to the Horn of Africa region to meet with representatives of the Eritrean People's Liberation Front (EPLF) and the Government of Ethiopia, as well as the Sudanese People's Liberation Front (SPLF) and the Government of Sudan. On the first list created at our Secretaries-General meeting at the Carter Center, these conflicts had been identified as among six "hot spot" high-priority targets for peace seeking interventions.

In October 1988, President and Mrs Carter led an INN delegation to the Horn of Africa, including Ethiopia and Sudan. Those on the trip included Secret Service agents; Dayle, Bill Ury; Richard Joseph, the Carter Center fellow for African Studies; Leah Leatherbee, Director of the Center's Human Rights Program; and Gayle Smith, from the Coalition for Peace in the Horn of Africa. We traveled to Nairobi, Addis Ababa, and Khartoum. The undertaking itself and the settings were alluring. It was exciting, unusual for all involved and a real first, at least for the INN. At the same time the background study we had done on the conflicts and the skills we were prepared to use grounded us. On our trip we had both content experts on the history and cultural aspects of the region, and process experts on the negotiations we hoped to enter.

We were provided the use of a private jet to facilitate our ease of travel in the region as we moved around among several countries. On our first visit to the region we were successful (and lucky) to earn the agreement of the four disputing parties to enter a peace seeking process in two of the longest running civil wars in Africa. After much preparation and further international consultations, President Carter invited representatives of Eritrea and Ethiopia to the Carter Center in Atlanta.

The conflict between Ethiopia and Eritrea had gone on for nearly twenty-nine years, creating a deadly famine in the mid-1980s and generations of suffering and destruction due to the war. Since 1974, more than one half million people had died due to the combination of the war and famine. Now, due to the intervention of President Carter and members of the INN Secretariat, twenty-two disputants were sitting in the same conference room of the Carter Center where the SGs had sat two years earlier.

Dayle and I asked the Carter Center conference planning staff remove all of the furniture from the meeting room we were going to use during the negotiations. We brought in a large oriental carpet from Dayle's home, along with side tables, low wattage lamps, plants, and low coffee tables. The room was designed to be comfortable, informal and conducive to making agreements. During the twenty-four days of negotiation, we never once turned on the overhead lights in the room. During the Atlanta negotiations, we strategically spent time dining with members of the two teams separately and we planned casual events such as pick-up basketball games with the Eritreans and tennis with the Ethiopian delegates to establish more personal relationships with each team member.

We did everything we could to create an intimate and casual atmosphere for the talks. But we could only do so much, as the gathering of disputants created a tense and emotional environment. Many of the people in the room had lost family or countrymen at the hands of others across the room. At breaks in our sessions we heard stories of human rights abuses from both sides. We learned how members of the opposite negotiating teams knew one another.

At one end of the meeting room was a couch where President and Mrs Carter sat, with Dayle and me sitting in straight chairs on either side. Along each side of the room were eleven chairs for the members of the negotiating teams from Eritrea and Ethiopia. Two chairs were included for UN interpreters who sat nearest the leaders of each delegation. Only low coffee tables and small side tables for beverages were between the disputants. The maroon and beige carpet lay outstretched between the delegations like an ocean of space representing the differences between the delegates. The armies of these men (and there were only men) were still killing one another back home as the meeting convened. Although some had gone to grade school together, most in the Eritrean team were former combatants. The leader of the rebel forces, Isaias Afwerki, the General Secretary of the EPLF, stayed back at his hotel. His first lieutenants, who checked back with him at breaks in the discussions, represented Mr Afwerki. The chair of the government team was actually the Attorney General of Ethiopia and an ally of the dictator President Mengistu Haile Mariam, who came to power after the death of the venerated Ethiopian leader Haile Selassie.

The first session was awkward and stilted. No one had participated in a session like this. The stakes were high and the delegations were very guarded. As I looked down each side I could see hatred and anxiety in the eyes of the men. For nearly thirty years they had been at war and now each man found himself 7,600 miles from the war zone confronting their enemy across the room for the first time without a weapon. It was tense.

Even in a business environment it is hard to get people to talk at the start of a meeting. In these first few minutes, the delegation chairs were asked to make opening statements, which they did with stale formality and rehearsed iteration. The delegates stared across the room or downward at the carpet. The UN interpreters rephrased each spoken line from the Arabic, as in the case of the Eritreans, or Amharic, as spoken by the Ethiopian delegation chair. Although most delegates spoke at least conversational English, the delegations had chosen to address one another and President Carter formally in a language representative of their independence as in the case of Eritrea or the state-adopted dialect of Ethiopia. Once the opening statements were over there was silence and again, tension. The task at hand was now to get the parties to agree to an agenda if we had any hope of starting down a path of dialogue and eventual agreements. The next few minutes would be critical to the success of the negotiations. If the mediation team took too great a lead, the negotiations could fail, and the stated projection by several of the delegates would become a reality—a powerful country would try to tell the delegates what to do. We were cautious about our next move for we did not want to alienate the delegations by showing any favoritism or unappreciated guidance in what they saw as their problem, not ours. Time passed in a stifling quiet. Eyes scanned the rows of eyes looking back across the room. Throats cleared and people shifted in their seats.

After further silence and disconcerting nervousness, Dayle, Carter, and I looked at one another in anticipation of what would come next. I slipped the President a Post-it note with these words: "Ask each delegate to list on a Post-it an issue that needs to be addressed in the meeting." The President glanced up. He knew that I was saying, if they won't speak to one another, let's get them to write down an issue. The President rose up and walked to the center of the room, saying to the chairs of each delegation: "I would now like the chairmen to distribute these Post-its to your delegations. Please write down in English the issues you would like to discuss in today's meeting. Is this acceptable?" The leader of each delegation nodded and distributed the small yellow sticky 2 x 2 inch notes down the row of men on each side of the room.

In a few minutes after surveying the room, President Carter astutely asked the chairs that if they had received all of the Post-its from their team members, would they please join him at a flip chart at the opposite end of the room from where the President had been sitting. Carter and the chairs began to rise to walk to the flip chart and easel. The President said, "Please, may I suggest we take a break while we review the Post-its? There is food and coffee outside the doors there."

The delegates started to file out using different doors and Dayle, Rosalynn, and I surged to join the President at the flip chart along with the two delegation chairs. Now standing in the mostly empty conference room, alone and in silence, the President placed each yellow Post-it on the large white chart, taking care to sort each by category. The chairs stood at his side watching and nodding as each Post-it was reviewed. The President, a very bright man who had been a nuclear engineer, crafted a successful President campaign, and served as leader of the free world, now tentatively stumbled through a slow reading of each hand written Post-it. He was strategically taking his time. His speculative consideration of each note drew in each chairman to assess the situation for them. What did each Post-it say? Where did it belong? How were the categories shaping up? How many topics were there? The President glanced up at the chairs and inquired about the topic: Should it go here? Was it a duplicate topic? OK, it would go there.

In a brief few minutes the task of sorting had been completed. The President looked to the chairs and said, "That looks good. Is this list acceptable to you? Is the order OK?" The chairs stated their agreement. The President suggested the chairs join him outside in the break area for refreshment. Dayle and I were left in the room to thoughtfully read through the list. The process had created an agenda.

Upon reentering the conference room, the President spoke first. "During the break, the chairs of each delegation met with me and they have agreed on the topics submitted by you to be considered by this gathering and the order in which each will be considered." Turning to the chairs on each side of the room, he asked, "Are you in agreement with the list as proposed at the front of the room?" The chairs nodded, and again speaking in their chosen language, their responses were reported in English by each interpreter. The President said, "We have a proposed agenda. May I review for the delegations the topics and order of their consideration?" Many of the delegates responded with nods or verbal agreement.

At that moment, I moved to the flip chart. Using clear Scotch tape, I placed two strips of tape down the vertical row of the thirteen Post-its arranged on the chart. Now the list was locked in.

For the next month of negotiations in Atlanta and in the following second round of peace talks in Nairobi, the flip chart served as our North Star. It was taped to the wall of our meeting room and displayed as the map for our peace negotiations. Following the outline of topics, our team and the delegates achieved what would be an eleven-month cease-fire that ended only when another rebel group routed the dictator's troops from Addis Ababa, ending the war. Mengistu, who had led Ethiopia from `977 to 1991, fled to Zimbabwe. Shortly thereafter, the chair of the EPLF delegation to the peace negotiations, Isaias Afwerki, became President of the newly independent country of Eritrea. Meles Zenawai, the former head of the Tigrayan People's liberation Front, TPLF, the sister rebel group to that commanded by Isaias, became President of the Country of Ethiopia.

The successful negotiations were to be recognized as the first international peace talks to use laptop computers. As in the Camp David peace talks, a process of single-text negotiation was utilized. In Atlanta and Nairobi, President Carter would carry a laptop between the negotiating delegations, asking them to make changes in the growing texts of agreement defining the terms. Some would say later that it was the first use of a laptop as an electronic tool of single text negotiating. It was certainly new for President Carter, and back in the staff room, we would gather around the computer to participate in subdued coaching about getting the right words and phrases onto the laptop.

In other regional conflicts we were equally successful in getting the parties to into a range of agreements—in one case, Sudan, arranging for the vaccination of children and the arrival of much-needed foodstuff in the war zone.

In the coming months and years, I was fortunate to actively promote conflict transformation in the former Russian republics; establish early earning and conflict prevention systems in Africa;

continue my work supporting societal change efforts among indigenous peoples in Alaska and facilitate large-scale change in several Fortune Fifty companies. All of these different cultural environments provided a great opportunity to practice collaborative skills that could also be applied in the international stage. My work in nuclear energy and technology had taught me to help retool industries and address issues of economic conversion in defense-related industries. I worked to promote regional cooperation in Sudan and the Horn of Africa, and post-conflict reconciliation in Ireland and Northern Ireland. We learn by integrating the experiences that shape us.

I was fortunate to have assisted President Carter and Dayle in a peace-seeking mission to Korea and North Korea, and between Eritrea and Ethiopia as described. I taught conflict resolution training in parts of the former Yugoslavia and in Russia. I did not only value these opportunities, they each represented the realization of the institutional marriage of process skills and organizational mission, in this case, the INN and International Alert.

Once on a peace undertaking in Africa, I shared an elevator with a Ugandan military advisor on site at our Nairobi negotiations between Eritrea and Ethiopia. The role of the tall, handsome colonel was as a liaison of his government to the host nation of Kenya, where the negotiations were being held. We had been together in briefings and meetings off and on for a week, but never together just the two of us. We entered the Hotel Serena elevator and stood on opposite sides, both looking at our feet, each separately contemplating, I am sure, the next activities of our day. After a few short moments, our eyes lifted and we greeted one another. He was not much older than I, and the whites of his eyes intensely set off his penetrating pupils. Ugandan army uniforms appeared different to me than the ones I was used to in America, or even in Europe for that matter. Ugandan uniforms had oversized epaulets, almost comical insignias, and odd color combinations.

Why I did what I did next, I do not know. In an effort to be humorous, I suppose, and in an ugly American, ill-advised manner, I reached up to touch one of the decorative elements on his uniform. As I did, I commented on it, and in that moment knew that I had made a huge mistake. The colonel instantly frowned down at me and said sympathetically, but with a cold sternness, "You have never been in the military, have you son?"

I quickly backed off and said, "No sir," trying to get off a smile but receiving nothing but a glare in return. "Please forgive me, I probably should not have done that, touched your uniform, I mean," I stuttered.

The colonel immediately said, "That would be correct sir."

In my effort to recover from losing face in touching his uniform, I bashfully suggested we have a drink together before dinner. I said I would be interested in talking with him about the negotiations, particularly some of the cease-fire provisions that were under consideration. He agreed.

The Serena Hotel, one of the loveliest in Nairobi at the time, had a wonderful bar near the sizable pool area. It was a verdant location with many blossoming trees and carefully maintained gardens. We met there and each ordered drinks. The colonel was now out of uniform and although the conversation started with a perfunctory tone, it soon eased into a comfortable dialogue. I apologized to him again for my mistake in touching his uniform. I said I had felt quite bad about it since my inappropriate action. That confession drew us into a more in-depth talk about the military.

The colonel said,

> "I joined the military at a very young age as it was one of the few options open to me to leave the poverty of my village and move to the city. It was never something I really wanted to do, but farming was not an option and city dwelling was very foreign to me. The army became my whole life. It saved me from being lost as a young man and has served me well as a profession."

I shared a bit of my background and he was surprised to learn that I was in fact a business consultant, not a professional diplomat. I confided, "I am really more of a problem solver than a diplomat. Perhaps that is why I did not understand the protocol regarding your uniform. Again, I am very sorry." This time he said, "Look, if you did not grow up in the culture, it might be hard for you to understand the culture. I get that." Then he smiled a wide, easy grin, almost chuckling, "Just do not do it again." We both laughed and raised our glasses in a mock toast.

The colonel said,

> "It's a system, it is, the army. It's a way of life. We have a job to do and we are trained to do it. It's not complicated. It's simple. It's expected. Sometimes we are asked to do things that we are not trained to do or should not be asked to do. That is where it gets complicated."

He swallowed and reached for some nuts across the small cocktail table. "My job is no less patriotic than yours, but in some cultures the military receives more credit than those who seek the peace like you, than those who defend the peace like me."

I told him that I had been to all of the national military service academies in the United States and all of the staff and command colleges of our military leaders. I had gone to graduate school with intelligence officers on leave for further education and, although I had never been in the military myself, I felt that I had been in the service of my country not unlike him. He smiled and looked down, and said,

> "The military is a tool, you know. In my country of Uganda, that tool has been misused at times, you know? At times it is hard to be a solder. In the military, we all live in a history book of heroes and villains."

Just then, one of the trainers from the hotel health club walked up to our table and greeted the colonel, tapping him on the shoulder. The colonel rose and exchanged a congenial fist bump, then palm slap with the spa employee. The colonel turned to me to introduce his friend, but it was clear we had all met while visiting the club during some part of our stay. He joined us.

With the sun going down, we were done with our second drinks and parted for dinner plans with others at the hotel. Although out of uniform, the colonel startled me with a surprise salute. I came to mock attention and returned his gesture. We left as friends and had learned something from each other.

♖ ♗ ♞

In the years after the USIP was authorized, I remained close to Bryant and continued to learn, enjoy and be grateful for our friendship, although usually by telephone. During the period immediately after the work of the commission Bryant had grown impatient about the slow progress in establishing a national peace academy or the USIP. He felt there was an urgent need to provide professional training in the field and he bolted into his entrepreneurial mode once again and set out institution building. Bryant set out to establish the Center for Conflict Resolution and Analysis at George Mason University, where he served as its first Executive Director. The program Bryant inspired became the first institution in the world to offer a Masters of Science degree. In 1987, the Center changed its name to ICAR, Institute for Conflict Analysis and Resolution, and in 1988 offered the world's first PhD program in conflict resolution. (The Institute changed its name again in 2020 to become the Jimmy and Rosalynn Carter School for Peace and Conflict Resolution.)

On our calls, we would discuss his current, or past papers; share what we were each doing and moreover, what we had recently read or learned about *"advancing international understanding,"* a pet phrase of Bryant's that he had begun to use in 1962, following his experience as an Eisenhower

Fellow. He was selected for the yearlong Eisenhower Fellowship while at Yale University because he was seen as "an innovative, ascendant leader who can have a positive impact on society." Bryant still met that description twenty years later.

In one such exchange we talked about the role of psychiatry and international relations, a theme of Bryant's life work and contribution. He had recently sent me an archival copy of a 1968 reprint from the *International Journal of Psychiatry*[86]

In the article from the late 1960's, Bryant argued that there was a role for specially trained psychiatrists to play a consultant role, and make unique contributions to the solution of problems in international relations. He wrote,

> "The idea that 'wars begin in the minds of men' and that 'it is in the minds of men that the defenses of peace must be constructed" is as old as the history of relations between societies. It has been restated most recently and authoritatively in the constitution of UNESCO. Why has the scientific profession most concerned with helping the individual with the troubles of his mind fail to contribute to problem solving the most significant problem in all human behavior? What could psychiatry contribute? How should the profession make the contribution to better management of international affairs which is theoretically capable of making?"[87]

Bryant's essay went on to develop his thesis. As was the custom in those days, qualified reviewers often added a critical evaluation following the article in the journal. Bryant's essay was critiqued by three colleagues, all expressing opinions largely skeptical of his vision for added training in psychiatry, and a new profession to advise leaders and apply principles of psychiatry to international affairs. In general, the evaluating psychiatrist's comments each addressed the theme that "it is unlikely that first-rate individuals four or five years' post-residency would be likely to switch careers and begin the necessary work for the training Dr Wedge proposes."[88] His colleagues all commended Bryant, for his innovative thinking, and they each firmly took a "wait and see" attitude.

One of the reviewers, Eugene B. Brody, MD, and Director of the Psychiatric Institute at the University of Maryland School of Medicine in Baltimore commented:

> "At this time, (1968) Dr Wedge is in the position of most pioneers, having carved out a unique area of competence for himself. I'm not at all sure if, without further experience, a training program leading to the kind of international psychiatry he describes is possible."

Another reviewer, Dr Nathan Kline added,

> "A similar knowledge of the country, its history, and its current political and economic situation is absolutely prerequisite not only to dealing with those in author but to devise any kind of sensible plan for clinical research or service."[89]

A third reviewer, Dr Henry P. David, Associate Director of the International Research Institute, American Institutes for Research wrote,

> "Bryant Wedge stands alone, one of the very few Western psychiatrists who, on a career basis, have chosen to forego the rewards of an extensive private practice, university tenure, or government civil service to adapt and apply psychiatric approaches to problem solving in international transactions."

Bryant seldom took a "wait and see" attitude. Caution was not part of his character. Bryant was a pusher of ideas. For more than fifty years, the Group for the Advancement of Psychiatry, GAP,[90] and its two hundred members has kept up this debate. Should psychiatrists comment on the mental health of our Presidents? What role should psychiatry play in terrorism and political violence? Bryant not only continued to provide articles to GAP and other publications on subjects such as these, he contributed to energizing the field of psychiatry to add value and insight to other professionals in international relations.

Bryant's persistence in going against social convention to create the political will to advance innovation can easily be appreciated by his efforts: he widely diffused the principles of the CRIS-CROS program we had envisioned; his leadership of NPAC directly contributed to creating the USIP; and in his imaginative thinking shepherded the initial programs at George Mason University. He may not have proven his fellow psychiatrist reviewers wrong back in 1968, but his life accomplishments certainly stand as a tribute that his vision could be implemented and sustained. Today, urban cross cultural communication initiative focused on gangs, gender identity, religiosity, and racial tolerance by example, are commonplace, and continue to be effective; the USIP exists and the graduate programs of 200 colleges and universities around the world thrive on nearly every continent.

If you met Bryant today on a street corner or coffee shop to personally thank him for these examples of his life's work and contribution, he might not even acknowledge your compliment; he would, however, share his latest narrative about causing change and creating the political will to do so, as he so often did. "And by the way," he would say, "here is how you can help."

Bryant was fond of quoting an icon of history's most recognized intellectual figures: "Albert Einstein was certainly correct when he observed that 'Peace cannot be kept by force. It can only be achieved by understanding.'"

♜ ♝ ♞

Bryant Wedge died in 1987. I was asked by Bryant's former wife, Dorothy, and brother Tom to deliver his eulogy along with others at a small memorial service we put together for him in Washington. Above the many who worked to bring USIP into existence, Bryant Wedge was certainly central to the success of the campaign. Without Bryant, there would be no USIP.

Bryant's passing at sixty-six was another major loss for me. Bryant's charm was his authentic devotion to understanding national behavior and its centrality to who we are as a people.

The small service for Bryant was in a fairly plain room. I don't even remember any windows. There were about thirty people in attendance, far fewer than the many multiple of the thousands his life had impacted upon. When I rose to speak, I was sad, grateful, and intent on honestly acknowledging the essence of this man who had meant so very much to me.

> "Bryant was our friend, husband, brother, and mentor. We are grateful for his life and the accomplishments that have been of great benefit to each of us, and our country. When I saw Bryant most stressed-out and concerned was when he was making a decision and professional mental health diagnosis that would affect the commitment of an individual to a mental institution. As we all know so well, he worked for many years with the courts, indigents, youth, veterans, diplomats, and others in his psychiatric practice.

> "Bryant cared about people, but more than that, he believed in people. He was always asking someone he did not know to do something of greatness. He would pluck them up and shove them into a task. As such he was a generous man, always giving people a chance, drawing them out, paying them from his own funds when necessary, and encouraging them to take steps to be responsible for their own path. Years later, I thought, "All along, we should have been paying Bryant!"

I described how each of those gathered knew Bryant as an entrepreneur.

> "Bryant was always starting something. He would get an idea, put names down on a piece of paper, and bam . . . there stood a new institute, committee, social

movement or newly born cause. Bryant's genius was that he never stopped creating. His weakness seemed to be more in those around him not being able to understand his lead, or direction of thought.

"Bryant would probably have considered himself a follower of religious humanism, which he saw as the integration of humanist ethical philosophy, yet he had the sincere appreciation for the spirituality of all cultures.

"Bryant had a way of pulling together people who shared in their own ways a desire for change and a desire for a better world. Often, it was Bryant who was the connection between people. Bryant Wedge was the force that drew people together—each operating in their unique ways— but still connected through this one man.

"Bryant expressed his own uniqueness in several ways. He used his training in psychiatry as a healer. He was a humanist and believed in the dignity of the individual. As an entrepreneur he was a creative force, a free spirit, an optimist and wide-ranging thinker. Bryant often used Freud as a point of reference. Freud, he said, felt that if aggression was irrepressible in man, 'what we may try is to divert it into a channel other than that of warfare.' He stated that reason and cultural change, as well as fear, might bring this about, pointing out that psychic changes accompany cultural development. Bryant always saw Freud's letters to Einstein as both hopeful and useful.

"Bryant came to believe that new American institutions like USIP could serve as a rudder to gradually move society to view group violence again human persons as unattractive and unneeded psychologically as a practical means of resolving conflicts. If the United States could migrate as a people to seeing war as obsolete, other nations would follow. The establishment of a national peace academy or USIP could become a fulcrum for change."[91]

Once Bryant and I were arguing such points in his Wisconsin Avenue office. With dimmed lights and the smoke of Bryant's cigarettes lingering, he said:

"In my judgment, we can 'cultivate the science of human relationships' at the intergroup level as President Roosevelt appealed to us to do. One of the principle strategies for the psychiatric sciences is to experiment with techniques designed to establish contact, communication, and cooperation between conflicting groups.

Such a strategy will not only allow us to refine theory and technique, but may also contribute substantially to more peaceful relations between groups."

That day with the hum of traffic and sunlight piercing between the dark blinds, I pushed back,

"So the question of how to change the war system we are currently part of is to redirect the natural tendency for man to fight?"

Bryant said, "No, no, no."

"You ask the wrong question. Psychoanalysis examines the human motivation to demonize our enemies; to project that violence is a positive image of masculinity, or to seek identity in pseudo-masculine illusions. The key at the psychiatric level is to support society in devising ways to use the myths of creation to supplant myths of destruction and death. It's a head game, it really is. If we are to become more humane and more civilized, further moral development is needed."

Trying to provoke him, I asked, "What are you talking about—church?"

"No. Another way of putting it is to say that the world needs to lower its threshold of revulsion. We need to encourage, any way we can, that violence is not acceptable. The question you should ask—the question all of us should ask is, "How can this revulsion be encouraged? It's like a force in physics but cognitive."

"OK," I said, "So if we try to find systemic ways to push back on the forces that lead to violence and we lower our societal tolerance for violence. Is that it?"

I tried to summarize. "So I am reminded of Kenneth Boulding metaphor, 'If I break a piece of chalk, did it break because the strain was too great or because the strength was too little?' "[92]

I continued,

"You are saying, Bryant, that the strength comes from our sense of what is acceptable, not from the ill-perceived power of force. You are saying we reduce the strain by tying down those forces among groups and in life that lead to destructive conflict. You called that once the Gulliver Effect. Right? Tying down Gulliver."

Bryant threw his arms out, flinging ashes:

> "Yes…. and institutions like USIP can push out that 'revulsion' – delegitimize violence –and highlight alternatives to the use of violence. It's a 'sales job', no doubt. It is precisely because it's a 'sales job,' that a new institution like the USIP can make a difference and society will see the benefit.

Bryant lived his life quite a ways ahead of the resulting enterprises he helped to create. The USIP was in its infancy about the time of Bryant's death. One of their earliest efforts was to establish a National Peace Essay Contest to bring visibility to their work and contribute to their public outreach mission. Concurrently, the Institute began making plans for the development of a physical headquarters. Respectfully, each of these initiatives represented low bars for the high hopes and expectations that Bryant had set. He wanted more attention to causing social change, and one of the most enduring qualities of his character was that he always did.

♖ ♗ ♘ ♞

By this time, the grief of Connie's illness and death was either hidden away or supplanted by my desire to find a familial environment for my son, Matt. Dayle and I had been working together for five years. We each recognized that we shared many of the same life experiences; professional interests and a commitment to one another. In the late fall of 1990, we decided to marry and we set about blending our new family of three children in Atlanta.

In the early 1990s I was asked serve on the Board of Directors of the British charity International Alert, and for the next six years devoted time each quarter for a board meeting in London and participated as much as possible in its programs as an advisor and consultant.

International Alert, or ALERT, had been formed in 1985 by the human rights campaigner Martin Ennals and others to combat the widespread violations of human rights inherent in violent internal conflicts. During my six-year relationship with the charity I performed an active role to assist the organization to develop worldwide networks, which work to prevent and resolve violent conflict within countries, and to reconcile parties at war with each other through mediation, facilitation and education. Our mission was to advance preventive diplomacy, influence the global community, generate political will, build strategic alliances, and create clear and effective peace-building policies. Our programs were focused on the former Soviet Union, Central and Eastern Europe, Latin America, Asia, and the South Pacific.

One of the conflicts we were monitoring at ALERT was the Bougainville crisis, involving Papua New Guinea and the Solomon Islands. As I had to be in Australia for business, I flew to the region on behalf of ALERT for a fact-finding mission at the request from some of the disputants involved. My trip started with meetings in Honolulu; then traveling to Sydney. After my client meetings there, I flew the four-hour flight north to Queensland and the town of Cairns. Cairns is about an hour boat ride to the Great Barrier Reef that extends 1,500 miles off the eastern coast of Australia. From Cairns it is a 1,000-mile stretch of open ocean to the Solomon Islands.

Bougainville is the largest Island in the North Solomon's and is a bit larger than the island country of Cyprus but smaller than the island state of Hawaii or the island country of Fiji. Beginning in 1988 several thousands of people had lost their lives to violence and thousands of others had succumbed to diseases due to a lack of access to medicine and basic services. The fighting was largely off the screen of international organizations like the United Nations or the Association of Southeast Asian Nations (ASEAN), and they had failed to intervene to stop the violence.

The direct origins of the Bougainville violence stemmed from the failure to renegotiate a mining agreement, which resulted in the landowners forcing closure of the Panguna mine by blowing up one of the main power bearing pylons. The Papua New Guinea Defense Forces responded to the disruption and were turned away by resistance forces on the island that became known as the Bougainville Revolutionary Army, BRA.

New Guinea, the second largest island in the world after Greenland (Australia is considered a continent), was divided in colonial days in two halves claimed by the Netherlands and Germany. Following World War II, the eastern half of the island, Papua New Guinea (PNG), became a territory of Australia. The Dutch Western half came to belong to Indonesia after their independence and became known as Irian Jaya, now West Papua. After Papua New Guinea obtained its independence from Australia in 1975, it assumed political control over Bougainville, although they are separated by six hundred nautical miles. Papua New Guinea wanted control of Bougainville as it contained one of the largest copper mines in the world producing more than one third of Papua New Guinea's national income. The 160,000 people who live on the island of Bougainville have long made claims of independence but have fallen under the heavy hand of Papua New Guinea, which resisted any separatist movements due to their economic interests. Ethnically, the Bougainville Islanders are more closely related to the race of Micronesians who inhabit the Solomon's. Melanesians largely make up the population of Papua New Guinea. So Bougainville developed into a political, economic, and ethnic conflict that nobody was really paying any attention to resolving.

During my time in the region I met with representatives from the Pacific and World Council of Churches, members of the Australian High Commission, and the Minister of Home Affairs of the

Government of the Solomon Islands in Honiara, the capital of the island of Guadalcanal. I spoke with the Minister of Foreign Affairs of Papua New Guinea, representatives of the Commonwealth Secretariat, US Embassy personnel, the President of the Court of Appeals of the Supreme Court of New South Wales, numerous academics in the region, and NGO humanitarian assistance groups including Save the Children, and Médecins Sans Frontières. At the time I reached the region there were no peacemaking or peace-seeking efforts being made to deal with the crisis.

Past agreements had not succeeded in part because the Government of Papua New Guinea was not able to control its military or act in good faith to introduce supervisory neutral international observers to the island of Bougainville, as had been agreed in March 1990. Conditions on Bougainville had deteriorated to the point where there were several factions within the armed resistance groups and it was nearly impossible for the Government of Papua New Guinea to conduct talks without a unified negotiating partner.

Upon departing the region I shared my observations and recommendations with all of those whom I had met, and of course my sponsor International Alert, as well as the appropriate parties at UN, ASEAN, the US State Department, the governments of Australia, Papua New Guinea, and the Solomon Islands.

One of the most unforgettable parts of the trip was an evening encounter on a beach facing the shore of Iron Bottom Sound just outside the town of Honiara. The sea was partially illuminated by a half moon, covered on and off by high clouds. There was just enough light to see the distant swells making their way along the coast to the small rippling waves that came in at my feet. I was alone. In the darkness, there were no stars and no man-made noise, only the intermittent coming and going of the tide. It was not just that I was by myself, eight thousand miles from home. I felt the moment, the isolation and the forsaken history of the place. On August 7, 1942, the Allies launched the first big offensive of the Pacific War by landing seventeen thousand men on Guadalcanal and at nearby Tulagi to drive back the Japanese. That was fifty years and forty-three days before I had come to stand on that darkened beach.

The historical significance of the place was palatable. I had played army as a kid, dressing up as a soldier carrying an army surplus canteen belt and worn canvas pack. Back then I knew the word Guadalcanal. It was such a strange word, and I recognized it had the import of similar words like Gettysburg, Bastogne, or Pearl Harbor. I had just not known where it was, or exactly what had happened there. Now I knew. I could feel it; feel the sanctity of the place, and imagine the noise, smells and flashes. I had been other places in my life, but this spot was different.

In 1971 I had slept huddled in my VW bus beside a burned-out church in East Berlin, and later overlooked the beaches of Normandy from cliffs disguising former German gun fortifications. I had watched the moon rise over the confluence of the White and Blue Nile Rivers in Khartoum in route to Addis Ababa, and had stood handing flowers to East Berliners passing West through the crumbing Berlin Wall in 1989. But this was different. I was alone, on my own mission. I was reaching out to seek a peace without back up or regional logistical support.

Fifty years of history had passed since the shoreline where I stood and the nearby channel were the center of the world's attention as the Japanese and Allied Forces fought to control these islands, airstrips, and airspace. Twenty-four thousand Japanese soldiers died here in less than five months, nearly twice the entire number of the local indigenous population at the time. Over one-third died from disease. Forty-seven naval ships sunk just offshore from where I tossed pebbles into gentle waves. Three enormous sea battles occurred over just several months and that was how Iron Bottom Bay had earned the name, because there was so much iron wreckage on the bottom of the bay. Countless islanders were mistreated and died; hundreds of aircraft crashed into the seas or jungle.

Nearby, the famed boat PT-109 skippered by Jack Kennedy sunk off the island of Lubaria near Rendova. On the plane over from Cairns, Australia, I had reread the story of the Japanese soldiers who were found in the mid-1970s hiding in caves thinking that Japan was still at war. There was much history here, all involving war. The Japanese general who had planned the vicious attack on Pearl Harbor had in fact been killed in an airplane crash near the site of the Panguna mine on Bougainville. The moment was surreal as the images of history flashed by in the darkness.

Off in the distance was The Slot, the deadly sea channel strategic to the war, and once so closely observed by the courageous coast watchers. Behind me was Henderson Field, Bloody Ridge, and Red Beach, where Japanese ships had to be run aground at night to bring supplies to their stranded forces, held down by the superior air support of the Allies. The darkness held these secrets of the past. It felt unexpectedly awesome to be there; standing on the sand, looking out to sea.

That very morning, two people, one adult and one child, thought to be sympathetic to the BRA had been killed, one adult and one child, and another kidnapped, on Shortland Island in the Western Province by PNG forces. It was the evening of my fifth day on Guadalcanal and I had spent the morning trying to connect with officials by telephone and interviewing the local Archbishop, a relief worker, and an embassy representative who was frustrated by the inaction of the world's governments to act on a conflict that was causing the unreported deaths of so many. I had met for more than an hour with several aggrieved islanders who were upset by the increasing economic power of ethnic Chinese merchants and storeowners who, they felt, threatened the local economy and traditions. At midday I ate lunch with a local dive shop owner in a fish shack overlooking the sea. Early in the afternoon, I paused to watch an Australian navy engineer, whom I had met on the plane flying in, oversee the construction of a new dock for the Solomon Island police boats that helped patrol the area in conflict between the Western Province and Bougainville.

I had what I needed for my report, but by evening was feeling unfulfilled and thwarted that I had not been able to do more. The next day I would begin the last twenty-four hours of my flight home after my 29,051-mile trip that had taken me literally around the world in sixteen days. I felt lucky, sad, and tired—all at the same time. I was pensive in the moment; thinking about the history; contemplating the dead, and being grateful that wars like that might never be fought again.

Just then, I heard footsteps in the sand behind me. I turned to see that it was a Western woman whom I had earlier noticed at the lobby desk of the small bungalow hotel where I had been staying. Our eyes met and we greeted each other, cautiously, as the location was so remote, dark, and foreboding. She looked more comfortable than I felt at that moment. I instantly assumed she was there as a relief worker or health professional. She just appeared to be more relaxed on the sands of a faraway, distant beach than I. I was suspicious of our backwater chance meeting, apparently more than she.

Our comfort level improved as we introduced ourselves. She introduced herself as Virginie. We exchanged stories of why we were each there. She was a representative of Médecins Sans Frontières— French, and assertive in her opinions regarding the troubles in the region. She, like me, was undertaking an assessment to analyze the situation in order to help prompt a greater humanitarian response. My interests were future actions to address the root causes of the conflict and seek regional validation or an invitation for an appropriate process of dispute resolution. Virginie was more concerned about humanitarian assistance.

At first she had thought I was Australian or perhaps an oil and gas manager from Singapore. After I spoke a bit, it became clear to her I was an American. Suddenly she overreacted to my presumed motivation in being on the ground there in such a remote place. Virginie went from casually strolling on a beach to being a prosecutor. She asked, "Who do you work for, exactly? I am not sure I understand why you are here?" Her soft French accent seemed incompatible with her probing words. I explained again that I was a business consultant who served on the board of a British charity and I was doing an assessment because no one in particular seemed to be paying attention to the conflict. She did not conceal her skepticism.

There on the quiet beach she suddenly fired off like a Roman candle, accelerating in an instant – prosecuting, accusing and probing.

"You Americans possess such economic strength and reach that you think you can go anywhere in the world to exert your power. Your government increases the likelihood of catastrophes around the world and you think of yourselves as above or beyond the reach of democratic institutions or international law. You are always trying to extradite terrorists from every part of the globe to take back to America to put on trial. It is the United States who instigates and controls much of the violence in the world as you pursue your own perceived national self-interests."

Waving her arms she said, *"C'est incroyable que."*

I interrupted her with a gesture of my own. I remembered enough from my college French to sense that she thought the actions of the American government were quite "incredible."

I offered a beleaguered, *"Un moment, s'il vous plaît!"* trying my best to slow things down. Switching back to English, I said, "Whoa, whoa, whoa."

She replied in a demandingly sharp tone, "Again, I ask you. For whom do you work?"

Not quite understanding why this chance encounter with an unknown woman on a beach was getting so out of hand, I became frustrated myself. "Who do you think I work for, if I might ask? I have told you twice. What is it that you think I do, or why do you think I am here, standing on a darkened beach of Guadalcanal looking out at the sea?" I backed off a couple of yards and sat on a fallen tree trunk overhanging the beach and water. She lit up again,

"You Americans are on some sort of messianic mission to bring democracy to a suffering world and I do not trust you. You say you do not want to control other nations or their affairs, but you also act very much like you do not want developments to get out of control – your control. You want other nations to act independently, except when doing so affects US interests – *'avoir un effet négatif'*— adversely. I think you are some sort of spy. Why else would you be here?"

"No, I am not a spy," I said with a smirk. "I am flattered that you would think I am here for God and Country to somehow take advantage of, well, God knows what? But I am not."

I moved off my log and we started to walk along the tide line. "I totally agree with what you are saying. I understand your perspective. But please do not confuse the actions and policies of a country with its citizens who try to act in different ways. I am like you, I suspect. I work for peace and do what I can, where I stand, to try and make a difference in the world. Much of the hard work I have to do is in my own country."

As I was walking away, I turned and faced her, "I agree. America has such potential to be a world leader in causing peace, and we fail miserably at it."

Virginie softened her tone. "I am sorry. I guess I really snapped at you. Being here, seeing these things makes me sad and discouraged." She caught up to me.

I stopped walking and said,

> "I feel the same way. I leave these Islands tomorrow and fear that my time here has only been about my own ego trying to help. I have little to show for being a peacemaker other than a story to tell when I get back home. I have already written half my report and the rest I will finish on my plane. I'll send it off and hope somebody or some organization will step up to do more. I know that it will take new institutions and time for America to overcome our hegemonic past. Believe me I have tried. It makes me sad. We are partners with the world and could serve other nations better by being more facilitative and not so dominating. I understand what you are saying, Virginie. But I am not my country. I am one person in a country."

It was quiet between us for a while and when we reached an impasse of palm trees too close to the water to pass, we turned and walked back toward the hotel.

"It's late. It was nice to meet you," I said. "Bonsoir!" She replied "Bonne nuit." We shook hands and each went into the shadows of the buildings and palms above the beach.

On the plane the next day, I rethought the depth of Virginie's feelings about America, and the truth about America sometimes overusing force, and the failed objectives and damage to our reputation it brought.

In 1992 the leaders of USIP went back to Congress to secure an amendment authorizing USIP to raise and accept private donations to design and construct its headquarters facility. In the process of writing early drafts of the enacting bills, we encouraged Congressional staff to include language authorizing the new institution to be able to raise private funds. The language was removed in committee by legislators, I believe, who feared USIP would grow in size and influence beyond the vision they held for its scope. It was an odd move, as much of government at the time was trying to engage the private sector as financial partners.

Jim Laue died on September 25, 1993. The last time I saw him he was in the hospital and I found it was very difficult to be there. Connie had died three years earlier in a similar circumstance. I cared greatly for Jim and his wife Mariann. When I was asked to be a speaker at his memorial service in Virginia, I almost declined. It would just be too hard. Finally, I agreed, as I not only owed it to Jim but felt I had something to say, to him and those who loved him as I did. We had known each other for seventeen years.

When I took the stage of the campus auditorium, tears filled my eyes as I walked up the stairs to the podium. There was just too much for me to say to the many gathered who loved him and were influenced by his kindness, inspiration, and action. I looked out into the elevated seats and saw faces that had dotted my career in Washington. I tried to compose myself, and then began by saying these words:

> "It's Jim Laue on the telephone line. 'It's Jim. Can you take the call?' Those words would always light up my face with a smile."

I tried to smile, but could not bring myself to grin, I could only make an otherwise contorted expression.

> "Those words were the daily, weekly, monthly, or quarterly harbinger of a conversation I was about to have with one of the most optimistic and kind persons ever to grace our field."

I went on to address how much Jim had meant to others and me, and provided a quick overview of some of the special moments we had shared. I knew that everyone in the audience had their own memories. I spoke only ten minutes or so and then turned to step off the stage.

Jim was gone. The man who was responsible for my meeting both of my wives, served as the best man in my first wedding, and who had tried so hard to flee a Washington snowstorm to attend the memorial service for Connie. Jim had been there for me—now he was gone.

By early October, I was on a plane a month later to Moscow to co-teach a seminar on conflict resolution. He was still very much on my mind. The three-week residential program took place outside Moscow at a former Communist party retreat center. The participants were thirty-seven scholars and civic leaders from eleven of the former fifteen Russian republics, representative of a dozen different ethnic groups. The program was sponsored by the United Nations University (Tokyo), the Russian Academy of Sciences' Institute for Ethnology and Anthropology, and International Alert. There were eleven faculty and six Russian translators in attendance spread out over the three-week period. I had responsibility for the advanced conflict resolution-training portion during the third week. It was brutally cold in Kliazma, the site of the seminar more than an hour's drive from Moscow, and a wintery park right out of Doctor Zhivago surrounded the postmodern, dorm-like building. There were walking trails and a children's play area covered in heavy snow. The tall pines held ice-encrusted snow formed oddly shaped cartoonist characters that loomed over the grounds.

The participants came from the Russian Federation, Kazakhstan, Georgia, and Latvia and were from a wide range of backgrounds: politics, journalism, university teaching and research, and nongovernmental organizations. In most cases, representatives from both sides of current conflicts were present. The long-range goal of the seminar was to support the development of institutional capabilities for peaceful conflict resolution.

In order that participants could express themselves freely on all issues, we requested that all who attended the seminar not quote the individual statements to the media or to nonparticipants. We emphasized that all statements during the sessions should be seen in a training context. The organizing committee, teaching staff, administrative and support personnel stressed that training was not negotiation. Participants were asked to explore alternatives and ideas beyond their current positions on many issues. We stressed that such explorations should not be interpreted as a change in positions.

The immediate purpose of the Moscow seminar was to train committed individuals in practical conflict resolution skills—including mediation, conciliation, and problem-solving techniques. We wanted to prepare the participants for a future role in peacemaking and conflict transformation. This we believed might take many forms, ranging from research, analysis, and education to policy-making, mediation, and conciliation.

All of the trainers and lecturers on case studies worked in English, although the staff was from America, Sri Lanka, Philippines, Azerbaijan, Australia, Norway, and Russia. As I trained in the highly interactive program, I paused after each phrase or new concept to hear it immediately interpreted by my partner who stood next to me as we walked around the teaching floor. His name was Pyotr Patrushev. After the persecution of his family as a late teen he escaped from Russia by swimming across a part of the Caspian Sea to Iran, and he eventually made his way to Australia.

Prior to my arrival at the conference site, the participants had benefitted from eight case studies presented by experts in each of the regions of the former Soviet Republics, including North Ossetia, Tatarstan, Northern Caucasus, the Urals, and Siberia of Eastern Russia, the problems of Russian minorities in Latvia and Kazakhstan, and potential ethnic conflicts in Bashkortostan and Dagestan. Note: You may not recognize the Republic of Bashkortostan, as it is a small and lesser know state and has no autonomy. These very detailed area studies formed a foundation for discussion among all of the participants. After my arrival, we had a lot to talk about and I worked each of the case studies into my training exercises and simulations.

Although with disputants so directly involved in the disputes of their homeland regions, it was hard to separate the content from the conflict resolution techniques I was teaching. In the end however, their familiarity and ability to express true emotions regarding the conflicts made the sessions all the more meaningful. The fact that the roughly fifty-person learning community ate meals and slept in the dorm-like environment for such an extended time drew the participants and faculty together. The program was indeed transformative for all of us.

I was delighted on a subsequent trip to Moscow to be able to meet with several of the participants and learn how they had applied what I had taught to the conflicts in their regions. At home in Atlanta one evening, I was particularly pleased to see a news story from the region where the spokesperson for the North Ossetia government was one of my students, Lev Dzugaev.

After a day of training, the participants would gather after the evening meal and sing, drink, and tell stories in the common areas of the building. One evening toward the end of my stay and after more than adequate consumption of the beverage of choice—a locally concocted vodka apparently made from sticking a pear or orange into any kind of bottle of what tasted like jet fuel—a few of us ventured outside into the cold. Leaving the glass doors of the main building we passed the night guards and facility caretakers who were leftover veterans of the days when only senior Communist party members and their families were allowed at the center.

In greeting us they sternly reminded us that we had to be back in the building before 9:00 PM when the doors would be locked tight for the night. No exceptions. We smiled and perhaps laughed disrespectfully at the drama of their old Communist behavior.

We made snow angels in the fresh powder and attempted to slide down the iced-up slides in the children's playground area. Three of us finally settled to sit on the canvas seats of a swing set and consume a bottle that one of them had hidden under his coat. I was sandwiched between a sociologist from Chechnya and a Cossack who was an architectural historian, more recently active in a sovereignty movement. It was so cold that zippers would not work due to ice build-up and the fabric of our jackets turned to fiberglass-like sheets of ice. As we tried to swing, kicking our feet in the powder, the subject turned to how communism had captured the politics, economics, and, for many, the hearts and minds of the people living in the Soviet Republics.

With difficulty speaking due to the frozen scarf around this mouth and no doubt lips and jaw muscles that were deeply chilled, Vakhit shared his views with a benumbed English-Russian accent:

"The people of Russia had a big bag over their heads for eighty years."

I asked for clarification as I thought he had said, "The steeple of crushed hats begged over eggs for eight deers." I was finally able to understand Vakhit when he temporarily pulled his scarf away from his beard and could speak more clearly.

Rarely in our informal training sessions had I engaged the participants in political discussions involving the Cold War, capitalism, or communism, or other subjects integral to Soviet-American relations. In graduate school, much of our national security focus was about the Soviet Union. They were the Evil Empire as some described, and even some academics wrote essays about how all Russians wanted to own lakefront property along the shores of our American Great Lakes. I had never believed it—and our discussion that evening in the snow and ice confirmed for me that most Americans had been hoodwinked into believing the myth of the Soviet threat, just as most Russians had been deceived into believing the West was the enemy.

As I swung on a frosty child's play set I regretted that the eighty years of the Cold War had been such a reality for so many in Russia and the West. It should have been avoided. Was I naïve, or was I realistic? What had happened? The arms race that drove much of the fear and limited economic prosperity had been such an unfortunate and unnecessary chapter of world history. It had been less of a story of different ideology than a narrative driven by political elites, military-industrial pressures and poor utilization of conflict resolution technology. The diplomatic focus on arms agreements and border issues had only addressed the symptoms of the conflicts and little progress was made in really understanding the root causes until the 1980s. It was sad, particularly as I enjoyed the evening with comrades in peaceful thinking rather than with the Cold Warriors that populated both of our countries.

When we returned to the main conference center doors of Kliazma, they were locked. It was as if the old communist guards had heard our conversation and resented our frivolity. In below zero temperatures, the eleven peacemakers stood on the freezing side of the one-inch glass doors, banging and pleading to be let in. The custodial gatekeepers still were playing out their old roles and glared at us from inside the building, unyielding to our post-midnight request to be let in. After forty-five minutes, the grounds security people happened by and unlocked the single entry door. It was a vision of the past.

♖ ♗ ♘

Back in Washington, the USIP presented Ronald Reagan and Jimmy Carter with their first "Spark M. Matsunaga Medal of Peace" and the Institute staged its first major conference, entitled, "Managing Global Chaos."

In the spring and summer of 1994, Rwanda was the scene of a massive ethnic genocide where the Hutu-led government slaughtered an estimated five hundred thousand to a million Tutsi and moderate Hutus in just a hundred-day period. The deaths represented as much as 20% of the country's total population and 70% of the Tutsi population living in Rwanda. A deep ethic rivalry and long history of violence was at the origin of the disastrous event. I was riding in the back seat of a London taxi with the international Chairman of Oxfam and a former British Labour Party member who had been Secretary-General for the International Voluntary Service in Great Britain. Both were members of the House of Lords and served with me on the Board of ALERT. We were deeply concerned about Rwanda and wondered what our small NGO could do, if anything, to have a direct impact on the ground in the region.

We were particularly concerned about the neighboring country of Burundi that was a possible ethnic powder keg due to its shared past with Rwanda. The two independent countries of Rwanda and Burundi were south of Uganda and west of Tanzania and shared an intertwined ethnic history. At the business meeting of the charity that afternoon we discussed the concern and the director of the organization, Kumar Rupesinghe, said he would follow up on the best course of action.

Back in Atlanta the following week I received a call from Kumar. He asked me to facilitate a gathering of humanitarian agencies and conflict prevention experts at the International Alert headquarters in London in September. Kumar had approached Bernard Kouchner, former French cabinet minister and current director of the Paris-based Action Humanitaire (Association for Humanitarian Action) to organize a meeting to take the first steps towards the creation of an effective conflict prevention capacity among several humanitarian and development agencies.

The initial meeting at the ALERT offices included about fifty NGO representatives. The offices were located immediately behind the MI-6 building on the Thames River that has been featured in so many James Bond movies. To reach the offices from Westminster it required crossing the Vauxhall Bridge, slipping under the Vauxhall elevated rail complex and walking along Kennington Lane into a side alley. When traveling to the ALERT offices every calendar quarter for six years, it required passing under many security cameras that are part of the CCTV system. It always gave me a strange sensation to walk between the very visible cameras posted on the corner of buildings, power poles and overpasses. Today, the seven and one-half cameras for every 100 individuals in the UK seem much more visible than the more than fifteen cameras per 100 individuals in the US. These cameras remind me that we have exploited technology to monitor urban unrest, but failed in many ways to capitalize on the social technologies of peace that are available to us.

The meeting started out quite chaotically, as each NGO wanted to have its story told about how they were helping in the region. After a while it became apparent that the full time of the meeting would be spent with each participant describing what solutions they were addressing and there would be no time to address any of the current problems that had been created by the lack of coordination among the aid agencies. Due to the conflict in Rwanda, international concern drove an expanded NGO presence in the Burundi capital that resulted in literal traffic jams of aid worker vehicles moving around the streets of Bujumbura. The agencies were admittedly, literally bumping into one another as they tried to address the needs of those most at risk in the countryside. One participant at the meeting described being caught up for hours each day in cues of white Toyota SUVs sporting freshly painted organizational logos.

Meeting space is ego space, and each representative was unrestrained in his or her personal reports about their own individual work effort. Soon after Dr Kouchner kicked off the meeting, it was apparent that at that slow rate of individual introductions the group would never get to the real issues before them. If each individual only took five minutes of introduction time and provide an overview of their NGO or agency, four hour would pass before anything might be said about the Burundi situation. I got the meeting on track by asking everyone to take a break. When the participants came back into the room, I suggested that everyone *remain standing* until all of the NGO reports were completed. After each standing participant would finish their introductory remarks about everything their agency was doing, I would ask them to sit down, leaving only those who had yet to speak. The facilitative intervention created a sort of human countdown clock that changed the mood in the room. While respectfully listening to each speaker, participants in the room actually began to eagerly anticipate the end of the introductions. This tactic caused the individual introductions to be very brief and we were able to move on to problem solve the important concerns expressed by the participants. People were amazed how effective the meeting became, expressing surprise that they were able to cover so much ground in such a short period. One State Department representative said in her closing remarks that she had never thought of good meeting and planning processes as such effective instruments of peacemaking. The meeting ended on time.

The meeting was judged to be very successful in realigning the priorities of the relief and conflict prevention agencies, so much so that the work of the initial working group expanded to include not just Burundi, but Kenya and a more regional early warning and early action group. The meeting was a good example of coalition building and international cooperation.

The representatives of the NGOs and government agencies met on five other occasions to outline the roles that each agency could play, as well as concrete actions that could be taken to prevent tension and conflict from escalating. Following the session, members of the State Department delegation that had been represented at the session, initiated their own Burundi Working Group.

Over thirty years have passed as the USIP has struggled to find its own core organizational philosophy and operating principles. It has quite naturally taken its time to get its act together. USIP may one day find new opportunities to further support sister national and international institutions in peace- and nation building. USIP resources can be leveraged and its mission expanded by new coalitions among academic centers within the US and in other countries. That was the intent of the commission findings and it still makes sense. Diffusion of ideas is based on broad-based strategies of working through the innovating and early adopter academic institutions across the land. The commission had seen the conduits for such work tied to the land grant college system. The legacy for USIP always appeared to be what it could push out rather than what it created within. It was built to be a lever, not a barrel. And we envisioned it as a fulcrum, not as some sort of intellectual reservoir, disconnected from policy makers or citizen activists.

My own journey had taken me from student to advocate to practitioner. I was able to become proficient at many of the tools conflict resolution and peace seeking. Among these techniques are the foundation of the USIP and its legitimacy. A country can never be what its people are not. I had told Virginie back on that beach, "I am not my country." But I am my country. We all are. I believe it is our responsibility, and obligation to be a country of peace.

As such, USIP was designed to raise American awareness and utilization of conflict management skills. Its mission was conceived to pursue the nation's advancement and use of alternatives to force in scholarship, policy, practice, and the aspirations of citizen life.

Societal change takes time, but it can be accelerated. The history of science proves this to be true. Pharmaceutical companies draw insights from rain forests; few people say that is not science. We learn about human behavior from observing other species; few people say that is not science. We learn about the mysteries of earth from studying far away galaxies; few people say that is not science. Peace research is a science, and has demonstrated the breath of the field. As society continues to make scientific breakthroughs in genetic and behavioral research, new fields of study and application may work their way into the USIP arena of research and applied practice. For example, USIP could conduct research in areas such as eusociality. Eusociality is a word invented in 1966 and refers to a cooperative groups; the study of animal societies where individuals work together to create specialized tasks and cooperative care. Kin selection theory is a narrative of evolutionary biology where animals recognize their own and provide mutual benefits. Forms of altruism are all around us and may become new areas of study as we continue to learn more about genetic expressions of cooperation. Science breaks down things into small parts in order to understand dynamics, patterns and motivations. Peace research does just that, with human behavior, systems dynamics, and political sociology. We need not be doomed to violence. Research produces insight and insights can lead to creating political will.

In my view the USIP must expand further to politically preserve its mission and future. The history of government departments and institutes is a textbook for remembering the struggle required for the power of bureaucracy to evolve. It is possible that more conservative legislators might move to limit the future scope of the USIP based on what I believe would be misguided perceptions of misalignment with their ideological or fiscal philosophy. More progressive members of Congress might move to expand the scope and reach of USIP over the next thirty years out of necessity to better manage community, national and international conflict. Equally possible, progressive legislators might react to the social unrest catalyzed in the spring of 2020 and take the view that USIP's research orientation is not activist enough to warrant its funding. It is not out of the question that one day the USIP may be invigorated to incorporate into its mission the worlds of community and national conflict, not just international peace. The USIP might well progress to be the pivotal part of a restructured federal department including reorganized entities such as USIP, the Arms Control and Disarmament Agency, Community Relations Service, Peace Corps, AmeriCorps, and other agencies. This type of federal reorganization has occurred in recent years with TSA, Homeland Security, the Department of Energy, and others.

The aspirational mission of an organization should always exceed practical expectations, but perhaps more importantly, the vision and capabilities of its people *must advance also to keep pace with the times.*[93] This is how the USIP will continue to be successful and enduring.

Chapter 11 Review and Reflection

Task

- Believe in yourself.

Challenge

- Set boundaries on your willingness to sacrifice.

Gift and Opportunity

- Find the gift of focus of what is most important to you.

Reflection

- If you cannot be all things, what can you be?
- Who or what do you pretend to be, but are not?

CHAPTER 12

Malibu

2011 - Malibu is a roughly one-mile by twenty-one-mile strip of land bound between the Santa Monica Mountains and the Pacific Ocean. It is a small place with a disproportionate amount of beauty – and for me holds a lot of memories. It is also 2,700 miles from Washington, DC.

Although Dayle and I had made the decision to relocate our family to live full-time on the island of Maui in Hawaii, I often had to be on the West Coast for business. I traveled to support clients wherever they were holding executive meetings or team retreats. I was in Los Angeles meeting with an executive team in Pacific Palisades. Being in Southern California got me thinking about my earlier days in Malibu. I was back where I had started.

On the last evening with the client, we celebrated with a cocktail reception on the hotel terrace overlooking the Pacific. Once again, T. S. Eliot came to mind: "And to make an end is to make a beginning. The end is where we start from."[94] The words had become a kind of life mantra.

As chance would have it my consulting schedule had me finishing up with the client in LA and boarding a red-eye for Dulles to work with a technology company in Washington, DC. I had not been to DC in a while and was hoping to look in on the new USIP building that had opened in 2011. Knowing that I had to be back in LA again the following week, I called my former Malibu housemate Sam to see if we could meet for dinner in five days. We had not seen each other in twenty-five years and I instantly looked forward to seeing him upon learning he was available.

Meanwhile, checking in at LAX, I made my way to the gate and proceeded to board the plane when I ran into one of my former business partners, John, who was also making the same overnight flight to the East Coast. We embraced, traded greetings, and made arrangements with another passenger to exchange seats so that John and I could sit together and visit on the long flight.

Like any chance encounter with a former colleague, we were excited to catch up. We had spent many evenings together on the road, often talking late into the night when we were away from family. Suddenly we were back in that former groove. We caught up on our families and the type of client work we had each been doing even before the plane lifted off the runway. Once in the air, the cabin darkened and other travelers began to sleep. We flipped on our reading lights and in that subdued, private space we began to explore more deeply the time that we had been apart. Knowing each other as we did, egos and judgment faded into interest and acceptance of where our lives had led us. We reconnected with a special level of trust built over the years.

John jumped in first and shared that he had remarried after a wounding divorce. His client work had been mixed, a lot of travel and repeat business with major companies, but it took time from his real love of mountain climbing. He did not do technical climbs anymore, but enjoyed walk-up adventures on some of the world's most notable peaks in Asia, Central Europe, and other far-off places when he could add on a side trip off a client assignment. He provided more detail on some of the more memorable trips. When the second drink service came through it was my time for storytelling.

A flight attendant interrupted to ask if we needed anything. "Are you guys brothers or something?" she asked. "Excuse me for breaking into your conversation, but we are going to turn the seat belt sign on and I wondered if you'd like anything else?" Waving her off, I began to share my part of the catch up conversation.

I told John about Connie's illness and death, and that I had remarried to a wonderful woman named Dayle. "I hope you get the chance to meet soon," I said.

> "I am still working with companies on their conflicts and, you know all of that work I was doing on the peace academy? It paid off and the government has created a new agency called the United States Institute of Peace. That happened about five years ago."

John acknowledged the somber parts of my story; congratulated me on my marriage and the formation of the USIP. Then John turned the conversation to what he had remembered about my advocacy work on peace. He asked, "Do you think people are now tuning into peace like they did in the 1960's?" he said.

I replied,

> "I really think that people see peace as black or white, and then they kind of glaze over. If we are in a war, it's on their minds. If no war, no real concerns about peace. Actually, the fact is that there is no sense of 'peace fidelity,' or a pure, final state of peace. Peace is an ongoing process. We want to see it as an end state, but it is a living thing. There will always be conflict. Folks still have a lot to learn if society

is ever going to change their interest and attitudes toward peace. Here, let me read you something."

I reached under the seat in front of me and grabbed my briefcase. I opened my Day-Timer and from among a few photographs I pulled out one of several 3 x 5 cards of favorite inspirational quotes I usually carried along with me on trips. "This is a quote from my friend Herb Kelman who used to teach at Harvard:

> 'Positive peace does not imply an ideal, utopian situation, but merely a livable world; a world in which peace is probable, so that individuals and groups everywhere can have a sense of security about their survival, and trust that their basic needs will be met and their basic rights protected.'

John said, "What other goodies do you have tucked away in that Day-Timer?" I just glared at him; then sat quietly for a while. A flight attendant walked by and we both looked up. With the distraction, I decided to take a different tact:

> "John, You are a hiker and climber. A lot of your gear is made of rip stop nylon. You know, the fabric with a heavier thread every twenty or so stitches. It's there to stop a tear from getting worse. The equipment manufacturer anticipates the abuse you will give the product, right? Well, we just don't think that way about the fabric of society. Most often we don't think about preventing violence. We just think about intervention or enforcement after the fact. We don't try to ensure that a tear in our social fabric will be self-managed by a built-in mechanism like rip stop nylon."

I picked up my plastic cup from the seat tray as I adjusted to the motion of the passenger in front of me who was reclining his seat. We were both quiet for another moment.

I started to explain again,

> "In our cities we have traffic lights and traffic lane lines, curbs to separate the pedestrians from the vehicles. We have rules. In war, we talk about rules, too. But we seldom talk about the rules of peace. That is what I have been working on since I saw you last: how do we get society to create the political will to seek peace by establishing better guidance on how to prevent violent conflict? We have 'Walk, Don't Walk' signage on nearly every busy intersection in this country, right?"

Ping, the seatbelt sign rang off. John put up the tray table where his drink had been resting and shifted in his chair. "I have got to go to the bathroom. Be right back." When he returned, John asked, "Where were we?"

> "OK, Let me just finish up. The scary part is that younger generations are beginning to see war and global conflict as the new norm. It's getting acceptable to fight several wars all the time. We get blowback from the wars we do fight. People see fighting in the cities; they see a political system that divides us not flexible enough to pull us together. Folks don't ask what the problems really are, of if the do, people feel we have lost our ability, or will, to deal with the solutions. They see racism, disparities and injustices that you would not expect of a top tier nation. We don't know what peace means at home or abroad. We still have about thirty-five internal wars going on each year, I can go on…"

I looked over at John to check in and saw that he had fallen asleep.

I eventually dozed off as well and when we landed in Washington, we said our farewells and each went our own ways.

♖ ♗ ♘

After my DC meetings, I traveled back to LA and to ensure I would be on time for the Monday meetings, I flew out on Saturday to settle in—and to have dinner with Sam as planned. Sam was a pediatrician, now married, and still lived in the area. We agreed to meet at Alice's Restaurant on the Malibu Pier. I had not seen him in twenty years.

Landing at LAX, I soon found myself passing through the tunnel at the end of the Santa Monica freeway. I began to get nostalgic. The drive up the coast began to put my personal journey of discovery in perspective. I had left this place in the summer of 1975, and moved on from a great job and a safe lifestyle. I left to learn things; perhaps get credentialed, and meet people who shared my interests. I had achieved two of the three. As I drove, the ocean was beginning to glisten in the afternoon light.

The drive up the winding Pacific Coast Highway was a photo album of memories and insights mixed in with the beauty of reappearing cliffs, sand, surf and sea. At each turn, the landscape changed. The road left one scene behind only to disclose another.

Sometimes, too, we have to let go. I had let go of Malibu. I had let go of Pittsburgh, and I had let go of Washington, DC. Those of us who worked so hard to create a national center for training and research in conflict resolution, had to let go in order to continue; each in our own ways. The people who had inspired our campaign; and the staffs of NPAC and the commission had moved on. Bryant moved on to push George Mason University to adopt and develop a program in conflict resolution, in much the way he had hoped a national peace academy would legitimize and train professionals. Jim moved on to redirect his focus to academia and conflict resolution practice and applications through the Conflict Clinic. Andy returned to politics and had moved through his second term as Atlanta's mayor to run for Governor of Georgia. I had served for a decade as a Managing Partner of a boutique consulting practice where I was able to address social issues and provide guidance to management executive teams dealing with change.

♜ ♝ ♞

The concept of a national peace academy had moved on, as well. One difference between our visions for the Peace Academy, and how the USIP was eventually enacted, had to do with a change in the political climate of the country and the popularity of Ronald Reagan. Our vision was of what would be positive for the future, was not necessarily acceptable to the country at the time. We worked hard to create the political will to create a starting point. USIP became, and is still becoming.

Our institutions change and twist with time. The Supreme Court evolves with the individuals who are appointed to it, and changes the laws of the land. It is a remarkable dynamic of our American society that though the members are appointed by different Presidents, the court functions to lend stability and structure to our democracy. Decisions of the court weave their way through history. The law of the land is based on principles of our Constitution, yet the process of interpreting, understanding, and applying laws flows with the changing advancement of society. So too, I suspect, the USIP will ebb and flow. But in the end, it is there: a beginning.

The American service academies did not happen all at once. In some cases they were nearly eliminated by Congress, just as they had begun. The traditions that surround the academies have taken hundreds of years to develop and mature. We felt that this same sort of evolutionary path might be a similar developmental course for a National Peace Academy; National Peace Institute; or one day, with a Department of Peace.

We become the architects of our own futures when we gather the means in our social toolbox to create political will. The ability to inspire short-and long-term solutions to social and political issues is a reoccurring prerequisite for changing history. In doing so, we enable communities to become the shapers of their own futures. Whether a neighborhood, a city, a business, or a nation, when we learn to influence others in collaborative and sustaining ways, we can harness the will, skills, and mindsets that can cause transformational change.

More recently, conflict resolution scholars like John Paul Lederach have moved the vision of conflict management even further to "conflict transformation," where the perspective changes from "How do we end something not desired?" to "How do we end something destructive and build something desired?"[95]

My belief is that each of us can cause change. That belief started early in my life and grew with my education and work experiences. As my interests in the sciences grew, I came to realize that most of life could be defined as systems that ever so slowly can change. I look back at what we did, and I see the cohesive five strategies for creating political will, at least for getting out of the tough spots when other tactics fail.

The tools we thought we used then were typewriters and the legislative process. Computers, the Internet, fax machines, and cell phones were not yet widely available, if at all. In contrast, the tools for change today in the twenty-first century have grown to include social media and video conferencing, instant communications, and web-driven access on any subject matter, worldwide. Yet the strategies for driving those tools remain the same. Today, the game is the same, but the playing field has been dramatically altered.

♖♗♞

With the sun starting its downward angle, I looked out at the flat horizon, now taking on more of a dramatic hue. Oceans elicit both remembrances and future thoughts for me. The sight reminded me of people in the old world who used to believe the world was flat. They, too, looked out to sea and embraced the edge they saw as the end. Today, we know better. Their playing field began to change, albeit very slowly. In 340 BCE, Aristotle wrote that the earth was a round sphere rather than a mere plane or plate. Aristotle made three observations that informed his thinking. First, he recognized the earth's shadow on the moon was always round. Second, he noticed that the mast of an approaching ship appeared on the horizon before he saw the ship.

Finally, Aristotle's third realization was that from the equator, at the middle of a sphere, the North Star appeared just over the horizon.[96] The Greeks spent a lot of their time navigating on the sea. It was pretty common knowledge that the North Star appeared lower in the sky when viewed from the South than it did when viewed from the north. Since the North Star lies directly over the North Pole, the star appeared to be directly above an observer at the North Pole. It is understandable today, but hard to grasp back then. Aristotle did the math, sort of speak.

These three pretty convincing examples were more than enough evidence for Aristotle, but not so for the rest of the world. It took roughly 1,200 years longer for the population to generally agree that the world was round. This consensus finally occurred in 1519–1522 when Ferdinand Magellan made his first circumnavigation of the world. Some things just take time to be believed. Knowing and convincing others of what you know to be true, are very different things.

Sometimes a group effort is needed to help people and society to see things differently. Actually, after Aristotle's work on the heavens, people still debated why there were tides and why ships did not fall off the presumed flat earthly plate. But a few thoughtful individuals figured it differently. One imagined and mapped the position of the planets; a second described the movements of the planets; a mathematician advanced the heliocentric view of the solar system; one guy figured out so much stuff, he is thought of as the Father of Modern Science; and then there was the man who conceptualized the laws of motion. They were all great thinkers: Ptolemy, Copernicus, Kepler, Galileo, and Newton – and they all agreed with Aristotle. Even their insights and beliefs that the world was, in fact, round did not sway public opinion until Captain Magellan finally won folks over by circumnavigating the globe. His voyage proved what Aristotle had espoused. Magellan became famous for a boat ride, but his journey contributed more to our understanding and acceptance of science. He proved what others had thought. He fought to take five ships and 270 men around the world. In doing so, he not only had to muster the political will to undertake the voyage; the outcome changed society's views on the world. Magellan demonstrated the imagination of Aristotle. As it worked out, both of them influenced society. The sciences and creating political will, go hand-in-hand.

The "will" of science is to know what questions to ask; the political part is in having the courage to ask them. New understanding brought on by the efforts of scientists, necessitate the knowledge of creating political will to gain acceptance of a new fact. Peace, too, can be seen as a science.[97] For those who might skeptically ask, "Wait a minute, you are kidding me, right? Is peace a really a science?" I wish those people had been with me one day when Kenneth Boulding cajoled: "I know peace is a science because I can give a test in it."

♖ ♗ ♞

If we believe that the earth is round, many of the mindsets and perceptions we have about the world change dramatically from what we would believe if we think that the world looks like a plate. So if we believe peace is possible, then our perceptions change from those we hold if we believe that peace is not possible.

Most of the entire world believed that the galaxy in which we live, the Milky Way, was the only galaxy up until the day of December 30, 1924. On that day, astronomer Edwin Hubble announced the existence of another galaxy in space. The people on planet earth were shocked because they thought they knew that our home galaxy was the only one. Instantly, when earthlings learned that there was more than one galaxy in the universe, our thinking, perspective and openness to the concept of existence changed. Our paradigm of the universe was changed forever. Since Hubble discovered the spiral nebula Andromeda, technology has enabled scientists to estimate there are more than 170 billion galaxies in the universe.

USIP was created to be a ladder, if our global village can learn to use it for its intended purpose, as Dr Schweitzer had sought to do with that village down river from Lambaréné. To paraphrase Winston Churchill, "First we shape our institutions, thereafter they shape us."[98]

The power of new discoveries to change our thinking – and cause us to be open to possibilities – has direct relevance to the creation of the USIP. By illustration, consider Aristotle's discoveries in 340 BCE and those of Hubble in 1924. One mind-blowing set of observations took centuries to be accepted while the other astounding discovery gained acceptance instantaneously. Indeed, technology shortens the time it takes for discoveries to be known and understood; diffused and accepted; and integrated into common practices.

The primary barrier, it would seem, to humans embracing the existence of a more peaceful world is our mind set that peace is not possible. As scientists, institutions, and civic leaders provoke the possibility of peace, even with certainty of the forces pushing back on that hope, society is influenced to be open to such realities. It is no longer our skill sets or technology that holds us back; it is the presence of the political will necessary to make the case. Paradigms can change; our thinking can get turned upside down; and science can be more impactful than mere hope.

America is a changing country. It is not what it was one hundred fifty years ago. It is not what it was fifty years ago. It is not what it will be in ten years. In fact, with the arrival of COVID-19 in the winter of 2020, the world, not just our nation changed in mere weeks. Conflict and change are defining us as a people. How we as individuals adjust, absorb, influence, and find meaning and the identity of who we want to become is defining—and will define—our national future. How we as a people come together as a nation to define and problem solve our future will be dependent on how evolved and well integrated our skills become as a citizenry and community of dispute resolvers.

We are each our own story. Each reader will choose to create his own political will for his own cause and beliefs. Each of us stands on our own Farragut Square. My story in helping to create the United States Institute of Peace was my own voyage of discovery.

Robert Theobald, the transplanted English economist and futurist, sent me a copy of a speech he gave at Kent State University in 1976 as his written testimony to the Commission. It was entitled, "Is Peace Possible?" He shared:

> "If present circumstances continue there will inevitably be an increasing number of recruits to terrorists causes, for there is a growing feeling of injustice throughout the world which cannot be removed, as in the past, by the catharsis of war.[99]

Theobald wrote in his testimony, that peace is not possible in the conditions in which we presently exist; the structures of the present world are not sufficient to nourish it.

> "The creation of peaceful conditions would involve not only fundamental change in the way we think and act but also the creation of new management systems in the world. These management systems would have to be clear about the directions needed to ensure our development and also have the necessary skills to work to attain them effectively.[100]

The work to understand such changes, structures, attitudes, and insights will is a necessary task for America in the decades ahead as we strive as a country to manage our way into a more peaceful world, part of the challenge and future legacy of the USIP.

♜ ♝ ♞

These thoughts and remembrances filled my mind and heart as I drove along the route. I caught myself making an audible sigh. The sun was beginning to set, my road seemed long, but it had been a beautiful ride. I was tired from my travel, but exhilarated to be back where it had started.

I turned on the radio and on came one of my favorite songs, "River of Jordan," by Peter Yarrow, formerly of the group Peter, Paul, and Mary. It was never more poignant for me:

> There is only one river; there is only one sea
> And it flows through you, and it flows through me
> There is only one people, we are one and the same
> We are all one spirit; we are all one name [101]

I turned the radio off after the song to be with my thoughts. I drove by many of my old haunts as I followed the winding road up the coast, humming the song over and over again.

I arrived a little early and walked out onto the pier. I checked in at the restaurant and then slipped outside again to stand by the pier railing overlooking the ocean to await my friend.

I looked out over the ocean and instantly saw the kelp beds, leaves flipping in the wind; shimmering in the golden light. I realized that my own journey had been a river. It had been a river of people, ideas, dreams, and many highs. Much of the shoreline I had passed was punctuated with triumphs and losses, friends, and adversaries. My mind and heart filled with the memories of the many others I had encountered on the journey. They too had made the choice to participate, to hope, to believe, to act. Without them, the passage through the shoals and rapids would not have been possible. I thought of Connie, and of Jim, Bryant, and Mike Mapes, mostly of those who had passed. I held these thoughts, and watched the kelp playing in the fading light.

My focus broke as it started to mist, and I turned as my friend Sam walked up the boardwalk of the pier to greet me. We exchanged a bear hug and pats on the back. "Hello, hello", we said.

We unfolded from our embrace and Sam said, "A lot of water under the bridge, or should I say pier, my friend? It's been a long time." I smiled, and we shared an enthusiastic fist pump, as I said, "Indeed."

We made our way into the iconic Alice's Restaurant, a place we had often sought a casual dinner during my time in Malibu twenty years earlier. It appeared obvious that the local landmark café was waning. The place was named after Arlo Guthrie's song by the same name. Unfortunately, Alice's would close not long after our visit. All good things come to an end.

With the quaint restaurant affording us an evening of nostalgia, we were able to revisit the depth of friendship we shared from many years earlier. Dinner conversation flowed.

Our conversation continued on as the tables around us emptied, and the wait staff began to hover. We settled our bill and walked for a brief while back down the pier, listening to the waves batter the pilings and run up onto the sand.

Suddenly, Sam stopped our progress back to our cars, and said, "Hey, look over there!"

I looked over the pier's railing and saw the moon rising, casting its magical light over the ocean. But the sight offered more than that, as the rain clouds were parting and the moon was illuminating not just the sea. The light of the rising moon was creating an arc of moonbeams across the clouds and down through the mist below.

Standing on the pier in that moment, we both were quiet. It was hard for me not to think about the familiar words "bending the arc of history", as the crescent rays interplayed with the changing cloudscape. Then, the clouds moved on; the sky lightened; the episode was over. It all had happened in a fleeting moment.

After a few more minutes of savoring the meaning of the experience, Sam spoke first, and asked with a flash of recollection, "Hey, do you still have that yellow kayak? I forgot to ask."

"Always", I said. "It's part of me."

Chapter 12 Review and Reflection

Task

- Identify your lessons and repeat.

Challenge

- Evaluate what works.
- Integrate learnings.

Gift and Opportunity

- Leverage meaningful, altruistic acts with integrity and gratitude.

Reflection

- What areas of your life demonstrate your current ability?
- What quality of your character is your foundation?

AFTERWORD

2020 – It has been forty-one years since my appointment to Director of the Commission, and forty-six years since my drive down Pacific Coast Highway to the UCLA Research Library to discover the world of peace.

Just a few years ago, Dayle and I were at the Lorraine Motel in Memphis, Tennessee, site of the King assassination on April 6, 1968. Dr King, Andy, Jim and others were in Memphis in support of striking African American sanitation workers.

This was where Jim held Dr King and Andy pointed out over the railing in the agony of his loss. Photos of both Jim and Andy appeared in the somber *LIFE Magazine* article documenting the shooting in the weeks following the tragedy. That moment in American history stands as a poignant reminder of the inseparability of justice from peace. I am reminded of the unfinished work of Dr King and of Andy, Jim, Bryant and the others who worked so tirelessly to create the USIP. It is a continuation in the pursuit of refining the American dream. Just as those who followed Dr King and have contributed to his legacy, those who follow in the wake of the founders of the USIP add dimension and further momentum to the wave. That critical wave of consciousness, indeed new mechanisms for peace, will serve to nourish the ongoing political will necessary to advance the cause. Too often, politics, elitism, and pressures within bureaucracies detach our institutions from the inspiring visions that lead to their foundation. Let us hope that the years will be good to the USIP.

Dr Martin Luther King, Jr, wrote, "In the end, we will remember not the words of our enemies, but the silence of our friends."[102] We each have the responsibility and obligation to seek the political will to find peace in our communities and world. Long-held attitudes can be adjusted when the behaviors of people are obliged to change due to laws or the pressures to conform to the values and aspirations of culture. For in the end, culture changes when the silent speak up.

In our schools, our communities, our state houses, our workplaces, we must come to understand that the process of peace, the road achieving culture of peace, is dependent upon all of us sharing the same vision of a country and world, united in non-violence and the pursuit of justice. In foreign policy, we must rise to the principles that hold non-violence and alternatives to the use of force above our available technology of war.

We can ask, which comes first, the pursuit of a culture of peace or the social realization of what that looks like? Ultimately it will be the leaders, who develop the political will for change; leaders who are equipped with skills, mindsets and the passion for working to change the culture. As in any change management initiative, there are barriers to be understood and overcome. There are strategies that inform the best practices we must embrace.

Racism, poverty, religion, technology, economics and resource allocation are all representative of the challenges we face in the journey toward creating a culture of peace. Religion, that language of symbols and metaphors, can co-exist within the framework of the shared higher values of non-violence and justice. Technology, the breakdown of time, space and simplicity of function, can be harnessed to the advance of peace when guided by the socially value-driven ambitions of the marketplace. Poverty, resource allocation and racism are manageable challenges when the aspirations of people for a culture for peace trump the attitudes and economics of the past.

How do we create a culture of peace? A culture of peace is a set of values, beliefs, attitudes and traditions that evolve through education; sustainable economic and social development; respect and tolerance for all forms of human rights; equality between men and women; participation in democratic processes; tolerance; and free flow of information and knowledge. Society must structure itself with the necessary institutions to influence progress in each of these areas.

A sustainable culture of peace is characterized by the belief that peace can be achieved. Believing that peace can be achieved is like getting the parties to the table; it is the hardest part. Building the culture of peace is easier. Both of these things benefit from our knowledge of what it takes to create political will.

There is social technology to impact on creating cultures of peace. It is different from what the State Department does or how police services carry out their duties. Implementing a vision of peace requires new competencies that integrate skills and tools for change that effect the elements and standards listed above.

Marcel Proust thought and wrote extensively about the vast changes that occurred in France in his lifetime, including the decline of aristocracy and the rise of the middle class. His writings both documented and challenged the establishment of his day. The metaphor of Proust's "new eyes" was the vision of Bryant, Jim and Andy in our efforts to establish a national peace academy and the USIP.

The importance of the USIP is that it serves as a practical lever and aspirational commitment to further our understanding and application of alternatives to the use of force in solving community, national and international problems. The USIP was created when many thought it could not. It was intended to concentrate on the fundamentals of changing the "terms of reference" within which the entire question of international peace is considered. To this extent, the USIP represents a significant step in an on-going change management process to grow and develop in our people what we as a country aspire to project, apply and achieve. Its mere existence is a symbol that peace can be achieved when many think it cannot.

There remains an urgent need to examine the psychological aspects of conflict, ongoing small arms races, and the over-dependence on weapons system that define most common measures of our national security. Concepts such as sovereignty and deterrence should be reexamined to explore the limits of power and projection in an ever more dependent international community of nations and regional identities.

American society is still struggling with how to better manage conflict and cooperation; how to conduct civil discourse at home and as a world leader, engage in dialogue abroad. The size and scope of the American military complex has increased in the last four decades. I have always taken this fact to be a profound statement of the need to institutionalize at the federal level the on-going search for practical alternatives to the use of force. Continued racism, poverty and increased political partisanship have made it even more difficult to problem solve social issues. The growing voice of various extremists around the world, including in America, make the art of Democracy and dialogue – let alone peacemaking and nation-building, more difficult, but not impossible. It is important to continue to focus on new tools, fresh perspectives, changing contexts and the on-going creation of political will. A story such as this illustrates not only the anatomy of a successful effort, but the perseverance required for effective and lasting social change.

I recently engaged conflict resolution scholar Lou Kriesberg in a telephone conversation about his views on how society and the field had changed since we had first met in 1976. Lou said, "I think things are getting better in terms of our social understanding of conflict resolution." I expressed surprise. He added, "Well, we (the US) have made progress, but most of the world is not there yet." Lou was speaking about the field of professionals, American institutions, associations and university programs.

The field of conflict resolution has become institutionalized, with many universities offering Masters degrees and a half dozen or so offering PhD programs. The language of the field has spread throughout society, although at times, it seems, people differ on the meaning of basic terms like 'win/win' or core processes that yield negotiated results. Lou reflected that there still exists many gaps in the global translation of skills to policy makers and NGOs.

Many of the policy makers and professional diplomats who grew up during the past decades understand the new skills and mindsets, but often have difficulty applying them as they are so caught up in the fast pace of work, incremental decision making and the necessary pursuit of American interests. Meaningful international change – and transformative change within the US foreign policy apparatus – requires a sustainable infrastructure that works to grow the networks necessary for diffusion of the peace and conflict resolution sciences. It takes time.

♖ ♗ ♘

Every reader is the author of his own story in finding personal meaning and identity in the pursuit of their goals. Mine was a search for a way to further peace and social justice in a lasting and systemic way, to contribute to the cause of peace; to seek a better, more peaceful tomorrow. It can be a self-actualizing voyage of the soul and of the mind. It is indeed, a special calling of the heart. It is my hope that telling my part of the story will inspire readers to focus toward similar ends, in any way they can. It is my wish that this account of the people, strategies, events and accomplishments of a decade of work to bring about a national center for training and research in peace and conflict resolution will influence further progress.

USIP is but a beginning. It is not yet all that its founders and those who supported their efforts intended it to be. However, it is a charge and a rallying cry.

My memories now are flavored with the essence of the work we shared together and the mutual cognitive legacy that became the formulation for the new institution. We envisioned the USIP to be like a wheelbarrow - modeling the three greatest tools of early man: the wheel, the incline plane and the fulcrum. Like these innovations that enabled the wheelbarrow, the USIP has the basic elements to leverage and diffuse, transport if you will, a new culture of thinking and behaving as a nation. It can be that simple, if we choose to create the political will.

Those of us, who were part of the peace academy, and peace institute movements, were fortunate to see our efforts reach fruition. Others come together everyday to create the political will necessary to bring attention and action to their own cause.

The will of one person to make a difference is the beginning of the exercise of creating political will. The will of one institution can make a difference as well. The gathering of others, perhaps also so moved, builds and grows into a common commitment or campaign.

Fortunately, in the decades of the 1970s and 1980s, thousands of people worked to establish the United States Institute of Peace. Some lent the modest financial support that facilitated the on-the-ground work of others. Some inspired the concept with their ideas, research, activism or direct leadership of the campaign and Congressional action. This entity, now in existence for over thirty years, had many names along the path to its creation. Whatever the name, the desired objective has always been to build an institutionalized Federal bias into the thinking and actions of the US government to actively define and seek peace in the full measure of the science and best practices of current research, theory and activism. One day, the USIP may go by another name, as was true of the State Department, several of the service academies and many federal agencies. Time and history change our perspective. Perspective changes our understanding; and understanding changes the scope of the problems we need to prepare to resolve.

We in America are the sum of our diversity and that 'special sauce' that inspires who we are as a nation. Those of great insight who have studied Americans over the years often get to know us better than we know ourselves.

Again turning to Alexis de Tocqueville for insight, he wrote:

> "The greatness of America lies not in being more enlightened than any other nation, but rather in her ability to repair her faults."[103]

As individuals, we search for most of our lives to understand who we are; what we do and how we chose to structure our daily routine and our path to accomplishing individual life goals. Citizens of these United States simultaneously romanticize and argue over what we perceive our roots as a nation to have been, and we constantly make decisions to redefine, re-invent and reshape our national attitudes and behaviors at home and our national brand as seen in the world. We do grow as a nation in awareness and resolve for those things we seek to further our democracy and the liberties we enjoy.

So it is with a nation. Our national political will is the sum of numerous moving parts constantly at play in our national life, working together to confirm or alter how we see ourselves and define ourselves as a people. How a country becomes something different grows out of how the political will of each of us is gathered in, like the drawstring of a net, to embrace a cause, a candidate, a vision, or a commitment to a specific solution.

In early 1980, I asked a small carload of staff members of the commission to take a car ride with me. I did not tell them where we were going. I drove from our offices on M Street, down past the Lincoln Memorial on the National Mall and directly to the Jefferson Memorial. It was just a few miles. We walked around to the entrance and looked out toward the Capitol. The cherry blossoms were not yet blooming, but had started to bud. Thomas Jefferson wrote many things, but that day – and today for me – one of his most important was this paragraph, enshrined on the southeast portico of the memorial.

> "I am not an advocate for frequent changes in laws and constitutions, but laws and institutions must go hand in hand with the progress of the human mind. As that becomes more developed, more enlightened, as new discoveries are made, new truths discovered and manners and opinions change, institutions must advance also to keep pace with the time. We might as well require a man to wear still the coat which fitted him when a boy as a civilized society to remain ever under the regimen of their barbarous ancestors."[104]

We stood in silence before the marble wall.

The quote is a condensed excerpt from a rather lengthy letter dated July 12, 1816 to Samuel Kercheval regarding equal representation. The text of the full letter reveals a set of strategies and tactics suggested by Jefferson to secure self-government, to structure its organization to afford every citizen the opportunity to exercise their political will in the administration of public affairs. Our actions to establish the USIP were inspired by such grand thoughts. The five strategies you have read about coalesced from our own efforts to create political will.

Much has been written about the "fog of war," that confusing and unruly collection of mindsets that pervades actions and the conditions found amid the violence and horror of war. Its peacetime corollary might be labeled the "cloud of peace," that shadow of doubt and disbelief that obscures the image of a stable peace. One day, we can hope that an image such as that will be as ingrained in our minds and hearts as our understanding of gravity. Perhaps this is the greatest challenge to lasting peace – our personal belief and communal resolve that it is possible. Believing is seeing.

There is a need to reframe the concept of peace to reposition its meaning – and so the sense of identity that people feel with it. Peace is a concept that is too often associated with war, when in reality peace is more about the pursuit of social and economic justice; the application of conflict resolution processes, than the preparation for war or the use of force to pursue political aims. Americans often view peace as something achieved by a strong national security apparatus, versus something achieved by the application of peace seeking, peace building and peacemaking processes. The military is an extremely important institution in American society. When we traveled to all of the military staff and command colleges and service academies, seeking advice and input on the importance of new ways of peace seeking, peace making and peacekeeping, we were met with considerable enthusiasm and support. More than most, the military agrees that force should never be the leading response or tool to address conflict. In early 1976, before the hearings on the George

Washington Peace Academy Act, Bryant wrote to General Andrew J. Goodpaster, who was then a professor at the Citadel in Charleston, South Carolina, inviting him to take an active part in support of the National Peace Academy Campaign. He responded that he had just been recalled to active duty and assigned as Superintendent of the US Military Academy at West Point and was not in a position to take an active role, but would lend his support for our objectives, and he did. The Ugandan Colonel who was observing our Eritrea-Ethiopia negotiations in Nairobi knew, despite the military being his way out of poverty, that peace is the nobler path. Warriors pay the greatest cost for war, and they are among those who have the highest regard for peace.

♖ ♗ ♞

Too often we forget that that humans cooperate far more than they fight; we collaborate far more than we quarrel; and we enjoy peace far more than we go to war. So why don't we have more of a sense of permanent peace? Moreover, what can we as a society do to cause peace?

When I lived in Boston, my friend and colleague Gene Sharp and I both had dogs. He had two Great Danes, and I a Keeshond-Shepard mix. We would often extrapolate their non-violent behaviors to gesture and get what they wanted from us. We would laugh at the thought that our dogs were negotiating their needs and interests with us in real time. They did it well, and it was instructive to watch them. Now, our puppy Winston is a seven-year old King Charles Cavalier spaniel. He is a pretty pampered pooch, and receives a lot of love and play; food and exercise. Yet, he like many dogs is programmed to bury bones and rawhide chew toys. Winston has no other reason to do this than it is in his DNA. Genes influence behavioral traits. The Ugandan Colonel who was observing our Eritrea-Ethiopia negotiations in Nairobi knew, despite the military being his way out of poverty, that peace is the nobler path. Warriors pay the greatest cost for war, and they are among those who have the highest regard for peace. He has a genetic link with wolves and other prehistoric canines that lived in very harsh conditions. Winston's ancestors either hid their food from other animals, or stored it in the ground to keep it moist for when they might need it again. Winston has neither need.

Clearly a modern puppy has genetically inspired behaviors that link it to its past. It is debatable whether we humans are more programmed to fight or flee; cooperate or resist; change or remain the same. Sometimes the simplest observations tell us the most about life. I believe people need, and want to collaborate.

Today, Darwin's arguments can reasonably be extended to imply that the momentum of evolutionary biology may one day lead us to greater societal cooperation. More peaceful ways of solving social problems may well become the guiding principle of "natural selection." Military solutions alone will not solve the many challenges we face. We will become extinct if we do not "select" for peace, and all that it means. The biological compulsion to survive dominates human existence. Our natural selection will depend on our ability and instinct to cooperate. The USIP exists as an advocate of that reality and vision. These days it is a little more complicated than fight or flight. In our shrinking world, we can't really flee, and we can no longer fight if we wish to survive.

The Cold War had us worried about nuclear weapons, a horrific fear and reality. In 2020, the world fights both the biological pandemic of COVID-19 and an environmental war with the planet. The odds may be with us to eventually live with the virus, but the odds are clearly against us to defeat the planet and the forces of climate change.

Recent work by scientists studying animal behavior conclude that we humans have been successful as a species due to our spirit of cooperation rather than our capacity for violence. Cooperation does not require family ties or shared national origins in primates or humans. Most often cooperation is based on reciprocation – as with chimpanzee simulations at the Yerkes National Primate Research Center in Atlanta -- and as famously translated into social-psychological human terms, by political scientist Charles Osgood's theory of Graduated Reciprocation in Tension-reduction, GRIT. Osgood's work helped to redefine American patterns of international behavior during the arms race with the Soviets in the early sixties. Simply put, positive unilateral initiatives create reciprocal action, as evidenced in the Cuban missile crisis.

Humans have the capacity to create highly complex collaborative structures such as collective terraced farming irrigation systems, or the CERN's collider that was built to find the Higgs-Boson particle. As our understanding of genetic and evolutionary biology progresses, we may one day discover ways that can be more healthy, disease-free – as well as capable of increased cooperation in discovering a "peace gene." The cost of conflict managed by war is so high that we may have no other alternative. America urgently needs to invent and advance the technology of peace, just as it did the technology of war.

♜ ♝ ♞

A nation is made up of individuals who share values and actions that define our national behavior. Understanding who we are as a nation is about appreciating how our national behavior validates or rejects the historical roots of our American experiment. If we seek to be more peaceful in our approach to global issues, then we must come to define the meaning and identity of what the concept and process of peace is all about. To achieve these ends, we must learn to structure society to better manage and adjust to creating the mindsets, skill sets and infrastructure required to nurture and sustain the culture of peace so needed in the world today.

To every extent possible the USIP should be encouraged to do the type of controversial, groundbreaking work intended by its founders. Recognizing that it is extraordinarily difficult to do such work when so closely tied to the federal bureaucracy, continued steps should be taken to fund external efforts through other institutions across the country.

Adlai Stevenson was the Democratic candidate for President in 1952 and 1956. Twice, Dwight Eisenhower defeated him. John Kennedy defeated Stevenson in the 1960 Democratic primary. After Kennedy defeated Nixon in the general election, President Kennedy appointee Stevenson to serve as the US Ambassador to the United Nations. Stevenson is credited with helping influence Kennedy to create the Arms Control and Disarmament Agency (ACDA) in a speech he had delivered on June 2, 1960.

> "Who is doing the homework of Peace? Who is drawing up the blueprints of disarmament, studying inspection and detection systems, making plans for eventual reconversion of our economy to fulltime, non-military production? Who is studying the political, judicial and psychological obstacles that must be overcome before Peace can be effectively enforced? … I think the time has come to put this important business on a permanent and professional basis."

In early 1961 the newly elected President John Kennedy invited many of the sponsors of past Peace Agency bills to the White House for a consultation. The failure of earlier bills was due in part to their vagueness and imprecision. The Department of Peace bills in particular failed in their arguments and recommendations to spell out the conceptual framework that lay behind any proposed governmental reorganization anticipated by the bills. These failures were due mainly to inadequate research. Few of the bill sponsors gave the bills the time necessary to develop concrete, well-written, publically supported legislation. The failure was also due to inadequate Congressional staff and expert resources to push the legislation through the Congress. But most importantly, the bill failed to get reported out of committee because the legislation lacked sufficient public support. American society lacked the proven models to illustrate the effectiveness of alternatives to force in resolving conflict. And those efforts simply lacked a sustained political will to cause the changes necessary in the legislature to redefine our concept of peace. It is taking a while for Americans to look beyond the "flat horizon of peace," as viewed through the old lens of peace or war. Admittedly it is difficult to see the new world and the terrain ahead when it is a process not a place. Aristotle was not proven right until Magellan demonstrated with his voyage, what Aristotle had sought.

In the 1960s, the Congress and White House were reluctant to appropriate monies for research or institutions responsible for developing policies in line with the stated national goal of pursuing peace. Finally, the lack of citizen pressure was partly due to the infancy of the "peace sciences" that were still emerging from World War II. But now, the "system" of war spending and its impact on society was becoming more evident. Quincy Wright wrote in *A Study of War* in 1964:

> "The nature of warfare had changed dramatically since the sixteenth century: 1) wars had increased in occurrence; 2) wars had increased in destructive capability; 3) wars had increased in intensity - numbers killed or injured in proportion to total population; 4) wars had increasingly usurped human and natural resources; 5) wars had increasingly disrupted the civilian sectors of society; 6) wars had increased military capitalization; and 7) wars had militarized society, to the point of transforming models of government."[105]

Wright's observations are as true today as they were in 1964.

From the end of World War II to the year we started NPAC, there had been 103 wars with an estimated twenty million deaths and an untold number of refugees. By far, most of the fatalities of war were women and children, not soldiers. War poses a problem not only for international stability but domestic stability as well. Social scientists like Harold Lasswell - with whom Bryant had corresponded in the late sixties – had predicted 37 years before our campaign began that out of war would arise 'garrison states' in which the specialists of bargaining and diplomacy would be replaced by the specialists of violence.

The control of violence has been a critical problem of all social systems irrespective of their models of government, level of economic development, scale of the violence, or its occurrence within or between nations. Violence has been around a long time, and the types of violence witnessed have changed over time. Seeking peace has been redefined over the centuries, too, as we have learned more about what peace means. The point is to minimize violence and manage conflict in positive ways. In the 2020 world, peace is a lot more than the absence of violence. Peace is defined in broader terms than only a world of no violence. Our approaches to both curtailing violence and seeking peace have changed as we evolve.

The case can be made that weapon systems do not always protect the peace. More often than not, the presence of weapons contributes to violence. Some might argue this point, but that in itself represents yet a separate problem, and often leads to different definitions of peace. There is agreement, however, that institutions do influence social outcomes, and how our institutions define peace determines the factors that sustain it.

Indeed as has been said, first we shape our institutions, and then they shape us. The mission and level of funding of our institutions influence the success of achieving the desired outcomes of our

American public policy. Investment in early childhood education, for example, positively correlates with lowering the incidence of adult violence later in life.

Another example of how institutions shape us might be the Defense Advanced Research Projects Agency, DARPA. DARPA was created in 1961 with the authority given to it in Section 31 (e) of its mandate to research: "the scientific, economic, political, legal, social, psychological, military, and technological factors related to the prevention of war with a view to a better understanding of how the basic structure of a lasting peace may be established." DARPA was clearly established in the minds of many to contribute to peace. Still, a person might ask, "Does DARPA contribute to what we today might call Stable Peace?" Opinions on this question will, of course, vary as well.

DARPA's mission has always been interpreted as the development of emerging technologies for use by the military. With all due respect to the men and women of DARPA, the institution was born in an age of retaliatory force resulting from the Cold War.

Do we need force to create peace? That's an interesting question.

Since the early 1960s DARPA's research and programming has concentrated almost exclusively on technical, scientific and economic topics without addressing basic premise of the arms race or seeking alternatives to the use of force in determining the outcomes of international conflict. DARPA has been reorganized and refocused several times since its creation. Its mandate has remained the same, the prevention of war. I have no doubt over the importance of DARPA. I do not question the dedication, or contribution of the many DARPA professionals. As has been stated, our civilian defense and military establishment is important to America. The contributions of our veterans have been significant to the freedoms Americans enjoy. These facts are not in question here. The relevant question I believe is this: when we imagine a peaceful world, will it have been brought about by force, or through the power of alternatives to the use of force?

How we *seek* peace will always come down to our definition *of* peace.

Whatever your answer, this important dilemma suggests further inquiry about the scale, intended result, and balance of alternative approaches. How does America make the best investment to create peace? In the year, 2019, DARPA and the USIP had nearly the same number of employees: 220 for DARPA and 262 for the USIP. It should be noted that DARPA's 2019 budget was $3.427 *billion*, while the 2019 budget of the USIP was $38.6 *million*.

Most people will argue that hardware is more expensive to produce than thinking about; writing about; proposing ideas; planning peace talks, or actually getting disputants together. It could be said that the USIP's mission is the development of emerging technologies for use by those who seek alternatives to the use of force in seeking peace. In fact, the USIP's current mission is "*to "increase US capacity to manage international conflict – to think, act, teach and train."* Both DARPA and the USIP are respected institutions. And both have unique, and quite different missions in the pursuit of peace. Perhaps both are needed to secure the peace, but at what level of investment or scale? Importantly, how should the desired outcome of peace be defined? Which institution will bring America and the world closer together? These are certainly things to ponder.

The USIP should take full advantage of its founding mandate and take steps to expand the scope to include community and national conflict, and other aspects of conflict that extend beyond its current portfolio. Reorganization and renewal should be expected and planned. Circumstances change. The USIP cannot be allowed to fail. Its mission must be renewed and nourished.

♖ ♗ ♘

Soren Kierkegaard was a Danish philosopher and theologian. He once wrote, "Life can only be understood backwards; but it must be lived forwards." Looking back helps us to understand why the USIP was created. Looking forward helps us to define what it can become. The Final Report of the commission was clear on where the commissioners stood in their final decisions regarding the creation of a peace academy.

After all the work, airing of views, research, and internal debate, the Final Report of the commission put forth a design that reflected their primary belief that:

> "The absence of a coordinated national commitment to research, education, and training, and information services from the field of peace learning has caused neglect of peace making knowledge and skills to the detriment of the nation's effectiveness in policy making and policy implementation in international affairs, conflict and war."[106]

The report stated that the commission felt it established *the need, the demand and the potential contribution* to world peace to support a recommendation of federal action in creating an academy. In proposing draft legislation, and detailing the specific design aspects of the proposed academy, the commission felt it useful to leave open certain flexibilities to the academy's initial Board of Directors.

In summary, the Commission on Proposals for the National Academy of Peace and Conflict Resolution found:

- There was broad public and government interest in a federal institution devoted to the nation's peacemaking capacities and that it should serve people in and out of government – and would be sheltered from undue government or private domination.
- The Academy should develop programs for peace research, education and training and information services, which include centralized and outreach capacities; should be an independent, nonprofit, federally chartered corporation; and should not engage in government or nongovernment policymaking or in active dispute resolution. It would not lobby, but could receive nonfederal funds in furtherance of its purposes.
- The three specific functions of the Academy could be detailed and described, as they were in the Final Report, including example relationships, and services.
- The proposed independent governance structure of the Academy was paramount in creating a concentration of resources and visibility sufficient to develop a critical mass capable of impacting its purposes.
- In order to establish national and international visibility and to remain sensitive to the federal government including Congress, the academy should locate its central facilities and administrative offices within easy reach of Washington, DC. The legislation drafted by the commission included the authority to establish subsidiary regional sites to achieve greater accessibility and partnership affiliations.
- When Americans have found the opportunity clear and the needs pressing for fusion between the worlds of learning and public affairs, the nation has responded.
- The needs for a new American stewardship of peace has never been more clear.

♖ ♗ ♘

In 1987 I was in Atlanta attending a conference on the Middle East that I had helped to design and facilitate for President Carter and his Middle East expert, Ken Stein. The planning for the event had been extensive and the participant list was impressive.

During a break, I found myself standing at a urinal in a crowed restroom. Participants were sharing side conversations that had carried over from the breakout sessions. Off to the side I heard a voice say, "Hello Sam! How are you doing? What are you doing now?"

The "Sam" was Samuel Lewis, who had just been appointed President of the USIP. A former US Ambassador to Israel, Ambassador Lewis was well known to those scholars and experts at the symposium. I did not know him. The Ambassador's reply was "Oh, I have a new thing up in

Washington. I have been asked to lead that new institute for peace. I guess I will give that a try for a while and see how it goes."

Emotions came streaming into my head. I had to bite my tongue. I literally did. *I guess I will give that a try for a while and see how it goes?* I thought. More than one hundred months of effort replayed in my head. And all you can say is, *I guess I will give that a try for a while and see how it goes?* It took me more than a few minutes to digest what I had just heard. What should I do next? Should I zip up and follow him? Should I walk up to the Ambassador and introduce myself? What would I say?

I thought to myself: what do I want, or need in this moment? I could not fathom the words I had just heard. I could not grasp the unlikely odds of a moment happening like the one I had just experienced. I tried to understand the Ambassador's response, although it was obvious.

On the one hand it felt terrible that all of my hard work – and the thoughtful efforts of thousands of others – was now being handed over to someone who had just acted so cavalierly about it. On the other hand, the comment by the ambassador meant that what we had worked so hard to create was indeed launched, much like a small yellow kayak, charting a yet unknown course. After I exited the men's room, I did not encounter Ambassador Lewis again.

♖ ♗ ♞

In the end, President Reagan supported the USIP for a variety of reasons which were most likely not in line with the motivations and efforts of the activists who sought to establish it. Such is the nature of governance and the changing cycles of political and ideological power.

Upon reflection, to contemplate how the USIP might evolve in the future is to understand its possible shortcomings in living up to the vision and expectations of its founders. I hesitate to offer advice to an organization that I have never been a part of, and my intent is not be critical but constructive. After years of working hard to enable its success, I feel I would be remiss if I did not share my "mana'o", the Hawaiian word for a belief that a person has formed about a topic or issue. Mana'o is also the Hawaiian word for hope. Here are a few thoughts on where the leadership of the USIP might consider placing their efforts to sustain and make more vibrant their future.

1) Work with members of Congress to incorporate the study and application of community conflict resolution skills and experiences into the USIP mission. By community, I mean community-based and business skills and techniques. Conflict resolution skills are of the same species whether they are for consumption by international allies, or street gang-police relations.

2) The full range of conflict resolution skills are informed by practitioner skills at every level, not just the international. The USIP should include conflict resolution scholars and practitioners from every level of society and every type of social interaction. By blending the expertise of multiple disciplines, the institution and its mission will be better served.

3) The USIP should seek to link its programming and outreach to land grant colleges around the country. In the fulfillment of its 21st Century mission it should find new channels of distribution, diffusion and advocacy for its programming, scope of discipline and reach.

4) The USIP should foster the development of deep cross training with the service academies and staff and command colleges in all service areas.

5) The USIP should explore the creation of extensive programming to impact on all levels of executive leadership service in federal government positions.

6) The USIP should work with Members of Congress and the executive branch to amend its mandate to include the raising of private funds to support developing new programs.

7) The USIP should be encouraged to live by the principle of giving away more than it consumes – meaning that the institution can best extend its reach by supporting, influencing and working through the efforts of other institutions.

8) Scholars at the USIP should not be expected to have tenure in their service to the nation. Rather, there should be an expectation of a constant flow of scholars, and members of the management team, in and out of the institution. The USIP should be viewed as a temporary pedestal not a perch.

9) The USIP should be encouraged to undertake a vibrant program of executives on loan to serve in various leadership roles throughout the organization.

10) The USIP should fund scholarships designated to partnering universities across the United States to encourage the academic pursuit of peace studies, and related fields such as cross-cultural communication, cultural change management and public policy marketing.

11) The USIP should undertake plans (and private donations) to create a residential campus within three hundred miles of the District of Columbia. The sense of community that can be created and sustained by residential programs, and the strength of an alumni base will help to ensure the vitality of the institution and its goals. Co-located researchers and area experts do not form a critical mass or esprit de corps sufficient to protect the institution politically, or act to revitalize its mission.

12) The USIP upon altering its mandate, should solicit corporate funds to support its programming along the lines of the successful model of the Aspen Institute and others.

13) The USIP should expand or develop training programs for entering members of Congress. Not only will this breed loyalty to the Institution, it will help to diffuse the innovations created by research, experimentation and new ways of thinking about conflict and dispute resolution.

14) The USIP should undertake programming meant to serve parliamentarians around the world.

15) The USIP should develop sustainable clearinghouses for what others are doing – matching the results of community and international intervention experiences, noting skills, strategies and resources used in easily available online and regional libraries.

Fortunately USIP has been growing, learning and maturing its mandate over the years. It is my hope that many of the suggestions on this list have already been implemented with success.

♖ ♗ ♘

Former long-time editor of the *Saturday Review* and member of the NPAC Executive Committee, Norman Cousins was helpful on several occasions in lending a hand or call to move our legislation forward. His reputation, like other members of the Executive Committee went a long way to bring the concept legitimacy and support. In his 1981 book, *Human Options*, he wrote,

> "There is no single formula for human survival, but the approach to survival has two main elements. The first is that we ought never to minimize or underestimate the nature of the problems that confront us. The second is that we ought never to minimize or underestimate our ability to deal with them." [107]

Norman Cousins was a thoughtful and highly influential force in his time. His optimism and enthusiasm for the road ahead and the fate of the human condition was his hallmark. Mr Cousins, like other Executive Council members did not gain fame by supporting the efforts to create a national peace academy, rather they took the risk to be a part of our efforts and in doing so, provided legitimacy and a foundation for our success.

Many of the individuals who stepped up to enable critical actions along this path remain anonymous. One example was an aide to Father Ted Hesburgh who made Father Hesburgh highly accessible to NPAC and our efforts. Many times during the campaign when I reached out to him, I came to believe he and Father Hesburgh were the same person, as the response time and quality of the action requested was so amazing. I never met this man, although I met Father Hesburgh. Not everyone was so responsive, but many, many famous, and not so famous people were. Those who are served by USIP and those who lead USIP today remain in their debt.

Bryant's vision is still an unfinished dream. It will only be judged by the test of time in how the USIP develops and evolves.

Jim's legacy - to inspire the personal connections of professionals and a citizenry informed by the lessons of the civil rights movement - is very much alive.

Andy went on to fight many battles for peace and social justice. He has continued to advance economic justice, human rights and the greater inclusion of minorities in creating the political will of communities and nations to aspire and grow.

As for me, my discovery of the meaning of peace and how to create political will represents the possibility that the many who try – and the many who will succeed – can also inspire others along the way.

Two years before I watched Robert Kennedy stand on the roof of a station wagon in San Gabriel, he said this in Cape Town, South Africa.

> "Let no one be discouraged by the belief there is nothing one man or one woman can do against the enormous array of the world's ills – against misery and ignorance, injustice and violence… few will have the greatness to bend history itself, but each of us can work to change a small portion of events, and in the total of all those acts will be written the history of this generation… It is from the numberless diverse acts of courage and belief that human history is shaped. Each time a man stands up for an ideal, or sends a tiny ripple of hope - and crossing each other from a million different centers of energy and daring - those ripples build a current which can sweep down the mightiest walls of oppression and resistance."

Some readers may believe that peace is illusive and unattainable. I differ in my opinion.

Whether it is gun control, urban policing reform, race relations, HIV prevention, agricultural production reform or efforts to recognize the importance of early childhood education: public policy and practice is determined by the efforts of those who create a change in the political will. The Great Chicago Fire caused social innovations relating to fire prevention so profound, they altered the way we view basic urban infrastructure.

Each year – year-in and year-out – there are between 30 and 40 wars going on around the world where more than 1,000 die. Far more loss of life occurs in the civilian populations. This is a barrier that we as a society can and will one day overcome. We must all work to lower the threshold of our revulsion to violence. As with the success we have had with managing the destruction force of fire, or in the athletic pursuit of running a four minute mile, peace can one day be better understood and managed than it is today. The choice to do so is ours and in the institutions we create to provide the bias and political will to bring the vision about.

Political will is what enables advocacy to work. When the legislative bill authorizing the federal commission was put forward in 1977, there were just 12 co-sponsors in the House of Representative, largely assembled due to the joint participation of the Congressional offices in the DC Summer softball league on the National Mall. There were just three cosponsors in the US Senate. Five years later when the USIP enacting legislation was first introduced in 1982, there were 163 Congressional co-sponsors in the House of Representatives, and 54 Senate members had signed on as co-sponsors. These events happened as a result of a clear strategy and very hard work. How do you get from a softball field to a new American institution? It was a demonstration of creating political will.

In 2011, the USIP moved to the site of its permanent headquarters adjacent to the National Mall in Washington, DC, creating a living symbol for peace in the form of a professional training center for practitioners in conflict prevention, management and resolution.

Go visit it. Stand on the steps of the Lincoln Memorial and look east toward the Capitol. Pause, and think of the speech by Dr King, made from the risers where you stand.

Take a walk north for two hundred yards, passing on your right the solemnity of the Vietnam Memorial.

At the corner of 23rd Street, NW, and Constitution Avenue, you will find the United States Institute of Peace. It was found in a voyage of discovery. It stands as a tribute to those thousands who worked to create its arching rooftop and solid foundation. It belongs to you. Care about it.

The concept of the USIP is that it becomes an institutionalized voice that will inspire, influence, educate, and act to foster international understanding to lead to a more peaceful and just world.

We learn from one another, and the history that goes before us. As was said in the Introduction, creating political will is what enables advocacy to work. We bend the arc of history toward peace and social justice by becoming more skillful at creating political will.

Remember, peace is to war, as chess is to checkers. Both are played on the same game board, but peace is a more difficult game. One is a game of power and political will; the other a scrimmage of force and coercion. One leads to causing social change; the other tears down and shatters. Both are precarious and risky to pursue; yet one builds hope and the other despair.

Why do we choose chess over checkers? Edward R. Murrow wrote, "Difficulty is the excuse that history never accepts." History does not forgive. Nor should we. We all have a part to play; an obligation to one another.

John Maynard Keyes wrote, "Ideas shape the course of history."

Peace is conceived in the mind; first and foremost, peace is an idea. It is a process, a place felt in the heart and sustained by our institutions. Learning to play chess inspires trust, reason and optimism that lead to understanding. Peace arises, and is sustained by the *capability* and *capacity* of political will. Each bends the arc of history toward justice.[108]

Each of us is part of the nation we aspire America to be, and the expectations we hold for our planet. Our responsibility of membership rests with influencing the political will to redeem the promises we share with one another.

Political will is defined as the art and science of influencing society. That was our hope in the effort to create the USIP. That is my desire for you today, as you discover the personal quest to make a difference in your world.

Listen to your own calm sea.

Set Sail.

ACKNOWLEDGEMENTS

We benefit from the prismatic encounters of those who bring light and energy into our lives. My thankfulness is expressed not only for those who inspired the writing of this book, but for the personal life commitments of those I know contributed to the creation of the United States Institute of Peace. I was once asked by a representative of the USIP to provide a list of the twenty-five most influential players in our efforts to create the USIP. I could not.

I am extraordinarily humbled to have played a role in the efforts to establish what resulted in the USIP. The story described in my writing would not have been possible without the dedication of the Congressional staff people who inspired their members to action: Cary Peck was such an aide to Senator Claiborne Pell; Steve Cloud and Jack Wicks were in the service of Senator Vance Hartke; Birdie Kyle and George Lawless worked diligently for Senator Jennings Randolph; Lon Fendall, Riki Poster and Tom Imenson worked for Senator Mark Hatfield; Elma Henderson served with Senator Spark Matsunaga, Connie Grice was the key legislative aide to Congressman Andrew Young; Tim Lovain kept the bills active with Congresswoman Helen Meyner, and there were of course, many others. The legislators themselves are to be thanked for without the focused work of a very few, Congress would not have acted to create the USIP.

During my eight-year journey of working to create the United States Institute of Peace, my colleagues and I would often say, "You can cause social change or take credit for it, but you can't do both." Stated another way, when you are striving to make a fundamental difference in something, it is important to be modest in your intentions to take credit for what you are doing or you risk falling short of the goal you are trying to accomplish. I am grateful to Bryant Wedge, MD, for inviting me to take this path. Bryant's passionate understanding of psychiatry, international relations, human behavior and the root causes of conflict became central in my own grounding. Jim Laue's passion in modeling an honorable and steadfast activist life was a determinant in my success. I am grateful to Andy Young for his inspiration, incredible contributions to social justice and to the pursuit of peace. Senator Spark Matsunaga entrusted me to guide the commission and he exemplified the constancy, along with Senators Hatfield, Randolph, and Hartke, to make a legislative difference.

Tom Westropp and Nachman Gerber would become early financial supporters of the National Peace Academy Campaign in 1976 and were present with me in 1984 when its board voted to end the campaign after the passage of the Defense Authorization Act of 1985 that contained the language establishing USIP. There were numerous academics without whose inspiration or encouragement I would have not completed my journey. Among them were Louis Kriesberg, J. David Singer, Ed Azar, Herb Kelman, Hanna and Alan Newcombe; Kenneth and Elise Boulding. Many times the individual encouragement of Father Ted Hesburgh, Rabbi Marc Tanenbaum, Congressman Dante Fascell, Jack Dunfey and Jack Dover made a profound impact on my confidence and effectiveness.

Many of these people have passed, but their published works and contributions to peace continue. I salute them, as I do the thousands of citizens who took action to enhance the capacity of our nation to advance along the path to justice and peace. More than 1,800 individuals contributed to the commission process; many of their names are listed in the Appendix of the commission's Final Report as witnesses and public seminar citizen participants. Even more Americans participated as supporters of the National Peace Academy Campaign and earlier efforts. I am personally indebted, and the USIP beholden, to those dedicated individuals listed later in this book as the Activists in the Campaign and Commission, who served on the staffs of the National Peace Academy Campaign; its Executive and Steering Committees, and the public seminar regional coordinators, commissioners and staff who served to facilitate the work of the commission.

Early on, Beverly Orr, Joan Mann, Mike Mapes, Bob Paley, Paul Ottens, Laurie Silver, Kathy Kozar Smith contributed heavily to the foundation of work begun in 1976 that lead to the passage of the enacting legislation of both the commission and the Institute itself. Each of these individuals in effect set the cornerstones of the USIP.

I sincerely appreciate those who thoughtfully provided comments on early drafts of my manuscript including Mariann and Frank Baker, Claudine Perrault and Howard Rifkin. I am grateful to Kathy Strickman who lent her fresh, professional eyes to read and make editorial suggestions to the words I began writing down in 2011. Dayle Spencer provided the loving scissors to instinctively cut, shorten and sharpen the manuscript.

I am grateful to Jim Laue, Dayle Spencer, Michael Doyle and David Straus, former President Jimmy Carter, Bill Ury, Bill Lincoln, Charlie E. Smith, and all who helped to model the craft that led to my experiences as a practitioner. All are gifted in their facilitative techniques.

Certain individuals in a life are the bedrock you return to when you seek grounding. Architect James S. Moore has guided me in the world of business for fifty years, and introduced me to integrity of selling ideas that you believe in. I am thankful to Jim, as I am Jack Dover, who has known me well enough to gracefully say: "*No, you cannot do that.*" I will always look to Jack for his political knack; dry wit, loyalty and upbeat crankiness.

President and Rosalynn Carter especially honored me by their confidence during the years 1984 to 1998, and for their continuing friendship to this day. President Carter provided me the gift and amazing opportunity to support him in reaching for his vision, and provided the phenomenal platform upon which to undertake the mediation of warring parties.

I am equality indebted to Dayle Spencer for her openness, collegiality, and acceptance of contributions I may have made to the Conflict Resolution Programs at the Carter Center of Emory University. Dayle's leadership of the INN, and amazing negotiation skills, are a privilege to behold. In those gifts, disputants and other professionals see her humanity and ethics. Both are uncommon assets, as is Dayle in helping others to understand one another, and find practical, fresh solutions.

This book has been about the individual efforts of all who contributed to the development of a peace institute for the United States. As colleagues and mentors, I gratefully acknowledge Bryant Wedge, Jim Laue and Andy Young for their reliance on me, and their vision for America and the world. They lived their lives creating political will. The splendid commitment of each of these individuals bore incredible results and enduring friendships.

I will always be extraordinarily grateful to Constance Grice, whom I married and with whom I started parenthood. Connie was a fellow traveler on my journey, as I was on hers. She was a teacher and advocate, with legislative skills and progressive values that enabled my continued dedication to our campaign.

Without the love of family none of us would be who we are. I am thankful for the love of my parents, Bud and Ruth Spencer, my sister Susan, brother-in-law John, and my sons Matthew Spencer-Grice and Geoffrey Powell. My daughter Allison Powell, who died in 2011, suggested the title for this book and encouraged me along the way. Any professional in this field knows that we do our work for our families, whether they are the few closest to us, or the larger family with whom we share our planet.

In the years since my involvement with the campaign and commission, I have benefitted from the love and inspiration of my spouse, Dayle. Even more than my words of Dedication at the beginning of this book, I am delighted and appreciative of her remarkable sparkle, intelligence, and the embracing breeze she brings into my life everyday.

ENDNOTES

In the writing of this book, the author referenced meeting notes, key dates and outcomes from his personal calendars kept at the time. The legislative history of events, congressional and commission testimony is well documented in archival documents in special library sections at several universities. The oral testimony provided to the commission at the time of its twelve public hearings, and the record of commission business deliberations were transcribed and are filed with the Library of Congress. The written testimony provided to the commission is part of these archival files. Campaign documents, academic conference proceedings, the notes of fifty commission special meetings and photographs were also referenced in preparation of this manuscript.

Prologue

[1]   The Daily Diary of President Ronald Reagan, White House; October 14, 1984

Introduction

[2]   David Cohen, Rosa de la Vega, Gabrielle Watson, (*Advocacy for Social Justice*, Oxfam and the Advocacy Institute, Kumarian Press, Inc., Bloomfield, CT, 2001)

[3]   Public Law 95-561, Education amendments of 1978, signed into law on November 1, 1978, establishing the United States Commission on Proposals for the National Academy of Peace and Conflict Resolution.

[4]   David R. Hawkins, MD, PhD, *Power vs. Force: The Hidden Determinants of Human Behavior*, (Hay House, Carlsbad, CA, 2012.)

[5]   Steven J. Rosen, *The Logic of International Relations*, (Winthrop Publishers, 1980, originally published 1974)

[6]   Final Report of the commission: *To Establish The United States Academy of Peace*, Report of the Commission on Proposals for the National Academy of Peace and Conflict Resolution to the

President of the United States and the Senate and House of Representatives of the United States Congress, (US Government Printing Office, Washington, DC, 1981.) Summary of commission process and principal recommendations; highlights of testimony; history; commission staff and Witness lists, bibliography, Library of Congress catalog number 81-600088.

[7]   The Final Report of the commission is 386 pages in length and contains an Appendix that includes: Draft legislation for a National Peace Academy; Public Law 95-561 creating the commission; biographies of the commissioners; a review of the commission Process; commission activities and participant Lists and a bibliography of some of the works consulted during the tenure of the commission.

[8]   The phrase "My heroes have…" was adapted from Daniel J. Boorstin, *The Discoverers*, (Random House, New York, 1983.) Boorstin's book is about the many types of human discoveries and is a part of a trilogy that includes *The Creators* and *The Seekers*.

[9]   In 1940, Ellot wrote the poem, "Little Gidding". It is the fourth and final poem of his Four Quartets, a series of poems that discuss time, perspective, humanity, and salvation. Eliot suggested that what we call the beginning is often the end, and to make an end is to make a beginning. The end is where we start from.

Introduction

[10]   Alexis de Tocqueville, *Democracy in America*, (Alfred Knopf, 1945.) Tocqueville was born on July 29, 1805 in Paris and died on April 16, 1859. The two volume *Democracy in America* (first published respectively n 1835 and 1840) was written as a philosophical history of the US, The book followed the tradition of political sociology perhaps begun by Machiavelli (1469-1527), whose best known work was *The Prince*, written in 1513.

[11]   Power comes from equality, and in the pursuit of equality, most often used as language of the underdog, power and force collide. To influence the balance between them is the challenge of pursuing peace. Fifteen years after he penned his Introduction to Volume One in 1835, Tocqueville wrote in his Introduction to the Twelfth Edition of *Democracy in America*, "Let it be read over again and there be will be found on every page a solemn warning that society changes its forms, humanity its condition, and that new destinies are impeding. It was stated in the Introduction to the work that 'the gradual development of the principle of equality is a providential fact. It has all the chief characteristics of such a fact: its universal, it is durable,

it constantly eludes all human interference, and all events as well as all men contribute to its progress.'" (p. lxiii) "I think it may be admitted as a general and constant rule that among civilized nations the warlike passions will become more rare and less intense in proportion as social conditions are more equal." (p.264) After describing why Democratic armies desire war, Tocqueville continues: "We thus arrive at this singular consequence, that, of all armies, those most ardently desirous of war are democratic armies, and of all nations, those most fond of peace are democratic nations; and what makes these facts still more extraordinary is that these contrary effects are produced at the same time by the principles of equality." (p. 266) Hawkins wrote: "The only way to enhance one's power in the world is by increasing one's integrity, understanding, and capacity for compassion."

[12] George Lakoff, *Moral Politics: How Liberals and Conservatives Think*, (University of Chicago Press, Chicago, 1996.) And George Lakoff, *Don't Think of an Elephant: Know Your Values and Frame the Debate*, (Chelsea Green Publishing, White River Junction, VT, 2004.)

[13] MLK preached his last Sunday sermon on March 31, 1968, "Remaining Awake Through a Great Revolution" at the National Cathedral in Washington, DC.

[14] Marcel Proust in 'La Prisonnière', the fifth volume of 'Remembrance of Things Past', also known as 'In Search of Lost Time'. Proust's original citation read: "A pair of wings, a different respiratory system, which enabled us to travel through space, would in no way help us, for if we visited Mars or Venus while keeping the same senses, they would clothe everything we could see in the same aspect as the things of the Earth. The only true voyage, the only bath in the Fountain of Youth, would be not to visit strange lands but to possess other eyes, to see the universe through the eyes of another, of a hundred others, to see the hundred universes that each of them sees, that each of them is; and this we do, with great artists; with artists like these we do really fly from star to star."

[15] Two books that have influenced me are Judith Korb and Jürgen Heinze, Editors, *Ecology of Social Evolution*, (Springer-Verlag, Heidelberg, 2008) and *The Evolution of Cooperation*, Robert Axelrod, (Basic Books, 1984.)

[16] If there is one book you ought to own to better understand the conceptual underpinnings of the efforts described in this story, see Kenneth Boulding, *Stable Peace*, (University of Texas Press, Austin, 1978.)

[17] Quote by President Grant in Ron Chernow, *Grant*, (Penguin Press, New York, 2017.)

Copenhill

18   The story Brian Urquhart shared on the bus to the Carter Center on May 28, 1987 about this experience in the British Airbourne Forces is a true one. I later realized the story was recounted with more detail and color on pages 54-55 of his book, *A Life in Peace and War*, (Harper & Row, New York, 1987.) The next several paragraphs of this chapter conform to Brian's own narration. The quotations are intended to capture more of his humor and accuracy.

19   Earl Foell, *World Monitor Magazine*, 1988.

20   William L. Ury is a gifted practitioner, teacher, author and inspirational pioneer in the field of dispute resolution. Bill's kindness, intellect; extraordinary bandwidth in the process tools of mediation have made him a mentor to many, and a very dear friend. We have shared backpacking trips, weddings, many moments of deep reflection, as well as shared speaking platforms at the Russian Parliament, United Nations, academic conferences and to one another's hearts. As far as the definition of good friend and colleague goes; Bill Ury's gift to all who know him are rare.

21   The direct result of our work was the Comprehensive Smokeless Tobacco Health Education Act of 1986 that directed the Secretary of Health and Human Services to establish and carry out a program to inform the public of any dangers to human health resulting from the use of smokeless tobacco products. The law (S. 1574) Directs the Secretary to: (1) develop educational programs and materials and public service announcements respecting the dangers to human health from the use of smokeless tobacco; (2) make such programs, materials, and announcements available to States, local governments, school systems, and other entities; (3) conduct and support research on the effect of smokeless tobacco on human health; and (4) collect, analyze, and disseminate information and studies on smokeless tobacco and health. The agreement we negotiated permitted the Secretary to provide technical assistance and make grants to States to assist in the development and distribution of educational programs, materials, and public service announcements on the dangers to human health from the use of smokeless tobacco, and to establish 18 as the minimum age for purchasing smokeless tobacco. It further specified warning labels on all smokeless tobacco products and advertisements; required manufacturers, packagers, and importers of smokeless tobacco products to annually provide the Secretary with a list of the ingredients added to tobacco, and a specification of the quantity of nicotine contained in each product.

22   Foell, *World Monitor Magazine*.

Chapter 1. Malibu

23   The work based on this research was reported in the *Journal of the National Cancer Institute*, 35.823-827, 1965, by Harry B. Demopoulos, Martha A. Gerving and Helen Bagdoyan, Department of Pathology, School of Medicine, University of Southern California, Los Angeles, CA, The title of the article was "Selective Inhibition of Growth and Respiration of Melanomas by Tyrosinase Inhibitors." It is mention here as this experience, my first job, provided the opportunity for me to feel I was, and could continue to make a difference in the world.

24   Lakoff, *Moral Politic, and Don't Think of an Elephant.*

25   Albert Schweitzer, *Out of My Life and Thought: An Autobiography*, translated by C.T. Campion, (Henry Holt and Company, New York, 1949.) 157.

26   Karen Horney (1885-1952) and Abraham Maslow, (1908-1970) The Tyranny of the Shoulds – we can have two views of our self: the "real self" and the "ideal self". The real self is who and what we actually are. The ideal self is the type of person we feel we should be. The real self has potential for growth, happiness, will power, realization of gifts, etc. but it also has deficiencies. The ideal self is used as a model to assist the real self in developing its potential and achieving self-actualization.

27   James Allen (1864-1912) was a British philosophical writer and known as a pioneer of the self-help movement. His best-known work was *As a Man Thinketh*, published in 1903.

28   Matt Steinglass is a journalist who covers Vietnam for the *Global Post*

29   The popular story, Two Wolves, is of unknown origins. First People American Indian Legend. Firstpeople.us.

30   Karl W. Deutsch, *Journal of Conflict Resolution* 14 (4) December 1970, "Quincy Wright's Contribution to the Study of War", 473-8.

31   Hanna and Alan Newcombe, *Peace Research Around the World*, (Canadian Peace Research Institute, Oakville, Ontario, Canada, 1972.)

Chapter 2. Grindstone Island

32 Lloyd J. Dumas, *The Peace Keeping Economy: Using Economic Relationships to Build a More Peaceful, Prosperous, and Secure World*, (Yale University Press, New Haven, 2011.) 5

33 Ernest S. Lent, Legislative Reference Service assessment, Library of Congress, October 22, 1968.

34 Ambassador George F. Kennan, *Realities of American Foreign Policy*, (Norton & Company, Toronto, 1966.) Kennan served as Ambassador to the Soviet Union, 1952, and Yugoslavia, 1961-1963.

Chapter 3. Pittsburgh

35 Bryant Wedge, "Khrushchev at a Distance – A Study of Public Diplomacy", (*Trans*-action, Washington University, St. Louis, 1968.) 24-28.

36 See Everett M. Rogers, with F. Floyd Shoemaker, *Communication of Innovations: A Cross-Cultural Approach*, (The Free Press, Macmillan Publishing, 1971), and Everett M. Rogers, *Diffusion of Innovations*, (Fifth Edition, The Free Press, Simon & Schuster, New York, 1995, originally from 1962.)

37 Karl W. Deutsch, John Hamilton Fulton Memorial Lectureship in the Liberal Arts, "Peace Research: The Needs, the Problems, and the Prospects". Middlebury College, Middlebury Vermont, 1972; and see Karl W. Deutsch, *The Analysis of International Relations*, (Englewood Cliffs, NJ, Prentice-Hall, 1968.)

38 William J. Spencer, "Perceptions of Force", GSPIA 296, The Role of Force in the Nuclear Age, University of Pittsburgh, winter 1976.

Chapter 4. Farragut Square

39 Robert K. Greenfield (1904-1990) was the founder of the modern Servant Leadership movement and the Greenfield Center for Servant Leadership. According to Greenfield's essay, "Essentials of Servant Leadership," he developed the philosophy after reading Hermann Hesse's *Journey to*

the East, Hesse was a German-born Swiss poet and novelist whose best-known works include: *Demian, Steppenwolf, Siddhartha* and *The Glass Bead Game.* Hesse's writings explore the individual search for authenticity, self-knowledge and spirituality. Hesse received the Nobel Prize in Literature in 1946. The books of Hermann Hesse have all been important books in my personal development. Larry Spears described the "Ten Characteristics of the Servant-Leader" (1998) as "listening, empathy, healing, awareness, persuasion, conceptualization, foresight, stewardship, commitment to the growth of people, and building community." To see how of these characteristics is defined: spearscenter.org. These are all words that describe Jim Laue.

40   Boulding, *Stable Peace,* p. x

41   Bryant Wedge, "The Individual, the Group and War", p. 79, essay and book chapter, personal library of William J. Spencer.

Chapter 5. Georgetown

42   Boulding, *Stable Peace,* p. 18.

43   Hawkins, *Power vs. Force.*

44   James H. Laue, *Direct Action and Desegregation, 1960-1962: Toward a Theory of the Rationalization of Protest,* (Carlson Publishing, Brooklyn, NY, 1989.)

45   Laue, Ibid, p. xv.

46   Henrik Ibsen, *An Enemy of the People,* (1ˢᵗ World Library, 2004, first published in 1882)

47   See NPAC Steering Committee listed at the end of the book.

48   See NPAC Executive Council members listed at the end of the book.

49   NPAC Executive Council, Ibid.

50   In the late 1970's NPAC was able to place full-page advertisements in both *Newsweek* and *TIME* that advocated for public support of our efforts to create ta national peace academy. Individual donors had previously paid to run similar ads in local newspapers, including the Cleveland Plain Dealer, but the exposure from these major American periodicals was significant in terms

of increasing the legitimacy of the campaign, raising the moral of our supporters and enabling us to reprint the ads to share with members of Congress. We initially tried to partner with the Ad Council, who had a history of public service campaigns, on issues such as polio and had actually worked with my dad when he was part of the efforts to get the Smokey Bear campaign off the ground in 1944. Unfortunately in 1978 there was a long "wait time" to be approved and develop an initiative with the Ad Council, but fortunately we were able to speed things up a bit using the personal contacts of NPAC staff person John Holman, whose father worked at *Sports Illustrated* magazine, part of the *TIME* family. It was quite an accomplishment for a small non-profit, and both *TIME* and *Newsweek* were generous in the space they provided. The *TIME* ad ran once and the *Newsweek* ad ran on two occasions.

[51]   See multiple works of Chalmers Johnson, including *Blowback: The Costs and Consequences of American Empire*, (Holt Paperbacks, 2004.)

[52]   The 24th Amendment prohibits Congress and the states from conditioning the right to vote in federal elections based on failure to pay a poll tax.

[53]   Spark M. Matsunaga and Ping Chen, *Rulemakers of the House*, (University of Illinois Press, Urbana, IL, 1978.)

[54]   James H. Laue, National Academy of Peace and Conflict Resolution; Hearings before the Subcommittee on International Operations of the Committee on International Relations, US House of Representatives, HR 10192, (US Government Printing Office, Washington, DC, 1978), p. 29.

[55]   Bryant Wedge, Ibid. p. 54.

[56]   Wedge, Ibid. p. 55.

[57]   Dante Fascell, Ibid, p. 77, 80.

[58]   Carlton Coon, Ibid, p. 181.

[59]   Andrew J. DeRoche; *Andrew Young, Civil Rights Ambassador,* (A Scholarly Resources Inc. Imprint, Wilmington, Delaware, 2003), p. 174.

[60]   Andrew Young, National Academy of Peace and Conflict Resolution; Hearings before the Subcommittee on International Operations of the Committee on International Relations p. 50.

61   DeRoche, *Andrew Young, Civil Rights Ambassador.*

62   Kenneth Boulding, Letter to the Editor, *Washington Post,* June 13, 1977

Chapter 6. Union Station

63   William J. Spencer, Personal notes, Dirkson Senate Office Building.

64   Spencer, Ibid.

65   Development Alternatives, Inc., The First 40: A History of DAI.

66   David Halberstam, *The Best and the Brightest,* (Fawcett Crest Book, Greenwich, CT, 1969).

67   William J. Spencer, personal diary.

68   William J. Spencer, Ibid.

69   William J. Spencer, Ibid.

70   Andrew Young, Comments made at Department of State, Special Briefing, August 15, 1979.

71   Young, Ibid.

72   Young, Ibid.

73   Young, Ibid.

Chapter 7. 2100 M Street

74   Joel Garreau, *The Nine Nations of North America,* (Avon Books, New York, 1981.)Garreau turned his 1979 article into a still fascinating book that has interest and implications even in 2020 as COVID-19 interacts with the nine nations he described.

75   Stephen Sawyer, private correspondence with author.

Chapter 8. Ala Moana

[76]   "Interim Report of the United States Commission on Proposals for the National Academy of Peace and Conflict Resolution"; 9/11/80 Public Law 95-561, (Education Amendments of 1978 Title XV – Part B 96th Congress)

Chapter 9. Rayburn

Chapter 10. China Basin

[77]   Norman Cousins, *Human Options*, (W.W. Norton & Company, New York, 1981.) Cousins was the Editor-in-chief of the *Saturday Review* from 1942 to 1972.

[78]   R. Buckminster Fuller was an American architect, systems theorist, author, designer and inventor. He published more than thirty books, and popularized many terms such as "Spaceship Earth."

[79]   Michael W. Doyle and David Straus started Interaction Associates in 1969. They entered the field of collaborative problem solving with a small 95 page notebook called *Tools for Change*, based on their research in observing "how students become more aware of and learn how to use process to help them become more productive, self-confident, and flexible in the solving of problems." This work grew into educational consulting, and then to corporate and community consulting in the areas of facilitation and problem solving. Their subsequent book, *How to Make Meetings Work: The Interaction Method* was published in 1976. After joining the firm, I rose to become the Managing Partner for the business consulting practice. I owe much to Michael and David, as well as Charlie E. Smith and Everett Rogers for the concepts and approaches that became central to my own management consulting and mediation practice.

[80]   Mahatma Gandhi, ***"Be the change you want to see in the world"***- Although this familiar quote is often attributed to Mahatma Gandhi, he is reported to have expressed a similar idea in the longer quote below. The origin of the longer quote, apparently can be found among the one hundred-volume record of his speeches, letters, and editorials organized by years by Arun Jaitley. The collection is called the *1964 Collected Works of Mahatma Gandhi*. It is reported that Gandhi actually said: "We but mirror the world. All the tendencies present in the outer world are to be found in the world of our body. ***If we could change ourselves, the tendencies in the world would also change.*** As a man changes his own nature, so does the attitude of

the world change towards him. This is the divine mystery supreme. A wonderful thing it is and the source of our happiness. We need not wait to see what others do." Emphasis added to highlight the two quotes. This explanation is included here as it is an important concept to peacemaking. The process of how you do things should be consistent with the objective you are trying to achieve.

81 Fuller, Ibid.

82 Rogers, *Diffusion of Innovations.*

83 Boulding, *Stable Peace.*

84 Each of these macro-strategies were first introduced to me, or invented by Michael Doyle, David Straus, Everett Rogers or my Interaction Associates colleagues during the consulting work we did together from 1981 to 1990. In 1989 I began to apply the tools and strategies in my international mediation work.

85 Spencer, personal correspondence.

86 Bryant Wedge, "Psychiatry and International Affairs", *International Journal of Psychiatry*, (April 1968, Volume 5, Number 4.) p. 330.

87 Ibid.

88 Nathan Kline, MD, "A Second Career for Psychiatrists," *International Journal of Psychiatry,* (April 1968, Volume 5, Number 4.) p. 345.

89 Ibid, p. 344.

90 Group fort the Advancement of Psychiatry, GAP, formed in 1946 under the leadership of Dr William C. Menninger, "and "the young Turks' in American psychiatry who were eager to professionalize the field." Bryant published many times in the GAP publications.

91 Spencer, eulogy of Bryant Wedge.

92 Boulding, *Stable Peace*, p. 18.

93 Thomas Jefferson, Southeast Portico inscription, Jefferson Monument, Washington, DC. Excerpted from correspondence to Samuel Kercheval, July 12, 1816. Kercheval was a Virginia

lawyer and wrote A History of the Valley of Virginia, published in 1833. Jefferson's letter to Kercheval was regarding Jefferson's concern about holding the Constitution to such a high standard that its words might become too rigid or fixed to serve the country.

Chapter 11. Cambridge

Chapter 12. Malibu

[94] Eliot, "Little Gidding".

[95] John Paul Lederach, *The Little Book of Conflict Transformation*, (Good Books, Intercourse, PA, 2003)

[96] Stephen Hawking, *A Brief History of Time*, "On the Heavens'" by Aristotle (Bantam Books; New York, 1996), p. 1-3.

[97] Theodore F. Lentz, *Toward a Science of Peace*, Peace Research Association, 1955. See William Eckhardt, "Pioneers of Peace Research IV: Theo. F. Lentz: Apostle of Attitudes", p. 179-211, *Journal International Interactions - Empirical and Theoretical Research in International Relations*, January 9, 2008, published online. William Eckhardt was on Grindstone Island in 1975 at the time of my visit. He was very close to Hanna and Alan Newcombe as a peace researcher at the Canadian Peace Research Institute.

[98] Winston Churchill, said "We shape our buildings; thereafter they shape us." – is rephrased in my text to apply to how an institution like the USIP may one day shape the lives of Americans. Churchill's use of the original phrase referring to architecture dates back to October 1943 when after the destruction of the Commons Chamber during the Blitz, the Commons debated the question of rebuilding. With Churchill's approval, they agreed to retain the adversarial rectangular shape of the chamber rather than a semi-circle design favored by some legislative bodies. Churchill insisted that the shape of the old chamber was responsible for the two-party system, which is the essence of British parliamentary democracy.

[99] Robert Theobald, Written testimony to the commission.

[100] Ibid.

[101] Peter Yarrow, River of Jordan, 1972.

Afterword

¹⁰² Dr Martin Luther King, 1965 speech on civil rights.

¹⁰³ Tocqueville, *Democracy in America*.

¹⁰⁴ Thomas Jefferson, Southeast Portico inscription, Jefferson Monument.

¹⁰⁵ Quincy Wright, *A Study of War*, (University of Chicago, Chicago, 1964.) p. 69-76.

¹⁰⁶ Final Report of Commission, Ibid.

¹⁰⁷ Norman Cousins, Page 21, *Human Options*, (W.W. Norton & Company, New York, 1981.)

¹⁰⁸ The historical arc we wish to bend is a long one, and the arc extends to our past and, of course, into our future. The power of our ideas shapes the course of history. Our capabilities to create political will for the good, and our capacity to sustain it, define not just who we are as individuals, but our character as a nation.

When the Reverend Theodore Parker first referred to the arc notion in this phrase, it was in a Boston sermon delivered in 1858 in which he said: "I do not pretend to understand the moral universe; the arc is a long one, my eye reaches but little ways; I cannot calculate the curve and complete the figure by the experience of sight; I can divine it by conscience. And from what I see I am sure it bends toward justice." Rev Parker's words influenced Dr King's reinvention of the phrase, as King influenced us.

To learn more: see Theodore Parker. Susan Manker-Seale (2006-01-15) "The Moral Arc of the Universe: Bending Toward Justice". Retrieved 2008-02-29. Archived from the original, Unitarian Universalist Association.

According Parker's biographer, John White Chadwick, Reverend Parker (1810-1860) was an American Transcendentalist and Unitarian minister who was a reformist and abolitionist. His American roots ran deep and he, like many in his generation, defined what we commonly think of today as the American Experience. His paternal grandfather was the leader of the Lexington militia at the Battle of Lexington, and another relative arrived in North America from England to help form the Massachusetts Bay Colony in 1634. His historical relevance in the pursuit of political will for the common good included many of the reform movements of his time: "peace, temperance, education, the condition of women, penal legislation, prison discipline, the moral and mental destitute of the rich, the physical destitution of the poor." These are struggles that continue to challenge us.

To learn more: see J.W. Chadwick (1840-1904 was a clergyman of the Unitarian Church. He wrote about Parker as a preacher and reformer. Parker, T., Cobbe, F.P. (1863) *The Collected Works of Theodore Parker: Discourses of Politics*, in the Collection of 14 Volumes by Frances P. Cobbe.

ACTIVISTS IN THE CAMPAIGN AND COMMISSION

National Peace Academy Campaign Chairs and Staff

James H. Laue, Co-chair

Andrew J. Young, Co-Chair

Bryant M. Wedge, Co-chair

Lupe Anguiano, Co-Chair

William J. Spencer, Executive Director

Marcia Harrington

Paul Ottens

Marilyn Hill

Robert Paley

John W. Holman

Mark Rilling

Kathy Kozar

Laurie Silver

Joan Mann

Ellen Speicher

Martha Manning

Richard Sullivan

Milton C. "Mike" Mapes, Jr.

Sara Swartzendruber

Robert L. McCan

Patricia Washburn

National Peace Academy Campaign Executive Committee

Ambassador Andrew Young – Honorary Chairman, US Ambassador to the United Nations

Rev. John P. Adams, Director, Department of Law, Justice and Community Relations, Board of Church and Society, United Methodist Church

Mr Harry Ashmore, Center for the Study of Democratic Institutions

Dr Roland Bainton, Professor Emeritus, Yale University

Professor James D. Barber, James B. Duke Professor, Duke University

Senator Julian Bond, Georgia State Senator

Professor Elise Boulding, Institute of Behavioral Sciences, University of Colorado, Boulder

Professor Kenneth Boulding, Department of Economics, University of Colorado, Boulder

Mr Paul Carrington, Attorney, Dallas, Texas

Mr Harlan Cleveland, Director of International Affairs, Aspen Institute for Humanistic Studies

Mr Robert Coulson, President, American Arbitration Association

Mr Norman Cousins, Former Editor, Saturday Review

Ms Frances Farenthold, President, Wells College

Dr Jerome Frank, Professor Emeritus, Psychiatry, Johns Hopkins University

Mr Buckminster Fuller, Author, Architect, Educator, Futurist

Mr Najeeb Halaby, President Halaby International, Inc.

Senator Mark Hatfield, (D-OR) United States Senate

Mr John Hersey, Author, Professor, Yale University

Father Theodore Hesburgh, President, Notre Dame University

Ms Ruth Hinerfeld, President, League of Women Voters of the United States

Mr Vernon E. Jordan, President, National Urban League

Mr Herbert C. Kelman, Cabot Professor of Social Ethics, Harvard University

Ms Coretta Scott King, Martin Luther King Center for Non-violent Social Change

Senator Spark Matsunaga (D-HI) United States Senate

Ambassador George McGhee, former Ambassador to German, Turkey

Dr Karl Menninger, Psychiatrist, Chairman, The Villages

Congresswoman Helen Meyner, (D-NJ) United States House of Representatives

Mr Paul Newman, Actor

Ms Claire Randall, General Secretary, National Council of the Churches of Christ

Senator Jennings Randolph, (D-WV) United States Senate

Representative Irma Rangel, Texas House of Representatives

Mr Ogden Reid, Former Ambassador to Israel, Former US Congressman

Mr John Richardson, Jr., Director, Center for Strategic and International Affairs

Mr Warren Robbins, Director, African Museum of Art, Washington, DC

Dean Albert M. Sacks, Dean, Harvard Law School

Dr Jonas Salk, M.D., The Salk Institute, San Diego, California

Mr Sargent Shriver, Attorney, Washington, DC

Rabbi Marc H. Tannenbaum, National Director of Interreligious Affairs, American Jewish Committee

Dr Jerome Wiesner, President Massachusetts Institute of Technology

Mr Roger Wilkins, The New York Times Editorial Board

Dr Herman Will, Associate General Secretary, Board of Church and Society, United

Methodist Church

Dean Colin Williams, Dean, Yale Divinity School

Mr Jerry Wurf, International President, American Federation of Sate, County and

Municipal Employees

Dr Herbert York, President, University of San Diego, Consultant to the US Department of Defense

National Peace Academy Campaign Steering Committee

DeWitt Baldwin, Rockville, MD

Robert Boggs, Ithaca, NY

Florence Block, New Fairfield, CT

Elise Boulding, Boulder, CO

Thomas Burke, Fairfield, CT

Steve Cloud, McLean, VA

Walter Corson, Arlington, VA

Eric Cox, Wayne, NJ

Paul Deets, Boston, MA

Allen Deeter, North Manchester, IN

Frances Farenthold, Aurora, NY

Jerome Frank, Baltimore, MD

Nachman Gerber, Baltimore, MD

H. Lamar Gibble, Elgin, IL

Richard M. Gray, San Rafael, CA

S. Spencer Grin, New York, NY

Sen. Vance Harke, Evanston, IN

Miyo Hayashi, Chicago, IL

Barton Hunter, Nyack, NY

Sidney Jacobs, St. Louis MO

Leah R. Karpen, Huntington, NY

Neil Katz, Syracuse, NY

Bernard LaFayette, St. Louis, MO

Linda Lawton, Washington, DC

Mary Liebman, McHenry, IL

William F. Lincoln, Boston, MA

Lowell Livezey, Chicago, IL

John Oliver Nelson, New Haven, CT

Joseph Nixon, Wabash, IN

Glen Olds, Kent, OH

Alaba Peters, New York, NY

Robert A. Smith, Huntsville, AL

George Sommaripa, Cambridge, MA

Frank Stone, Storrs, CT

John Wallace, Brattleboro, VT

Thomas Westropp, Cleveland, OH

Nelson Woodward, Alexandria, VA

Robert Ziener, Chicago, IL

Commission Appointees

(Biographies can be found in the Appendix of the Final Report)

Senator Spark M. Matsunaga, Chair (D-HI)

James H. Laue, Vice-chair

Arthur H. Barnes

Elise Boulding

John R. Dellenback

John P. Dunfey

Congressman Dan Glickman (D-KS)

William F. Lincoln

Congressman John Ashbrook (R-OH)

Commission Staff

William J. Spencer, Director

Wilma Bryan, Secretary

Judy Bunnell, Asst. Dir. Operations

Rev. Leslie H. Carter, Dir. Operations

Steve Cloud, (Research Consultant)

Marge B. Dahlin, SA* to Rev. Carter

Mary Downs, Receptionist-Secretary

Ruthe Farmer, Dir. of Administration

Mimi Gerdes, Student RA**

Jacqueline Goldberg, Student RA

Ruth Gutama, Editorial Associate

Michael Hayes, SA Public Education

David C. Jensen, Deputy Dir.

Diana Jones, Executive Secretary

Laurellet Kirby, Administrative Asst.

Bernard LaFayette, Research Consultant

Lee Lawrence, Public Affairs Coordinator

Donna Lee, Student Assistant

Brian Lepard, Student Assistant

Jeffrey Miller, Student Assistant

Marianna G. Paige, Dir. of Communications

William Pryor, Student RA

Betty Reardon, Research Consultant

Ann Richardson, Program Operations Analyst

Ina J. Riesman, Research Coordinator

Charles D. Smith, Editor, SA to Senator

Marcia Smith, Student RA

*SA denotes Special Assistant

**RA denotes Student Research Assistant

National Peace Institute Foundation Staff

Lili Bermant

Robert J. Conlan

Gretchen M. Dursch

William W. Woods, Jr.

Bruce Bishop

Elizabeth C. Corn

Harry J. Hogan

HISTORY OF THE CONCEPT

Some feel the relay race for an American establishment of peace was begun by George Washington, who wrote in a circular to the States on June 9, 1783: "There can be little doubt but Congress will recommend a proper Peace Establishment for the United States." The "Peace Establishment" Washington mentioned here was most probably in reference to a standardized militia. The American Revolution was fought by troops from the various geographic and qualitatively different militias from around the Colonies. Just as Washington saw a need to unify and coordinate America's defense establishment, he also advocated for a "National University" concept and that was at the core of many of the proposals made between 1787 and 1846. Many leaders from the former colonies saw the value in a shared educational center to help bind the new nation together. Many too, wrote in favor of establishing and growing a national center to address issues of peace and sustainable civil society.

Following the American Revolution there was a period of uncertainty regarding how the new nation would solidify its fragile union. John Quincy Adams labeled these years, the 'critical period', knowing that sustaining the union of separate Colonies would be a difficult task. The Continental Congress was left with a debt crisis following the war years and each new state had its own ideas of how to formulate not only the fiscal foundation of the new country, but many were concerned about ways to manage differences among the states, provide for the future defense of the nation and diffuse a common set of principles for dealing with inter-state or domestic issues. This start up period of the democracy, if you will, was a low point following the high point of revolutionary radicalism. The hard part of learning to govern was afoot and its leaders knew that it would not be easy. Adams called this low point, working out the 'bonds of union'.

Benjamin Rush, M.D., proposed "a United States Peace Office" in 1789. In the fall of 1792, an essay by Dr Rush appeared in the first edition of 'Banneker's Almanack (sic) and Ephemeris for the Year of Our Lord 1793' in Philadelphia. It began,

> "Among the defects which have been pointed out in the Federal Constitution by its antifederal enemies, it is much to be lamented that no person has taken notice of its total silence upon the subject of an office of the utmost importance to the welfare of the United States, that is, an office for promoting and preserving perpetual peace in our country."

As President Washington laid the corner stone of the new US Capitol building a year later, the population of the new nation had grown to about four million people, plus an additional 600,000 people who were slaves. The nation was just beginning to work through the process of getting its governing principles and structure right. Not only was were the nation's leaders worried about protecting the country from international intrusion, there was an equal amount of concern for how the country would hold itself together from within. The "internal" peace of the coalition of new states was by no means secure. Many feared and wrote about a lack of transcendent institutions to serve to hold the new nation together. Very slowly such institutions were planned, and even more slowly the bills enacting their purpose were considered by the new Congress.

While the United States struggled to find internal mechanisms to promote peace, the international community floundered as well. Institutionalizing organizations to advocate for and promote peace proved to take time – a lot of time. In 1889, one hundred years after Benjamin Rush's proposals, US President Benjamin Harrison opened the First Pan American Conference in Washington, DC. The conference, nearly a decade in the planning, required Congressional urging to finally get it off the ground. Its purpose was to harness the special role of the nations of the New World to find more effective ways of avoiding or resolving conflicts among American states, as well as develop greater commercial inter-dependence that would lead to growth and stability.

The conference was attended by twenty-seven delegates from thirteen countries, but failed to achieve significant agreements. It did however set the precedence for establishing a new culture for periodic meetings and greater respect and understanding among the participating nations. This helped to create the environment to formally establish the Organization of American States in 1948. The League of Nations was founded in 1920 as a result of the Paris Peace Conference that ended the First World War. It became the first international organization whose principal mission was to prevent wars through collective security, disarmament, and dispute resolution through arbitration and negotiation. The League of Nations had some notable successes but ultimately proved incapable of preventing the aggression of the Axis powers and with the outbreak of the Second World War, showed that it had failed in its primary mission. The League of Nations did last for twenty-six years, however, until the United Nations replaced it in 1946. These institutions failed in part as they largely lacked any concept of the types of transferable skills and mindsets that would later come to define peace making and peace building in the modern era. Structures were beginning to change; but little cultural change was occurring in a world still caught up in the limiting formalities of diplomacy and the antiquated views of national self-interest, defined by imperialism over internationalism. Simply put, form was not following function, as the technology of peace making had not yet been developed.

During the course of the 19th Century, various publicists and legislators spoke out about creating a department of peace, peace agency or educational institution. Franklin Roosevelt urged the development of a "science of peace" in 1945, and Presidents Dwight Eisenhower and John F. Kennedy both called for alternatives to military might to achieve and maintain world peace. Historically, there had been bi-partisan support for efforts to improve America's peacemaking capability. Eisenhower warned in his memoirs, 'Waging Peace', that there is an imbalance in our national means of seeking security and liberty and an undue reliance on methods of power and force in managing conflict. Who would know better than former General Eisenhower? In his farewell address, President Eisenhower advocated a fervent search for "the proper meshing of the huge military and industrial machinery of defense with our peaceful methods and goals." It is fitting that the autobiography of the Supreme Commander of Allied Forces in Europe in World War II would be about waging peace. At the end of World War II serious alternatives to warfare were discussed, even as the nation's stockpile of armaments grew. Citizens were both afraid of losing another war with the Russians and worried that creating a militaristic society would defeat our democracy. New language to describe peace and peace movements to avoid any future war began to emerge in the American scene. The nation talked more about the importance of peace, even as we engaged in war.

President Kennedy, in a 1963 speech delivered at the American University in Washington, DC, said,

> "The pursuit of peace is not as dramatic as the pursuit of war… But we have no more urgent task. Peace is the necessary rational end of rational man…based not on a sudden revolution in human nature, but on a gradual evolution in human institutions."

Searching for a 'stable peace' remained a national challenge. As the forefathers had observed, regional issues would increasingly test the strength of national bonds brought on by external threats. Congress, as well as the international community, sought to find ways to institutionalize their concerns for peace.

In the same year the United Nations was formed in 1945, Senator Jennings Randolph of West Virginia offered a Department of Peace bill. Between the 84th Congress and the 90th Congress (1955-1968) no less than 85 bills were introduced in the House or Senate to create a Department of Peace. The establishment of the Air Force Academy in 1954 and the expansion of other uniform service academies were seen by many as an obvious model for Federal sponsorship of peace education as well as advocacy. Continuing concerns about the Cold War spiked interest in better managing international peace, and in 1960, Senator Hubert Humphrey introduced a bill to create a National Peace Agency. In 1961, the Arms Control and Disarmament Agency, ACDA, was set up to study the "scientific, economic, political, legal, social, psychological, military and technological factors relating to the prevention of war." Unfortunately the momentum of these efforts seemed to fail in successive administrations. Despite ACDA's expansive mandate, underfunding, understaffing and a lack of forceful advocacy in the White House marginalized its programs and influence. ACDA took on a technical orientation, detached from the American people, and never developed a sufficient political base to influence policy makers.

Activists from many organizations continued to raise the visibility of these concepts during the sixties and seventies, including many from the Council for a Department of Peace (CODEP), Another Mother for Peace, and other grassroots anti-war advocacy groups founded in opposition to the US war in Vietnam.

On June 28, 1968, Senator Vance Hartke of Indiana introduced Senate Bill 3708 to establish an International Peace Institute. On September 11, 1968, Hartke again introduced a bill, S.4019, to establish a Department of Peace. Thirteen other Senators joined Hartke as did 65 Congressman led by Seymour Halpern of New York. They saw value in creating an executive department of the government to house and develop a professional workforce, solely dedicated to promoting and preserving peace inside and out of the country. All efforts failed.

President Nixon at the time expressed his opposition to the idea in a press conference. When asked about it, the President said, "In fact, one of my task forces recommended a Department of Peace. I think, however, that derogates and improperly downgrades the role of the Department of State and the Department of Defense. I consider the Department of State to be a Department of Peace, and I can assure you that at the White House level, in the national Security Council, there is where we coordinate all of our efforts toward peace. I think putting one department over here as a Department of Peace would tend to indicate that the other departments were engaged in other activities that were not interested in peace." (War/Peace report, May 1969)

Senator Hartke wrote in response in May 1969, "I find it difficult to think of the Department of Defense as a Department of Peace, and I would say the same for the Department of State. I think we must move forward and do everything we can to get our bills enacted into law. Old proposals, old institutions, old establishments have not worked. We need something new. The people are sick of Vietnam. They are sick of war. And either we purge ourselves of this disease, or the disease will take over this country and tear us apart." Many share Hartke's view today.

This debate highlighted the tension between the Realpolitik of the existing American foreign policy and military establishments -- and the aspirations of a growing number of citizens that there was a more urgent need to establish a Federal institutional counterweight to seek alternatives to the use of force or coercion in preventing or addressing conflict.

On October 14, 1969, Congressman Charles Vanik of Ohio reiterated his support for a national peace academy by inserting in the 'Congressional Record' the story of a banker from his Congressional District, Thomas C. Westropp, who had been advocating for such an institution.

Later Senator Hartke also inserted into the 'Congressional Record' an article published in the February 1973 issue of 'Current Magazine' by another businessman from Maryland, Nachman M. Gerber. Gerber had formed an organization called Peacefully Yours, Inc. to raise consciousness about peace education and new institution building, including the creation of a Department of Peace, a Peace Research Institute and a Peace Academy.

In fact, from 1935 to the early 1970s there were 140 unsuccessful bills introduced in the United States Congress to establish a Department of Peace or an academy of peace. Innovations in conflict resolution skills arising out of the civil rights, environmental, and labor-management movements were leading to a new appreciation for their further application, codification, and diffusion. However citizens, scholars and legislators remained unclear how to accelerate the benefit of these emerging skill sets to the international, national and community sectors.

The introduction of a Senate bill to establish a 'George Washington Peace Academy' by Senators Vance Hartke, Mark Hatfield and Jennings Randolph, served to further mobilize citizens. In the summer of 1975, Bryant Wedge called Tom Westropp in Cleveland and Nachman Gerber in Baltimore. An Ad Hoc Committee for the National Peace Academy was created. Soon other individuals from around the country were made aware of the bill and were engaging their elected leaders. On May 13, 1976, Senator Claiborne Pell, Chairman of the Education Subcommittee, of the Senate Committee on Labor and Public Welfare, convened the first public hearings on the idea.

As an outcome of the hearings, two breakthroughs occurred. The first was the formation of the National Peace Academy Campaign (NPAC) in July 1976 and the second was the decision to "get the nose of the camel under the tent", as advised by Senator Pell, to move the cause forward with the modest approach of creating a federal commission to study the idea further *rather than* continuing to seek the more robust strategy of asking Congress to establish a Cabinet-level Department of Peace or a National Training Academy along the lines of the existing service academies. The creation of NPAC and the decision to seek a commission as an interim step changed the game.

NPAC's grass roots efforts focused on a single, non-partisan issue and its membership grew to include thousands of citizens nation-wide. It resulted in an effective lobbying campaign that drove more than fifty legislative actions by the Congress in the years 1976 to 1985. Congressional momentum grew, but legislative efforts resulted in cycles of success and failure as bills moved in and out of four Senate and House committees on education and international relations. In August 1976, Senator Mark Hatfield offered an amendment to the Higher Education Act to establish a commission. It passed the Senate, but failed a month later to clear a House conference committee meeting.

In January 1977, Representative Andrew Young of Georgia and twelve co-sponsors introduced a bill in the House to establish the Commission on Proposals for the National Academy of Peace and Conflict Resolution; Senators Randolph, Hatfield and Spark Matsunaga introduced an identical bill in the Senate. In 1979, Hubert Humphrey and Andrew Young co-authored a widely distributed dear-colleague letter of support of a bill introduced to create the Federal Commission. It was Humphrey's last legislative act as a Senator before his death a month later in January 1980.

Following hearings by the Senate Foreign Relations Committee, the Senate Human Resources Committee and the House Committee on International Relations, Congress enacted the proposal to create the Commission as part of the Education Amendments of 1978, signed into law on November 1, 1978. Further lobbying ensued, and in 1979, Congress proceeded to appropriate $500,000 for the one-year Commission study. Soon, three commissioners were appointed by the Speaker of the House; the President Pro tempore of the Senate appointed three commissioners; and finally, President Jimmy Carter appointed three commissioners for a total of nine as allowed in the legislation.

During the first seven months of the commission's work American citizens and organizations across the country testified that there was a need for a dramatically increased commitment of resources in the areas of peacemaking and conflict resolution training, research, and public information. Commission members met with President Carter in the Cabinet Room at the White House in July 1980 to deliver the Interim Report of its work. President Ronald Reagan received the Final Report of the commission entitled: *'To Establish The United States Academy of Peace'* in 1981. Several more years of campaign and legislative efforts culminated in 1984 when the United States Congress acted to create the independent, nonpartisan, publicly funded national institution to be known as the United States Institute of Peace.

USIP was chartered to "serve the American people and the federal government through the widest possible range of education and training, basic and applied research opportunities, and peace information services on the means to promote international peace and the resolution of conflicts among the nations and peoples of the world without recourse to violence." President Ronald Reagan signed the bill into law on October 19, 1984.

In 2011, the USIP moved to the site of its permanent headquarters in Washington, DC on the National Mall, approximately 200 yards from the site we had envisioned in 1979. After 195 years in the making and with 30 years under its belt, the USIP will soon be entering its young adulthood as measured in government organization years. Its future and contribution to America's pursuit of peace are just beginning.

Summary of Key Chapter Points and Reflections

Chapter	Task	Challenge	Gift & Opportunity	Reflection
1. Malibu	Chose one piece of a vision of the "world to be" that appeals to you.	Find your source of power to cause change.	Follow your heart, not your head. Let go of your left brain.	What feels so wrong to **you** that you want to change it? *What has heart and meaning to you? What is most important to you?*
2. Grindstone Island	Search for ways to market a noble idea.	Engage in advocacy.	Invite new experiences.	*What idea generates hope and questioning in you? What is a good fit given your background, skills, and passions?*
3. Pittsburgh	Know what you are doing.	Evaluate a dream against practical and attainable results.	Find wisdom in curiosity; self-acceptance of your skills.	What barrier must be overcome for you to make a sizeable contribution? *What motivates your search to act?*
4. Farragut Square	Create a well-rounded team to help you get there.	Sort through the attributes and strengths of the team in hand.	Develop meaningful relationships.	*How can you meet others that feel the same way? What strengths do you have? What do you respect in others?*
5. Georgetown	Explore your vision of change? Define how do you get there?	Be clear on your objectives and strategies.	Broaden your confidence to be authentic.	What or who affirms your creative spirit to cause change? *Who are the people who have most inspired you? How are you like them? How are you different?*
6. Union Station	Discover how to use the power of the system.	Be clear on influencing change versus causing change.	See your life in new ways. Seek to influence by giving power away.	List 5 things that you feel are root causes of the situation or problem you wish to change. *What prevents that change from occurring? What sociological or ideological forces drive the change you are seeking?*
7. 2100 M Street	Create a culture of change.	Taking credit for change versus giving credit away.	Seeing your life in service to others.	The word "inspire" comes from the term in-spirit; what motivates you in-spirit to be of service to others? *Where do you find joy in giving credit Away?*

Summary of Key Chapter Points and Reflection

Chapter	Task	Challenge	Gift & Opportunity	Reflection
8. Ala Moana	Develop your message and the ways to deliver it.	Understand your audience.	Expand the generosity of your character by developing or enlarging your tolerance	What lessons can you learn from those with whom you do not agree? What wisdom do others offer you?
9. Rayburn	Learn to manage failure and loss.	Find your resilience.	Learn to be fearless, with non-attachment to self-importance, ego or absolute control.	What do you trust unshakably in yourself? *How can you help others change themselves?*
10. China Basin	Manage people up and down the leadership	Manage mentors, allies and the people who do not agree with you.	Become facilitative, not forceful. Strive to influence not intimidate.	Where do people say you lead by example? When are you a good follower? *What of your gifts help others?*
11. Cambridge	Believe in yourself.	Set boundaries on your willingness to sacrifice.	Find the gift of focus on what is most important to you.	If you cannot be all things; what can you be? *Who or what do you pretend to be, but are not?*
12. Malibu	Identify your lessons and repeat.	Evaluate what works. Integrate learnings.	Leverage meaningful, altruistic acts with integrity and gratitude.	What areas of your life demonstrate your current ability? *What quality of your character is your foundation?*

ABOUT THE AUTHOR

William J. Spencer has focused his career on advancing the practice of how business and society manage cooperation, conflict and change. Will has served as a management consultant to Fortune Fifty companies, and family businesses, in strategic planning, collaborative problem solving and conflict resolution. He graduated from Occidental College in Los Angeles and attended the University of Pittsburgh Graduate School on Public and International Affairs. He served as the founding Executive Director of the National Peace Academy Campaign and was the Director of the Unites States Commission on Proposals for the National Academy of Peace and Conflict Resolution, whose work resulted in the creation of the United States Institute of Peace.

Throughout his professional life Will has been involved with companies, social initiatives and international organizations that have made a difference in the way we work together to resolve issues, seek justice and prevent violence. He has worked to advance the field of conflict resolution, conflict prevention early warning systems, human rights and peace building measures in many regions of the world. Will and his spouse Dayle live in the Wood River Valley of the Rocky Mountains.

To learn more about the author, his publications, and work that is important to him, search the author at: Linkedin.com

CPSIA information can be obtained
at www.ICGtesting.com
Printed in the USA
LVHW101640211020
R16350700001B/R163507PG669248LVX1B/1

9 781982 254056